Environmental Policy in an International Context

ENVIRONMENTAL PROBLEMS AS CONFLICTS OF INTEREST

ENVIRONMENTAL POLICY IN AN INTERNATIONAL CONTEXT

EDITED BY
Pieter Glasbergen and Andrew Blowers
Open Universiteit, The Netherlands, and Open University, UK

PERSPECTIVES ON ENVIRONMENTAL PROBLEMS
P. Glasbergen and A. Blowers

ENVIRONMENTAL PROBLEMS AS CONFLICTS OF INTEREST
P. B. Sloep and A. Blowers

PROSPECTS FOR ENVIRONMENTAL CHANGE
A. Blowers and P. Glasbergen

Environmental Policy in an International Context

ENVIRONMENTAL PROBLEMS AS CONFLICTS OF INTEREST

EDITED BY
PETER B. SLOEP AND ANDREW BLOWERS

Open Universiteit, The Netherlands, and Open University, UK

A member of the Hodder Headline Group
LONDON • SYDNEY • AUCKLAND
Copublished in the Americas by Halsted Press
an imprint of John Wiley & Sons Inc.
New York – Toronto

First published in Great Britain in 1996 by
Arnold, a member of Hodder Headline group,
338 Euston Road, London NW1 3BH

Copublished in the Americas by Halsted Press,
an imprint of John Wiley & Sons Inc.,
605 Third Avenue,
New York, NY 10158-0012

British Library Cataloguing in Publication Data
A catalogue record for this book is available from the British Library

Library of Congress Cataloging-in-Publication Data
A catalog record for this book is available from the Library of Congress

ISBN 0 340 65260 8   ISBN (US only) 0 470 23584 5

Typeset in 11/12 pt Times by GreenGate Publishing Services, Tonbridge, Kent
Printed and bound in Great Britain by
St Edmundsbury Press Limited, Bury St Edmunds, Suffolk and
J W Arrowsmith Limited, Bristol

Contents

BOOK 3: PROSPECTS FOR ENVIRONMENTAL CHANGE

EDITED BY
Andrew Blowers and Pieter Glasbergen

BOOK 1: PERSPECTIVES ON ENVIRONMENT

EDITED BY
Pieter Glasbergen and Andrew Blowers

About the contributors

Dr Nick Barnes is an ecologist with particular interest in the utilisation of population information for assessing and monitoring environmental quality. He has undertaken research and lectured at Coventry University and The Open University, UK. Dr Barnes is currently working on an amphibian conservation project as part of the IUCN's Task Force on Declining Amphibian Populations.

Pieter van Beukering is an economist at the Institute of Environmental Studies at the Free University of Amsterdam, The Netherlands. His major fields include international economic relations, development economics and climate issues. He recently completed a study on emission registration in the United States. He is currently studying the impact of international trade between the North and the South on the environment and the economic value of natural resources in developing countries.

Dr Andrew Blowers is Professor of Social Sciences (Planning) at The Open University, UK. Most of his teaching, research and publications have been in the fields of environmental planning, politics and policy. He is particularly concerned with the politics of sustainable development and the problems of radioactive waste. Among the books he has written are *The Limits of Power*, *Something in the Air* and *The International Politics of Nuclear Waste* (as a co-author); he has also edited *Planning for a Sustainable Environment*. A former Dean and Pro-Vice-Chancellor of the Open University, Professor Blowers is currently Chair of the Interfaculty Studies Board. He is also a member of the government's Radioactive Waste Management Advisory Committee (RWMAC), former Vice-Chair of the Town and Country Planning Association and has served as an elected county councillor in Bedfordshire since 1973.

Dr John Blunden is Reader in Geography at The Open University, UK. A graduate in social studies of the University of Exeter, his doctoral thesis investigated spatial and temporal variations in the impact of agricultural support policies on farm enterprise. He has published widely in the field of rural resource management and, with Nigel Curry, has written and edited a number of books on rural change. His most recent research work, undertaken for the European Commission, looked at environmentally acceptable ways of stimulating rural development in the wake of changes to the EU's Common Agricultural Policy.

Emmy Bolsius is a senior rural planner at the National Spatial Planning Agency of The Netherlands. She is mainly concerned with research into and planning for Dutch rural areas in their European context, ranging from marginal use to highly intensive occupation. Her most recent publication in this field is called *Pigs in Space* and is an examination of spatially acceptable solutions to the problem of the overconcentration of pig farming in various European regions.

Dr Nigel Curry is Professor of Countryside Planning and Head of the Countryside and Community Research Unit at the Cheltenham and Gloucester College, Cheltenham, UK. From 1992 to 1994 he was Visiting Professor in Environmental Planning at the Queen's University of Belfast, Northern Ireland and in 1995 he was a Visiting Research Fellow at the Institut d'économie rurale Antenne romande at the University of Zürich, Switzerland. His most recent book, *Countryside Recreation, Access and Land Use Planning*, was published by Chapman and Hall.

Dr Jaap Frouws is a senior lecturer in rural and political sociology at Wageningen University of Agriculture, The Netherlands. Most of his work has been concerned with intermediation and policy formation, primarily in the fields of agriculture and environmental policies. His politico-sociological study on Dutch manure policy, entitled *Mest en Macht (Power and Manure)*, has aroused a great deal of interest in both academic and political circles.

Dr Pieter Glasbergen is Professor of Environmental Studies – Policy and Management – at the University of Utrecht and at the Dutch Open universiteit, The Netherlands. He specialises in planning and policy issues, with particular reference to environmental policy, physical planning, water management and landscape and nature conservation. He has conducted research for various government bodies, including the Ministry of the Environment, the National Physical Planning Agency and the Ministry of Public Works and Water Management. Dr Glasbergen has authored, co-authored and edited 12 books. He recently edited the fourth edition of *Milieubeleid; een beleids-wetenschappelijke inleiding* (*Environmental Policy: A Planner's Perspective*), Vuga Publishers, and *Managing Environmental Disputes. Network Management as an Alternative*, Kluwer Academic Publishers. He chairs the Environmental Policy Section of the Dutch Institute for Physical Planning and Housing.

Dr Colin Sage is a lecturer in international environmental policy at Wye College, University of London, UK. He currently has research interests in Indonesia, Mexico, Bolivia and China; these centre primarily upon issues of rural resource management and livelihood security. He recently co-edited (with Michael Redclift) *Strategies for Sustainable Development: Local Agendas for the South* (John Wiley & Sons, Chichester, UK).

Dr Peter Sloep is a senior lecturer in theoretical biology at the Open universiteit of The Netherlands. He is primarily interested in conceptual and modelling issues in relation to ecology and environmental science. His most recent publication is a study on the relevance of the notion of sustainability to the interdisciplinary nature of environmental science, in G. Skirbekk (ed.), *The Notion of Sustainability*, Scandinavian University Press, Oslo.

Dr Jan van der Straaten is a senior lecturer in environmental economics at the Department of Leisure Studies at Tilburg University, The Netherlands. He is also on a secondment as a senior researcher at the European Centre for Nature Conservation at Tilburg University. He is interested primarily in the effects of economic theories on policies in the area of nature and the environment, particularly in a European context. His specialist field is the problem of rural development with respect to nature conservation, agriculture and tourism. He recently edited, with Jeroen van den Bergh, *Toward Sustainable Development: Concepts, Methods and Policy*, published by Island Press, Washington DC.

Dr Egbert Tellegen studied sociology and is now Professor of Environmental Science at the University of Amsterdam, The Netherlands. His main fields of study are organisational aspects of waste minimisation and energy conservation and environmental problems and policies in Central and Eastern Europe. He recently published 'Interdisciplinary and problem-oriented environmental education at the University of Amsterdam', in R. Ernsteins *et al.*, *Environmental Science and Management Studies*, *Yearbook '93*, Ecological Centre, Publisher Vide, Riga.

Dr Pier Vellinga is the Director of the Institute of Environmental Studies at the Free University of Amsterdam, The Netherlands. He received his PhD in technical studies (coastal zone management and morphology, and fluid dynamics) from Delft University of Technology in 1986. Professor Vellinga has broad international experience in global change science and governmental policy. He is a bureau member of the Intergovernmental Panel on Climate Change (IPCC) and Vice-Chairman of STAP, the Science and Technical Advisory Panel of the Global Environmental Facility of the UNEP, UNDP and World Bank. He is a board member of and advisor to a number of international and national institutions in the fields of energy, the environment and land use management.

Preface

Environmental Policy in an International Context or, to use its familiar acronym, *EPIC* is a course that developed as a result of discussions between the Dutch and British Open Universities in 1991. Eventually a collaborative project emerged which now consists of three textbooks, a workbook/study guide and six video programmes. The course has been written by an international group of experts able to bring together the latest thinking on a subject area that is relatively new but of immense importance to our future.

The course takes a critical and analytical look at contemporary environmental issues building up a discourse around four key questions. In Volume 1, *Perspectives on Environmental Problems*, the key question is, 'What are international environmental problems, and why have they become important politically?' The question is examined from the different viewpoints of the natural sciences, sociology, politics, law and economics. It is emphasised that a multidisciplinary approach is necessary if we are fully to understand environmental problems. Volume 1 covers various themes. One is that environmental problems have both physical and social aspects and that, therefore, the social context must be understood. A related theme is that environmental problem solving is both a scientific and technical and an economic and political matter. There is a need to assess the relationship between scientific evidence and policy. The scale of contemporary environmental problems is such that policy must be addressed through international arrangements. Volume 1 focuses on conceptual and theoretical analysis, illustrated by a range of environmental issues. Especially it adopts a critical perspective on the concept of *sustainable development*. It is stressed that sustainable development should be seen in terms of the conflicts of interest that arise out of development and distribution problems.

Volume 2, *Environmental Problems as Conflicts of Interest,* considers the interaction between political power, policy making and environmental consequences. The organising principle of Volume 2 is the question, 'What are the causes of international environmental problems, and what are the conflicts surrounding their definition and potential solution?' Volume 2 consists of case studies of specific environmental problems. The logic of the case studies is that they move from the local to the global, analysing the nature of problems in the western world, the former communist countries and the South, concluding with those problems that are truly global, such as the threat of nuclear proliferation, the onset of global warming, and the loss of biodiversity. In Volume 2 it is emphasised that conflicts of interest often have both local and global implications in relation to policy and that resolution of the conflicts must be related to the social context of the problems.

Volume 3, *Prospects for Environmental Change*, goes on to discuss the possibilities for influencing environmental policy at the international level. The question addressed here is, 'What are the major constraints and opportunities that influence environmental policy making in an international context?' The opening chapters consider the role of major international actors, the nation state, non-governmental organisations and the business community in setting the policy-making agenda. The following chapters examine the importance of international relations (trade; West and East; North and South) in setting the context for environmental policy making. From this analysis the book turns its attention to the prospects for achieving sustainable development. The key question here is, 'How far can international action achieve sustainable development and in whose interest is such action taken?' The problem of translating the concept of sustainable development into practical policy and its implementation is considered before, finally, the book speculates on the social changes that are necessary if a sustainable society is to be secured.

Although *EPIC* is designed as a course with integrated components, each of the course books is also freestanding so that it can be read by those who are not taking the course. The three books, both individually and together, are intended to provide a context and body of knowledge of interest and importance to both social and natural scientists and a wider audience beyond.

Andrew Blowers (The Open University, Milton Keynes, UK)
Pieter Glasbergen (Open universiteit, Heerlen, The Netherlands)
Course Chairs – April 1995

Acknowledgements

The present book is part of a course which is taught by the open universities of both The Netherlands (Open universiteit) and the UK (Open University). The course has been developed by a joint course team from both universities.

Particular thanks go to the senior administrators and staff in both institutions who made this book possible by providing the necessary funding and administrative support to permit the venture to go ahead. The editors wish to extend their thanks to the members of the course team and to the many others who have in some way or other contributed to the present book. Without wanting to seem ungrateful to those who contributed in small yet important ways, we would like to thank a number of people explicitly:

John Bennett, Dr John Blunden, Ron J.M. Cörvers, Dr Bernard Eccleston, David Potter, Dr Alan Reddish, Varrie Scott, Dr Peter B. Sloep, Paul Smith, René van Veenhuizen, Dr John Wright, Anke H. van der Zijl for their services as members of the core course team. Professor Michael Redclift, the course's External Assessor, is thanked for his comments, and assessments of the course materials. Also, the services of the Tutor Panel (Fenella Butler, Mike Gordon, Gordon Jones and Miles Litvinoff) in the UK and Dr Wim Westera and the Student Testers in The Netherlands were invaluable and indispensable.

We further thank Miek A.M. Wierts-van Helden for logistics support, Ommo E. Smit for editing the manuscript and Tony Parr for his editing of the English language. Finally we must thank Evelin B.A. Karsten-Meessen for typing up the manuscript and all the secretaries who provided their services over the years.

This book, Environmental Problems as Conflicts of Interest, is volume two of the series Environmental Policy in an International Context. First published in 1996, it is part of the Open universiteit course N.22.2.1.2. The following photographs were provided by:

- ❍ ABC Press, Amsterdam: 3.2
- ❍ Andrew Blowers, United Kingdom: 6.2
- ❍ Michiel Cornelissen, The Netherlands: 2.3
- ❍ Environmental Picture Library Ltd, London, United Kingdom: 5.3, 6.1
- ❍ Greenpeace, Amsterdam, The Netherlands: 6.3, 6.4, 6.5
- ❍ Lineair/Derde Wereld Fotoarchief, Arnhem, The Netherlands: 1.1, 1.2, 1.3, 1.4, 3.1, 3.3, 4.1, 4.2, 4.3, 5.1, 5.2, 7.1, 7.2, 7.3, 8.1, 8.2, 8.3
- ❍ Mike Read, Ringwood, United Kingdom: 2.1, 2.2

Introduction

Pieter Glasbergen

The concept of sustainable development played a central role in the first book of this series on environmental policy in an international context: *Perspectives on Environmental Problems* (Glasbergen and Blowers, 1995) It did play that role because of its capacity to integrate the natural with the social. First, it recognises the natural limits imposed by the ability of the biosphere to absorb the effects of human activities. Second, it underlines the threat to environmental resources created by the present state of technology and social organisation. In other words, the term 'sustainable development' suggests a desire to ensure that social developments are compatible with the needs of the environment. As Opschoor and Van der Ploeg argue (1990, p.102), the environmental capital must not be allowed to depreciate. Natural resources are not only a source of human prosperity, they are also essential to the survival of the human race. As long as some specific conditions are met, natural resources should be able to continue to perform this function.

Firstly, the rate at which *renewable* resources are used should not be greater than the rate at which they are replenished. Secondly, the rate at which *non-renewable* resources are used should not be greater than the rate at which alternative, renewable resources are developed. It seems feasible to satisfy these conditions for an international community which feels a need to treat its natural environment in a sensible manner, particularly since it is clearly in its own interests to do so. After all, the bottom line is the preservation of the very conditions that enable us to live.

The day-to-day political reality is, however, rather different. In many cases, people simply fail to realise (or choose not to realise) that some of their actions are solely in their own interest and not in the interest of our common environment. Not surprisingly, therefore, there is a very close link between environmental problems and conflicts of interest. One of the main conclusions drawn in the first book of this series reflects this very situation: 'Sustainable development should be seen in terms of development and distribution problems that involve conflicts of interest' (Blowers and Glasbergen, 1995). Various types of conflict of interest were discussed in this connection, e.g. between short-term and long-term interests, between the interests of the present generation and the potential interests of future generations, between rich and poor, between North and South, East and West and (on a more abstract level) between the environment and the economy. It should be said, however, that many of these conflicts of interest were only mentioned in passing, i.e. in the course of analyses of environmental problems each of which started out from a highly specific perspective. As a result, a fairly diffuse picture of the significance of conflicts of interest was presented and reference was made to totally different phenomena at different levels of abstraction.

An exception, perhaps, was Potter's contribution (Potter, 1995), which linked conflicts of interest not just with environmental problems but also with environmental policy. He claimed that environmental policy always works in favour of certain interests at the expense of others. In his view, the best means of illustrating the conflicting interests is by asking the following questions: Who benefits? In whose interest is a particular environmental policy? This first attempt at a more systematic analysis of the conflicts of interest surrounding the definition and potential solution of international environmental problems forms the basis for further analysis in the present book. The great complexity of the issues involved is reflected in the following questions, which will be discussed below:

○ How can one identify conflicts of interest?
○ In what light should conflicts of interest be seen?
○ In what way are the conflicts of interest tending to change?
○ How can one classify conflicts of interest?
○ How far are conflicts of interest manageable?

The discussions take the form of tentative answers. They are based on viewpoints which may be described as the prescientific intuitions to which we readily adhere. As we study the answers closer, however, they'll prove to be in need of adjustment. From the discussions, then, a description arises of the structure of the present book in the series on environmental policy in an international context.

How can one identify conflicts of interests?

The term *conflict of interests* tends to suggest the presence of two or more parties who are engaged in active, open combat. Yet not all such clashes actually express themselves in the form of conflicts; conflicts of interest may occur without there actually being any evidence of conflictive behaviour. This is the case, for example, where a researcher concludes that the interests of the parties involved in a given environmental issue are at odds with each other and are thus theoretically conflicting. In other words, conflicts of interest may be *manifest*, with the parties concerned displaying some form of 'destructive' behaviour, in the sense that each tries to undermine the other's position to a greater or lesser degree. Equally, conflicts of interest may also be *latent*, with the parties concerned refraining, at least temporarily, from active, open conflict. In the latter case, the parties may or may not themselves experience the conflict of interests as an actual conflict.

As far as environmental problems are concerned, both types of conflict occur. Manifest environmental conflicts may arise, for example, over the control of certain natural resources such as water, fertile soil or fish stocks. The Gulf War is a good example of a very serious conflict in which the struggle for the control of a natural resource (oil) played a key role. If we examine crises such as these, we can gain a clear idea of the precise interests which are at work and the consequences this may have. Other conflicts may be of a less cataclysmic nature, e.g. the disagreements which have arisen between the countries of the Northern and Southern hemispheres during the international climate talks. Nevertheless, they are manifest and an analysis of the conflicts of interest may help to understand the social implications of global warming.

Interestingly, the conflicts of interest which have arisen as a consequence of the desire to achieve sustainable development should be regarded more as the results of an analysis. The process of change which this desire involves is likely to lead to certain vested interests being undermined, certain established rights being restricted and traditional property rights being questioned. To some extent, these effects are already visible. However, it is researchers who are trying to quantify the implications of the term 'sustainable development'. In doing so, they also try to identify latent conflicts of interest and to determine how they can best be avoided, precisely in order to prevent the occurrence of a destructive conflict.

In what light should conflicts of interest be seen?

Conflicts of interest are generally cast in a poor light. It is not clear, however, whether this is entirely justified. After all, conflicts of interest can just as easily be seen as a general feature of human activity, i.e. as inherent to human life. This is in itself a good reason for not instantly associating them with bad news. Social scientific studies intended actively to encourage certain population groups to become more aware of their own interests in order to improve their social standing reflect particularly clearly how conflicts are part and parcel of human life. Some Marxist literature and the feminist approach to scientific thought are both good examples of this. Researchers working in these schools base their work on an explicit value judgement, i.e. the consideration that certain interests are not recognised and certain groups are not sufficiently organised, with the effect that social inequality is sustained. However, even where there is less direct evidence of a normative perspective, one may still conclude that conflicts of interest may be productive vehicles of social change. In fact, one could even argue that positive social change is not possible without some form of social conflict.

One could, in this connection, compare the development of environmental issues with that of social issues at the beginning of the century (Bressers, 1992). It was at that time that a new form of social ethics began to develop, in the West in particular, which had the effect of altering the current ethics surrounding social conduct. However, the establishment of organised trade unions and progressive political parties was needed before the new ethics could be translated into new social legislation.

The scale of the challenge which society is now facing as a result of environmental problems is of more or less the same order. Today's environmental problems also require us to adopt a new attitude (and hence a different type of conduct) towards the way in which we provide for ourselves. Here, too, it is likely that the forces of change will have to organise themselves. The environmental movement is already playing a pioneering role to an increasing extent, together with non-governmental organisations which are concerned with the problems of developing countries, as well as with certain political groupings. It is reasonable to assume that, as the quality of the environment progressively deteriorates, we shall see ever closer co-operation between such environmental activists and political parties. The conflicts which will ensue may be an incentive for international action, thereby taking us a further step forward in the continuous process of formulating interests which need protection. This is the case, for example, where a conflict is institutionalised, i.e. talks are held, negotiations conducted and conflicts regulated by certain bodies established specially for this purpose. Within the field of international environmental protection, a first, albeit hesitant step has recently been taken in this direction.

In what way are the conflicts of interest tending to change?

The term 'conflict of interest' is often readily associated with clearly definable *material interests*. Here, too, the conflicts surrounding environmental problems are somewhat at variance with the usual picture. This is largely a result of the shift which has taken place in the nature of environmental problems and in the way in which they are viewed by society. For example, there has been a dramatic change in the nature of environmental pollution over the past few decades. At the beginning of the 1970s, when modern environmental policy was still in its infancy, people tended to regard environmental issues as problems of a general hygienic nature which posed a threat to human health and which could be solved with the aid of modern technology.

We now know, however, that high concentrations of toxic emissions produced by large-scale polluters no longer constitute the most important problem facing us, at least not in the industrialised countries. As far as these are concerned, it is fairly easy to identify the interests involved and hence to take action to reduce the threat. The key problem today is rather that of controlling all the diffuse, mobile sources of pollution (such as traffic) which emit low concentrations of a wide range of substances, many of which are not immediately harmful. Pollution is tending to be spread over a much wider area, to accumulate and to affect the quality of environmental 'stocks', e.g. the ozone layer, the atmosphere, the soil, the oceans, the rivers and the ground water.

A secondary complication is the increase there has been in the scale of environmental problems. Alongside local and regional environmental problems, we are now faced with cross-border problems and even issues on a global scale.

Thirdly, because of the changes in the nature and scale of environmental problems, the time span of cause, effect and (where feasible) recovery has been greatly extended, thereby increasing the degree of scientific uncertainty (Verbruggen, 1995, pp.3–4). A further factor which could also be cited is the intensive use that is now made of the land, which has resulted in a decline in biodiversity. In the developing countries this has become a particularly desperate problem. It is a problem which is caused by a low, rather than a high, standard of living and is now also regarded as having a global dimension.

As a result of all these various developments, environmental policy has undergone a sea change, reflected in a switch in thinking away from a hygienic perspective (in which environmental problems are perceived primarily as a threat to public health) towards the adoption of a framework based on the conditions which need to be met in order to ensure the survival of ecosystems. According to current thinking, there is only a limited role for technology to perform in solving environmental problems. The central theme now is the need for a change in the attitudes and habits of producers and consumers (see also Weale, 1992).

As a result of these trends, we have also seen a change in the pattern of interests surrounding environmental issues. First of all, it has broadened. As environmental problems have crossed (national) borders, so there has also been a concomitant increase in the variety of interests involved. In addition, the interests themselves have grown more diffuse. It is becoming increasingly difficult, for example, to decide which interests benefit and which interests suffer from particular methods of dealing with environmental problems which are themselves clouded in uncertainty. As a consequence of scientific uncertainty, procrastination and the protection of interests are likely to occur while long-term fundamental threats are mounting. Particularly where global environmental problems are concerned, the arguments in favour of certain solutions are often based on an assessment of the potential risks and the degree of irreparable damage which may possibly be caused in the future. There are very few material interests which are either served or damaged as a direct result of such action.

Finally, it should also be pointed out that immaterial interests have also begun to feature more prominently. Some of the arguments used today, for example, claim that the intrinsic value of Nature and the uniqueness of certain ecosystems are in themselves sufficient grounds for protective action.

How can one classify conflicts of interest?

The next question is linked to our tendency to think in terms of simple categories and often even in terms of dichotomies. I referred to a number of these at the beginning of this introduction: short-term interests as opposed to long-term interests, present versus future generations, rich and poor, etc. In the previous section, we talked about local, regional, cross-border and global environmental problems. Because such classifications present the complex reality in easily understandable chunks, they may help us to build up a theoretical insight. At the same time, they are often such oversimplifications of the social reality that they ignore certain essential aspects. In other words, these types of classification may in fact tend to conceal the truth. In any event, they are virtually always contestable. Take, for example, the supposed conflict between the environment and the economy to which experts frequently refer. Economists are not in agreement about the resolution of the problem. Some claim that economic growth is needed in order to enable environmental problems to be tackled. Others, on the other hand, point to the need for a slowdown in economic expansion. Others again argue that the presence or otherwise of economic growth is a total irrelevance.

As a second example, how about the supposed North–South dichotomy? The relationship between the two hemispheres involves a number of highly complex interdependencies that are by no means always unidirectional. In economic terms, many Southern states may be said to be dependent on Northern states and yet in practical terms this is not always the case. Economic growth in rapidly developing countries has been achieved through the development of low cost production in industries like textiles, once the preserve of the North. This has resulted in a painful process of restructuring in the North. This sort of pressure is likely to become even more intense in the future.

In political terms, the situation is again different. Is it not true that the prosperity of the North depends, *inter alia*, on the political stability of and democratic progress in the Southern states? There are also various complex interdependencies in evidence if one looks at the situation from a cultural viewpoint. This means, for example, that different cultures may view the same phenomena (such as environmental issues) in an entirely different light and that the same phenomena will therefore have a totally different impact on societal behaviour in different cultures (see Liberatore, 1995).

We also need to give special thought to the popular system of classifying environmental problems on a spatial basis. This is often deceptively convenient, particularly if it implies that a problem which can be described in certain spatial terms also needs to be resolved within the same framework. This applies, for example, where it is suggested that a so-called 'local' environmental problem needs only to be tackled on a local level and that a 'global' problem basically needs a global solution. In fact, problems that may appear at first sight to be local are often of a completely different nature. Even if the adverse environmental impact manifests itself on a small scale, it may nevertheless be the case that the roots of the problem are actually far removed from the same scale. To give an example, the environmental pollution which is caused by intensive agricultural production in The Netherlands is closely linked with international agricultural policies. Here, the solution of a local problem requires action on an international level that even goes beyond the confines of environmental policy. Similarly, a series of minor, local sources of pollution may give rise to an international environmental problem. This is not simply due to the fact that there may be a cumulative adverse environmental impact. In many cases, local action is possible only once certain steps have been taken to safeguard the competitive balance of international business relations. By the same token, many issues which are perceived to be global problems are in fact essentially local or regional problems. The felling of tropical rainforests, for example, causes tremendous problems in the vicinity of the forests. Equally, any restrictions which are placed on the trade in tropical hardwood have an intense local impact. And yet the issue is neatly compartmentalised as the global problem of a decline in biodiversity.

Other global environmental problems, such as the depletion of the ozone layer and the phenomenon of global warming, require action which may have completely different effects from region to region and which therefore tends to differ from region to region. For this reason, it is actually wrong to try and determine, as many people tend to do, the optimum scale on which policy action should be taken to counteract a particular environmental problem. Many environmental problems need concurrent forms of interrelated action on differing spatial scales.

How far are conflicts of interest manageable?

Finally, we are often at pains to translate cause and effect relationships affecting environmental problems into conflicts of interest involving an 'offender' on the one hand and a 'victim' on the other. In this scenario, the 'offenders' are those who are responsible for the problem in question and who need to change their behaviour accordingly. In many cases, however, the situation is not as simple as this suggests. The chief reason for this is that, in certain respects, environmental conflicts are highly specific social clashes (Glasbergen, 1995, p.6). What we see is that, although there is often a broad acceptance of environmental policy aims at an abstract level, it is difficult, and sometimes even impossible, to follow this through to its logical conclusion and actually adapt one's behaviour in the manner which is needed.

There is a broad consensus as to the direction in which the necessary process of environmental renewal should proceed, i.e. that of sustainable development. There are no social forces urging us to step up the level of pollution, to quicken the speed at which the supply of natural resources is being depleted and to launch fiercer attacks on flora and fauna. To this extent, the term 'sustainable development' has the same force and appeal as words like 'freedom' and 'equality'. Everyone is in favour and it is not until words need to be turned into action that certain conflicts of interest emerge.

Yet there is one essential difference. There is no one – with the obvious exception of criminal elements who are intent, for example, on making money from the trade in contaminated waste and who know what environmental impact their activities have – who may be said to be seeking deliberately to cause environmental problems. Farmers are not in business to raise the levels of soil acidity. Traders do not operate for the sole purpose of jeopardising public health. Indeed, many farmers and traders will claim that they support the aims of nature conservationists. In other words, the social activities which lead to environmental problems do not stem from a desire to damage the environment. In fact, virtually all conflicts of interest come into being around social activities which are regarded as being beneficial from a non-environmental viewpoint. Agricultural and industrial production and personal mobility are examples of such activities. There is no sense in which their very existence and purpose have been called into question. What is at issue is their adverse environmental impact.

Who, then, are the offenders and the victims here? This question can be answered in different ways. We could, for example, hold individual farmers and traders responsible for the pollution which they produce. But are they not more or less obliged to do so in order to stay ahead of the competition? We could also designate the agricultural and industrial sectors as a whole as the 'offenders', with the general population taking on the role of innocent 'victims'. But are we not all consumers of agricultural produce and users of industrial products? A third possible answer is that we are all both offenders and victims alike.

It would seem that we are trapped like prisoners in social systems which force us to act in a manner which causes effects we have no desire to cause. Or is this just an easy way of renouncing our responsibility and ignoring the ethical and normative aspects of our own role? If, however, we do attempt to take account of the ethical side, we find that there are differences in the degree to which different actors may be expected to initiate change.

In countries with a high standard of living, for example, there are in theory plenty of opportunities for changing production and consumption processes. In many of the poorest countries, on the other hand, where intensive use of the soil has sparked off a process of desertification, there are simply no alternatives available. The people in such countries are both offenders and victims at one and the same time and environmental degradation there is the result of a situation of *force majeure*. For this reason, it is reasonable to expect the richest countries not only to take the lead in instituting a process of environmental regeneration, but also to help solve the desperate situations in which other countries may find themselves. In fact, this brings us back to one of the key arguments presented in the first book of this series: the only way of solving environmental problems is by learning to regard them as international development and wealth distribution issues. It requires us to think of alternatives for the ways in which we currently provide for ourselves, based on the assumption that there must be other ways of securing a reasonable standard of living. In short, the issue is primarily a political one.

The structure of the present book in the *Environmental Policy in an International Context* series

The above is no more than the opening speech in the debate which we should like to initiate in this book. The key question is '*What are the causes of international environmental problems* and *what are the conflicts surrounding their definition and potential solution?*' I have tried to make clear that, by choosing to study environmental problems as conflicts of interest, we have adopted a perspective which can further our understanding of the issues introduced in the first book. Conflicts of interest represent major concerns of the parties involved in international environmental issues. By studying these, we can build up a clearer picture of current preoccupations. We have decided to do this in this book by means of *problem-oriented case studies*.

The logic of the case studies is that they generally work from the local to the global in terms of the type and scale of the problems addressed. Chapters 1 and 2 begin by examining local environmental problems in Western Europe, i.e. problems whose impact is confined basically to one single country. Despite this, it is in international political and economic structures and relationships that we can find both their causes and their solutions. Bolsius and Frouws (Chapter 1) look at the ostensibly local problem of environmental pollution caused by intensive agriculture as practised in The Netherlands. A closer analysis reveals, however, that there is a clear international dimension to the problem. Blunden and Curry (Chapter 2) then demonstrate that conflicts of interest of different types are played out at different levels, including internationally, in respect of the protection of the Broadland area in the UK. Local policy is shown to be greatly affected by international conventions.

Chapters 3 and 4 address environmental problems in Central and Eastern Europe and in the Southern hemisphere respectively. Tellegen (Chapter 3) discusses the transition from an authoritarian, planned economy to a democratic, market economy, which has given rise to new forms of conflicts of interest in relation to environmental problems. They are particularly complex in that some of them are bound up with ethnic conflicts. Sage (Chapter 4) argues that, contrary to popular belief, there is no simple causal relationship between population growth, poverty and environmental degradation in the South. The pattern is more complex than that. It is possible to identify a range of conflicts of interest whose impact is felt way beyond the limits of the South.

Chapter 5 deals with a regional issue while the remaining three chapters focus on global issues. Van der Straaten (Chapter 5) looks at the problem of acid rain and centres on the cross-border effects of this environmental problem, showing how cause–effect and cost-benefit relationships can affect the way in which the problem is tackled. Expressing the problem in economic terms is a process that is clouded in ambiguity.

Global environmental problems provide the theme for the final three chapters of the book. Blowers (Chapter 6) establishes various links between conflicts over waste disposal and the politics of power. The hierarchical relationships which are seen to be at work in connection with hazardous waste are not the same as those which are involved in the disposal of nuclear waste. For this reason, the management issues also differ. Van Beukering and Vellinga (Chapter 7) discuss the question of global warming, with all its attendant uncertainties. These have not, however, stifled recent attempts to bridge a number of international gaps created by conflicts of interest. Barnes (Chapter 8) demonstrates, with reference to the problem of the decline in biodiversity, that environmental problems are frequently closely linked to social problems. This makes them difficult to quantify. There are also both national and international factors at work which have an impact on such problems. The question is whether it is possible to find an effective means of dealing with them.

The case studies have both an internal rationale and a rationale in the context of the book as a whole. Their internal rationale is that they each represent a major environmental issue in an international context. Together, they cover a broad policy spectrum. Their rationale in the context of the book as a whole lies in their link with conflicts of interest. The case studies in question have been chosen with the specific aim of inviting the reader to give further thought to the points which have been raised in this Introduction and to formulate his or her own point of view on them. In doing so, I have tried to clarify two other abstract views which transcend the specific points at issue here. The first is that conflicts of interest have both local and global implications in relation to policy. The second is that any resolution of such conflicts must be related to the social context of the problems. For this reason, the analysis of each case includes international policy and management issues.

1

Agricultural intensification: Livestock farming in The Netherlands

Emmy Bolsius and Jaap Frouws

1.1 Introduction

Agriculture in The Netherlands represents one part of the most intensive agricultural production system in the world. The Netherlands, although one of the world's smaller countries in terms of its area, is the world's third largest exporter of agricultural products after the United States and France. In 1992, it accounted for 10% of world exports of agricultural products. As a consequence, The Netherlands is as densely populated with animals as it is with people. The number of pigs, for example, at 14 million almost equals the number of human inhabitants.

The agricultural production system in The Netherlands is based on a complex and extensive national infrastructure. It supplies feed, artificial fertiliser, farming machinery and fuel; it processes milk, meat and sugar beet; and it provides key services such as trade and transport. Imports also take place on a large scale. Six million hectares of agricultural land outside The Netherlands are needed to produce the raw materials for the feed consumed by Dutch livestock. This international dimension means that changes in Dutch agriculture and horticulture have a direct bearing on agricultural producers and traders elsewhere in the world. The effect on the environment of such an intensive production system demands action. Major national and international economic interests are at stake, however, and reconciling environmental interests, economic interests and agricultural trade policy with one another is no easy matter.

This chapter is in the form of a case study, focusing on an environmental problem in an advanced Western society. It demonstrates that even apparently localised or national environmental problems have much wider international ramifications. The case focuses on three aspects that arise out of intensive livestock farming. First of all, it addresses the question of *ecological and economic interdependencies*. The large number of animals involved in the agricultural production system accounts for vast amounts of manure to be disposed of somehow. The traditional solution of using it as a natural fertiliser only offers partial solace: there simply is too much of it. As the manure surplus nevertheless is still largely applied to the soil, environmental pollution results. Indeed, closer inspection reveals that the Dutch manure surplus is an international problem too. Not only does pollution cross national borders, but the production of the required animal foodstuffs causes problems in developing countries. Moreover, possible solutions to the problems in The Netherlands in turn have economic and environmental effects elsewhere.

Second, both the definition of a problem and any attempts which are made to solve it involve numerous *conflicts of interest*. These problems come at all levels, from the local through the national to the international level. In part, these conflicts are ideological. 'General' interests (such as the economy, the environment, Nature, animal well-being) may collide but so may administrative interests, as between different governmental and public organisations. A sizeable fraction of conflicts, finally, concerns distributional issues: who benefits and who bears the costs of the problem or its proposed solutions?

The third aspect is the *role of technology*. 'Faith' in specific technologies is ideology-laden; it is connected with particular interests. The bearers of these interests are keen to portray the technical solution (in this case industrial manure processing) as being in the public interest. Others, however, argue that in the final analysis the technology has damaged socioeconomic and environmental interests.

The following section (1.2) describes intensive agricultural production and its environmental problems in The Netherlands. Section 1.3 deals with the international dimension of Dutch pig farming and discusses the international environmental, economic and political implications. From this discussion it becomes obvious that a solution needs to be found. However, all attempts to tackle a problem of the present proportions stumble upon a web of conflicting interests. Section 1.4 charts the main conflicts of interest, that are mainly of a national scale. Against the background of these varying and conflicting interests, section 1.5 presents three possible development scenarios for Dutch pig farming, with special attention to their political, social and technological consequences. The conclusion (1.6) summarises the discussion by listing the dilemmas facing the intensive livestock farming industry in The Netherlands.

1.2 Intensive pig farming in The Netherlands

Development of the sector

The pig population in The Netherlands has increased substantially since the 1960s. Figure 1.1 shows a six-fold increase since 1960, when the total was 2.5 million. The period between 1970 and 1980 saw the largest increase, 8% a year. The number of pigs has stabilised at around 14 million in recent years. The average number of pigs per agricultural holding rose during the same period from 20 in 1960 to 476 in 1990 (see Figure 1.2). The number of piggeries fell during this period from 146,000 to 29,000. There are two main branches of the pig-farming industry: breeding piggeries where sows produce a constant flow of piglets and farms where pigs are fattened until they reach the weight at which they are slaughtered.

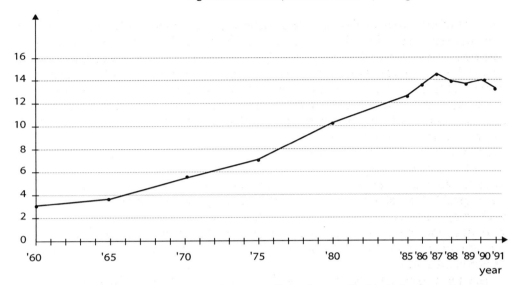

Fig. 1.1 Trends in the Dutch pig population in millions. Source: De Nederlandse varkenssector tot de eeuwwisseling [The Dutch pig-farming sector during the period up to the end of the millenium], P.V.V. report No. 9104A, p.50

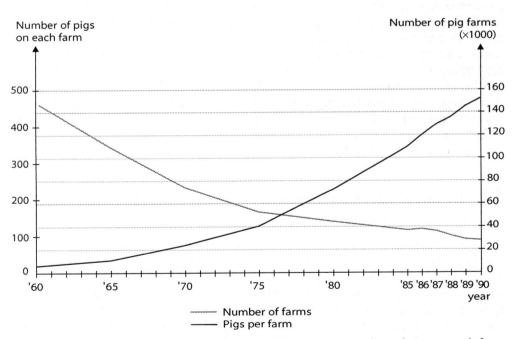

Fig. 1.2 Trend in the number of pig farms and the average number of pigs on each farm. Source: De Nederlandse varkenssector tot de eeuwwisseling [The Dutch pig-farming sector during the period up to the end of the millenium], P.V.V. report No. 9104A, p.50

The 14 million pigs are not distributed evenly throughout The Netherlands. Intensive farming is concentrated in a number of areas, mainly the sandy soils of the Southern and Eastern regions of the country (54% of the pigs are located in the south alone). In the same regions farms are located that produce veal calves and chickens and keep dairy cattle. The reasons why Dutch pig farms have developed in size to such an extent are largely historical. The sandy soil is relatively infertile. By tradition, each of the children in a pig-farming family inherited an equal share of a small, mixed farm. This resulted in intensification. Imported livestock feed was another key factor, because it allowed the farms to became 'independent of the soil'.

Plate 1.1 Intensive pig farming in The Netherlands. Photo: Ron Giling/Lineair

Nowadays, virtually all the pig farms in the southern part of The Netherlands use mixed feed, the composition of which has changed considerably over the years. Grain (i.e. barley and maize) now accounts for only 10% of the feed. The rest of the feed consists of tapioca (30%) and by-products such as soy bean meal, which are known as grain substitutes (see Table 1.1 for the composition of pig feed). Ninety percent of the raw ingredients are imported. In 1960, imports amounted to around 1.5 million tonnes. Imports peaked at 7 million tonnes in 1988 and now fluctuate at around 6.5 million tonnes. The feed contains many additives, some of which are zoo-technical, i.e. designed to promote growth or prevent sickness, while others are technical additives such as emulsifiers and antioxidants. Additives which have been used by the original growers, such as heavy metals, and other substances such as fungi, bacteria, the seeds of poisonous plants and pesticide residues sometimes find their way into the feed. These substances can form a threat to human health.

	1970/1971	1980/1981	1986/1987
Grain	43	17	10
Pulses	2	2	8
Tapioca	10	28	29
By-products of milling		14	7
By-products of sugar production	37	5	5
Corn gluten feed		4	5
Animal and dairy products	5	5	7
Other	3	4	7

Table 1.1 Average percentage composition of mixed feed for pigs (annual feed statistics published by Agricultural Economics Institute). Source: De Nederlandse varkenssector tot de eeuwwisseling [The Dutch pig-farming sector during the period up to the end of the millenium], P.V.V. report No. 9104A, p.79

In 1992, 2.6 million piglets were exported, 2.9 million pigs were shipped to foreign slaughterhouses and 900,000 tonnes of pork left the country, producing total earnings of 6.3 billion guilders (Agricultural Board, 1993, p.23). This figure represents only part of the sector's role in the Dutch economy, though. The production of livestock feed, the trade in livestock, the processing of pigs into pork, the transport industry, the construction of animal pens, climate control systems and related machinery and veterinary care are all linked to the sector.

The environmental problems

Livestock farming has numerous side effects. The buildings in which the animals are housed must comply with certain standards; they must be heated, for example. Special machines are needed to feed the animals and distribute the manure. Roads and physical space are required to accommodate incoming and outgoing products. Where the land is

Plate 1.2 The fertilisation of agricultural land in The Netherlands with manure obtained from livestock farming. Photo: Ron Giling/Lineair

marshy, the water level must be regulated so that heavy machinery can be used. Because the raw ingredients for livestock feed are imported, this generates a high concentration of minerals in a very small area, where the energy and minerals are converted into meat and manure. The majority of the meat goes abroad in the form of live animals and carcasses. A large proportion of the minerals are still present, however, in pig manure, which is a by-product of the pig-farming sector and affects the quality of the soil, water and air.

Intensive livestock farming not only has an impact on the soil, water and air, it also affects other types of land use. The odour creates serious problems for the living and working climate, not just in the vicinity of agricultural holdings but also in areas where the manure is distributed. The Dutch Environmental Protection Act has led to the creation of a system of *odour zones*, as a result of which it is now forbidden to build new housing in certain areas or further to develop certain villages. In some cases, such as in the Peel region (in the vicinity of the Southern city of Eindhoven), the concentration of intensive pig farming is so high that the countryside looks like an urbanised, industrial landscape rather than a rural area. The cornfields are among the main natural features during a large part of the year.

The odour from pig farming has meant that certain parts of The Netherlands are now less suitable for recreation and tourism than they used to be. Clearly, the attraction of water-related leisure activities tends to pale if the water in question is covered with algae because of eutrophication (i.e. a nutrient surplus). The economic viability of river and coastal fishing has been undermined by poor water quality and excessive algal growth. The pollution of water systems through nitrate leaching, both above ground and underground, affects the vegetation, fauna and drinking water for several decades.

The vitality of nature reserves and woodlands is affected by emissions of ammonia and the eutrophication of the water, especially in naturally low-nutrient environments. Biodiversity declines where heavy metals and other nutrients from animal feed enter the soil through manure. Organisms are damaged, as is the quality of agricultural products in the final analysis. The acidity of the soil may change to such an extent as to depress harvest yields.

The high concentration and arbitrary location of agricultural holdings have the effect of fragmenting the available space and hampering efficient delivery and collection. On the other hand, agriculture is often the economic locomotive of a region and an important source of direct and indirect employment. If stringent environmental requirements were to be introduced, such as a maximum number of pigs per unit area of land and a drastic reduction in ammonia emissions and energy consumption, 5 million fewer pigs would have to be produced every year. This would mean a loss of 28,000 jobs (Agricultural Economics Institute, 1994).

The environmental effects of pig farming are particularly acute in the south of The Netherlands because of its high human population density (431 inhabitants per square kilometre) and high concentrations of chickens, beef cattle and dairy cattle. This has the effect of threatening other types of activity. The geohydrological composition of the soil (i.e. the type of soil and its drainage properties, the circulation rate of the water and the ability of the soil to neutralise dangerous chemical substances) is such that the environment is overburdened. If the high concentration of livestock farming continues, the only way to counteract the environmental impact will be by spending a great deal of money, for example, on enclosed animal pens, fully industrialised manure processing and a further concentration of scattered businesses.

Reducing the manure surplus

The high density spots on a map of Europe that show the number of pigs per hectare in Europe correspond with areas with excessive nitrogen levels. The highest density of pigs and level of nitrogen is in the south of The Netherlands (compare Maps 1.1 and 1.2). In 1986, animal manure was responsible for the presence of 410 kilos of nitrogen and 240 kilos of phosphate per hectare of Dutch soil (Stolwijk *et al.*, 1992, pp. 28–30). Clearly, much higher values are encountered locally. Set against the background of the increase in the number of pigs, legislation on manure has been very late in coming.

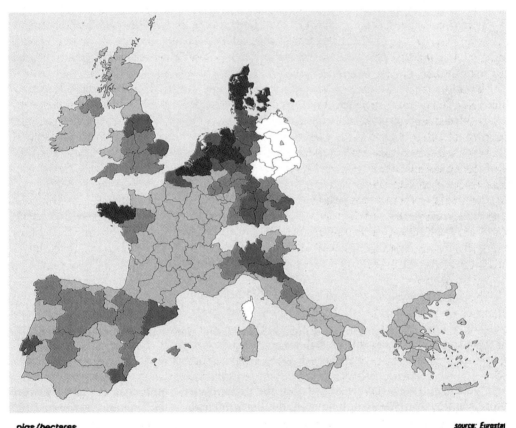

source: Eurostat

pigs/hectares

- ■ *2 to 11*
- ■ *0.5 to 2*
- ▒ *0.25 to 0.5*
- ░ *0.0001 to 0.25*
- ☐ *no data*

Map 1.1 Number of pigs per hectare in each NUTS1 and NUTS2 region in 1988. Source: De Hamvraag, E.Bolsius. Ruimtelijke verkenningen, 1993, RPD-VROM, Den Haag

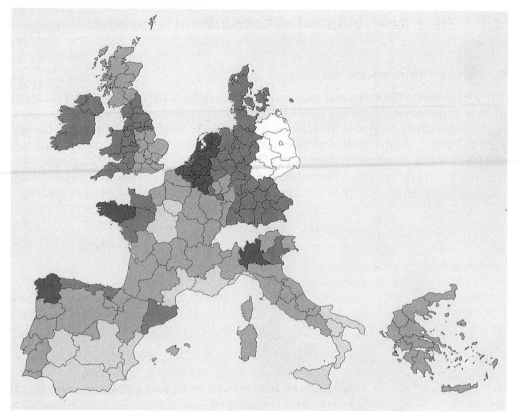

source: LEI (Agriculture Economics Research Institute)

N-production per hectare
kilos N/hectare UAA

■ > 150
■ 75-150
▨ 25-75
▢ < 25
▢ no data

Map 1.2 Nitrogen pollution in Europe. Source: De Hamvraag, E.Bolsius. Ruimtelijke verkenningen, 1993, RPD-VROM, Den Haag

For years, nutrients have leached into the groundwater; and toxic substances were stored in the soil. The Dutch have gradually tightened up their manure laws. In 1995 even stricter regulations were introduced, which also covered the dissemination of minerals through artificial fertilisers. Under these regulations, attempts were made to reduce soil pollution by establishing maximum levels per hectare. Measures to limit emissions of ammonia were also prepared. Discussions in the Dutch Parliament (September 1994) with the then new Minister of Agriculture, however, confirmed that all these regulations did not do enough to alleviate environmental pollution. The need for reducing the number of pigs therefore proved even more pressing. In section 1.4 we will go further into this matter.

1.3 The international dimension

Intensive livestock farming in The Netherlands is connected with *international interests* in numerous ways. Imports of raw materials for animal feed affect the interests of Thai cassava producers, soy producers in the United States, Brazil and Argentina and arable farmers in Western Europe. Exports of livestock and meat affect the interests of livestock farmers and meat-processing companies in Italy, France, Germany and Denmark. Dried poultry manure and granulated animal manure are exported to France, where they are used by arable farmers and wine growers. A high percentage of the ammonia in Dutch animal manure is exported abroad, where it contributes to the acidification of the environment in countries like Germany (see Chapter 5). The pollution of the groundwater and surface water by nitrates from livestock farming ultimately affects the quality of the water in the North Sea. This section deals more closely with these international aspects of the problem.

Animal feed imports

Pigs are fed with specially grown crops or by-products of crops produced for other purposes. The fodder is mixed so that it contains sufficient energy-producing raw materials (such as tapioca, maize and wheat bran) as well as proteins (such as the by-products of soy and citrus fruits, copra and fish meal). This feed compares favourably with grain cereal in terms of quality and is cheaper than European grain feed despite the cost of transport.

The prices of raw materials on the world market affect the composition and price of animal feed in The Netherlands. Most incoming shipments arrive at the port of Rotterdam, from where they are taken by inland waterways or by road to the livestock farming areas. Imports of grain substitutes are not handicapped by high *tariff barriers* at the borders of the European Union (EU). Some EU member states, notably France, are pressing for external tariff barriers to help dispose of the sizeable surplus of grain produced in the EU. In 1992, the EU reduced internal grain prices and this depressed grain substitute prices on the world market. Prices could be set to fall to a level that would make it impossible to export the products to the EU and cover the costs. Rising transport costs, due to rising energy prices, could place suppliers of raw materials in an even more difficult position in the future.

Many of the by-products used in mixed feed are from the United States (40%). The rest comes from developing countries, including Brazil and Argentina, as do the specially cultivated crops. Thailand is the biggest supplier of tapioca. The developing countries are extremely dependent on EU demand. Other countries, such as the states of the former Soviet Union, Russia and others, and Japan, are only interested in high-protein substances such as fish meal and soy bean meal.

The changes in EU policy have had a particularly sharp effect on developing countries and their ability to trade with the West. Many non-governmental organisations (NGOs, i.e. organisations of citizens concerned about the fate of the environment, the peoples of the developing countries, etc.) welcome the end of the trade. In their view, European agriculture makes too heavy a demand on scarce agricultural land which developing countries need to produce food for themselves. Additionally, the

Plate 1.3 Tapioca cultivation in Thailand. Tapioca is a raw material for animal feed, and The Netherlands is one of its main importers. Photo: Ron Giling/Lineair

increased production of raw materials for animal feed in Thailand, Brazil and Argentina has resulted in large-scale *deforestation* (see also Chapter 4). The cultivation of soy beans in the South and South-east of Brazil is said to have led to serious nutrient depletion and soil pollution resulting from the use of pesticides.

Another reason for welcoming further trade restrictions is the manure surplus in the EU, which contains many fertile elements from the soil in the developing countries. We have already mentioned that a number of developing countries are highly dependent on the foreign currency they earn from this trade. It is not so much the countries which produce by-products like soy bean meal or citrus pulp which suffer, but rather those which export primary raw materials for animal feed. In Thailand, for example, production is in the hands of small farmers. Some 700,000 families earn 40% of their income from the cultivation of tapioca (Sprang *et al.*, 1990, p.17). Whether their production methods are sustainable is open to debate (soil nutrient depletion is an additional problem on top of deforestation and erosion), but they have no alternatives. In all fairness, it should be added that pig feed consists to a large degree of by-products that would otherwise be wasted such as soy bean meal, maize bran, sugar beet pulp and brewery waste. It thus solves an environmental problem for exporting countries.

Animals and meat

The Netherlands is a leading producer of live pigs. The main export markets are Italy, Spain, France, Belgium, Luxembourg and Germany (see Figure 1.3). The southern part of The Netherlands tends to specialise in the supply of piglets, partly because of certain unintended side effects of the legislation on manure. In 1987 legislation came into force which included a ban on the expansion of livestock together with restrictions

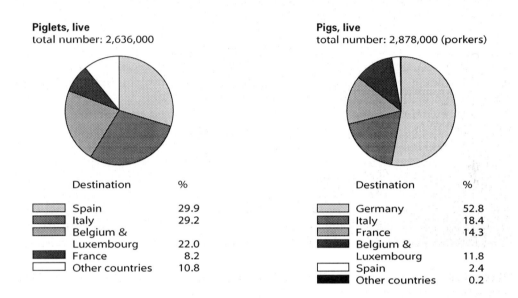

Piglets, live
total number: 2,636,000

Destination	%
Spain	29.9
Italy	29.2
Belgium & Luxembourg	22.0
France	8.2
Other countries	10.8

Pigs, live
total number: 2,878,000 (porkers)

Destination	%
Germany	52.8
Italy	18.4
France	14.3
Belgium & Luxembourg	11.8
Spain	2.4
Other countries	0.2

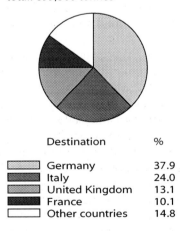

Pork
total: 899,500 tonnes

Destination	%
Germany	37.9
Italy	24.0
United Kingdom	13.1
France	10.1
Other countries	14.8

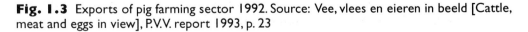

Fig. 1.3 Exports of pig farming sector 1992. Source: Vee, vlees en eieren in beeld [Cattle, meat and eggs in view], P.V.V. report 1993, p. 23

on switching from one type of livestock to another. It has produced a situation in which the large-scale production of fattening pigs has been replaced by the production of piglets. The rationale behind this was in the phosphate production of the livestock and not in considerations of profitability.

The main countries to which meat from The Netherlands is exported are Germany, Italy, the United Kingdom and France. Large-scale exports have been facilitated by the Common Agricultural Policy of the EU and the absence of internal trade barriers. For example, exports to the United Kingdom rose substantially in the years after Britain joined the EC in 1973. The EU also operates a system of export rebates or price subsidies for agricultural products sold outside the EU. The idea is to stimulate exports on the world market, although some people regard the practice as dumping. Intensive dairy cattle farming in The Netherlands has taken wholesale advantage of this scheme but new trading arrangements under the General Agreement on Tariff and Trade (GATT) have put a stop to the practice (see also Faber, 1996).

Transported meat is usually refrigerated and severe hygiene standards are imposed. However, the transport of live animals is subject to much less stringent rules. It involves problems connected with the animals' physical welfare, such as exposure to extreme temperatures, lack of food and water for lengthy periods while travelling long distances and stress during transport. Disease is more of a problem with exports of live pigs and piglets than with meat exports. Clearly, the more live animals are imported the greater the risk of disease. The risk is also greater if the animals are moved between agricultural holdings. Exporting regions may also be penalized if it is established that a disease has been transferred to another region or country. For instance, Brussels is empowered to ban exports and countries and regions can close their borders to one another. In 1994, Brittany and Spain closed their borders to imports of Dutch pigs in order to prevent the spread of swine vesicular disease.

The instability of an export-orientated pig production system is greater the more live animals are moved from place to place, the higher the absolute number of pigs per hectare (because the consequences of an outbreak of disease are more serious) and the less strictly hygiene regulations are observed. For these reasons, it has been suggested that The Netherlands should not export any live animals to southern Italy.

The international dimension of the manure problem

Some of the manure from areas in The Netherlands where there is a high concentration of livestock farming is supplied to arable farmers in other parts of the country under long-term contracts. The regulations allow them to use some of it on their own land, but the rest must be industrially processed. As policies are tightened up, a higher percentage of the manure will have to be processed. Industrial plants separate the nutrients from the water using a process that requires a great deal of energy. The clean water is discharged into the surface water. The nutrients are converted into powder or granules and are then fit for reuse. Unfortunately, these products cannot compete with artificial fertiliser in terms of price.

Many ideas have been put forward over the years about how to deal with the 'manure mountain'. Dumping it at sea and incinerating it are among the least environmentally friendly options. If it is fed to chickens, the nutrients enter a new cycle, but the problem remains in The Netherlands. Another suggestion is to export the manure to the developing world countries so as to prevent nutrient depletion in soil which is being used to grow raw materials for animal feed. This would be an extremely inefficient and expensive way of practising agriculture, however. It would be better to raise pigs in Thailand and transport the meat from the other side of the world. The manure granules could be sold to French wine growers, as is already done with dried chicken manure. But if the entire manure surplus which cannot be used in The Netherlands were to be processed industrially, many more granules would be produced than the wine growers could possibly use in the short term. Moreover, the end product must be able to compete with the cheaper artificial fertiliser which has been used to date.

Industrial manure processing is only viable if it is heavily subsidised. It has even been suggested that the Sahara could be made fertile with the aid of Dutch manure granules or that liquid manure should be exported to India, dried in the sun and sold. The response by Indian farmers to this idea confirms that conflicting interests are at stake, as Box 1 indicates.

I

Farmers in India angry over plans to import Dutch manure

(Wednesday) Angry farmers brought traffic to a halt in parts of New Delhi as they marched in protest against plans announced by a Dutch businessman to export manure worth millions of guilders to rural India. The farmers claimed that the Indian government was willing to pay an annual figure of 5.5 million guilders for the manure and that this was a complete waste of money.

'We wish to make clear that there is no need to import manure,' said Rajiv Vora of the Ghandi Peace Foundation. He accompanied the hundreds of fist-shaking farmers, assembled in a long procession of carts and lorries. 'It is a ridiculous proposal,' he added.

Men and women raised handfuls of manure in protest. For centuries, dried manure has been used in India as a fuel and as a construction material for huts and floors. It is also an important trading commodity. Villagers smear manure mixed with straw on the walls of houses; it is claimed that the chemicals in it act as disinfectants and protect public health.

Mr P. Hamoen of the Dutch embassy in New Delhi confirmed that Mr H.P. Prins of the Dutch Seaswan company was investigating the possibility of shipping surplus manure to India. The plan was intended to make good use of the manure surplus that existed both in The Netherlands and elsewhere in Europe. He pointed out that manure was used in India in many other different ways. In addition, he said that cows in India were not fattened to the same extent that they were in The Netherlands. The Indians regarded them as sacred animals and did not eat their meat.

The union representing 200,000 cow and bull owners in the vicinity of New Delhi claimed that there was enough manure, but not enough money to distribute it over the country. A spokesman said that their cattle produced 1500 tonnes of liquid manure every day, but that the owners had no way of disposing of it.

The well-known activist Ms Niru Vora accused the Indian government of plotting with international aid organisations to solve the Dutch manure problem.

Source: Reuters, New Delhi.

Finally, European environmental policy has a significant bearing on the Dutch manure problem. Despite the promptings of the European Parliament, the EU has decided, partly because of pressure from The Netherlands, not to force intensive livestock farmers to adopt a fixed animal-to-land ratio as is the case in Denmark. The imposition of such regulations would have sounded the death knell for Dutch pig farming. However, a *nitrate directive* has come into force which establishes an upper limit for permissible levels of nitrates in ground and surface water (50 mg per litre). Compliance with the directive is also required as part of the commitments under the *Rhine and North Sea Action Programme*, but it is extremely unclear as to whether The Netherlands will succeed in meeting the nitrogen requirements. The pollution of ground and surface water from agricultural sources will continue to rise for a number of years despite the lower manure utilisation standards, because the nitrate takes a long time to leach away (Ministry of Agriculture, Nature Conservation and Fisheries, 1982). Years of overfertilisation mean there are already high concentrations of nitrates in the soil. Sooner or later, they will end up in the water.

Plate 1.4 Algal bloom in the Wadden Sea, a wetland off the Northern coast of The Netherlands. Extensive studies have shown increased algal bloom caused by the run-off into the sea of nutrients from farms and sewage treatment plants. Photo: Mark Edwards/Lineair

We have now sketched both the national and international economic and ecological dimensions of Dutch intensive livestock farming. They form the backdrop to the stage on which the conflicts over the environmental impact of manure are played out. Box 2 summarises the resulting picture as a balance of negative and positive effects.

2

The economic and environmental effects of Dutch pig farming in a national and international perspective

	Positive	Negative
National	Employment (in the agricultural, industrial and service sectors) Revenues Revenues from foreign currencies Absorption of waste products Supply of animal manure	Water and soil pollution Exacerbation of acidification Damage to flora and fauna caused by ammonia Foul smell Damage to landscape
European	Supply of piglets and pigs Supply of pork Supply of animal manure (granulate)	Pollution of North Sea Export of ammonia
International	Supply of pork Purchase of foodstuffs Absorption of waste products	Soil erosion/nutrient depletion Deforestation Pesticide, etc. pollution

---

1.4 Conflicts of interest

The Dutch agricultural model

The climate, the soil, the proximity of major sales areas, a highly developed infrastructure, the availability of advanced water management technology and agricultural know-how are some of the factors which have contributed to the economic success of Dutch agriculture. One clearly important factor which is sometimes described as the *secret of Dutch agriculture* is the social, economic, institutional and political organisation of the agricultural sector or the *Dutch agricultural model*.

The model is characterised by a high density of organisations and a high degree of organisation. Virtually every important part of the agricultural sector which includes interests extending beyond those of individual enterprises is organised. Many issues, ranging from the health of animals to the amalgamation of scattered plots of farmland, from quality control to the supply of labour in the case of illness, are handled on a collective basis. Issues which are not dealt with by private farmers' organisations and professional bodies are handled by the Agricultural Board, to which all Dutch farmers and market gardeners pay an annual levy. The Agricultural Board is a statutory body which is empowered to lay down binding collective regulations.

The degree of organisation is also high in economic terms. On average, every agricultural producer is a member of four co-operatives involved in deliveries, marketing, processing, services, etc. The co-operatives include several huge agro-industries. They are owned by farmers; many directors of agricultural organisations are also directors of co-operatives. The interests of the co-operatives are therefore easy to reconcile with those of the farmers. A strong sector ideology has developed; the agricultural industry and agricultural trade are both part of the agricultural sector, which has its own sectoral interests to uphold in society, for example in relation to the environmental movement. Another feature of the agricultural model is the characteristically Dutch combination of elitism and pragmatism. The leaders of the farmers' organisations (which are established along denominational lines like much of Dutch society) find it relatively easy to do business with one another and with the government because their members are so passive. Consultations at the highest level are pragmatic, concern technical and economic problems and rarely degenerate into political conflict.

This brings us to the final feature of the Dutch agricultural model: the symbiosis between the highly organised agricultural sector and the government in the shape of the Ministry of Agriculture. For a long time, the agricultural sector was regarded as the Ministry's mainstay of support. There was consensus between the government and the industry on how agriculture in The Netherlands should develop and on agricultural policy. The most important issue was regarded as being the maintenance of the international competitiveness of an industry which depends on exports to survive. Market and pricing policies, as well as sectoral policies, were designed to develop the most productive businesses operating at the lowest cost. The government and agricultural organisations worked closely together to prepare and implement agricultural policy with this objective. For a long time, they encountered virtually no problems from 'outsiders' such as representatives of non-agricultural interest groups, ministries other than the Ministry of Agriculture or members of Parliament other than agricultural specialists closely associated with the agricultural sector. This tightly organised and relatively isolated stronghold, the heart of which was formed by the Ministry of Agriculture and the Agricultural Board, has often been described as the Green Front.

Conflict on the manure problem

For a long time, the Green Front turned a deaf ear to warnings about the manure problem. As early as the late 1960s, agricultural experts had warned against overfertilisation with manure and the dumping of animal manure (Frouws, 1993). They pointed to the danger of nitrogen leachate and eutrophication of the soil and groundwater. 'Critical' agriculturists and the environmental organisations which emerged in the early 1970s suggested that the number of animals per hectare should be limited and that this should also apply to intensive livestock farming (i.e. pigs, poultry, calves and red meat production). Other agricultural research workers, the government and agricultural organisations refused to see the dangers. They insisted that manure surpluses were a regional problem which would disappear by transporting the excess to areas where there was a shortage. Manure 'banks' were set up in the early 1970s for this purpose.

In hindsight, the political and social climate at the time was not ripe for tackling this growing environmental problem. The animal sector and allied industries were a source of increasing prosperity and employment. There was a great deal of faith in technical solutions, i.e. not just manure distribution, but also a better utilisation of animal feed and manure processing, by oxidation, for example. The critics, especially the agriculturists among them, were accused of indoctrination. Genuine attempts at dealing with the manure problem were postponed in various ways. Research was carried out into the nature and size of the manure surplus and potential technical solutions. A succession of committees of civil servants and advisory committees in the private sector were set up to consider policy measures. A fierce and extremely lengthy struggle was waged with the Ministry of the Environment about who should be responsible for which aspects of the manure legislation. The combined efforts of the Ministry of Agriculture and the Agricultural Board sometimes succeeded in preventing information about manure surpluses and possible manure utilisation standards from being made public. Clearly, ideological conflicts were at the roots of such administrative conflicts. Box 3 describes a typology of these conflicts.

3

A typology of conflicts

Conflicts of interest about the manure issue have an ideological component in that they involve a clash between *environmental interests* (i.e. clean water, energy savings and nature conservation) and *economic interests* (i.e. employment and export revenues), both of which are justified by invoking the common good. The administrative dimension of conflicts of interest is a matter of authority (i.e. who regulates what), the stringency of rules, and the expediency with which measures are taken.

With the manure problem, as with any environmental problem, the allocation of costs and benefits leads to distributional conflicts. These are played out at an international level (for instance, between the suppliers of foodstuffs inside and outside the European Union), at a national level (for instance, between the fertiliser industry and the industries responsible for processing and distributing manure), at a regional level (for instance, between the cattle farmers in areas with a manure surplus and those in areas with a manure shortage) and at a local level (for instance, in relation to plans for expanding a particular farm or disposing of manure).

However, the pressure placed on the agricultural sector was gradually intensified. It was difficult to ignore the results of research which confirmed that serious environmental damage would result from overfertilisation. The Ministry of the Environment could no longer be placated. Having introduced environmental legislation to deal with air and water pollution, it decided to tackle the third and remaining area, i.e. soil pollution. Pressure was growing in society (from environmental organisations, the media and scientific research institutes) and in political circles, where the environment was developing into an important issue. The trend was accentuated by alarming developments in the early 1980s, such as the nitrate pollution of drinking wells and an explosive growth in the number of pigs and chickens.

Policy development

The first regulations that came into being as a result of the growing pressure consisted of interim legislation to halt the growth in the number of livestock. In the short term, this government intervention actually exacerbated the problem. Pig and poultry farmers made extensive use of provisions that allowed them to expand if they had obtained a municipal permit or made investment commitments before a certain date. As a result, in the three years after the announcement of the interim legislation, the number of pigs went up by 28% and the number of poultry by more than 16%.

All the legislation on manure which was enacted after the interim legislation announced in late 1984 was prepared by the Ministry of Agriculture acting in conjunction with the Ministry of the Environment. It was difficult for the ministries to work together to begin with. Each part of the legislation produced a fierce struggle, whether about the level of the standards of enforcement, the arrangements regarding when and how manure should be spread, or 'manure bookkeeping'. The result of this first period of policy development was, apart from a considerable delay, legislation with a clear agricultural bias (see Box 4).

The development of legislation on manure | 4

After a long tug-of-war, it was decided in the mid-1980s to approach the problem of manure in stages. Stage 1 (1987–1990) centred on stabilisation or restraint and was designed to prevent the problem from getting any worse, and to find solutions in the form of livestock feeding, manure distribution and manure processing techniques. In 1987, an upper limit for phosphate production by agricultural holdings was established, thereby creating manure production rights. Regulations were introduced to prevent an increase in manure production. Limits were imposed on the quantities of animal manure which could be spread on the land and on the periods when this could be done. However, the limits were so generous that it was possible to dispose of all the manure produced throughout the country without exceeding them. The manure surplus had been defined out of existence.

The aim of stage 2 (1991–1994) was gradually to reduce the impact on the environment by tightening up utilisation standards. The idea was to adopt a timetable so that the manure surplus resulting from the tightening up of regulations could be dealt with by the solutions that were being developed (such as manure processing). Stage 3 (1995–2000) seeks a further tightening of standards so as to achieve balanced fertilisation in due course, at which stage the mineral quantities added to the soil by animal manure and artificial fertiliser will equal those taken from the soil by crops, taking acceptable losses into account. It was not clear at the end of 1994 what the final levels would be. However, it has become increasingly apparent that industrial manure processing is not developing fast enough to handle the additional manure surpluses which are being produced as a result of the gradual tightening of standards. A reduction in livestock numbers is therefore inevitable.

The manure utilisation standards were very flexible to begin with, the transitional period leading to less and eventually no overfertilisation was very long and there was initially no question of reducing livestock numbers. In fact, only excessive overfertilisation was halted and a definitive solution to the manure problem was made dependent on the availability of technical instruments such as improved methods of distribution, better use of animal feed and industrial manure processing, some of which still had to be developed. The Green Front succeeded in channelling hundreds of millions of guilders of government funds into the stimulation of technical solutions.

The Green Front achieved its 'victory' because of its ability to represent the interests of the agricultural sector, the power of the economic argument and its superior knowledge of fertiliser and livestock issues as compared with the environmental lobby. But its triumph was short-lived. The confrontation with such an extensive environmental problem as manure brought the Green Front into serious difficulties. Development and distributional issues were at stake which not only divided environmental and agricultural organisations, but also created conflicts of interest between the government and the agriculture lobby, as well as within the agricultural sector.

The *development problem* is about the nature and size of the intensive livestock farming system. There are numerous related issues. What standards must the system comply with as regards the degree of environmental pollution? What losses of minerals into the soil and groundwater are acceptable under which circumstances? What levels of ammonia emissions are permissible in which areas? What restrictions should be imposed on transport (of animal feed, animals and manure) and energy consumption (for heating animal pens, producing animal feed, transport and manure processing)? What standards should apply to the health and welfare of animals, the smell and the use of space? There are no objective answers to these questions, for they all involve the reconciliation of conflicting interests and hence political debate.

Ultimately, one has to make choices, for example between the value attached to the quality of woodlands and to the economic activity associated with pig farming. What is more, potential solutions to the manure problem can work against one another, so that here too priorities must be established. An example of a measure which has raised many questions is the method of mixing manure directly into the soil using turf spreaders and manure injectors. It limits ammonia emissions from the distribution of manure, but also has unintended effects which clash with the aims of government policy on environmental protection and nature conservation. The leaching of nitrates into groundwater is exacerbated by working manure deep into the ground, whilst on grasslands, birds' nests are destroyed by the machinery used to mix in the manure.

Furthermore, any solution to the development problem will involve sharing the costs and benefits to some extent. The development issue is therefore inextricably linked with the *distribution* issue. If it is decided to make drastic cuts in the pig sector, the immediate question is: which enterprises will have to go and which can or may continue to exist? For example, the pollution of groundwater by minerals can be counteracted by limiting the amount of manure which is spread on the land or by removing phosphates and nitrates at water treatment plants. In the former case, it is the farmers who foot the bill; in the latter case, the consumers of drinking water. The next section outlines these conflicts with reference to policy options, some of which have already been realised in part and some of which are still being developed.

Sharing the costs and benefits

The subject of reducing or restructuring the number of livestock has been a virtual taboo for many years. However, shortly after a new government came into power in the autumn of 1994, it became a serious option. The reason was, among others, that it became clear that other solutions such as large-scale manure processing would not make enough difference. Many interests are at stake here, often conflicting ones. The agricultural organisations have always fiercely rejected reductions by saying they would be contrary to the sector's interests. Now that some form of restructuring is unavoidable (either by allowing market forces to prevail or with government support), some farmers' leaders are prepared to start thinking about what would be the most desirable form. The *ideological* conflict that initially concerned the reduction in the number of livestock has now been followed by a *distributional* conflict.

A drastic reduction in the total number of animals in The Netherlands would appeal to pig and poultry farmers with good prospects because they would have more scope to dispose of their manure and the cost would therefore go down. Clearly, a reduction would damage the interests of suppliers (of animal feed and buildings for animals) and service firms connected with pig farming and poultry farming (e.g. contractors, the cattle trade, transporters of raw materials, manure, animals, etc.). If a reduction in the primary sector were accompanied by a reorganisation of the economically weak slaughterhouse sector, it would certainly benefit the surviving slaughterhouses and meat-processing companies. At an international level, a reduction in intensive live-stock farming in The Netherlands would mean greater sales opportunities for competing production areas in France and Denmark and pig producers and meat companies in Central and Eastern Europe in the longer term.

It is not inconceivable that The Netherlands will be prepared to make trade policy concessions in relation to this sector, which is in an awkward competitive position because of its environmental problems, in exchange for trade policy benefits for other agricultural or non-agricultural sectors. However, less pig and poultry production in The Netherlands will inevitably mean a shrinking sales market for raw materials used in animal feed obtained from Thailand, Brazil and the US. Finally, there is the problem of the way in which the reorganisation of the industry should be achieved and financed. Major interests are at stake, which means that there is again plenty of scope for conflict. The issues here are the degree of government intervention, the scale of government support and the degree to which the pain (caused by the reductions) and the costs (for example, of a fund to buy up production rights from the market) should be distributed over the sector as a whole and within the category of primary producers in particular.

A second option which is similarly accompanied by major conflicts of interests concerns the organisation and financing of manure distribution and processing. The 'surplus' levy used to finance research into manure processing and to support the manure bank created conflicts from the outset between the areas where there was a manure surplus and those where there was a shortage. Livestock farmers and organi-sations in the North and West of The Netherlands were against paying the levy because they felt they were being asked to foot the bill for a manure problem caused by livestock farmers in the areas with a surplus. On the other hand, the view in areas with a high concentration of intensive livestock farming was that the problem was a *national* one and that large-scale processing increased the opportunities for individual farms with a surplus in the shortage areas to dispose of manure. The conflict of interest clearly emerged in the dispute about the proposed 'manure centre.'

Farmers and organisations in the South of the country took the view that all livestock farmers in the areas with a manure surplus should be obliged to offer their surplus manure to a central organisation known as the manure centre. The centre would charge the same price, irrespective of the destination of the manure, and would manage the flows of manure as efficiently as possible, thereby saving money on transport and processing. This system would prevent livestock farmers from competing with one another to dispose of their manure. Competition would have forced up the price and would have benefited the arable farmers who received the manure. This is the reason why, in the first instance, the arable farmers were fiercely opposed to the compulsory nature of the manure centre. They saw their competitive advantage taken away from them. But there was also opposition from livestock farmers who had solved their surplus problems by extending their storage facilities, reducing the volume of manure on their farms or by entering into long-term contracts to sell manure to arable farmers.

The funding of large-scale manure processing has revealed yet other conflicts of interest. The artificial fertiliser industry was opposed to the subsidisation of the manure-processing plants by means of a system of levies. In other pig-producing areas of the European Union, these kinds of subsidies were regarded as distorting competition. The European Commission therefore only allowed the imposition of a *destination levy*, to be paid by farmers in areas with a high concentration of livestock farming to get rid of their manure surpluses, for a very limited start-up period.

The final conflict of interest relates to groundwater protection areas and the application of the *polluter pays principle*. Voluntary agreements have been reached between farmers in areas where water is extracted and the water companies to the effect that livestock farmers will be subject to stricter regulations than those in force in the rest of the country as regards the use of fertilisers and the distribution of manure on the land. The level of the payment they receive in return has been the subject of disputes between the agricultural organisations on the one hand and the water companies, the provincial authorities and the environmental organisations on the other. The latter have taken the view that consumers of drinking water are having to foot too much of the bill.

1.5 Possible solutions: the role of politicians and technology

In this section, we shall discuss the pig-farming industry as it may aptly serve as the main model for what many people refer to disparagingly as *the bio-industry*. Whenever the complex and long-lasting problem of manure comes up for discussion, the finger of accusation is immediately pointed at pigs. It should be kept in mind, however, that poultry and cattle make a sizeable contribution to the manure mountain too. In fact, cattle manure is the main agricultural source of ammonia emissions in The Netherlands.

In exploring the potential solutions for the environmental problems raised by pig farming in The Netherlands, it is possible to envisage three distinct scenarios or models, each of which has distinct developmental and environmental implications (Bolsius, 1993, pp.11–69). The first, which may be called the *global scenario*, involves concentration of production in an industrialised setting. The second is based on a *regional cycle* of manure and animal feed. Finally, the *local scenario* assumes maximum distribution, so there is no longer a region with a high concentration of livestock farming. After describing each of the scenarios, we shall give a brief analysis of the political and technological conditions which are required in order to put them into practice and describe the conflicts of interest which they involve.

The global scenario

In the *global scenario*, animal feed is imported on a large scale and converted by pigs into meat. The meat is supplied to consumers, who may live at a considerable distance from the production area. There is too much manure for it to be disposed of in the immediate vicinity so it must be processed at a central location or removed elsewhere and disposed of outside the region. If the incoming and outgoing flows are properly managed, there is in theory no limit to the number of pigs which can be concentrated in a small area. The costs of the environmental pollution are gradually passed on to producers and consumers. And although Dutch producers invest a great deal in order to comply with environmental regulations, by doing so they raise their production costs considerably and their competitive position deteriorates.

In a global scenario, raising pigs requires large-scale operations which manage incoming and outgoing flows efficiently. The model necessitates massive investment in buildings, infrastructure and allied environmental facilities in order to combat the smell, treat effluent, process manure on a large scale and market the meat. Large-scale operations of this kind should be located on industrial estates close to deep water and not in rural areas.

Transferring pigs to industrial estates does not produce any space gains in the sense that more land immediately becomes available. But it does mean that there are more opportunities for developing nature reserves, the recreation industry and drinking water supplies, because there is less pressure on the environment. A reduction in manure production indirectly creates more opportunities for other forms of land use. This model foresees attempts to reduce costs to a minimum by maximising the scale of the operations. The primary objective is high quality and homogeneous bulk production. There is little likelihood of the rural economy in the regions reaping the benefits of this kind of industrial process. Theoretically, the production chain could even be managed by multinational companies.

This global scenario has the effect of completely unfettering intensive livestock farming. It can easily move to areas where animal feed is produced or where processed manure is marketed, if that would improve the cost/benefit ratio. In it, productivity is maximised and is supported by an efficient distribution system between the various stages in the production chain and between the end stage of the production chain and the consumer market.

In political and administrative terms, the global scenario requires a business location policy that is subject to strict central controls so as to resolve numerous disputes about how space should be used and about the quality of the environment in a broad sense. It will result in an industrial sector consisting of a number of pig-producing businesses with employees on their payroll. It will mean restructuring the existing pig-farming industry and eliminating existing family businesses. Any policy which expressly seeks to achieve this objective will be unacceptable to the farmers' organisations, which still rate family businesses highly.

The question of animal welfare and related ethical aspects of this industrial form of livestock farming will result in critical public attitudes. The need for large-scale manure processing makes the global scenario highly dependent on energy prices. The model also requires the sustainable development of land in other countries which is used to produce raw materials for animal feed. Tariff barriers must not be erected against imports of raw materials and the more expensive European grain will not be used as animal feed.

Stringent technological conditions will have to be met in addition to political ones. The new pig farms will have to be far enough away from one another and the transport of live animals will have to be kept to a minimum in order to prevent diseases from spreading. The farms will be 'closed' establishments where piglets are born and pigs are fattened for nearby slaughterhouses. Productivity will have to be very high in order to produce a bulk product that can be sold at competitive prices in spite of the high cost of environmental measures such as emission-free pens, manure processing, etc. These requirements will reinforce the industrial nature of the farms even further. The ultimate question is whether Western European consumers will accept such industrially produced meat.

The regional scenario

An alternative scenario is provided by a *regional model*. Here, the feed comes from the region itself, possibly supplemented by grain from the closest grain-producing region. This scenario therefore creates problems for the producers of grain substitutes in the developing countries and elsewhere. The manure is not distributed any further than the area which supplies the feed, although the meat is exported much further afield.

The development opportunities for this system will depend on the claims made by other types of land use. Consultations will need to establish which land is to be used by each sector and the environmental quality which must be maintained will be laid down in the form of increasingly strict standards. The required level of investment will be high and will continue to rise, but will only be worthwhile if sufficient added value is created. A shift from bulk production with a low added value per unit of product to a method which does little damage to the environment and which offers a higher added value would be the best solution.

One way of achieving this would be by severing the link between pig breeding and the fattening of pigs for slaughter, i.e. by using specialisation to achieve greater economies of scale. However, this approach would conflict with the aim of creating closed farms and limiting the transport of pigs. Another way would be to raise the added value at all the stages in the production chain and to develop a variety of end products, especially for meat. In the regional scenario, it would be difficult to keep disease under control, which means a great deal of preventive vaccination would be required. Hygienic controls would have to be very strict; a certain degree of stress on the animals would be unavoidable.

If the regional model is used as the starting point, the environmental requirements will be stricter and the authorities will have to set limits for the number of pigs in each region. If there are transferable manure production rights, bigger farms will buy up the manure quotas of smaller farms. Environmental investment will be subsidised in exchange for the stricter requirements and farms will be given financial incentives to cease operating. The transportation of manure over long distances will be discouraged. Fixed contractual relationships between breeders, fatteners and processors will have the effect of keeping animal health problems to a minimum. This form of pig farming will make a major contribution to the socioeconomic sustainability of rural areas as a source of regional economic activity and income, but is clearly not without its problems.

The local scenario

A third scenario is offered by a *local model*. It centres around a purely land-based type of farm which is more or less extensive, i.e. a mixed farm with free-range animals. As pigs live in groups they could, for instance, be used in the subsidised management of semi-natural landscapes and forests. The feed comes from the immediate vicinity, which means that this model also has an adverse effect on producers of grain substitutes in the developing countries and elsewhere. Manure is also disposed of in the immediate vicinity. In principle, the pigs can make use of space out in the open air. The meat is sold at high prices because of the quality label it carries, which is why the farmers can afford to operate this type of system, with their income supplemented if necessary by income from other sources.

This system is entirely land-based, which means that the cost of land is the highest item of capital expenditure. For lack of food, pigs will be less concentrated and their numbers will be kept low. The impact on the environment of these types of farms therefore stays well below accepted environmental limits and virtually no investments are required to ward off or compensate for environmental damages. The system is also almost unaffected by energy prices and hygiene-related, stress-related and epidemic diseases are rare. However, additional income may be needed from other sources, such as the exploitation of the landscape and natural features, recreation and afforestation. The regional model also requires strong pig breeds capable of spending long periods in the open air.

In political and technological terms, the local scenario represents the most radical break with the established system of intensive production. It presupposes a drastic reduction in primary and secondary activities connected with pig farming. The volume of production is only a fraction of that at present. A system of local quality marks could guarantee that the pork had been produced with real concern for the welfare of the animals. It could stress that the pigs were raised with a guaranteed access to enough space both indoors and in the open air, as well as opportunities for natural behaviour and without the use of antibiotics.

1.6 Conclusion

In all likelihood, none of the scenarios described in the previous paragraphs will ever be achieved in its entirety. Each of them is a model which is designed to illustrate the development issues and different interests that are involved. If the models make anything clear, it is that restructuring intensive livestock farming with its detrimental effects on the environment is an enormous undertaking in both political and techno-logical terms. A drastic form of intervention is more or less unavoidable, but the question is: how should it be done?

The government is facing a dilemma in this respect. An enormous effort will be required to resolve the manure problem within the foreseeable future, whatever course of action the government adopts. If it does not provide substantial support, not only will there be a serious risk of widespread social unrest among the pig farmers who are forced out of business, but the surviving businesses will also try to recoup high levels of expenditure (on manure processing and/or modifying or moving their operations) in all kinds of ways, which will make it extremely difficult to enforce environmental regulations. At the same time, if the government organises and supports a restructuring process which gives viable pig farms sufficient scope to produce along environmen-tally acceptable lines without incurring excessively high costs, the funding required from general funds may be so high as to be regarded as unacceptable outside the agricultural sector and possibly even outside the intensive livestock farming sector.

The dilemma we have described has not yet been resolved. The government and leaders of the sector are making urgent appeals to the livestock farmers' sense of responsibility and resourcefulness and are urging joint initiatives, not just from pig farmers but from all those involved in the production chain. One idea, for example, is to use a *'mineral bookkeeping'* system, with levies and premiums to encourage livestock farmers to minimise the leaching of phosphates and nitrates into the environment. Farmers are also being encouraged by means of grants and licences to make joint plans for their own regions for the storage, transport and processing of manure (albeit on a small scale) and for reductions in overall ammonia emissions. As part of the sectoral debate described in section 1.4, a scenario has been proposed (Bens *et al.*, 1994) in which the added value at all the stages in the production chain would be raised by intensive co-operation between all the firms involved in the production of pigs and pork. Slaughterhouses and meat-processing companies are being asked to consult with one another and make arrangements for ceasing mutual competition. This would also involve entering into long-term contracts with both pig farmers and their customers. Exports of live piglets and pigs could decline and market prices could stabilise at a higher level. It would then be easier to finance environmental expenditure with the additional income.

A co-operative approach requires a degree of private planning and regulation which is difficult to reconcile with the spirit of free enterprise and free trade which is relatively strong in the pig-farming sector. An example of a collective initiative, the 'manure centre,' has already failed. One is still no nearer to defining what the future of the Dutch pig-farming industry will be. The question is decided by forces both inside and outside the sector. But how much more time and space will the politicians and the public give a sector which is balancing on the knife edge of government regulations as regards environmental pollution, hygiene and animal welfare?

Things are further complicated by the sector's close involvement in a number of international conflicts of interest. In the context of the EU and GATT, there is pressure on grain prices, which could eradicate the competitive edge enjoyed by Dutch pig farmers as a result of importing cheap grain substitutes. The interests of tapioca exporters such as Thailand, which would probably side with the Dutch, does not seem to count for much in this situation and may well be bought off with support for local food production in these countries. Additionally, growth in exports from Central and Eastern Europe in the next few years could represent a threat to bulk pork production in The Netherlands. Competition from Western European production areas, for example Denmark and Brittany, where the environmental problems are less acute and extensive, forms a further threat. Besides international interests, there are the international environmental problems. Large-scale soy bean cultivation, especially in the south and south-east of Brazil, has already been described as an ecological disaster (Besselial *et al.*, 1994). It is virtually impossible to comply with European standards on the quality of groundwater, surface water and the North Sea. And the opportunities for finding foreign markets for the Dutch manure surplus should not be overestimated.

For a long time, 'faith' in the technology of large-scale manure processing kept many people under its spell. A sizeable number of farmers, however, are apparently unwilling to submit themselves to a collective organisation that would co-ordinate manure transport and its financing. The distressed pig-farming sector cannot afford the high costs of this technology. It is clear once again that the role of technology can only be considered in its socioeconomic context. By clinging obstinately to the technological option of industrial manure processing, society has effectively blocked the promotion of other options, such as small-scale manure processing techniques and the gradual restructuring of the entire cattle and meat sector. In retrospect, both the cattle farmers and the environment in the areas of concentration have suffered from this technological optimism.

A drastic reduction in the number of agricultural holdings is expected, the impact of which will be softened by government support. The pollution of groundwater by minerals which are in the system as the result of years of overfertilisation (therefore necessitating the treatment of the groundwater before it can be used for drinking purposes) will remain a problem in The Netherlands for many years to come. For the time being, the competitiveness of the surviving pig-farming sector will also be under pressure as a result of the cost of dealing with the problems of manure and ammonia.

Alongside the large-scale, mainstream pig-producing companies, a subsector could develop which produces 'ecological' pork aimed at a limited segment of the domestic market. The strict environmental conditions under which they will have to produce mean that price differences need not form an insuperable problem.

2

Analysing amenity and scientific problems: The Broadlands, England

John Blunden and Nigel Curry

2.1 Introduction

The River Yare and its two major tributaries, the Waveney and the Bure, drain to the sea through Great Yarmouth in East Anglia (in the Eastern part of England). The low-lying land surrounding the tidal reaches of these rivers is known as Broadland, an area unlike any other in the country. Flat and low-lying, it contains a variety of landscapes and wetland habitats and supports a wide range of activities. Much of the area is devoted to agriculture but this co-exists with an extensive tourist indus-try, visitors being attracted by the opportunities offered for boating, walking, fish-ing and general sightseeing. The major town is Great Yarmouth, an active port and an important base for the offshore gas industry (National Rivers Authority, 1993).

This quotation encapsulates well the range of environmental values and economic activities that are to be found in the Broadland area. They undoubtedly represent a unique constellation in the context of the UK and are only rarely replicated amongst the wetlands of the rest of Europe. This chapter provides an in-depth study of Broadland in order to consider how conflicts of values and interests affect the definition of an environmental problem and the approach to its solution. The argument proceeds as follows.

First, the case study will be used to show how competing values and activities have evolved and to identify some of the principal environmental problems arising from *multiple land uses* in an area of extreme environmental sensitivity (section 2.2). Secondly, we will explore the conflict of interest between the private landowner, exercising his or her property rights , and the land user, including public bodies and recreational interests. In particular the conflicts and consequent negative environ-mental effects over water quality, water and river management and agriculture are discussed (section 2.3). This discussion leads to considering the attempt that has been made to mediate and resolve conflicts through the establishment of a Broads Authority (section 2.4). The international dimension to the study of Broadland is then elaborated by articulating the kinds of value systems that are commonly present in the processes of *environmental mediation*, many of which extend beyond boundaries of the nation state. Here particular attention is given to the attempt to establish commonly agreed value systems and a holistic approach to both scientific conservation and landscape protection for amenity purposes (section 2.5).

2.2 Broadland – a case study

Historical context

As a flood plain, the area of Broadland (see Map 2.1) owes its unique environmental and ecological characteristics to medieval peat workings. During the 12th, 13th and 14th centuries, peat digging was a major industry. The workings became filled with water, thus creating an expanse of 'broads' – large areas of water and shallow lakes. As the broads themselves were cut by hand, so were the dykes needed for the purpose of transporting the reed harvest and sedge and marsh hay from the wet marshes. Also ditches were dug to drain the wet areas for grazing, later to be made all the more effective by the introduction of wind pumps. The whole water system became a trading network for the otherwise isolated villages in Broadland.

In this state, a crude equilibrium was achieved between the human demands made upon it, particularly in terms of large blocks of grazing marshes from which a thriving wool trade developed in the 16th century, and the maintenance of a particularly rich ecology. For centuries, the Broads were self-supporting, providing food, buildings and transport for people living and working in the area. From the beginning of this century, however, threats to this equilibrium emerged. In terms of human impact, the population has increased and farming has intensified. At the same time other interests have gained ground. Recreation and tourism, which began in the 1870s with the arrival of the railway in Broadland, have made the Broads a destination for thousands of people ironically seeking the freedom and tranquillity of some 200 kilometres of waterway. Fresh water supplies are threatened by both increasing demands, through new house building in Norfolk and Suffolk, and reductions in the supply of good quality water through the pollution of water courses by intensive economic activity. Nature, too, is providing its own threats through the global phenomenon of sea level change with a rising and stormy North Sea threatening to undermine everything that makes the Broads special.

Today, then, there are many conflicting value systems that place pressures on Broadland. Private economic and commercial aspirations in both agriculture and recreation are often at odds with more public desires for high quality ecological and amenity environments. These have been generated at the local, regional and even international level with the values of different user groups and landowning and water interests increasingly difficult to reconcile. Indeed, the most recent draft plan for the Broads (Broads Authority, 1993), in being entitled *No Easy Answers*, recognises the particularly acute nature of competing interests and value systems that operate within the area.

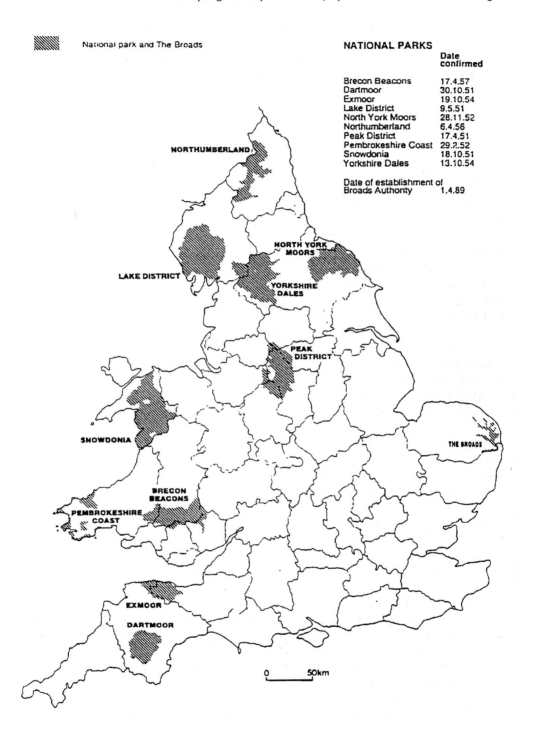

National park and The Broads

NATIONAL PARKS

	Date confirmed
Brecon Beacons	17.4.57
Dartmoor	30.10.51
Exmoor	19.10.54
Lake District	9.5.51
North York Moors	28.11.52
Northumberland	6.4.56
Peak District	17.4.51
Pembrokeshire Coast	29.2.52
Snowdonia	18.10.51
Yorkshire Dales	13.10.54

Date of establishment of
Broads Authority   1.4.89

NORTHUMBERLAND

LAKE DISTRICT

NORTH YORK MOORS

YORKSHIRE DALES

PEAK DISTRICT

SNOWDONIA

THE BROADS

BRECON BEACONS

PEMBROKESHIRE COAST

EXMOOR

DARTMOOR

0   50km

Map 2.1 National parks in England and Wales

Amenity values

The landscape of Broadland, with its vast skies, open water, vivid colours and rich wildlife, provides a unique sense of place – a place of peace, remoteness and contact with nature. It is distinctive in its landscape features. The rivers wind slowly between embankments, high above open grazing marshes and waterlogged areas of pond weeds, rushes and alder known as *fens*. Windpumps, church towers, white sails on the waterways and areas of carr woodland, with their predominant stands of alder as well as sallow, osier and willow, all provide striking vertical features in an otherwise horizontal landscape. The evocation of these landscapes has been expressed by a number of local authors (Dymond, 1990; Malster, 1993).

In valuing such landscapes, certain descriptive taxonomies can be deployed, as Box 1 indicates.

A landscape taxonomy   ▌1▐

The Broads Authority Landscape Group have classified the landscapes of the area into five principal types:

1 Broads that are fully enclosed by reed or alder carr providing short views opening out over small areas of grazing marsh.
2 Broads that are less enclosed offering a larger scale landscape but with a distinct valley form. Grazing marsh is dominant, but with occasional trees.
3 Open valleys that provide grazing marsh perspectives with views of villages on raised land, churches and windpumps.
4 Open flat landscapes offering large areas of water fringed with reeds.
5 Extensive open landscapes providing little open water, but large areas of grazing marsh, marsh gates, regulated dykes, birds and an immense sky.

Source: Broads Authority (1986)

But the overall *amenity values* of this area are greater than the sum of its landscape parts. They owe as much to cultures, local traditions and historical economic activity. The landscape has been fashioned by the working and living patterns of the people, exploiting the natural resources of the landscape for their own ends. Historically, fish and wildfowl provided a source of food, and reed and sedge, through thatching, gave them a roof over their heads. Marsh hay provided fodder for grazing cattle and the waterways were used for transporting goods. These economic and social activities, in turn, allowed wildlife and habitats to flourish. Much of the heritage of the area can be seen in the landscape today. The wherries that transported goods along the rivers may still be found alongside a great diversity of historic buildings which remain as the outward manifestations of the patterns of land ownership and economic activity of the past.

Amenity values are thus an intertwining of topographical characteristics, fauna and flora, and human tradition. Clearly, they are intrinsic public values, based as much on a sense of localness, resident culture and 'belonging' as on any more classifiable value

Items ISSUED to: 7604728238

Title: Local environmental policies and strategies

ID: 7608568863
Due: 21/01/2008 23:59

Title: Environmental policy in an international
context
ID: 7620149344
Due: 11/01/2008 23:59

Title: environmental history of Britain since the
Industrial Revolution
ID: 7620992041
Due: 11/01/2008 23:59

Title: Health and health care in the Third World
ID: 7604919920
Due: 21/01/2008 23:59

Title: New face of the NHS
ID: 7622001573
Due: 11/01/2008 23:59

Title: Health policy in Britain : the politics and
organisation of the National Hea
ID: 7623680946
Due: 11/01/2008 23:59

Total items: 6
1/12/2007 13:50

Thank You for using Self Service.
Please keep your receipt.

Overdue books are fined at 40p per day for
week loans, 10p per day for long loans.

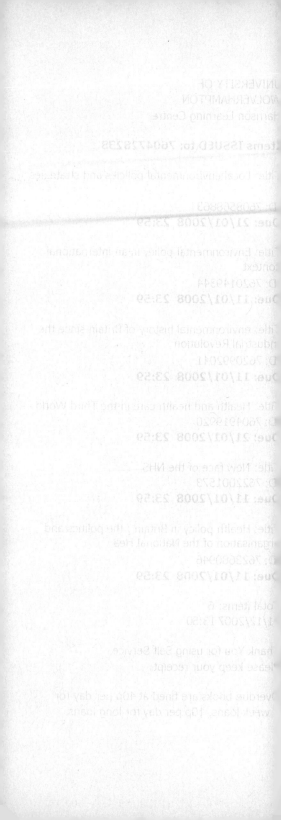

Plate 2.1 The River Ant, Norfolk. The Norfolk Broads are a unique region around a group of shallow lakes connected by a network of rivers. Photo: Mike Read/Ringwood

system. They are not represented through any market mechanisms (although they undoubtedly provide one of the core values of the leisure market) nor, of themselves, are they recognised through any statutory designation, local, national or international. Rather they are manifest through a sense of pride of place and 'ownership' of locality by the indigenous population, seen through a range of fond and nostalgic writings about cultures, customs and traditions (Calvert, 1993; Calvert and Calvert, 1992; Green, 1992).

The essential localness of amenity values has broadened to the wider population where it has been broadcast either through the landscape paintings of such as Turner and Sir Armesby Brown or more overtly through the positive marketing of Broadland as a leisure destination.

Nature conservation values

The Broads play host to many species of plant life that are fast disappearing from wetland habitats. This ecosystem provides essential sustenance and shelter for animal life. The fens alone contain over 250 plant species including the nationally protected fen orchid, the yellow loosestrife and the ragged robin. Aquatic plants too, such as the water soldier, the holly-leaved naiad, the hogwort and the bladderwort, do much to define the distinctiveness of the area. These plants provide scarce breeding grounds for butterflies such as the swallowtail, dragonflies, the Norfolk hawker and damselflies.

The Broads also are well known for their diverse species of birds. Coots, moorhens, ducks, herons and grebes are commonly seen in the region, but more remote areas of open water are important for breeding and overwintering birds such as the goldeneye, teal, mallard, widgeon, shoveller and poachard. Species such as the reed warbler, the sedge warbler, bearded tits and reed buntings are to be found in contrast, in the reedswamp of the fens. In other areas on the drained marshlands, snipe, redshank and lapwing nest and find food, whilst oyster catchers may be found on marshland nearer the coast (Jones, 1985).

This variety of fauna and flora provides a series of public values in stark contrast to those generated by the amenity values of the area. Rather than being prized for their localness, for their values as heritage or unique sense of culture, these are values that have a more ubiquitous currency. The diversity of species within Broadland has led to values that have been recognised through nationally and internationally accepted designations.

Specific sites in the Broads, for example, Bure broads and marshes and Upper Thame broads and marshes, were designated in 1976 as *Ramsar sites* under the Convention on Wetlands of International Importance signed at Ramsar in Iran in 1971. This has established their worth according to an international value system representing, as they do, two of only 13 such sites in England and Wales.

Values of national currency also have been established through the designation of *Sites of Special Scientific Interest* (SSSIs) in the area. These are defined by English Nature, the successor body to the Nature Conservancy Council, under a continuous process which attempts to safeguard ecosystems of unique significance. Moreover, three *National Nature Reserves* (NNRs) at Hickling Broad, Bure Marshes and Ludham Marshes have also been declared because of their biological and physiographic importance in the national context. But in addition, those SSSIs that include Bure broads and marshes, the Ant broads and marshes, the Yare broads and marshes and the Upper Thame broads and marshes have been recommended by English Nature for further designation either as Ramsar sites or as Special Protection Areas under the 1979 European Directive on Birds, or both. Clearly, both international and European value systems are being proposed to establish the nature conservation worth of the region as being of more than just national significance.

In seeking to formalise national nature conservation values too, the Broads Authority (1993) considers some 80% of the grazing marshes to be of SSSI quality in respect of their marsh dyke communities.

Recreation values

If the public and cultural values of amenity and nature conservation are themselves very different – the former being based on the uniqueness of locality and the latter on the ecosystem values of an international currency – they are also overlaid by powerful market or commercial values generated by the two main industries of the area, tourism and agriculture. The historical importance of waterways in Broadland for trade has all but disappeared with waterways today almost exclusively used for leisure. This principally takes the form of tourism with many people staying on the large number of hire boats in the area, as well as local hotels and bed and breakfast accommodation, but there are also considerable numbers of day trips from bases near Norwich and Great Yarmouth. The Broads attract in excess of 1 million visitors each year.

The unique drainage and river navigation system of the Broads is undoubtedly best experienced by boat. As one of Europe's most popular inland waterways, the Broads have the largest hire boat fleet of any waterway system in Europe and the private ownership of craft has grown considerably. In 1971 there were more than 10,000 boats registered on the Broads. By 1981 this had risen by more than 14% and by 1993 it had risen by a further 12%. This growth has spawned a large boat-building industry and a thriving export trade.

The 200 kilometres of safe waterways also allow ample opportunity for fishing and nature study. Land-based recreation is not extensively exploited although there is considerable scope for opening up more walks and rights of way since the wildlife and landscape interests accessible from the land are considerable.

All of this leisure activity adds up to a direct injection of between £20 and £30 million per annum into the local economy (Broads Authority, 1993), with ancillary industries generating economic activity that probably doubles this value. As well as expenditure on boat hire and accommodation, fishing licences and permits to fish generate considerable income. Indirectly, the boat-building and repair sectors, which alone have an estimated turnover in excess of £15 million per annum and employ over 1500 people, are supplemented by a large fishing tackle and bait industry. Indirect employment, too, is generated through the necessary employment of river bailiffs, ghillies and so on. In 1988, the Broads Hire Boat Federation estimated that between 5000 and 5500 jobs were in some way dependent upon the hire boat sector.

Recreation and tourism values are expressed in large part, then, by the operation of the free market with consumers demonstrating a willingness to pay through an established price structure. This market operation also generates *externalities*, impacts of market activity that are not fully accounted for in the price of commodities or in the processes of production (see also chapter 5). Not only are the externalities not fully internalised into the market (that is, recreators do not pay in full for the environmental change their activities cause) but they represent significant threats to the very different amenity and nature conservation values of Broadland.

As well as the monetary market values of leisure, there are hundreds of thousands of people every year who derive enormous pleasure from visiting the Broads. This pleasure represents further externalities, this time positive ones, to the leisure market, which economists have classified under the general term of *merit goods*. The spiritual and physical refreshment derived from a holiday in Broadland is rarely fully encapsulated in its market price. These intangible merit values derive again as much from the amenity and nature conservation values of the area as from its commercial infrastructure.

Agricultural values

The Broads historically have yielded a diverse harvest. Peat, reed and sedge, marsh hay for cattle, marsh litter for livestock bedding, wildfowl and fish for the table all provided sustenance for the traditional marshmen in their hand to mouth existence. Today, the marshes and fens still rely on marshmen, some looking after more than 400 hectares of land. They are invariably employed in summer by landowners (although land has historically been and is still today owned in small parcels) and as well as having responsibilities for livestock, they are charged with many aspects of the drainage of the area – the maintenance of dyke levels, the operation of sluices, the recutting of foot drains and so on. Many are also employed by landowners to cut reed and sedge in season.

This pattern of agriculture, which characteristically is still broadly grazing marsh with a few pockets of arable land, has done much to define the amenity values of the area. But it has been continually facing pressures for modernisation. From the 13th and 14th centuries the draining of the marshes began to allow landowners to raise and fatten livestock. By the 17th century this had become widespread.

Accession to the European Community in 1974, however, brought about much more far-reaching changes. Guaranteed prices for cereals made arable farming a significantly more profitable enterprise. By the 1980s dairy quotas had forced many farmers in the Broads to reduce their herds. The result was that grassland was fast disappearing under the plough. Conversion to cereals was made even more attractive by high rates of drainage grants available during the 1970s.

By the early 1980s the grazing marshes, one of the principal landscape features of the Broads, were in danger of being substantially given over to wheat production. The infrastructure appropriate to the production of wheat (concrete roads, storage barns, overhead cabling for supplying power to grain dryers) and fertilisers and pesticides seeping into the dykes were radically affecting the central amenity and nature conservation values of Broadland.

Agricultural values are also thus composite ones. At the farm level, the landowners and marshmen are operating within a market structure to maximise farm incomes from food production. But, unlike leisure and tourism, they are operating within a market heavily managed by the Common Agricultural Policy (CAP). Price signals arise not from the free market but from European policy priorities. The means of production are driven by policies on farm input subsidies rather than the free market for inputs. These market signals driven now by policy also generate negative environmental externalities. The increased use of fertilisers and pesticides threatens the pollution of water courses, affecting water quality. The draining of the grazing marshes threatens to change the amenity value of the landscape beyond recognition and to impair much of the diversity of the wetland-based fauna and flora of the region. As the monetary returns from agriculture increase, the impacts on the landscape and ecosystems can be devastating.

Composite value systems in Broadland

The value systems of Broadland are complex. They can be considered in at least two different ways. Firstly, there are tensions between *market values* based on the ownership of land, capital goods and *private property rights*, personal values based on the uniqueness of place and public values based on more widely recognised notions of the quality of the environment. These are summarised in Table 2.1.

Market values	Values from agricultural production based on the managed market
	Values from recreation and tourism based on the free market
Personal values	Amenity values based on custom and culture
	Physical and spiritual refreshment from recreation and tourism
Public values	Negative environmental externalities from agriculture
	Negative environmental externalities from recreation and tourism
	Nature conservation values

Table 2.1 Types of values in Broadland

In addition, however, such values can be classified in terms of scale. Amenity and refreshment values derive very much from the locality. Broadland as a tourism resource and its nature conservation values represented through Sites of Special Scientific Interest and National Nature Reserves provide values of regional and national significance. Food output driven by the Common Agricultural Policy and the recognition of Special Protection Areas for birds are very much concerned with the imposition of a European value system. Sites designated under the Ramsar Convention, however, are more fully international. These are summarised in Table 2.2.

Local values	Recreation values derived from spiritual and physical refreshment
	Amenity values derived from custom and culture
Regional and national values	Broadland as a tourism resource
	Nature conservation values recognised through SSSIs and National Nature Reserves
European values	Agricultural values driven by the market management of the Common Agricultural Policy
	Nature conservation values in Special Protection Areas under the European Commission Directive on Birds
International values	International wetlands under the Ramsar Convention

Table 2.2 The scale of values in Broadland

2.3 Conflicts of interest

The interplay of these value systems inevitably, and in the case of Broadland critically, leads to *conflicts of interest*, where the activities of the market place in leisure, agriculture and indeed aquaculture, together with water abstraction and supply, severely threaten the more personal and public values of amenity and scientific conservation. This has led to a spiral of decline, well summarised by the Broads Authority (1993):

> In many places, the water is murky where it should be clear; long stretches of river bank have lost their cushion of reeds; toxic blue-green algae outbreaks are more frequent, as are fish kills. Trees and scrub have invaded neglected fens threatening its rich wildlife and cutting off the breeze from sailing craft. And what more poignant symbol of misuse could there be than the prolonged absence of bittern, the talisman of the Broads.

In essence, these deleterious impacts of the market are caused by *negative externalities* which are no more stark than in their impacts on water quality and the consequent requirements for water and river management in Broadland.

Water quality

In 1982, a draft strategy and management plan, *What Future for Broadland?*, articulated clearly that the key to the future of Broadland was water quality. This quality had been declining over a number of years principally through the process of *eutrophication*, the fertilisation of the water through nutrient enrichment, mainly as a result of increasing amounts of phosphorus and nitrogen in the water.

The increasing amounts of phosphorus came in large part from sewage treatment works; the then regional water authority had seen the area as a principal destination for effluent disposal. This was a case of conflicts of interest coming from policies of the state, where one public policy objective – effluent disposal – was having significant detrimental effects on another – water quality – which itself was inhibiting the provision of potable water supplies, a responsibility of the same water authority. This situation was made worse by a degree of effluent disposal actually being imported into the area from a water authority that had a much larger catchment than that of just Broadland.

On occasion the overburdening of sewage arrangements led to a discharge of raw sewage into the waterways of the area. Even today, the discharge of domestic and industrial effluent is often considerable. Many water treatment works, which carry out primary and secondary treatment adequate for removing major pathological dangers such as disease organisms, are not equipped with tertiary treatment facilities for stripping or polishing nutrients from the treated water prior to discharge.

Phosphorus, too, came from the workings of the policy-driven market in agriculture, through the increasing amount of farm wastes that were generated by intensifying livestock production systems. Slurry, silage liquid, which is 200 times more polluting than domestic sewage, and other liquid wastes such as those from yard washing were beginning to show significant pollution impacts. Silage liquid was also producing significant amounts of ammonia, which was directly toxic to fish.

This policy-driven market in agriculture was more significantly responsible for the contribution of nitrogen to the process of eutrophication. The favourable price regimes for the production of cereals led to the increased leaching of fertilisers and pesticides from treated soils to watercourses. The extent of this problem has resulted in the whole of the Broads catchment potentially being designated as a *vulnerable zone* under the recent *European Directive on Nitrates.*

This nutrient enrichment through increasing infusions of phosphates and nitrogen as a result of both market activity and public policy essentially causes the phytoplankton, microscopic algae, to become dominant, making it harder for larger aquatic plants to grow, particularly in the marsh dykes. In turn, without these plants, aquatic inverte-brates, such as water snails and insects, are less common, which means less food for adult fish. Eutrophication has thus led to the impoverishment of natural fish stocks, but the loss of these larger aquatic plants, too, allows sediment to be more easily stirred up and then transported, causing increases in the rates of sedimentation. This requires increasingly expensive dredging if the silting up of open water is to be avoided. Siltation and sedimentation are often exacerbated by the drainage of certain acid peat soils, through intensive agricultural practices, that releases ochre into the dykes, rivers and broads.

By the time *What Future for Broadland?* had been produced, phosphate in domestic sewage, fertiliser run-off and indeed gull droppings had permeated the water to a point where only four of the 41 broads could support the traditional range of aquatic plants; 31 had lost virtually all of them. Nutrient enrichment had caused the water to become cloudy. By this process of eutrophication, the water lost its oxygen and the animal life supported by the plants was lost. Large numbers of fish died (MacEwen and MacEwen, 1987).

Eutrophication also has exacerbated the problem of bank erosion, through the loss of larger aquatic plants such as the rond, which had shielded the river banks against boat wash. The rivers were embanked hundreds of years ago and have been constantly under threat of erosion from wind, waves and tides. The operation of the private leisure market has compounded this. Water cruisers have made the problem worse and their wash now provides the main cause of erosion. Burrowing animals, bankside fishing, the unofficial mooring of water craft and dredging that removes river bed gradients also have made a significant contribution to the erosion of banks. Attempts to solve this problem have been less than satisfactory in terms of amenity values. The widespread introduction of piling, which is expensive, gives the banks a steep, linear, unvegetated canal-like appearance.

In addition to the significant pollution through phosphates, nitrogen and related infusions of ammonia and ochre, the use of lead for weights in fishing and shot in wildfowling, both associated with the leisure market, have caused significant lead poisoning to plants, invertebrates and animals. The leisure sector, too, has caused fuel pollution from boats both at times of filling and through spillage of diesel. The discharge of oily water through bilges is regulated within the hire fleets, but is more of a problem with private boats. Washing up water often causes foaming from unspent detergents.

Private industry generally was responsible for high levels of mercury being dis-charged into the watercourses of the Broads during the 1960s and 1970s. There are still isolated high concentrations in the River Yare today. Dredging can stir up mercury compounds which can have serious consequences for wildlife. Finally, in respect of influences over water quality, the introduction – through fish farm escapees – of exotic species or different genetic strains of fish to receiving water can alter the species or genetic diversity of the natural fish stocks.

These conflicts of interest relating to water quality have been made more complex by the difficulty of attributing their causes to specific actors in the Broads and therefore securing agreement amongst them about the nature of the problem that could ultimately destroy nature conservation and amenity values. At times, since accession to the then European Economic Community, now European Union (EU), and the Common Agricultural Policy, farmers had been reluctant to recognise any real problem at all. The then Anglian Water Authority remained unconvinced about the detrimental impacts of high phosphorus emissions, despite research evidence to the contrary. As a result, it was reluctant to take expensive corrective action. The water authority, in defence of its position, identified the farmers as the real culprits of declining water quality, as a result of nitrogen run-off. The National Farmers' Union (NFU), whilst acceding to the nitrogen issue in part, identified the main problem, phosphorus pollution, as being the responsibility of the water authority. The situation was made worse, the NFU contended, by recreation interests, where motorised craft had created turbidity and had stirred up silts. Indeed, a strong contingent of NFU members on the North Norfolk District Council succeeded in the late 1970s in having boats temporarily banned from two broads for this reason, despite the fact that research evidence showed that boats had had little real impact on turbidity.

Water and river management

In addition to the problems of eutrophication, silting, bank erosion and damages caused by a range of other chemical pollutants, the Broads also suffer from two more fundamental water and river management problems. On the one hand, river flows have become lower and groundwater has become depleted. On the other, there is an ever present threat of increased saltwater incursion and flooding from the sea.

An adequate freshwater supply to the dyke systems and a high summer water table are essential for the maintenance of traditional grazing practices. Good river flows are also important in reducing phosphates. Water levels and flows must thus be maintained if the ecological quality, or nature conservation values of the area, are to be sustained.

A range of practices, again driven by market criteria and public policy goals, have severely threatened the sustainability. As the marshlands have been drained by more effective pumping and drainage technology to allow a more intensive cereals-based agriculture, changes in the water table have developed, with reduced run-off rates and flow regimes. Arterial drainage schemes and irrigation projects have often been brought about through large-scale channel and engineering works and all of this has been with the full support of the Common Agricultural Policy.

Water abstraction for public water supply and aquaculture from watercourses and boreholes tapping aquifer supplies has also led to changes in the natural flow of rivers and reductions in water table levels. Activities in agriculture and water supply have

Impacts

Causes	Amenity values	Nature Conservation values	Recreation values	Agricultural values	Industrial values	Aquaculture values
Amenity values						
Nature Conservation values						
Recreation values	1	2				
Agricultural values	3	4	5			
Industrial values		6				
Aquaculture values		7				

1. Bank erosion from wash from boats, bankside fishing and unofficial moorings

2. Lead pollution from fishing and shooting
   Fuel and waste pollution from boats

3. Bank erosion from eutrophication
   Drainage and irrigation works

4. Phosphorous generation from livestock wastes
   Nitrogen generation from fertiliser and pesticide runoff
   Drainage from acid peat soils releasing ochre

5. Ammonia from silage liquid impairing recreational fishing

6. Phosphorous generation from sewage treatment works leading to eutrophication
   Mercury infusions from industry generally, stirred up by dredging
   Water abstraction, lowering the water table

7. Nitrogen generation from fish farming
   Introduction of exotic fish species

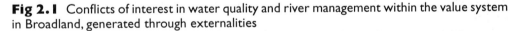

Fig 2.1 Conflicts of interest in water quality and river management within the value system in Broadland, generated through externalities

thus both served to impoverish the amenity and nature conservation values of the area. Much of the landscape has lost its traditional wetland character. Reductions in river flows have led to algae accumulation, again preventing the growth of water plants. Decrease in river flows also accentuates saline incursion into the freshwater ecosystem.

These saline incursions are made worse by a continuous threat of flooding from the sea which has periodically broken through the dunes along the coast since the 13th century. The coast between Winterton and Happisburgh is the most vulnerable, but is also the most protected. Flood alleviation will also entail the strengthening of river banks on over 200 km of river, where the river is higher than the surrounding land.

The resolution of river management conflicts suffers from the same problems as water quality. Various actors in the past have sought to identify the causes of the problems as being the responsibility of others. The Broads Hire Boat Federation, for example, has been insistent that the impact of boats on bank erosion and silt stirring has been negligible. They have asserted that bank erosion has arisen mainly as a result of the trampling of river and broad banks by anglers and cattle. The economic value of the water-based leisure industry far outweighed any damage that boats might have caused.

The activities of the market place and of public policy can thus generate negative externalities that are often hard to attribute directly (in Broadland these are largely environmental in nature) which lead to significant conflicts of interest amongst the value systems inherent in the Broads. These are summarised in Figure 2.1. But the interests of private property rights are also notorious conflict generators and these have been particularly contentious in the agriculture sector.

Agriculture

With the increasing intensity of agriculture since the accession of the UK to the European Economic Community in 1973, traditional fen and marshland management practices were being used less and less. The fenland reeds were no longer cut for thatch and the fens themselves were no longer used for the cultivation of marsh hay. As a result, the scrub advanced and the fens receded. The interests of private property rights, invested in the farmer and landowner, were beginning to have a detrimental impact on both amenity and nature conservation values, essentially driven by European policy. Significantly, however, these rights extended to the control of internal drainage boards.

With this control, farmers had been seduced by drainage grants to introduce electric pumps to drain fields in hours that would have taken traditional wind pumps weeks. High subsidised cereals prices and the prospects of big profits were theirs if they could switch from traditional livestock grazing to cereals. It was this degree of subsidisation of agriculture that was to induce one of the most notorious agriculture-versus-conservation controversies in Britain in the 1980s.

The bigger expanding farmers in the area had a rational financial interest in the installation of more powerful pumps to lower the water table and facilitate conversion from livestock grazing to more subsidised cereals production. In one part of the Broads, the Halvergate marshes, it proved impossible to persuade farmers to desist from these proposals by negotiating a management agreement with compensation for foregone profits under the 1981 Wildlife and Countryside Act. Some of the more entrenched farmers had to be restrained from draining, as a temporary measure, with the use of an 'Article Four Direction' under UK town and country planning legislation, forbidding a drainage project. This direction was confirmed by the then Prime Minister, Margaret Thatcher, only after the Secretary of State for the Environment and the Minister of Agriculture had failed to agree on its invocation.

As an interim measure, however, the Direction had not resolved the basic dilemma. The Country Landowners' Association and the National Farmers' Union, together with the internal drainage boards, continued to press for compensation for not lowering the water table, at the local level. In fact, though, they were more representative of a small number of large arable farmers than the larger number of traditional marsh grazers in the area. This second group was worried that the intensification that might ensue would force them to sell up or move into cereals production. Instead they preferred continuing grazing in the traditional way, with some smaller payment as compensation for not maximising output, for acting as custodians to tradition. It is clear here that the interest in private property rights amongst the largest farmers in the area, as well as creating negative environmental externalities, was creating conflicts not only amongst a number of actors in the mediation process but also within the farming community itself.

In the knowledge of this schism within agriculture, the Countryside Commission, with powers given it in another part of the Wildlife and Countryside Act, introduced an experimental conservation scheme, the Broads Grazing Marshes Conservation Scheme, between 1986 and 1988. This was administered and financed jointly by the Commission and the Ministry of Agriculture's advisory service. Payment at a flat rate of £120 per hectare per annum was made for farmers not to plough the Halvergate marshes, to maintain limits on stock numbers and nitrogen application and to take only one cut of silage a year. In short, they were to pursue traditional grazing practices in the marshes. Over 90% of farmers accepted these terms.

The scheme was to provide a blueprint for the introduction of *Environmentally Sensitive Areas* (ESAs) in England and Wales. In Broadland, the ESA is designed to ensure that landowners can derive a living from traditional marsh management. Through this system, the Grazing Marsh Conservation Scheme could be continued indefinitely. The Broadland ESA now covers about 16,250 hectares, some 90% of which by land area is covered by some form of agreement (see Map 2.2). Of this, about 32% is covered by the more environmentally friendly second tier agreement, where further rates of payment are made for eliminating fertiliser application and silage cutting altogether.

The mediation of ESA policy takes place through a Broads Agricultural Liaison Panel comprising representatives from the Broads Authority, farmers, landowners, internal drainage boards and the Ministry of Agriculture, Fisheries and Food. This panel played an important part in the review of the ESA, particularly since the Broads Authority under the Norfolk and Suffolk Broads Act of 1988 was given no direct powers to stop damaging farming and drainage operations directly. The review has lead to a revised Broads ESA introduced in 1992 which enlarges its boundary to include the Wensum valley, the Bure valley between Aylesham and Saxthorpe and the Waveney valley between Bungham and Redgrave. Agreements have been extended from five to ten years, offering more security to farmers and wildlife alike.

The issues at stake

Overall, then, conflicts of interest in Broadland are generated through a complex series of interactions driven by market activities and public policies, which themselves generate negative externalities, and private interests in land that invariably conflict with more public values in relation to the sustenance of public goods. Conflict in activity is exacerbated by a conflict in relation to an acceptance of responsibility, which means that a purely objective approach to management solutions is often not possible.

Such management systems need to take into account not only the inherent values in Broadland but also the perceptions of those values by different actors. To the water company, the Broads are just a residual outlying part of a larger system for which they are responsible, to be used for effluent disposal. To boat hire companies, the Broads may be a seasonal profit-making system. To the conservationist the Broads constitute

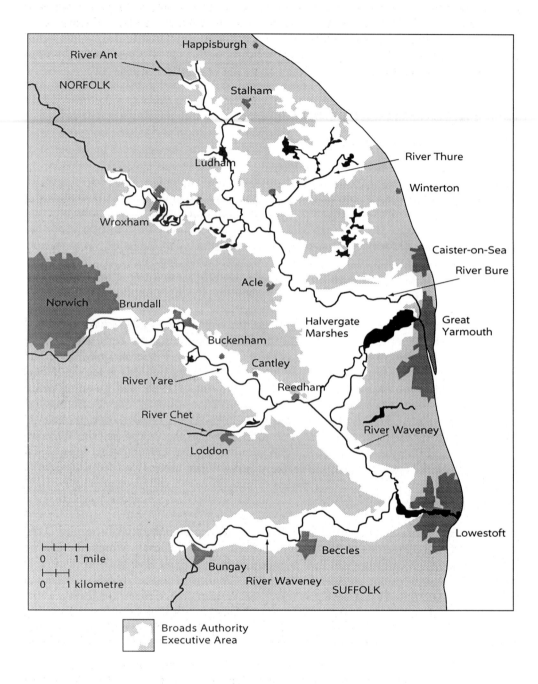

Map 2.2 The Broads Authority Executive Area

a unique ecosystem or a prized landscape. To some farmers, the Broads may represent a profitable source of income, but to others the Broads may be part of a system for the perpetuation of land ownership from generation to generation, for the preservation of a particular way of life or for the maintenance of a particular social status. Clearly, such varying perceptions and the complex nature of value systems and environmental conflicts in Broadland pose a particular problem for the management of this unique wetland. And particular problems often necessitate special solutions.

2.4 Regulating conflicts

The Broads and national parks

By the mid-1970s, Broadland was facing a significant deterioration in scientific or nature conservation values caused mainly by water pollution both from domestic sewage and a whole variety of run-off wastes from the agricultural sector transmitted from a very large geographical area. In line with national trends, too, there had been a significant growth in the use of the waterways in pursuit of recreation values from the mid-1960s which, because they were largely unrestrained, were also causing severe environmental problems. The conflict between amenity, nature conservation, agricultural and recreation values was coming to a head.

Plate 2.2 Pleasure boats on the River Bure near Acle, on the Norfolk Broads. Nature conservation and intensive water recreation are often at odds with each other. Photo: Mike Read/Ringwood

To a large degree in response to these problems, the then Countryside Commission for England and Wales, in 1976, proposed that the Broads should be designated as a national park. This was a controversial decision, since the national park system in England and Wales had not originally been conceived as a mechanism for crisis management. Rather, the administrative authorities of parks, certainly in terms of their conservation objectives, were seen as being passive, because farming and traditional land management would, allegedly, conserve the countryside (MacEwen and MacEwen, 1987).

The proposal to make the Broads a national park was not a new one. The Broads had figured in a 'reserve' list of national parks in 1945, when a report proposing the designation of parks was produced by John Dower. When the Hobhouse Committee recommended the specific location of parks in 1947, the Broads was again one of the 12 recommended. But the Broads were not included in the ten national parks designated between 1951 and 1957 chiefly because it was felt by many that the notion of a river and wetland park heavily used for boating and fishing did not fit well into Dower's original concept of wild and rugged open country. Even by the 1950s the Broads were considered to be too intensively used to be accorded national park status. By 1957, resistance to further designations had brought the general process of creating new parks to a halt.

By the mid-1970s, then, it was recognised by both the Countryside Commission and the then Nature Conservancy Council that their traditional remedies for the problems of the Broads, particularly in respect of a very intense cereals-based agriculture, were simply not powerful enough or met with strong local opposition. Even by the mid-1960s, a Nature Conservancy Council study of 1964 showed a surprising and worrying deterioration in the quality of the wetlands and their wildlife across the whole area of the Broads. But it was uncertain about how to resolve the problem since its traditional means of safeguard, particularly Sites of Special Scientific Interest and National Nature Reserves, were only site-specific. It had nothing in their armoury that would cover larger areas of the countryside or that could cover multiple land uses very effectively.

The Countryside Commission, on the other hand, could offer a solution to larger areas of countryside in the designation of a national park or an Area of Outstanding Natural Beauty, but these would not really allow any control over water management or water quality – the principal problems of the Broads – or over agriculture or land drainage – the principal causes of them. The two conservation agencies between them had no mechanisms that could resolve the problems at the right scale.

The Broads Authority

While not offering a very satisfactory solution, the proposal for a national park in 1976, then, was all that the Countryside Commission could offer. This was opposed immediately by the district councils in the area, since at that time, unlike county councils, they would have no representation on a national park authority under the traditional model for the administration of national parks. The districts instead proposed a joint planning committee of all local authorities in the area, on which the Countryside Commission and the water and navigation authorities would have representation. This original idea for an informal 'Broads Authority', which was actually designed by the districts to frustrate the idea of a national park, was formally instituted in 1978. It was funded by the local authorities, the Countryside Commission and a small contribution from the water and navigation authorities. It operated, less powerfully than national parks, only through the delegated powers of the local authorities that were its members.

The success of this authority over the ensuing eight years, particularly in the areas of research, management and public relations, provided it with a strong case for autonomy, both in terms of planning powers and resources. The Countryside Commission concluded that this autonomy would in many ways provide a better mechanism for administering the area than a conventional national park. After some resistance on the part of the navigation authority, the Commission and the county councils, led by Norfolk, were successful in persuading the government that such an authority should come into being. The Norfolk and Suffolk Broads Act received Royal Assent in 1988, placing three main duties on the authority: conserving and enhancing the natural beauty of the Broads; promoting the enjoyment of the Broads by the public and protecting the interests of navigation.

The resultant, now statutory, Broads Authority has introduced a number of innovations in both research and management that distinguish it from the rest of the national parks in England and Wales. In administrative terms, however, it is a national park in all but name. It has the same autonomy in financial terms, as well as equal control over administration and policy. It is financed by a 75% grant from the National Park Supplementary Grant fund, with the balance of the money being met by constituent local authorities. In expenditure terms, this income funds a general account, nearly half of which is spent on conservation action. A separate navigation account is funded through income from tolls. Indeed, in terms of national park status within the Broadland area, the Farm Grant Notification Scheme, by which farmers in national parks have to notify grant-aided operations to national park authorities, has applied to the Broads since 1985 – three years before the inception of the Authority.

In terms of representation, the authority has a similar structure of members to a national park but with the addition of a much wider range of interests than other park authorities. These include boating, fishing, tourism and voluntary conservation representation, particularly on the Broads Authority Navigation Committee. Local authorities are thus represented on the Broads Authority as a whole together with the Countryside Commission, English Nature, the Great Yarmouth Port Authority, Anglian Water and the Secretary of State for the Environment.

The mediation process

In mediating the local, national and international values of Broadland, described in the first part of this chapter, a large number of interest groups have had a significant role to play within the overarching strategic responsibilities of the Broads Authority. Such groups have been instrumental in at least three distinct spheres. Firstly, in bringing about pressures for change, the Countryside Commission and the local authorities in the area, in particular, have had an important role to play in the establishment of the Broads Authority itself. National pressure groups, such as the Council for National Parks and the Council for the Protection of Rural England, have had a significant influence on strategic developments, particularly in relation to exerting pressure on central government to switch resources from damaging land drainage schemes to providing positive support for traditional farming.

Secondly, interest groups have an important function in assisting with the ongoing management of Broadland in the context of measures developed to ameliorate the enduring conflicts in the area. In excess of 3500 worker days per annum are donated by volunteers, for example, in practical habitat management. The Norfolk Broads Conservation Volunteers, the Norfolk Naturalists' Trust, the Suffolk Wildlife Trust and the Broads Authority's own volunteer group, the Beavers, all receive grant aid from the Broads Authority and are co-ordinated through its employee conservation officers and riverside officers. The Royal Society for the Protection of Birds, too, has delegated management powers in areas such as the Berry Marshes Nature Reserve but also owns and manages its own land, for example the marshes at Cantley and Buckenham. This degree of voluntary involvement is not only cost effective, but provides an excellent means through which an understanding of, and sensitivity to, the different value systems of Broadland can be fostered.

Other voluntary groups concerned more directly with amenity values, such as the National Trust, the Norfolk Mills and Pumps Trust and the Wherry Trust, and recreation interests such as the Royal Yachting Association indulge in continuing dialogue with the Broads Authority and again often become involved in direct works.

Thirdly, a comprehensive web of consultation and liaison committees has evolved in an attempt to ensure that the strategic development of Broadland proceeds within a broad consensus of groups that individually hold very different values for the area. The Broads Consultative Committee provides a foundation for this, containing a wide range of interest groups that have an important input into strategic policy formulation. The Broads Authority also has set up an Agricultural Liaison Panel, with representation from farmers, landowners, internal drainage boards and the Ministry of Agriculture, a Broads Research Advisory Panel and a Water Recreation Liaison Panel, all of whom act as sounding boards for both policies and practice. Other independent bodies, such as the Broads Hire Boat Federation and the British Reed Growers Association, are consulted over more specific aspects of strategic development and invariably become involved with the Authority in individual management projects.

In addition to these interest groups, the unique administrative structure, in the UK context, for Broadland has been central to the process of mediation. The concerted efforts of the Countryside Commission and constituent local authorities have done much to bring this about and to make it work. To ameliorate the conflicts of interest within the area, the Broads Authority has undertaken a series of initiatives that provide a blend of existing legislation and policy and novel approaches to environmental solutions (see Table 2.3).

Indeed, as a unique wetland in the UK context, the Broads Authority actively looks to other areas with similar characteristics, particularly in Europe, for examples of good practice in the complex processes of wetland management, a theme to which we turn now.

Instrument	Use	Comment
1. *Direct action*		
Key authorities	Broadland restoration	Broads Authority and National Rivers Authority acting in concert but involving English Nature and Countryside Commission plus voluntary groups through membership of Broads Authority
Research and experiment	For example, phosphate stripping, suction dredging, biomanipulation, bank erosion, boat design	Broads Authority has spent 10% of its budget over last decade in successful research collaborations with English Nature and University of East Anglia
2. *Controls*		
Legislation	Restoration through the 1988 Norfolk and Suffolk Broads Act; water regulation through the 1991 Water Resources Act; defining rights of way through the 1981 Wildlife and Countryside Act	1988 Norfolk and Suffolk Broads Act provides the basis for much of the present action in Broadland
Regulation	By-laws for boating standards	These cover safety, size, insurance, speed etc., and are policed by river inspectors
Licensing	Of boats to ensure environmental standards; of water abstraction to control water levels	Enacted by Broads Authority, boat licensing ensures craft are environmentally friendly
3. *Land use planning and management*		
Plans and strategies	Stategic plans from Norfolk and Suffolk counties; management plans (e.g.'No Easy Answers', 1993) from Broads Authority, along with guidance on enhancement of landscape and buildings design; district and Broads Authority local plans detail the means of implementing the strategic plans – these are effected through development control	All plans go for public consultation and discussion and, once in place, provide a framework for action
Development control	Controlling new development, particularly in relation to recreation and tourism, and river usage	Exercised through granting or not of planning permission for holiday accomodation, moorings etc., and mediated by the Broads Authority local plan
Environmental Impact Assessment (EIA)	Examining the impacts of large scale developments or uses under EC Directive	EIA can be invoked by the planning authority and used to assess developments such as those for drainage or recreational carrying capacity
Land uses designations	Designation of Broads Authority area as a quasi-national park; ESAs; SSSIs; NNRs	These designations provide a tempering influence on developments which may affect landscape or nature conservation
Management strategies	For addressing particular management issues	E.g. Broads Authority and National Rivers Authority – control of discharges from acid peat soils; Broads Authority and English Nature – control of scrub invasion. Broads Authority – responsible for alder woodland management
4. *Incentives*		
Grant-aid	For a range of restoration and management measures	Used as an input to the Broadland restoration process in general and for ESAs in particular, these are provided by the EU. Broads Authority offers grants for the traditional management of carr woodland
Pricing	To encourage environmentally sensitive uses	Broads Authority operates different tolls e.g. lower for sailing craft than for motor boats
5. *Information, education and advice*		
Consultation and campaigns	To raise awareness about required action	Broads Authority and National Rivers Authority run consultation services in relation to grants; campaigns include those by Broads Authority and internal drainage boards to inform farmers about acceptable drainage practices
Information and interpretation	To provide an understanding of the complex web of the area's ecology and value systems	Exercised through the Broads Authority Information Centres and an education centre at How Hill, and by signposting public rights of way and navigable waterways

Table 2.3 Mediating environmental values

2.5 The international dimension

Nature conservation – the wider context

So far in this chapter emphasis has been laid on the particular example of Broadland. However, our examination of the different, often competing, interest groups and value systems that this has exposed in this area of Eastern England and the means by which a degree of resolution may be achieved in order to sustain the unique qualities of ecology and landscape has a resonance well beyond the United Kingdom.

To some extent this notion has already been touched upon in section 2.2 on nature conservation values. There we noted not only the recognition of many parts of the area as important within the national context as NNRs and SSSIs but some sites, in being recognised by the Ramsar Convention on Wetlands of International Importance, as having an international dimension. Although the Convention was not effected until the early 1970s, efforts to sustain sites of unique ecological importance worldwide have been backed by scientific communities in many developed countries since the Second World War. The experience of the UK is not untypical. During the passage through Parliament of the National Parks and Access to the Countryside Act 1949, those aspects touching upon scientific conservation, including the provision for SSSIs and NNRs, were largely uncontested. To a considerable extent this may be explained by the widespread deference to scientific expertise which was commonplace at the time and that, in attempting to conserve examples of unique ecosystems, the amount of land thus called upon to be 'sterilised' was relatively small (Blunden and Curry, 1989). It is easy to envisage such attitudes, largely divorced from any element of political controversy, being widespread in developed countries thus making international co-operation over the scientific issues, including ecological conservation, all the more likely. Indeed, the post-war period provides evidence of the growth of a plethora of international science-based conventions and councils, sometimes *ad hoc* (for example, the International Technical Conference for the Protection of Nature, held at Lake Success, New York in 1949), but more often than not with an ongoing remit and serviced by a secretariat. Examples here might include the International Union for the Protection of Birds or the Geosphere Biosphere Programme sponsored by the *International Council of Scientific Unions* (ICSU).

Recognising landscape values

Until comparatively recently attempts to conserve larger swathes of the country-side in the interests of maintaining landscape values have had, in contrast, a much more difficult time in the face of resistance from well-organised groups, such as farmers. Their broader economic interests in an approach to agriculture, which is often capital intensive, clearly runs counter to those who would espouse the cause of landscape conservation, a matter which calls for protection on a much greater scale. Attempts to bring pressure to bear in favour of conservationist objectives have rested largely upon the efforts of non-governmental organisations (NGOs), although in the case of England and Wales, the Countryside Commission has also been a key player.

Environmentally Sensitive Areas

2

Designated under the EC Structure Regulation 797/85, ESAs permit hectarage payments to be made for farming in ways which help to conserve landscape and habitat by resisting economic pressures for intensification. Their establishment introduced four important features into agricultural support:

1 a flexible means of protecting landscape, wildlife and archaeological features which can be integrated into agricultural practice;
2 income support measures which can be used to sustain traditional farm enterprise;
3 a limitation on the conversion of land to the production of high-yielding, food surplus-generating forms of activity;
4 general encouragement for low input/low output farming

(Blunden, 1987).

However, by the middle years of the 1980s, so far as the EC was concerned, it became only too apparent that widespread landscape destruction was an additional cost to that of producing highly priced food for which there was largely no market. Consequently, the notion of offering protection to larger areas of the countryside was realised. Here the Broads were important in pioneering the idea of offering financial support to farmers prepared to use extensive, traditional forms of agriculture practice, rather than aggressive forms of agribusiness based on monoculture and high levels of capital input as part of an intensive system. Since the ESA has now become part of The European Union framework for landscape protection it represents one important way in which the case study of Broadlands locks into an international context (see Box 2).

At the same time the Ramsar Convention, originally led by the concerns for scientific conservation, has moved on. When it was first established its emphasis was largely upon the idea of international co-operation in conserving key habitats for the survival of birds and other species, and the 'wise use of wetlands' to this end. However, the concept of 'wise use' seems to have been subjected to wider interpretation. Now there is a recognition of the 'need to relate indigenous uses of wetlands (not all of which are positive) to the wise use concept'. There is a realisation that 'the potentially damaging effect on wetlands caused by a higher density of human population and concomitant intensive use, whether in developed countries (reclamation, recreation) or in developing countries (over-exploitation)' underlines 'the urgent need for the zoning of activities' rather than total exclusion.

Although in the early years of Ramsar heavy stress was laid on international co-operation through the networking of common experience, it is no longer enough merely to foster more effective scientific knowledge of wetland functions and the protection of species and habitats in biosphere reserves. Today, the sharing of experience relating to both the scientific and the social scientific aspects of wetland management would appear to be germane (Marchand and Udo de Haes, 1991). This

59

Plate 2.3 Offshore industry close to the coast of Ameland, an island in the Dutch Wadden Sea. The Wadden Sea, off the Northern coast of The Netherlands, is an international wetland that is currently under threat from human activities. Photo: Michiel Cornelissen

brings Ramsar more into line with the approach of the *International Union for the Conservation of Nature and Natural Resources* (IUCN) to the designation of national parks as protected areas. While it maintains that these should contain central cores of wildscape where human intervention is minimal, these may be surrounded by 'harmonious land-scapes' which have resulted from traditional patterns of land use (Simmons, 1989).

Wetland problems

However, those parts of the Broads recognised under Ramsar are merely fragments of an area for which holistic approaches to management are a necessity. Likewise the protection offered by ESA status has to be seen somewhat in the same light and cannot be considered as an all-embracing solution for landscape protection. In this respect the Broads are no different from other wetlands areas around the world. Indeed, for many of them, the problems posed by the diversity of interests which they contain remain largely divorced from any progress towards the achievement of management solu-tions. Examples abound from the developing as well as the developed world, especially where the activities of people whose traditional occupations have for centuries been in harmony with wetland ecologies are no longer so.

In India, for example, two wetlands, the Keoadeo Ghana National park near Agra and Lake Kolleru on the East coast, are the product of centuries of interaction between the rural populations and their environment in which a system of small-scale rice cultivation, grazing, fishing and duck farming had evolved and was maintained in a state of relative equilibrium. In recent decades, however, increasing population pressure and the desire for rapid economic growth have led to the over-exploitation and degradation of the wetlands. Attempts to counter these problems by the park authorities first involved eliminating the direct impact of the people on the wetlands – until it was realised that it was the complex interactive nature of the traditional local economies with their surrounding environment that conserved the area. Subsequent attempts to combine the conservation of biotic diversity and representative habitats in some areas and permit the maximum economic activity elsewhere have also proved disastrous (Gopal, 1990).

In the European context, the Camargue, located at the mouth of the Rhone in Southern France, is amongst the most famous wetlands. Because of the natural and amenity values of the area, several protective measures, largely based on scientific conservation, have been taken. These include the setting up of the Réserve Nationale de Camargue in 1928; the parc Naturel Régional in 1972; various departmental reserves; the Conservatoire du Littoral; UNESCO's Biosphere Reserve and the voluntary reserve of the Tour du Valet. But, in all, the total protected area is about 19,000 ha out of the 145,000 ha which constitutes the whole Carmargue (some 13%). One characterisation of the area emphasises 'the subtle interpenetration of its distinct biotopes both in terms of space and time in a rather unpredictable way. From a scientific as well as an aesthetic point of view these patterns are predominant and from this the myth of the Camargue as a wild paradise has been born'.

However, it would seem that current realities are undermining such a picture since distinct social groups of users (into which the residents and tourists may be divided) are independently exploiting the potentialities of the area according to their respective value systems. Although a modest degree of conciliation between these groups has been attempted, each sector continues to pursue its own profit-motivated objectives in a largely uncontrolled fashion and to such an extent that deterioration is rapid. As in the Broadland area, support policies which have underpinned the agricultural sector, coupled with other forms of private market activity, often of a recreational kind, have generated environmental externalities which have affected those large areas not enjoying any form of protection. Certainly, no attempt has been made to try to address a common, legally binding framework of action that might conserve the Camargue with its specific natural and cultural characteristics in the interests of all. Nor, indeed, has any attempt been made to find 'new perspectives in terms of co-operation', perhaps, as has been suggested, through 'education and human interrelations rather than administrative rules and structures' (Tamisier, 1991).

Holistic approaches to management

The emphasis on personal interrelationships and the creation of better levels of understanding between contesting interest groups as a means of achieving holistic and effective management, which the Carmargue example discusses, is not new and has been the subject of work carried out in relation to Broadland in the mid-1980s. This aimed at improving understanding between the different interest groups or actors with their attendant values. It would be achieved through interactive sessions in which each of the different interest groups defined the nature of the Broads from their own perspective, thus promoting a learning process for all concerned and leading not just to more understanding between them and therefore reasoned debate, but also a diminishing potential for conflict (Blunden, 1987). Such an approach was advocated before the setting up of the Broads Authority with its aggregation of top-down powers aimed at achieving much the same end, if in a rather different way.

The problems of conflict resolution in wetland areas have more recently been addressed by others, this time in a more abstract context but based on wide empirical experience. They underline the key problems which may result from a multiplicity of players where 'it is very unlikely that all the actors regard all necessary measures (in the formulation of integrated management objectives) as equally urgent or seek solutions in the same direction'. In such a situation it is suggested that a *project approach* may provide the best route to harmonious integrated management. This involves not only a clear distinction between what is called *the problem field* and *the management field in relation to the problem field* (see Box 3), but as in Blunden (1987) and Glasbergen and Klijn (1991), it recognises wetlands are recognised as complex interactive systems in which the players view the nature, extent and purposes of the system in quite different ways. The last mentioned authors, however, discuss a more formalised approach leading to an integrated management plan. Having collected a total database for the area, the project approach then elaborates overall objectives in which these should be made 'specific for the various interests', at the same time paying attention to their interdependence. As the project approach facilitates the establishment of priorities, interventions are made explicit in the integrated management plan as this is a prerequisite for achieving the necessary co-operation.

European co-operation

From the evidence so far, it is clear enough that designating an area as a wetland and complying with the recommendations of the Ramsar Convention is not a sufficient conservation measure of itself. Whilst Ramsar now acknowledges the need to do more than conserve species and ecologies at a number of sites of modest size, it hardly suggests frameworks similar to those referred to above (Holistic Approaches to Management), within which the management complexities of a large wetland area might be tackled meaningfully.

Unfortunately within the European Union there is a notable absence of formal structures or, indeed, directives from the European Commission relating to wetland

Managing wetlands – an analytical framework **3**

'The problem field is a coherent set of problems, in this case (a set of) discrepancies between actual wetland qualities and requirements as to its qualities. The latter are defined by those who have an interest in its resources: the interest groups. Often, the interest groups also affect the wetland by their use (exploitation). The interest groups may therefore be considered as actors. The mutual relation between interest groups and a wetland is shown in (a) below.

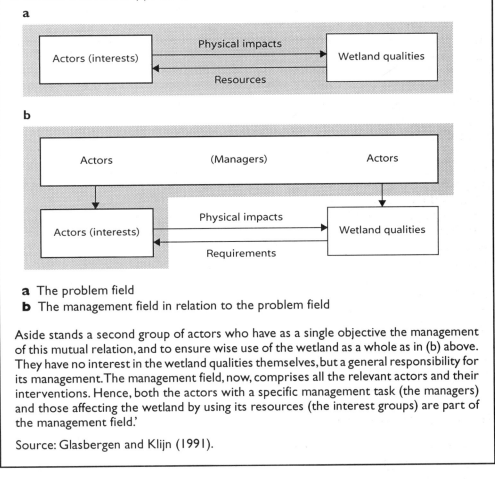

a The problem field
b The management field in relation to the problem field

Aside stands a second group of actors who have as a single objective the management of this mutual relation, and to ensure wise use of the wetland as a whole as in (b) above. They have no interest in the wetland qualities themselves, but a general responsibility for its management. The management field, now, comprises all the relevant actors and their interventions. Hence, both the actors with a specific management task (the managers) and those affecting the wetland by using its resources (the interest groups) are part of the management field.'

Source: Glasbergen and Klijn (1991).

management outside the *Habitats Directive* which deals only narrowly with endangered habitats or species. However, this has not meant that the Commission has had no role to play in this field. In the Mediterranean where wetlands are particularly under threat and few properly managed or protected, the Mediterranean Wetland Forum, which was formed in 1991, has established an action programme to begin to redress just these problems. Set in motion in 1993 and to last for three years, it uses grants from the EU's Financial Investment for the Environment fund. Although enabling rather than prescriptive in its approach, the Forum will require further funding later in order to ensure that the proper foundation for the implementation of the conservation and management of these wetlands can be built upon. Indeed, it hopes to apply further finance in a time frame that will allow its programme to continue well into the next century.

In Europe, other forms of international co-operation to share knowledge and expertise exist. The Action Plan for Protected Areas in Europe, sponsored by the Federation of Nature and National Parks of Europe, is a broader forum for sharing common problems including, but not exclusively, those of wetlands. However, as its president states, 'such plans only provide a framework for future action. Inevitably it will be the individual and collective responsibility of those who manage these areas across Europe to identify ways of working together to meet the right mix of local, national and international objectives' (Clark, 1993). Such an approach can be seen to be most immediately in evidence where wetlands form a contiguous whole across national boundaries. The Wadden Sea area, which falls within the jurisdiction of Denmark, Germany and The Netherlands, is an excellent example of such co-operation. However, it is an approach which also brings this discussion full circle since it well describes the networking activities of the Broads Authority. Not only does the Authority sponsor occasional international workshops such as that held in the Broads in October 1992 on assessing and monitoring changes in wetlands parks and protected areas, but it also works closely with other wetland authorities.

Of particular importance here is Le Marais Audomarois Regional Park near Saint-Omer in the Nord-Pas de Calais region of France and de Weerribben National Park in the North-west of the province of Overijssel near the town of Steenwijk in The Netherlands. Both parks, like the Broads, originated as a result of peat extraction; all three offer a similar diversity of environments which provide habitats for a variety of wildlife and all have similar management problems caused by the different needs of a range of different groups. Close co-operation between them has been in evidence since 1989. However, in June 1993 they agreed to join the *European Natural Sites Twinning Programme* (EUROSITE) sponsored by the European Union. This should be helpful in facilitating in a formal context an exchange of staff and act as a means of sharing the expertise so far developed independently in such fields as water quality, woodland, grazing and visitor management, and information, interpretation and education. Box 4 details these benefits as seen from the point of view of the Broads Authority. Perhaps equally important is the fact that twinning, as an EU enabling device and in the absence of a policy framework, offers the opportunity to bid for research and development funding from Brussels.

2.6 Conclusion

In line with other wetland areas, particularly in Europe but also elsewhere, Broadland offers a variety of value systems that hold a different and varying currency amongst different users of the area. The influence of the private market and of public policy goals aimed at assisting productive outputs in both the agriculture and water sectors has been one of generating externalities, particularly negative environmental ones,

---

Benefits of site twinning

4

The Broads Authority recognises a number of advantages to be derived from twinning with the Audomarois and de Weerribben as part of the European Natural Site Twinning Programme:

1　It helps establish the importance of the Broads in the European context and the contribution the Authority has to make to wetland management. It assists in obtaining EC funding for its research and management programme.

2　It allows access to four working groups established within the Programme which cover topics relevant to the Broads and enables the Authority to draw on the collective experience of 33 sites in the EU.

3　It provides an exchange mechanism for staff and access to grants to facilitate this, thus offering an unrivalled opportunity for the transfer of information between sites, especially in the following areas:

○ water quality – a problem for all three sites extending beyond the water itself to the marginal communities which are declining and into adjacent fen vegetation where such problems as falling reed quality are manifest.

○ fen and carr woodland management – de Weerribben has a well-developed management programme for these habitats. Its experience in the management of reedbeds and marsh hay meadows is particularly relevant to the Broads.

4　Grazing marsh management – large areas of Audomarois and parts of de Weerribben are under grazing marsh. Their management of these for birds and the resolution of pollution problems in the dyke systems offers useful guidance to Authority staff.

5　Visitor management – there is much to be learned from the Dutch on 'green tourism' and the recreational management of park areas. Canoe trails, nature trails and the management of visitors arriving by all methods of transport are well established in de Weerribben.

6　Information, interpretation and education – both de Weerribben and Audomarois have interesting visitor centres using a range of interpretative techniques. On-site interpretation is also being developed at both. Environmental education programmes are well established in both areas using specialist personnel.

Source: Broads Authority memorandum, September 1989.

---

that have severely compromised such value systems and have generated a range of land-use-based and particularly water-based conflicts. This situation has been exacerbated by difficulties in unequivocally attributing, if not identifying, the principal causes of environmental deterioration in the area.

These environmental problems have led to attempts at conflict resolution in the British context. The Broads Authority evolved into statutory status through a process of organisational and pressure group lobbying, first for national park status but subsequently for an organisational form that matches the problems of the area even more appropriately than a national park might have done, particularly in respect of research and experiment. Within this organisational structure, the full panoply of environmental mediation instruments has been deployed. The traditional demarcations, in Britain at least, between land use planners and resource planners have been set aside to allow the full range of direct action, plan making, development controls, economic controls, land use designations and information and advice to be harnessed together in pursuit of the common goal of environmental quality. And the integrative role of the Broads Authority, in assuming a range of delegated powers from local authorities and statutory powers from Parliament, has provided a means of exploiting such instruments.

Similar approaches have been advocated certainly in the context of the wetland areas to be found within the EU. This is because, as in the case of the Broads, many similar pressures resulting from the claims of the market and the landowners to pursue economic goals continue to pose problems of reconciliation with the needs of biological and amenity conservation. This in spite of the argument put forward by some that the diminishing emphasis placed on the EU's Common Agricultural Policy, which requires drastic reductions in production subsidies for farm crops, could assist in ameliorating some of the negative externalities of intensive agriculture.

However, the fact remains that statutory approaches to environmental conservation remain largely concerned with ecology and the protection of habitat and are applied inside the EU on a small scale, as is the concept of the ESA. Co-ordinated attempts to deal with these on a broader scale and within a wider interest group framework, which includes landscape protection, remain central to the national frameworks most countries offer for the administration of their national parks. However, in these parks the problems are generally less complex across a wide range of locations. Indeed, out of the 31 national parks outside the UK but in the EU as at the beginning of 1994, only one, the Tablas de Daimiel in La Mancha, Spain, is a wetland. But even this is very small at just under 2000 hectares. For wetlands the fine balance between the interests of the market and environmental objectives is undoubtedly much more difficult to achieve. Notwithstanding the financial support given by the European Commission for *ad hoc* voluntary co-operative initiatives of an enabling kind, the Commission has seemed singularly reluctant to involve itself in positively evolving a mandatory integrated management framework suitable for wetlands.

3

Environmental conflicts in transforming economies: Central and Eastern Europe

Egbert Tellegen

3.1 Introduction

The former communist states of Central and Eastern Europe (see Box 1) are currently undergoing a process of transformation, from authoritarian, planned economies to democratic market economies. One of the burdens of the past in this part of Europe is excessive damage to the environment. This chapter relates these environmental problems to the ideological, economic and political characteristics of the former societal system in this part of Europe. Another main theme is the environmental consequences of the current transformation from a planned to a market economy. The intention will be to show that environmental problems in Central and Eastern Europe have their origins in both the nature of the political system and the level of economic development.

  The chapter begins with a overview of three different types of environmental problems in Central and Eastern Europe: air pollution, nuclear disasters and hazardous waste. A feature which they all have in common is their international dimension (section 3.2). I shall then look at the main characteristics of the former communist states, compare Eastern and Western economies, and discuss the transformation of the former communist states (section 3.3). I shall go on to outline the conflicts of interest involved in the process of international co-operation on environmental issues (section 3.4) and subsequently examine environmental policies in the post-communist era (section 3.5). The chapter will finish with some concluding remarks (section 3.6).

3.2 Current environmental problems in the region

Publications on Central and Eastern Europe give numerous examples of excessive forms of environmental pollution and of wastage of materials and energy. Yet the environment is not in a poor condition in all parts of Central and Eastern Europe. There

---

Central and Eastern Europe

The terms *Central* and *Eastern* Europe will crop up frequently in this chapter. The term *Eastern Europe* is often used in the literature to refer to the former communist countries in Europe. However, it seems odd to refer to the very small part of Europe that lies West of the former Iron Curtain as 'Western Europe' and to use the term 'Eastern Europe' to refer to the immense area between Germany and Asiatic Russia. Moreover, people in countries like the Czech Republic, Hungary and Poland consider their country as belonging to Central Europe and not to Eastern Europe. We shall endeavour to respect this preference. Although there is no state border between the two, we will use the term *Central and Eastern Europe* to designate the area in question. The Eastern border of Europe is formed by the Ural mountains. Again, there is no legally recognised, formal boundary. The former Soviet republics of Ukraine, Belarus and Moldova, together with the Baltic republics of Estonia, Latvia and Lithuania, became independent countries within Europe after the break-up of the Soviet Union. Russia itself, consists of a European part, west of the Ural mountains, and an Asiatic part stretching out as far as the Pacific coast. Forms of environmental damage which have affected the Asiatic part of the Russian Federation will also be discussed in this chapter. The Caucasus forms the geographical and legal boundary between Russia and the republics of Georgia and Azerbaijan. Together with Armenia, these republics are sometimes considered as European and sometimes as Asian. For the purpose of this chapter, they will be considered as being part of Europe.

---

are large areas in countries like Poland and Russia which have been virtually untouched by human activities (see Box 2).

However, there are many *hot spots* of extreme forms of environmental pollution, nuclear risk and landscape destruction too. The *Environmental Action Programme for Central and Eastern Europe* distinguishes regional and local hot spots. The 'Black Triangle', the heavily polluted area on the borders of the Czech Republic, Germany and Poland, is one of these regional hot spots. Local hot spots are often to be found in places where lignite power plants and metal smelters are located. The town of Copsa Mica in Rumania is an apt example of a local hot spot. As a consequence of the presence of dust and gases, significant losses of lung function were found among children in this city. In the same sample of children 73% recorded either 'weak or very weak' scores in an IQ test, although only 30% would be expected to do so under normal circumstances. This extremely low score was ascribed to high lead exposures affecting neurobehavioural responses (Environmental Action Programme for Central and Eastern Europe, 1993, pp.II-7.).

This section, however, will not focus on local and regional hot spots; rather, it will present three environmental problems with a decidedly international dimension: air pollution, nuclear disasters and hazardous waste. The international effects of air pollution in the Black Triangle are evident, not only for the countries of Central and Eastern Europe but for the entire European continent. Without doubt, the nuclear disasters in Central and Eastern Europe have had a negative impact on an international, perhaps even global, scale. Finally, the transport of hazardous waste from Western European countries to Central and Eastern Europe is a clear illustration of the international dimension surrounding many contemporary environmental problems.

Poland's natural treasures   **2**

If one were to rely solely on statistical data describing the state of the environment in Poland, one would expect to find nothing more than a biological desert between the Oder, Vistula and Bug rivers. A glance at locally produced information leaflets advertising Polish treasures of nature (which are gloomy, greyish and far from paragons of the art of printing) would actually tend to confirm that impression. Nevertheless, in spite of the news about environmental disasters and the clumsily produced leaflets, the reality of the natural world of present-day Poland is surprisingly rich, beautiful and versatile. One might even go so far as to claim that Poland, with its beauty, uniqueness and rare specimens of fauna and flora, is a natural treasure house of European and even global significance.

According to the latest *Report on the State and Protection of the Environment and on Environmental hazards* (1990), an annual publication of the Chief Statistical Bureau, 5.5 million hectares of land, comprising about 18% of the total area of the country, were under various forms of protection in 1989. This is about five times more than in 1980.

Source: Ministry of Environmental Protection, Natural Resources and Forestry (1991), pp.28–29.

Air pollution: the Black Triangle

Air pollution has for many centuries been recognised as a source of nuisance. In the recent past, air pollution in Western Europe has changed from being primarily a health problem in the 1970s (caused partly by sulphur dioxide (SO_2) emissions), to an acidification problem in the 1980s (caused by sulphur dioxide, nitrogen oxides (NO_x) and ammonia (NH_3) emissions) and finally to a climate change problem in the 1990s (caused mainly by carbon dioxide (CO_2) emissions).

Compared with the situation in Western Europe, sulphur dioxide emissions are still high in Central and Eastern Europe. Air pollution, and in particular air pollution caused by SO_2 and dust emissions, is extremely high in the Black Triangle. The unfavourable natural conditions in the Black Triangle exacerbate air pollution. Western winds transport air pollutants from abroad, while the Giant Mountains of Northern Bohemia and Southern Silesia form a natural barrier, hindering the eastward transportation of locally generated air pollution (Knook, 1991, p.711). The local causes of air pollution are the concentration of electricity production and heavy industry in this area, the use of locally mined and extremely sulphur-rich lignite and brown coal and the use of technologies which are outdated by Western standards. A recent Polish report states that 'the situation within the Upper Silesian region is reminiscent of what prevailed 30 or 40 years ago in the Ruhr Basin in Germany, or the Pittsburgh area (United States), or in the English or Belgian coal mining districts' (Nowicki, 1992, p.13). Sulphur-rich coal is also one of the main sources of energy for household heating.

Concentrations of sulphur dioxide in the Black Triangle regularly exceed standards for maximum admissible concentrations. A Czech state report concludes from long-term measurements in Northern Bohemia that situations often occur more or less throughout the area in which the maximum admissible concentrations of 150 micrograms of SO_2 per m^3 are exceeded. The citizens of Chomutov can actually expect this critical value to be exceeded 117 days a year (Ministry of the Environment of the Czech Republic, 1990, p.122). There are many indications that air pollution contributes to the poor health of the population of this area (see Box 3).

3

Air pollution and health effects in the Black Triangle

Median life expectancy in Poland (67 years for men and 75 years for women) is low compared with Western European countries. In Silesia, life expectancy is at least one year shorter and infant mortality and premature childbirth are extremely high (Ministry of Environmental Protection, Natural Resources and Forestry, 1991, p.36). Although it is not clear to what extent air pollution in general and SO_2 pollution in particular contribute to the poor health of the local population, it is highly probable that SO_2 emissions do play a role.

In the Czech Republic, the lifespans for both men and women vary from 70.3 to 70.5 years. In Northern Bohemia, however, the average life span for men is 2.5–3 years shorter than in the rest of the Czech Republic (for women it is 1.5–2 years shorter) (Krivsky, 1991, p.18).

A study of the former German Democratic Republic (GDR) reports that, in areas with extreme SO_2 pollution, the prevalence of respiratory diseases doubled in the period from 1970 to 1989, although the number of children declined. In Saxony, respiratory diseases have been diagnosed among 50% of the children. Thirty per cent of the children in the extremely polluted areas suffer from eczema (Metz *et al.*, 1991, p.84).

Besides health effects, air pollution has damaging effects on natural features and buildings. In virtually no other region is the damage to the forests as visible as in the mountainous frontier area between the former German Democratic Republic and the Czech Republic. Air pollution is also damaging the historical monuments of the ancient city of Cracow (Poland) and is having a detrimental effect on agricultural production.

The combination of economic activities (i.e. the concentration of mining, electricity production and heavy industry) and physical conditions (i.e. mountains as barriers to the Western winds) in an area which overlaps three different countries makes the Black Triangle a typical example of an international environmental problem. The widespread long-range transport of air pollutants from this area into other parts of Europe has resulted in a further widening of the international dimension.

Nuclear disasters

The 4 November 1976 edition of *The New Scientist*, a popular British scientific journal, contained an article written by a Russian immigrant, a natural scientist called Zhores A. Medvedev. The article mentioned a nuclear disaster which hardly anyone had known about until then. It was supposed to have happened in the Urals in 1957 or 1958 and to have been caused by the discharge of an enormous quantity of radioactive waste (which had been stored underground) into the atmosphere. As a consequence, more than 1000 square kilometres in the Southern Urals had been contaminated, several hundred people had died and thousands of people had been evacuated and hospitalised. A large area would remain a danger zone for decades (Medvedev, 1980, p.4).

The story of this nuclear accident was either dismissed out of hand as pure science fiction or reinterpreted as being about a nuclear reactor blast, rather than an explosion of buried atomic waste. It was not until 1989, more than 30 years after the accident, that the Soviet government admitted that a tank of radioactive waste had indeed exploded at a weapons plant near Chelyabinsk on 29 September 1957. It is now estimated that 271,000 people were exposed to the radioactive cloud that was formed by the explosion.

Today, we know much more about radioactive contamination in this former 'closed' area of the Soviet military industrial complex. In 1947, ten years before the accident described above, nuclear waste was dumped in the Techa river. The dumping continued for several years. It is estimated that, as a consequence, 124,000 people were exposed to radiation (Monroe, 1992, pp.534–6). Less is known of the contaminating effects of several reservoirs containing radioactive waste. On 22 November 1990, the Russian government declared the Chelyabinsk district an ecological disaster zone. The nuclear disaster at Chelyabinsk was, unfortunately, not an isolated event. It paled into insignificance in 1986, when the Chernobyl catastrophe took place.

In the early morning of 26 April 1986, an explosion took place in reactor 4 of the nuclear power plant at Chernobyl, in the Soviet Republic of the Ukraine. Radioactive materials and gases were blown into the atmosphere, forming a plume which moved in a North-westerly direction. What is at present known as the Soviet Republic of Belarus being directly in the path of the plume, was affected even more than the Ukraine by the catastrophe at Chernobyl (see Box 4). The ecological, economic and socio-psychological damage caused by the Chernobyl accident can hardly be overestimated. People will suffer from its consequences for decades, if not centuries to come.

There was no way of maintaining secrecy about the Chernobyl catastrophe, if only because its consequences were felt abroad. On 28 April, 53 hours after the accident, the radioactive plume was detected at the nuclear power plant at Forsmark in Sweden. It was later found that 170,000 reindeer in the Swedish part of Lapland had been seriously contaminated as a consequence of the Chernobyl accident. Fall-out from Chernobyl was registered in every country of the Northern hemisphere (Medvedev, 1990a, pp.194–220). Although the era of *perestroika* and *glasnost* had started a year before with the appointment of Mikhail Gorbachev as Secretary-General of the

Consequences of the Chernobyl disaster in the Soviet Republic of Belarus

4

In Belarus alone, 257,000 hectares of agricultural land and 1.34 million hectares of forest were taken out of production (Marples, 1992, p.423). Hundreds of thousands of people had to be removed as a consequence of the catastrophe. The official number of human fatalities caused by the accident is 31. Unofficial sources, however, have estimated the death toll at between 6000 and 7000. There has been a sharp rise in recent years in the number of new cases of thyroid cancer, particularly in Belarus.

Region of Belarus	1986	1987	1988	1989	1990	1991	1992	Total
Brest	0	0	1	1	6	5	5	18
Vitebsk	0	0	0	0	1	3	0	4
Gomel	1	2	1	2	14	38	13	71
Grodno	1	1	1	2	0	2	6	13
Minsk	0	1	1	1	1	4	4	12
Mogilev	0	0	0	0	2	1	1	4
Minsk city	0	0	1	0	5	2	1	9
Total	2	4	5	6	29	55	30	131

The sharp rise in the number of new cases of thyroid cancer is generally regarded as being a consequence of the spread of radioactive iodine during the first eight days after the catastrophe. However, it will remain uncertain for decades as to whether people suffering from cancer are victims of the Chernobyl catastrophe. Illustrative of the uncertainties regarding the impact on human health is the situation among immigrants from Belarus, Russia and the Ukraine in Israel. They formed the association 'SOS Chernobyl'. According to this association 100,000 'victims of Chernobyl' arrived in Israel between 1990 and 1992. They are dissatisfied by what they consider a lack of concern for their medical problems by the Israeli authorities (Chernobyl Conference, 1992, p.21). As in the former Soviet republics it is not possible to determine how far health problems can be ascribed to the direct radiation effects, the indirect effects of the catastrophe disrupting living and working circumstances, other forms of environmental pollution or the disintegration of the former Soviet Union and its republics.

Uncertainty is also a consequence of suddenly heightened levels of radiation at unexpected times and places, caused by the Chernobyl accident. To give just one example, on 9 February 1991, Izvestia informed its readers that heightened levels of radiation had been registered as a consequence of the Chernobyl accident in the famous seaside resort of Sotsji on the border of the Black Sea. Radioactive particles were said to have been transported by rain.

communist party of the Soviet Union, information about the nature and impact of the Chernobyl catastrophe came late and remained limited. (See also Liberatore, 1995, in book one of this series, who discusses the responses made by different countries to the Chernobyl accident.)

Hazardous waste

In general, there are no vested interests involved in receiving polluted air or radioactive fallout from neighbouring countries. However, the same cannot be said of the receipt of waste from abroad. Waste may be imported legally or illegally, with or without the consent of the authorities of the receiving countries. I will not discuss waste in general, but focus on hazardous waste (including waste in liquid form) in particular. The term 'hazardous waste' covers both toxic chemicals and radioactive substances though usually they are treated as quite separate categories. Radioactive substances are subject to different regulatory processes. Hazardous and radioactive wastes are the subject of Chapter 6 in this book.

The implementation of legislation in Western countries on the processing or disposition of hazardous waste has led to steep rises in handling costs. To avoid these costs, hazardous waste came to be exported to countries where costs are lower. Since the revolutions of 1989, Eastern European countries have become a favourite destination for hazardous waste from Western countries. In fact, the transportation of hazardous waste to this area actually started earlier than 1989. The former German Democratic Republic (GDR), Poland and Rumania are among the countries to which hazardous waste from Western Europe has been (and indeed still is) transported.

Since 1979, different types of waste, including hazardous waste from Austria, Belgium, Italy, The Netherlands, Switzerland and West Germany, have been dumped at a landfill site in Schoenberg in the former GDR, near the West German town of Lubeck (Vallette and Spalding, 1990, p.218). Schoenberg is an important though not the only dumping site for hazardous waste of Western origin. Since 1982, when exports to Schoenberg started, more than half a million tonnes of hazardous waste of Dutch origin have been dumped in Schoenberg. The treatment of hazardous waste in The Netherlands would cost ten times as much as the costs of dumping it in Schoenberg (Ouwendijk and Musse, personal communication). In some cases, exports of hazardous waste from The Netherlands to Schoenberg have been stopped as a result of combined protests by German and Dutch pressure groups. However, incidental successes have not put a complete halt to the exports of hazardous waste to Schoenberg and other dumping sites in the former GDR.

Even before the fall of the communist regime, the Polish government tried to limit imports of hazardous waste from abroad. A ban on imports of hazardous waste has been in force since 1989. In that year, a new article was added to the Environmental Protection Act, under which illegal importers of toxic waste faced the prospect of imprisonment. Bernstorff and Puckett claim that what they call 'the vague definition of what constitutes hazardous waste' is one of the biggest problem, in preventing the export of hazardous waste. As they see it:

> When a waste is imported with a recycling pretext or destination, Polish law can allow its importation. This provides an extremely dangerous loophole as nothing, even with the best intentions, can ever be 100% recycled, and most often, vast quantities of hazardous residues will continue to be dumped in Poland. In addition, the new joint ventures with Western companies often make it difficult to decide whether the material crossing the borders of this large country is a raw material or a hazardous waste (Bernstorff and Puckett, 1992, p.35) (see Box 5).

Waste imports in Poland

The Poles were swiftly 'rewarded' once they opened their borders to industrial companies from the West. The preliminary findings of research conducted by Greenpeace indicate that 22 million tonnes of toxic waste have been offered to Poland during the period since 1989. Of that total, over 46,000 tonnes of toxic waste have actually crossed the open borders from countries like Germany, Austria and Sweden.

At least 72 foreign firms, disposers and brokers have been involved in 64 waste trade schemes with 13 countries. Half of the schemes originated in former West Germany. Complete plants for incinerating waste and 'recycling' used oil have even been offered free, on condition that the plant accepts imports and the residues from these processes necessarily remain in Poland.

Recycling and re-use are often used as pretexts for waste imports. In fact, of those waste schemes where the destination is indicated, 62% claim some form of re-use as a pretext.

Source: Bernstorff and Puckett (1992), p.3.

Notwithstanding the political loopholes, another Greenpeace report concludes that the Polish government had the problem of toxic waste import 'by and large' under control by 1991 (Bernstorff and Totten, 1992, p.5). As a consequence, other countries became targets for waste exports. One of them was Rumania. As in the former GDR in the communist era, the political establishment had vested interests in the import of hazardous waste. A number of officers belonging to the Rumanian Secret Service, the *Securitate*, who also held posts as managers of foreign trade firms, were among the importers involved in these deals (Bernstorff and Totten, 1992, p.9). The post-Ceaucescu regime was overwhelmed by proposals for waste imports from Western companies, often combined with offers to build waste incineration plants. According to Bernstorff and Totten (1992, p.12):

> Within a mere three months after Bleahu [the Minister of the Environment] had taken office, i.e. between October 1991 and January 1992, about 30 waste import proposals had crossed the Minister's desk. Along with several French, Dutch and US projects, the majority of offers were from German, Austrian and Italian companies and involved the construction of waste incinerators free of charge. During their first 10 to 15 years in operation, at least 50% to 60% of the total volume burned in these facilities was to consist of imported wastes. The incinerators were then to be turned over to Rumanian ownership.

One of the reasons why exports from Western European countries to Central and Eastern Europe are able to continue is the conflict of interests between the environmental and trade policies of the European Union. On the one hand, EU member states are encouraged to manage waste as closely as possible to the place where it is generated. On the other hand, waste is considered to be a commodity like any other commodity, whence it should be traded freely unhindered by national borders (Bernstorff and Puckett, 1992, p.38).

3.3 Environmental deterioration and communism

Communism and the exploitation of Nature

The cases of (extreme) environmental damage described above may be considered as symptoms of the damaging effect of the former communist regimes in the states of Central and Eastern Europe (see Box 6). This is without denying the environmental damage caused by other types of societies in other parts of the world. It also needs to be recognised that, during the communist regime, the countries of Central and Eastern Europe were undergoing rapid modernisation through industrialisation, a process which elsewhere has usually been accompanied by exploitation of natural resources and degradation of the environment. Three aspects are particularly important in order to understand the negative impact which communism has had on the environment: ideology, the economic system and the political system.

As regards the role of *ideology*, Marxism, the ideological foundation of the former communist regimes in Central and Eastern Europe, is an example of Western belief in progress by means of the exploitation of Nature. During the Stalinist period, Nature

---

6

Economic and health effects of environmental problems

The main differences between the forms of environmental damage as they occur in Central and Eastern Europe and those which are seen in Western Europe relate to their economic and health effects.

It is clear that some forms of environmental damage in Central and Eastern Europe have an excessive economic impact. In the Chernobyl case in particular, enormous areas of land had to be taken out of production and new housing facilities had to be found or constructed for thousands of people. This case is not the only example of great economic losses as a consequence of environmental deterioration. It has been estimated that, out of the 605 million hectares of land in the former Soviet Union which are available for agricultural production, 157 million hectares have been severely damaged by salination (Yablokov, 1990, p.4). This is one of the reasons for the dependence on imports of grain for the domestic food supply.

Whereas it is seldom possible to prove the existence of any relation in Western countries between environmental decay and negative health trends, Central and Eastern Europe offer an overwhelming list of examples of such relations:

○ Overexposure to lead among children (at 37 locations in seven countries).
○ Acute (short-term) respiratory/irritant conditions (at 46 locations in ten countries).
○ Chronic respiratory conditions (at 29 locations in nine countries).
○ Excessive infant and lung cancer mortality (at eight locations in three countries).
○ Abnormal physiological development (at 18 locations in seven countries).
○ Waterborne methaemoglobinaemia (widespread in six countries).

Source: Environmental Action Programme for Central and Eastern Europe (1993), p.II: 20–21.

was considered as an obstacle to further progress (Weiner, 1984, p.75). Scientific disciplines like genetics and ecology, which showed either the limited opportunities available to human beings for changing Nature or the damaging effects which human activities could have on the natural environment, were condemned as bourgeois and counter-revolutionary. Scientists working in these fields, and in genetics in particular, were dismissed, arrested and liquidated. Great projects were started which were aimed at transforming or correcting what were called 'mistakes of Nature'. The term *voluntarism* is often used to refer to the arbitrary and frequently impulsive manner in which sweeping changes in natural conditions were pursued, without any thought being given to the real possibilities for change and the damaging effects which such changes could have. One example of such a large-scale project is the attempt to change the direction of flow of certain stretches of rivers in Siberia and the European part of Russia from northwards to southwards to promote large-scale irrigation and hydro-power projects. The plan was abandoned in 1986.

Planned economies tended to underestimate the value of natural resources, as, parenthetically, market economies still do too. Planned economies, however, had a more severe impact on the environment than market economies as they were more extreme in their denial of value to Nature. According to Marx's theory of the value of labour, natural resources have only a *use value* and not the *exchange value* that market economies attribute to them. Unlike use values, exchange values are expressed in prices. Exchange values derive from the human labour which is invested in a resource's production. So scarcity of a resource, for instance, is reflected in its price. On the other hand, the free, unpriced availability of natural resources (their having a use value only) is considered as an essential feature of a socialist economy. Today, it is often cited as a cause of waste. Prime examples of this are the tendency constantly to shift mining activities in order to obtain easily accessible minerals without being hampered by financial barriers; the excessive irrigation of agricultural land as a result of the free distribution of water; and the quantities of materials and energy which are used in industrial production, which are relatively large by Western standards.

In centrally planned economies, furthermore, planning targets were often for-mulated in physical terms, such as the quantity of material inputs. Producers were therefore encouraged to use large quantities of materials. For many years, the absurd effects of the physical planning targets were featured not only in Western publications, but also in the Soviet press (Tellegen, 1986). As a consequence of the use of physical planning indicators, it was sometimes the case that only large saucepans or thick sheets of paper were available to consumers, as producing small saucepans and thin sheets of paper would require more time and effort in order to meet the same planning targets. Planning targets were generally unrelated to consumer needs. As a consequence, there were both shortages and surpluses of consumer goods.

The final aspect that affords an understanding of why communism had such an impact on the environment is the particular *political system* of these countries. Environmental problems may be conceived of as the 'external' effects of activities undertaken by widely different types of institutions. In general, these activities cannot be stopped, but need to be moderated or changed in order to avoid environ-mental damage. One cannot simply cease all industrial production, motorised transport or housing but one may limit them, at least in certain areas, or change them. Outward *countervailing power* is necessary in general in order to change the behaviour of institutions and thus to prevent or limit environmental damage. In the political system of the former communist states, countervailing power was weakly developed. The veil of secrecy in which the Chernobyl disaster and other nuclear accidents were shrouded is a typical example of a political strategy that is designed to avert countervailing power. Although there were certain institutional divisions between the government and the communist party, these did not generate any countervailing power such as would have prevented government decisions from having any damaging environmental effects. Environmental control was integrated within the ministries for different branches of industry whose prime task was the fulfilment of planning targets. In the national report to the UNCED Conference in 1992, this situation was described as follows: 'One of the principal drawbacks of that system in state management of the use of nature and environmental protection was that those functions were distributed among numerous ministries and departments, mostly working in the economy, which means they themselves were users of natural resources. In conditions where openness (glasnost) was a foreign term,

Plate 3.1 Woman sitting on the beach at a Black Sea resort near Constanta, Romania. Photo: Sean Sprague/Lineair

such a system could not be efficient, as outside supervision over their own influence over the state of the natural environment and resources was actually ruled out' (Ministry of Ecology and Natural Resources of the Russian Federation, 1992, p.61).

There was little scope for environmental protest by individual citizens or organised pressure groups. Environmental protest was also hindered by the strong local power of industrial enterprises. Not only did they provide jobs, but they also supplied housing and even built and operated cultural and recreational facilities.

A comparison of Eastern and Western economies

Both planned and market economies have common roots in Western culture as it has developed in Europe over the past few centuries. Their common weakness is a tendency to undervalue freely available natural resources in the form of materials, energy, plants, animals, ecosystems and clean soil, water and air. This weakness, however, is more characteristic of planned than of market economies.

In the former planned economies, prices played a minor role in the supply of material inputs to industrial enterprises. There was a tendency to keep large quantities of materials in stock in order to avoid future scarcity. Yet resource scarcity is a semi-permanent phenomenon in a planned economy. Kornai argues that the pure type of socialist economy is a *resource-constrained system*, where production is limited by the scarcity of resources. On the other hand, capitalism in its classic form is a *demand-constrained system*. Here, production is limited by the demands of consumers (Kornai, 1979, p.804). In the socialist economies, producers paid little or no attention to consumers' preference. Even before the era of *glasnost* and *perestroika*, the lack of financial stimuli to encourage people to make rational use of natural resources was recognised as a basic weakness of the planned economies. In the 1980s, for example, the Hungarian economy produced one unit of *gross domestic product* (GDP) using 40% more materials and energy (e.g. three times as much steel) as well as 50% more capital than the average OECD country (Government of the Hungarian Republic, 1991).

An important difference between the development of market and planned economies may be seen in the development of the price of energy. In the market economies, the two oil crises which occurred in 1973 and 1979 led to a sharp increase in energy prices. Planned economies were protected from this type of resource constraint. As a consequence, the sharp reduction in the energy intensity of production that took place in the West was not mirrored in the communist countries.

The difference in industrial energy use between the East and West is also a matter of difference in energy efficiency resulting, in part, from the different stage of economic development that has been reached. In general, Western countries need less energy than Eastern European countries to produce a given quantity of products. A well-known example is the production of steel. In 1980, Japan used 18.8 gigajoules to produce one tonne of steel, the United States 23.9 and the Soviet Union 31.0 (Chandler, 1985, p.12). The difference between Eastern European countries and OECD countries is not only caused by differences in energy efficiency, however. Another relevant development is the declining share of industrial production accounted for by various energy-intensive (and polluting) branches of industry, such as steel, concrete and fertiliser production. This is another area in which the OECD countries have left the Eastern European countries far behind (Janicke *et al.*, 1992). Nonetheless, the situation in terms of energy use in other sectors of society, in particular housing and transport, is quite different (Box 7).

In summary, we may conclude that, whereas in the former planned economies productive activities were major contributors to environmental pollution, in the market economies consumption patterns in fields such as housing and transport are important causes of environmental damage, with energy use providing a good indicator. Whereas environmental problems in the planned economies were often

---

7

Energy use in OECD countries and Central and Eastern Europe

Energy use and production
Between 1970 and 1990, the average annual growth in energy use was 1.3% in the Western OECD countries and 2.4% in the former states of the Eastern bloc. The main cause of this difference between the market and planned economies lies in the development of industrial production. Between 1970 and 1988, industrial energy use in OECD countries fluctuated around a stable level, whereas it rose sharply in the USSR and other Eastern European countries.

In the OECD countries, the share of manufacturing in total final energy use declined from 36% to 27% between 1973 and 1988. In the USSR, the share of final energy use accounted for by manufacturing industry was still 55% in 1985.

Energy use and consumption
Despite the cold climate in Eastern Europe, there is no great difference between OECD countries and the former Soviet Union in terms of the share accounted for by the residential sector in energy use: in both cases, it is approximately 20%. In the former Eastern bloc countries, the efficiency of energy use, in relation to both space heating and water heating as well as to consumption by electric appliances, was traditionally low and, unlike the OECD countries, it remained low in the 1970s and 1980s. However, people in Eastern Europe have far less energy-consuming residential space and fewer appliances at their disposal and this limits household energy use.

The share of passenger travel in energy use in OECD countries increased from 19% to 22% between 1973 and 1988, whilst in the USSR it was not more than 5% of final energy use, even in 1985. In personal traffic, energy intensity is lower in the East than in the West, because of the larger share of railway traffic and the smaller share of motor cars. Compared with Western Europe, the level of per capita travel is also low, even in the former Soviet Union with its large distances.

Source: Schipper and Meyers (1992), pp.73, 78, 79 and 130.

---

caused by the over-exploitation of natural resources and excessive quantities of pollution per unit of GDP, the environmental problems in the market economies are much more a factor of the continuing growth of consumption. In other words, the resource-constrained, planned economies of the East in fact generate environmental problems by their excessive use of natural resources per unit of GDP, whilst the demand-constrained economies of the West cause environmental problems by their ever-growing consumption.

The transformation of the former communist states

The communist regimes did not, it should be said, completely ignore all environmental problems. Some forms of environmental degradation were discussed in the scientific press and sometimes even in the popular press. One example is the pollution of Lake Baikal, which has been the object of regular criticism in the Soviet press ever since the 1960s. Indeed, the Soviet Union was one of the first countries to formulate environmental quality standards, which were in fact stricter than those later formulated in the United States. Environmental legislation and environmental inspections were developed. Natural areas were protected by awarding them the status of nature reserve. Progress was made in some areas, in particular in the reduction of surface water pollution (see Box 8).

Progress in environmental policies did not prevent excessive forms of environmental destruction, though. In official publications, environmental pollution was referred to as a form of *wastage*. Even before Gorbachev came to power, there had already been criticism of the excessive use of materials and energy in Soviet manufacturing industry as compared with the West. As early as 3 June 1981, a decision was taken by the Central Committee of the communist party and the Council of Ministers of the Soviet Union to step up efforts to save and make rational use of raw materials, energy and other material resources. This decision was later confirmed in other public statements and

---

8

Water management in the Soviet Union

There is evidence that the authorities began to pay serious attention to the Soviet Union's mounting water pollution problem during the 1970s and 1980s. The purification and re-use of water became common practice in industry. By 1990, 72.5% of the country's industrial water needs were met from this source, compared with a 56.9% recycling rate in 1976. Whilst only 63% of sewage and industrial waste water was purified in 1979, that figure had risen to 77% by 1990. Despite such progress, the lag in constructing new facilities and the introduction of more stringent water quality requirements meant that only 30% of the water treated in 1990 actually met the government standards set at the time. Indeed, there were definite signs of regression during the late 1980s. There was again an increase in polluted discharges into natural hydrosystems and a considerable reduction in the rate of construction of treatment facilities.

Source: Golitsyn (1992).

decisions (Tellegen, 1989, p.148). Economic stagnation and environmental damage were considered to be caused by the same factor: wastage.

As a consequence of the policy of *glasnost* in the Soviet Union and comparable developments in other Eastern European states, environmental issues were not only discussed more openly than before but were also presented in a different context. Instead of being regarded as symptoms of wastage, they were now considered as symptoms of *exploitation* by the central authorities, in particular the central government in Moscow.

Environmental pressure groups were very successful in the Soviet Union after 1985. An extremely important success was the cancellation of the project which had been designed to alter the direction of flow in a number of rivers (see 3.3: Communism and the exploitation of Nature). Various forms of action aimed at industrial enterprises also proved to be highly effective. Many polluting factories had to stop production for a period of time and in some cases there were lengthy shutdowns. The planning and construction of many nuclear power plants was halted after the Chernobyl accident.

Environmental issues played a major role in the fall of communist regimes outside the Soviet Union and the struggle for independence of the Soviet republics. In Poland, the Polish Ecological Club was founded together with the Solidarnoz trade union in 1980. In Hungary, the protest against the canalisation of the Danube, led by an action group called the Danube Circle, played a key role in the process of political change. In Bulgaria, the Ecoglasnost pressure group was one of the driving forces behind the takeover of power from the communists. In Estonia, the campaign for national independence began with protests against a new phosphorus mining project, which was considered to be of no interest to Estonia, actually damaging to its natural features and leading to changes in the groundwater level in a large part of the republic. In Armenia, protests against pollution caused by chemical plants marked the beginning of the struggle for independence. This revolutionary period is now undoubtedly a thing of the past.

3.4 Co-operation and common problem solving: conflicts of interest

Environmental problems, particularly international environmental problems, can only be solved through co-operation between the parties involved. However, the kind of co-operation needed depends on the problem at hand. There is thus a vast difference between co-operation needed to solve problems which are caused and felt in both Eastern and Western Europe and that required to solve problems which are caused in one part of Europe but which have an impact in another part of the continent. Also, co-operation may misleadingly suggest the existence of only common interests. We will see there are also conflicts of interest, particularly where one part of Europe has to be protected against another. This applies not only to Eastern and Western Europe in general but also to individual countries within Eastern and Western Europe which are involved in East–West environmental contacts.

I shall now discuss three types of environmental co-operation between Eastern and Western Europe: solving common problems, protecting the East against the West and, finally, protecting the West against the East.

Air pollution: a common interest of East and West

Some transboundary environmental problems are caused in both Eastern and Western Europe and felt in both Eastern and Western Europe. Air pollution and water pollution, for example, do not stop at the border between Eastern and Western Europe, they migrate in either direction. Because of their uniformity they require common problem solving, that is, they can only be solved when both parties take action. By way of an example, I shall discuss some forms of air pollution.

Polluted air is transported hundreds and sometimes thousands of kilometres by the wind, crossing many national borders. There are, however, great differences between countries in the extent of their contribution to and suffering from transboundary air pollution (see Box 9).

The reduction of air pollution has long been recognised as a common interest of Eastern and Western European countries, even though some countries suffer more from transboundary air pollution than others. Both natural conditions (in particular prevailing wind directions) and economic activities in neighbouring countries (such as energy production and other industrial activities) may contribute to these differences. Among the European countries, Russia is a net importer of air pollution, most of which originates from other members of the former Eastern bloc.

In 1979, negotiations within the framework of the *Economic Commission for Europe* (ECE) of the United Nations led to the adoption of the *Convention on Long Range Transboundary Air Pollution* (LRTAP). This convention was ratified by 32 countries in Eastern and Western Europe and Northern America (the United States and Canada). Even before 1979, the ECE had already initiated the development of a programme for monitoring and measuring transboundary air pollution, called EMEP. Under the umbrella of EMEP, Monitoring Synthesising Centres were founded near Moscow (known as MSC East) and Oslo (known as MSC West). Scientific research was concentrated in IIASA in Laxemburg (near Vienna), where the RAINS model was developed (see Box 10).

Within the framework of the LRTAP convention, various protocols were signed on different air pollutants. In 1985, 18 countries signed the Helsinki Protocol and thereby committed themselves to reducing SO_2 emissions by 30% by 1993, as compared with the level of emissions in 1980. Under the 1988 Sofia Protocol, the signatories are committed to stabilising NO_x emissions to 1987 levels by the year 1994. A third protocol, signed in Geneva in 1991, aims to limit emissions of volatile organic compounds (VOCs) in 1999 to a level 30% below that applying in 1988 (Hordijk, 1991; OECD, 1993, pp.179–81). All the Western countries and most of the Eastern European countries had reached the 30% reduction target in 1993. Many Western countries achieved a much larger reduction in SO_2 emissions.

In 1993, the member states of the LRTAP agreed upon a new SO_2 reduction plan. The new plan is not *emission orientated* but *effect orientated*. In other words, the aim is no longer to achieve equal reductions in emissions in all member states, but to reduce local depositions as far as is necessary not to surpass *critical loads*. The concept of a critical load has been defined as 'a quantitative estimate of an exposure to one or more pollutants below which significant harmful effects on specified elements of the environment do not occur according to present knowledge' (Amann *et al.*, 1992,

Transboundary air pollution in Europe

9

The long-range transport of sulphur dioxide in Europe has been well documented since the 1970s. It has more recently been ascertained that other contaminants, such as nitrogen oxides, ammonia and heavy metals, are also transported over long distances. The pattern of prevailing westerly winds in Europe implies that the main transport of pollutants is typically in an easterly direction. However, two other important factors influence the net flux of pollutants. First, the density of emissions per unit area is much greater in most of Eastern Europe than in Western Europe. Second, stagnant or easterly wind conditions sometimes occur; at these times, pollutants gather over Central and Eastern Europe and may be transported westward. For example, in the well-documented case of SO_2 smog in January 1985, pollutants accumulated in a stagnant air mass over Central Europe and were then transported to Western Europe by moderate winds blowing from the East. Owing to these factors, there is a flux of pollutants both eastward and westward (as well as northward and southward) in Europe. Various computer models have been used to estimate the atmospheric flux of different substances between European countries. Results from the EMEP (European Monitoring and Evaluation Program) model indicate a net westward flux (backflow) of atmospheric sulphur. In 1985, for example, the eastward flow of atmospheric sulphur was estimated at 463 kt (kilotonnes or millions of kilos) and the westward flow at 870 kt. This implies that there is a net flow from East to West: the high density of the emissions in the East surpasses the effect of the prevailing westerly direction of the winds.

Besides the long-range transport of air pollutants in Europe, there is also the problem of transboundary air pollution within Central and Eastern Europe itself. The net direction of the atmospheric flux of sulphur again follows the prevailing winds eastward. This is because substantial amounts of sulphur are emitted nearly everywhere in Eastern Europe and hence there is no substantial backflow of pollutants within Eastern Europe as there is from Eastern to Western Europe. Poland, for example, receives a much greater amount of sulphur across its Western border (for instance from the lignite-fired power plants in Eastern Germany) than it sends across this border. In the same way, Poland passes on considerably more sulphur to its Eastern neighbours than it receives from them. This flux, of course, is a function of the size of the receptor country; a small country will receive fewer kilotonnes of sulphur on its territory than a large country, all other factors being equal.

The annual flux of nitrogen (as the sum of nitrogen oxides and ammonia) also shows a general trend toward the East. However, the total mass of nitrogen is not as great as the mass of sulphur. In addition to the acidifying pollutants of sulphur and nitrogen, relatively large quantities of other more toxic pollutants, such as heavy metals, are also emitted to the atmosphere in Central and Eastern Europe. These substances are emitted as gases or small particles from power plants, metallurgical smelters, vehicles and other sources. Computer models show that there is a substantial transboundary flow of these substances. A fairly even exchange of arsenic and cadmium takes place between Poland and Eastern Germany, but the flow is much less balanced between other countries.

Source: taken from Alcamo (1992), pp. 88–101.

The RAINS model

The RAINS model focuses on the acidification of Europe's natural environment and on the deposition of sulphur and nitrogen compounds that lead to acidification. The model consists of a set of submodels that cover the cause–effect chain: pollutant generation (energy scenarios, emission abatement option, costs of control), atmospheric transport and deposition and environmental effects (forest soil, Scandinavian lakes and groundwater). The model covers the whole of Europe, including the European part of the former USSR, using a resolution of 150 × 150 km for emission and atmospheric processes and a grid system of 0.5° latitude × 1.0° longitude for environmental impacts. The pollutants included are SO_2, NO_x and NH_3.

The RAINS model can be used for the following purposes:

1 Given a certain financial budget, to maximise the number of kilotonnes of SO_2 that can be reduced in Europe as a whole.
2 Given a specific deposition target, to minimise the amount of emission reduction needed to reach the target. A different target can be set for each cell of the RAINS grid (150 × 150 km).
3 Given a specific deposition target, to minimise the costs of emission reduction needed to reach the target.

Sources: Amann *et al.*(1992), p.1187 and Hordijk (1991), p.599.

p.1186). This new policy is based on maps of critical loads for different parts of Europe (Hettelingh *et al.*, 1991). There are great differences in the critical loads applying to different areas, based, for example, on the different types of soils in these areas.

It is clear that this new policy makes international co-operation much more complicated. Local emissions are often highly dependent on emissions in other countries (Box 9) and the necessary level of reduction may therefore differ among member states because of the different effects in other member states. A logical consequence of the effect-oriented approach would be the creation of a common European fund from which investments in pollution reduction would be paid in order to reduce the most extreme deviations from the critical loads, wherever this is in Europe. The RAINS models could be used for this purpose.

As early as in 1985, the Austrian Minister of Environmental Protection, Kurt Steyer, suggested creating a common fund for SO_2 emission abatement in the framework of the LRTAP treaty. At the time, opponents of this idea argued that Eastern European countries should not be granted subsidies for taking environmental measures as long as a large part of their state budget was still devoted to military spending. However, even though the Cold War has now come to an end, such a common fund has still not been created. At the same time, Western financial institutions offer financial aid to individual countries to reduce local and transboundary air pollution. Co-operation within the LRTAP Convention remains limited to joint studies of the scale and effects of air pollution and the definition and evaluation of policy targets.

Hazardous waste: protecting the East against the West

Some environmental problems are caused mainly in the West, while their effects are transmitted at least partially to the East. For instance, there is a social 'law' that hazardous waste moves to places with weak environmental regulations and a high level of interest in foreign sources of income. Accordingly, waste is shipped both legally and illegally from Western to Eastern Europe.

The problem with the concept of co-operation here is that it suggests too much close harmony. In reality, environmental co-operation often means two or more bodies working together to fight the environmentally damaging activities undertaken by other bodies.

Various international agreements regulate the transport of hazardous waste and other dangerous substances. Among these agreements is the Basel Convention, which was signed by many Eastern and Western European countries and has now entered into force in a number of them (see Box 11).

The Basel Convention does not explicitly ban the transport of hazardous waste. While there is general agreement on the principle that waste should not be transported but be processed or dumped at the place where it was produced, this principle has not been put into practice to date. The vested interests which are involved in the export of waste are too strong for export to be banned completely. Further discussion of the transport of hazardous waste will be found in Chapter 6.

Nuclear power plants: protecting the West against the East

The relative backwardness of industrial technology and organisation and the weakness of environmental controls in Eastern Europe have resulted in forms of environmental

---

The Basel Convention | **11**

The Basel Convention on the Control of Transboundary Movements of Hazardous Wastes and their Disposal was adopted on 22 March 1989 and took effect on 5 May 1992. The main provisions of the convention call for the following action by states:

1 Information exchange with other parties on waste exports and imports, through designated national authorities.
2 The prohibition of waste exports to countries that are not party to the convention or to countries which are party to the convention but which have not expressly authorised waste imports.
3 The licensing and supervision of persons transporting or disposing of waste.
4 The packaging, labelling and transport of waste in accordance with international rules and standards.
5 Co-operation on the environmentally sound management of waste.
6 Mutual information in the event of accidents during the transboundary movement of waste.

Source: Environmental Action Programme for Central and Eastern Europe (1993), pp. VI–21.

pollution which are felt far across the boundaries of the Eastern European states. The spread of radioactivity as a consequence of the catastrophe at Chernobyl in 1986 is the most dramatic example of transboundary pollution generated in Eastern Europe and felt in Western Europe. Since the Chernobyl disaster, both politicians and the general public in the West have been acutely aware of the risks associated with the use of nuclear energy in the Soviet Union and the other former Eastern bloc states. A number of countries are particularly concerned about nuclear power plants which are either in operation or under construction. Finland, for example, is afraid of plants operating in nearby St Petersburg, while Austria fears the future operation of the nuclear power plant in Temelin (Czech Republic).

The disintegration of COMECON (roughly, the Central and Eastern European Economic Co-operation Platform) and the Soviet Union have made the risks associated with the use of nuclear energy in this part of the world even greater than they were in the past. Before the disintegration of the former Eastern bloc, Russia dominated nuclear energy production both within the Soviet Union and in other COMECON countries where nuclear energy had been introduced. Both the other Soviet republics and the various satellite countries were dependent on Russia for the construction and management of nuclear power plants, the supply of fuel and the disposal of waste. The old networks on which the use of nuclear energy was based were destroyed when COMECON and the Soviet Union fell apart. Those nuclear power plants which are still operating suffer from a lack of skilled staff and of facilities for disposing of nuclear waste. Another new risk involving the use of nuclear energy, whether for peaceful or for military purposes, is the outflow to foreign countries of both nuclear materials and nuclear experts.

The quickest short-term solution for reducing the nuclear risk in Central and Eastern Europe would be to shut down the nuclear power plants which are currently in operation. It has been argued by Western experts and politicians that there is a particularly urgent need to shut down the oldest type of VVER reactors as soon as possible so as to avoid new nuclear catastrophes (see Box 12).

12

Soviet nuclear reactor types

There are two basic Soviet power reactor designs: the RMBK and the VVER. RBMKs are boiling light-water, graphite-moderated, channel-type reactors which have only been built or operated in the former Soviet Union. The four reactors at the nuclear power plant near Chernobyl in the Ukraine are of this type. Other RMBKs have been built in Lithuania (2) and Russia (4).

VVERs are pressurised water reactors. They have been built in Armenia (4), Bulgaria (4), the Czech Republic (6), Eastern Germany (4), Hungary (4), Russia (31), Slovakia (8) and the Ukraine (15).

In addition, there are a number of other units of a different design that are used for district heating.

Source: UI (1993).

Four VVER plants in Greifswald (in the former GDR) have been shut down. The same has happened with two Armenian power plants of the same type, although it is possible that these may be recommissioned in the near future. Although all the power plants of this type, particularly those in Bulgaria, are considered to constitute a major safety hazard, most are all still in operation.

Another way of containing the risk associated with the use of nuclear power is either to improve both the technology and the management of existing nuclear power plants or to replace them with new, 'safe' nuclear power plants. There is growing resistance in Central and Eastern European countries to the closure of existing power plants. The West also has a strong interest in improving existing nuclear power plants or building new ones instead of closing them down. The Western nuclear industry has suffered from shrinking markets in Western countries for many years now. Nuclear equipment suppliers such as Westinghouse (in the USA) and Siemens (Germany) have strong interests in the continued use of nuclear energy in the former Eastern bloc countries. They are also interested in safety, however, because a second Chernobyl disaster would deal a severe and perhaps decisive blow to the future of nuclear energy all over the world. The provision of aid to improve technology and management may also pave the way for future investments in new nuclear power plants in Central and Eastern Europe (see Box 13).

One special form of Western aid that is designed to limit the nuclear risks resulting from the disintegration of the former Soviet Union is the creation of employment for nuclear specialists in subsidised nuclear research institutes in their home countries, thereby discouraging them from emigrating to countries which may use their expertise for military purposes.

3.5 Environmental policies in the post-communist era

Political independence, economic interest and environmental protection

The disintegration of the former communist states has led to a dramatic fall in local production levels. Reductions of 50% and more have become normal phenomena in the post-communist period. In the short run, this trend has led to a reduction in environmental pollution yet this can hardly be considered to be an environmental success story. The closure of factories or the drastic reduction of their output alone does not contribute to a long-term solution to environmental problems. Sooner or later, governments and firms will begin attempting to restore production levels to their former states. If a long-term reduction in environmental damage caused by productive activities is to be achieved, existing facilities will need to be modernised and particular economic activities will have to be replaced by others.

A lack of state control, however, hinders the development of environmental control. In that vein, the former Soviet Minister of the Environment, Vorontsov, has already warned against the environmental 'chaos' which would be the outcome of the collapse of all-Union institutions. Referring to both the political circumstances and the environmental situation in the Baltic region, he queried: 'Is it possible to declare the "independence"

Western involvement in Eastern nuclear power

13

A Friends of the Earth report distinguishes three types of involvement of Western firms in the nuclear industry in Central and Eastern Europe: selling technology or expertise; investing directly in the concerns which manage operations within the nuclear fuel chain; and buying electricity from the utilities which operate nuclear power plants.

The state of the nuclear industry in Central and Eastern Europe is an issue of global concern. However, despite all the political talk and corporate hype since the collapse of communist regimes in the region, little has been done so far to change the situation. Moreover, the limited level of finance and support which has been offered has tended to perpetuate the expansion of nuclear power programmes in Central and Eastern Europe, rather than address immediate safety concerns relating to existing nuclear reactors and develop more environmentally acceptable and economically efficient energy systems.

The key findings of this study are as follows:

○ More than twice as much government-backed money has been directed at completing partially-built nuclear power plants in Central and Eastern Europe than has been spent on making existing reactors any safer.
○ When all public and private Western financial involvement is considered, nearly three times as much finance is going towards expanding nuclear power generation in the region as towards making existing reactors safer.
○ Western electricity utilities are providing incentives to countries in Central and Eastern Europe to complete partially-built nuclear plants and to patch up existing ones by signing long-term contracts to buy the electricity output of the plants.
○ Western financial assistance programmes have ignored the need to target decommissioning.

Investments are made by buying shares in newly privatised concerns. Thus, Siemens owns 67% of the Czech Republic enterprise, Skoda Energy. Electricity companies in Switzerland, Austria, France, Italy and Germany import electricity from nuclear power plants in Central and Eastern Europe.

Source: Roberts (1993), pp.3 and 9.

---

of the atmosphere?' (quoted in Peterson, 1993, p.44). Although, as we argued, environmental control was already a weak element in the former communist states, many of the previously existing structures and mechanisms have now indeed disappeared without their being replaced by new, effective forms of environmental control. In the former Soviet Union, the concept of *perestroika* not only failed to give rise to an 'eco-perestroika' but, on the contrary, was actually accompanied by a marked increase in the pace of environmental destruction (Wolfson, 1994, p.77). In a number of countries and former Soviet republics, there is a strong tendency towards political decentralisation. Political power has been transferred from national to regional and local authorities. However, the new regional and local authorities often have little or no experience in environmental control. They also lack the financial resources to build up systems of local environmental control. Central funding has been drastically reduced and local authorities are now entirely dependent on the limited funds that they can raise locally through taxes or other tariffs (Environmental Action Programme for Central and Eastern Europe, 1993, p.IV–7).

The weakening of (internal) environmental protection measures is exacerbated by the splitting up of large firms and the privatisation of state enterprises. In the past, many large enterprises traditionally pre-treated the effluent they discharged into municipal waste water systems. Today, as firms are split up and privatised, the cost of industrial pre-treatment is felt to be too high and there is a risk that increasing amounts of industrial discharges will flow directly into municipal sewers, which are not equipped to handle them. On the positive side, the change in water pricing systems and the collapse and restructuring of the industry often diminish the earlier overloading of existing facilities (Environmental Action Programme for Central and Eastern Europe, 1993, p.II–13).

The important role which environmental protest movements played in the fall of communist regimes has already been mentioned. In the Soviet Union, polluting firms came under attack as being evidence of the exploitation of the country by the central authorities in Moscow. For the new, independent republics, the products of these very same companies have become a matter of economic survival and at times national pride. So it was that, in the 1980s, the Ignalina atomic power plant in Lithuania was the subject of criticism from both local environmentalists and nationalists. Yet as soon as Lithuania became an independent nation, the protests faded away. Vytautas Statulevicius, the founder of the Lithuanian Green movement, is quoted as having said about Ignalina: 'When Lithuania was in the Soviet Union, it was one thing. But now it belongs to us' (Peterson, 1993, p.243). Basically, the situation is no different in Armenia, where the protests against Nairit, a highly polluting chemical plant, marked the beginning of the struggle for national independence. The factory was closed at the beginning of 1990, but reopened in 1991 after Armenia became an independent nation (Peterson, 1993, pp.244–6). Contrary to earlier decisions, reactors 1 and 3 of the Chernobyl nuclear power plant have been kept open because of the shortage of electricity in the Ukraine.

In the meantime, the environmentalists have seen their position considerably weakened. Where there had previously been a common enemy, i.e. 'the System', environmental activists now face numerous regional and local systems which are no less dangerous. The environmentalists are being forced to divide their forces. Without having achieved any tangible changes and forced now to fight for their own survival, many of those who sympathised with and helped the movement have left it. Within the movement itself, conflicts have increased over the issue of whether groups should be political in character or concerned exclusively with protecting the natural heritage. Perhaps the most disturbing development is the division of a once united movement, operating within the framework of the USSR, into numerous isolated ethnic groups and movements. Politics today is undoubtedly stronger than ecology (Yanitsky, 1993, pp.100–1).

Environmental conflicts between states

As a result of the breaking of the old bonds between communist states and between Soviet republics, new tensions have developed or have at least come to the surface, as a consequence of transboundary environmental damage and risks. This section discusses two examples of environmental conflicts between states: the Gabcikovo-Nagymaros dam dispute and the Aral Sea conflict.

As far back as the 1950s, plans were made to canalise the Danube between Bratislava (in Slovakia) and Győr (Hungary). The main purpose of the proposed project at the time was to connect the two countries with the planned trans-European Danube-Main-Rhine waterway, which was to create a direct water link between the Black Sea and the North Sea. After the oil crisis in 1973, the original plans were changed and electricity production became the main aim of the project. In 1977, the Czechoslovak and Hungarian governments agreed upon a common project: the Gabcikovo-Nagymaros dam system (see Box 14)

At first, the project was delayed by economic difficulties in both countries, but it later met with growing opposition, especially in Hungary. Among the damaging environmental effects which it was claimed the project would cause were the extensive destruction of the Danube landscape, the degradation of groundwater quality and the loss of agricultural land, flood plain forests and fish stocks. In addition, it was feared that there was a risk of flooding further downstream, as well as a potential for disastrous flooding in the event of a dam burst.

The opposition in Hungary to the whole project became so great that the Hungarian government decided to stop work on the Hungarian part of the project in 1989 and in 1992 unilaterally withdrew from the 1977 treaty. The new, independent Slovak government, which assumed power on 1 January 1993, decided to persist with the project. Measures were taken to complete work on the project with the exception of those parts which were located on Hungarian territory. Conflicts between Hungary and Slovakia about the project continued after Hungary's withdrawal. Slovakia reproached Hungary for withdrawing unilaterally from the project. Hungary, in turn, tried to stop the project in Slovakia, because of its damaging effects on the population, flora and

---

14

The Gabcikovo-Nagymaros dam system

In 1977 the Austrian, Czechoslovak and Hungarian governments agreed to divert the Danube through a huge concrete tunnel in order that the river would generate electricity and provide a safe passage to barge traffic. Under the plan, upstream, close to the Hungarian village of Dunakiliti, a dam was to be constructed in order to create an artificial lake 25 km long with a surface area of 60 km². This lake is connected to a hydro-power plant in Gabcikovo by a canal which is 18 km long and up to 730 metres wide and which, at some points, is raised some 18 metres above the surrounding area. From the Gabcikovo power plant, the water flows through 8 km of canal before reaching the Danube, which is deepened over a distance of 20 kilometres downstream of the end of the canal. The construction of a second dam, in Nagymaros (Hungary), prevents wide fluctuations in the level of the Danube downstream as a consequence of the operation of the Gabcikovo power plant twice a day during peak periods of electricity consumption. Between 90% and 97.5% of the Danube water passes through the artificial lake and canals and only 2.5–10% follows the old bed of the river.

Plate 3.2 Construction work on the Gabcikovo-Nagymaros dam. Photo: Jacques Langevin/ ABC Press

fauna in Hungary. Both the Commission of the European Community and the International Court of Justice became involved in the conflict (see also Kamminga, 1995).

One of the main reasons for the continuing struggle between the two countries is the fact that the majority of those people in Slovakia who are likely to suffer most from the effects of the project are members of the Hungarian minority. The environmental conflict is therefore also an ethnic conflict. For the Slovaks, finishing the Gabcikovo project has become a matter of national prestige and a means of strengthening nationalist sentiments by blaming Hungarians both outside and within Slovak territory. Hungary is fighting not only for its environmental interests, but also for the interests of Hungarians on both sides of the Hungarian–Slovak border. Strong nationalist feelings are involved on both sides.

Political tensions, not only between the former communist states but also between former Soviet republics, are hampering the prevention or solution of other transboundary environmental problems. This is the case with the conflict surrounding the Aral Sea (see Box 15).

The divergent interests of the various republics surrounding the Aral Sea hamper the introduction of effective policy measures. The principal adverse environmental effects of the shrinking of the Aral Sea are:

1. the disappearance of important shipping routes, in particular between Aralsk in the North and Muynak in the South;
2. the end of the fishing of sturgeon and many other species of fish. Annual catches of fish used to range from 45,000 to 50,000 tonnes. The local fish factory, the Muynak Cannery Combie, now has to import its fish from the Atlantic;

The shrinking of the Aral Sea

15

Until 1960, the Aral sea , with a surface area of 66,000 km², was the fourth largest lake in the world, after the Caspian Sea (371,000 km²), Lake Superior (83,000 km²) and Lake Victoria (69,000 km²). For many centuries, the boundaries of the Aral Sea remained essentially unchanged and the water level fluctuated between approximately 50 and 53 metres above sea level. In the short period between 1960 and 1991, the average level of the Aral Sea went down from 53 to 38 metres above sea level and it was divided into a large and a small lake. The total surface area of the lake was reduced to half of its original size, decreasing from 66,000 km² to 33,000 km². Even more spectacular was the shrinking of the average volume of the lake from 1090 km³ to 290 km³. This process has not yet come to an end.

Year	Average level (m)	Average area (km²)	Average volume (km³)	Average salinity (g/l)
1960	53.41	66 900	1090	10
1971	51.05	60 200	925	11
1976	48.28	55 700	763	14
1993 (1 January)		33 642	300	
large sea	36.89	30 953	279	~37
small sea	39.91	2 689	21	~30
2000 (1 January)		24 154	175	
large sea	32.38	21 003	159	65–70
small sea	40.97	3 152	24	~25

In the past, the loss of water by evaporation was compensated for by the inflow of water from two rivers: the Syr(darya) and the Amu(darya). Between 1930 and 1960, the average inflows from the Syr and Amu in the Aral Sea amounted to 50 km³. In 1970, the inflows were reduced to 35.2 km³. They further decreased to 10 km³ (1980) and between 1 and 5 km³ in the 1980s. This reduction in the scale of these inflows was a consequence of the use of water for the irrigation of agricultural land. Yet irrigation as such is not the cause. For several millennia, water from the two rivers had been used for irrigation purposes without this substantially reducing the inflows into the Aral Sea. Traditionally, irrigation has been based on small farms and small irrigated fields.

In the 1920s, however, new irrigation techniques were introduced by the communist regime. New, powerful equipment became available and newly constructed, huge canals enabled land located hundreds of kilometres away from the rivers to be irrigated. The collectivisation of agriculture in the 1930s led to the development of large, state-managed agricultural collectives with irrigated sectors 7–10 times larger than before. In the 1950s, irrigation was further mechanised and the irrigated sectors of farms further expanded. The development of cotton production as a monoculture in Uzbekistan in particular required large-scale irrigation. The area of irrigated agricultural land in Central Asia and Kazakhstan grew from less than 3 million hectares in 1950 to more than 7 million today.

Modern, large-scale irrigation is a highly inefficient system of supplying water. It is estimated that 60–80% of the water is lost during transport. Excessive irrigation and excessive wastage of irrigation water during transport are encouraged by the free supply of irrigation water. The free availability of this natural resource was justified in the recent past by the communist ideology, according to which Nature has no price and should be freely available to everybody.

Source: Precoda (1991), pp.109–12; Micklin (1992), p.270.

3 a sharp reduction in the size of forests and reed banks along the borders of the lake. In the past, reeds were used by the local Kryl-Ordinsk cellulose and cotton combine; now they have to be brought in from Siberia;

4 the lowering of groundwater levels by 3–8 metres;

5 climate change. The vapour rising from the surface of the Aral Sea once formed a barrier against cold winds from the North. Dry winds and dust storms are now damaging agricultural land at large distances from the Aral Sea. They transport salts from the dry bed of the former sea, damaging not only crops but also electric power lines and concrete structures;

6 salination. Both wind and irrigation contribute to salination. Water losses during transport and excessive water use in irrigation cause groundwater to rise to the surface, carrying salt with it;

7 health damage. The health situation in the Asian republics surrounding the Aral Sea is extremely bad, even compared with other parts of the former Soviet Union. The excessive use of chemicals in the production of cotton has been cited as the main cause of exceptionally high rates of infant mortality, cancer incidence and other indicators of poor health conditions. The transport of chemicals by irrigation water contributes to the poor health conditions in the area;

8 the declining production of cotton. Although large-scale irrigation was primarily developed to enlarge the production of cotton, even the production of cotton itself is suffering from the modern methods of irrigation and the climatic effects of the shrinking of the Aral Sea. Soils used for the cultivation of cotton are salinated by excessive irrigation. This contributes to soil degradation and hence to the need for taking new land into production. As a result, there has been a decline in the production of cotton and the area of land that has had to be taken out of production has increased since the 1980s. The production of cotton nearly doubled between 1960 and 1980, but has declined since then. In 1989, a Soviet publication estimated the annual decrease in output at 4.9 million tonnes (Fesbach and Friendly, 1992, pp.73–88; Khazanov, 1990, p.20; Kotlyakov, 1992, pp.288–9; Micklin, 1992; Precoda, 1991, p.111).

Plate 3.3 Ship cemetery near Muinak City, Aral Sea. Formerly located on the seashore, the town is now more than 50 km away from the sea. Photo: Victoria Ivleva/Lineair

There were already certain conflicts of interest even when the republics were still part of the Soviet Union. On the issue of water distribution, for example, relations between Uzbekistan and Tadzhikistan have been strained for many years. Tadzhikistan and Kirgizia, which are located relatively close to the sources of the Amu(darya) and the Syr(darya), are able to use the water without having to spend additional funds on treatment facilities, while Turkmenistan, and especially Uzbekistan which is the largest consumer of water, are at a geographical disadvantage. The disappearance of the central authority in Moscow and of economic interdependencies between the different republics has only strengthened this type of tension.

Within less than a decade, the political context of environmentalism in Central and Eastern Europe has completely changed. In the 1980s, environmentalist action was closely linked with resistance to the central authorities in Moscow and was stimulated by the struggle for local and regional autonomy. In the 1990s, environmental issues are playing a role in conflicts between former Soviet republics and former communist states. Conflicts of interest between these independent political entities are hampering the solution of transboundary environmental problems. Where nationalism and environmentalism were allies in the 1990s, they have now become enemies in the 1990s.

New problems and new policies

The adoption of Western lifestyles in Central and Eastern European countries will lead to new forms of environmental damage deriving from Western patterns of behaviour.

Many Central and Eastern European countries have public transport systems which lack comfort, but which are superior to those in Western Europe in terms of the density of the network and the frequency of service. There is now a tendency to follow the Western example, however, and hence for transport to become increasingly a private rather than a public provision, even though people are broadly aware of the damaging environmental effects of such a development. In Central and Eastern Europe, systems of recycling household waste, for example by means of the use of returnable bottles, are now losing ground, while the use of non-returnable, disposable packaging as advertised by Western firms is gaining more and more of a foothold. Strange though it may sound, the culture of militarism and secrecy had certain beneficial effects on the state of the countryside in former communist states. Large tracts of land along borders (not only along the 'Iron Curtain', but also between the communist states themselves) and coasts were closed off and guarded against all forms of human influence. Now these nature reserves which developed secretly, as it were, during the communist period may be disturbed by a wide variety of human activity.

Although the environment is not in general a top priority in post-communist Central and Eastern Europe, a large number of government officials in these countries, sometimes working together with representatives from environmental groups, are now engaged in developing new and more effective environmental policies at national, regional and local levels. High priority has been given to the development of systems for monitoring environmental pollution. Forms of environmental impact assessment have also been introduced to incorporate environmental criteria in decision making on industrial activities and infrastructural works with major environmental effects. In general, much is expected of the use of financial instruments, which have indeed been given a prominent place in new environmental policies. In the past, the scales of fees and fines were too low and their payment was often not enforced. This means that fee and fine levels will have to be raised and enforcement procedures introduced. In Poland, for example, the level of pollution charges has been raised by a factor of about ten since 1990. What has now happened, however, is that these charges have been temporarily reduced by 90% to enable industries to adjust. The economic crisis and growing rates of unemployment have put both the level and the maintenance of pollution payments under great pressure.

3.6 Conclusion

The specific characteristics of the environmental problems in Central and Eastern Europe are related in part to the inferiority of the industrial development which has taken place in this region. During the past few decades, the Western industrial states have experienced a transformation in industrial production which is nowadays often referred to as *ecological modernisation*. One of the implications of this process has been a decline in both material inputs and polluting outputs per unit of gross national product. Fewer resources are now used and less pollution is generated per unit of product. Central and Eastern Europe has been left far behind in this process. In fact, the general stagnation in industrial development was one of the driving forces behind the process of societal change that started in the mid-1980s. But relative backwardness is not the whole story. *Voluntarism* has already been mentioned as one of the elements of the prevailing ideology in this part of the world. The ease of central decision making and the absence of feedback in the form of both scientific criticism and democratic control and public opinion were specific properties of centrally planned economies which created environmental problems of a magnitude that never existed in Western European countries.

Central and Eastern Europe has experienced the failure of central economic planning. As a consequence, political control by the state and its institutions has more or less disappeared. Environmental organisations in Central and Eastern European countries have recently lost much of the strength which they had acquired in the revolutionary period of around 1989. Environmental protection needs strong countervailing power exercised by both public authorities and environmental groups. East-West co-operation between public and non-governmental organisations can support the badly needed development of countervailing power in Central and Eastern Europe. Although inward investment by Western firms may contribute to cleaner and less wasteful production in the East, all new ventures should be critically screened by the public authorities and environmental organisations in order to avoid the transfer of pollution from Western to Eastern Europe.

Acknowledgements

The author is indebted to G.C. Boere, R. Brieskorn, P. Buijs, L. Gowatsikova, R. Hollander, J. Hontelez, L. Hordijk, Z. Karpowicz, D. Lehrack, L.S.J. Ogterop, W.J. Veening and others who have provided him with oral and written information on the subject of this chapter, and to R.J.M. Cörvers for his assistance in giving the chapter its final shape.

4

Population, poverty and land in the South

Colin Sage

In the 130 years from 1800 to 1930, the world's population doubled from 1 to 2 billion. In only 30 more years, it reached 3 billion. By 1975, 15 short years, that number was 4 billion, and only 12 years later, yet another billion had been added. Now we must contend with a global population multiplying by 250,000 each day ... (Shaw, 1992, p.119).

○ Two hundred million people depend directly upon depleted forest resources.
○ Eight hundred million people are affected by dryland degradation.
○ One billion people rely upon increasingly fragile irrigation systems, which suffer from inadequate supply of water and salinisation of soils.
○ Over 1 billion people lack an adequate, safe, water supply.
○ Nearly 2 billion people suffer from malnutrition or lack proper sanitation.
○ *Each day* 35,000 children die from environmentally related diseases, attributable to pollution and unsafe water (World Bank, 1992).

4.1 Introduction

The purpose of this chapter is to examine the linkages between population growth, poverty and environmental degradation in the developing countries of the South. The chapter will make clear that there is no simple causal relationship between these variables such that, for example, a sharp fall in human fertility would inevitably result either in an improvement in human prosperity or in environmental conservation. Rather, there are a wide range of powerful economic and political factors which influence the way in which different groups of people make use of resources, some in highly unsustainable ways. Consequently, we will need to consider the capacity of the North to consume alongside the growth in human numbers, the effects of widespread poverty, inequality and short-term survival strategies, which are typical of the South. Clearly, then, the North and South have conflicting interests. However, as we will see, it will not do to look upon the South as an area that is homogeneous in this respect: within the South different and conflicting interests may be discerned.

Population growth has proved a highly contentious and political issue, which has long divided North and South. At the World Population Conference held in Bucharest in 1974 many developing and socialist countries accused the North of focusing on the 'population problem' in order to distract attention from the structural inequalities of the existing international economic order. Yet in the United Nations International Conference on Population and Development held in Cairo in September 1994 there appeared a greater willingness by all 180 participating countries to recognise that current rates of population growth are unsustainable. Although there was a clash of cultures around the issues of contraception, abortion, sex education and the meaning of 'family', a new, if fragile consensus emerged. It was based upon acceptance of the need for gender equality and the empowerment of women to form an essential part of a more effective population policy.

However, as this chapter will argue, while it is important to bring human numbers into line with the capacity of the Earth's resources required to support them, it is myopic to believe that it is only population growth in the South that presents a threat to the global ecosystem. For this reason we will consider the consequences of high consumption levels in societies with low population growth rates, alongside the reasons behind high levels of fertility.

To provide a proper backdrop for our dicussions, first of all the differences between the environmental problems of the North and the South will be character-ised (section 4.2). This naturally leads into a discussion of how exactly population characteristics and environmental damage are related and what additional variables may be discerned (section 4.3). Although it is possible to draw up a typology of interactions, it rapidly becomes clear that there are important regional differences in the factors that are most prominent, not only between the North and South but also within the South. So, as expected, Northern and Southern consumption patterns and technology play their different parts (section 4.4.) but differing Southern regional trends in population growth are also important (section 4.5). Another important factor pertains to differences in income, again both between the North and South and within the South (section 4.6).

At this juncture, the discussion will have revealed a plenitude of factors and ways in which they may interact. A discussion of deforestation practices in Central America and South East Asia, a high profile issue which is often incorrectly attributed only to rapid population growth, will offer an opportunity to see many of these factors in action (section 4.7). The discussion serves to demonstrate the complex linkages between many diverse factors. It also shows that these factors are ultimately grounded in the often conflicting stakes available to the various players. The chapter will end with a few concluding remarks (section 4.8).

4.2 Environmental problems in the North and the South

We need to be cautious about the way in which we characterise environmental problems in the North and South (see Box 1 for a note on the terms 'North' and 'South'). For the purposes of this chapter, it is argued that land-based resource depletion is more prevalent in the South as compared to the North where controls over land use are generally tighter. Examples of such depletion include deforestation, the exhaustion of soil fertility and water resources, salinisation and desertification, processes which result in the lower productive potential of the land. On the other hand, environmental pollution resulting from industrialisation and urbanisation and involving the atmosphere, rivers and marine resources has long been a feature of the developed North. Yet such pollution has also become a significant feature of many regions and cities in the South and often occurs at levels which exceed 'safe limits' set by the World Health Organisation.

For example, in the case of suspended particulate matter (airborne dust and smoke) which causes respiratory disorders and cancers, recent levels in Bangkok and Delhi were 741 and 1062 micrograms per cubic metre of air compared to 77 and 97 in London and Brussels respectively. The World Bank estimates that excessive urban particulate matter levels are responsible for between 300,000 and 700,000 premature deaths annually. Yet national and local governments in the South have, until recently, treated such problems as an inevitable, even necessary part of the development process, to be resolved once the economy is strong enough to withstand tougher environmental controls and able to adopt cleaner technologies.

While the North has taken a disproportionate advantage of the global commons to dispose of and disperse its environmental pollution, it is the destruction and degradation of land resources in the South which has caused most concern amongst environmentalists and policy makers in the North. Moreover, this destruction is often attributed to high rates of population growth.

This has led to sharply contrasting international policy agendas where the North has argued for an urgent reduction in rates of deforestation and fertility while the South has emphasised the need for economic growth. As *The Economist* magazine put it in advance of the Earth Summit in Rio de Janeiro of 1994:

> Deserts are advancing, forests are vanishing, crops are failing, species are becoming extinct. The root cause of this damage is a continuation of population growth and poverty in the third world. These are the gravest threats to environment and development ... (*The Economist*, 1992, p. 11).

It is important to appreciate that such environmental concern often fails to understand the role of our own levels of consumption in the North. As we shall see, our capacity to purchase and consume tropical products can have far-reaching consequences for land resources in the South.

There is no general consensus that population growth causes environmental degradation despite the assertions of the vociferous advocates of population control and the popular media. This is not to say that population growth may not be an important

'North' and 'South'

In this chapter we use the terms 'North' and 'South' to distinguish the developed, industrialised world of Europe, Japan and North America from the developing economies of Africa, Asia and Latin America. There are several reasons why the term 'Third World' is no longer satisfactory:

1 The extraordinary diversity of countries lumped into this category, ranging from the very poorest countries, the majority of which are in sub-Saharan Africa (and which sometimes have been referred to as the 'Fourth World'), through the newly industrialising countries (the 'NICs'), to the high-income oil exporters.
2 With the collapse of the old political order in the Soviet Union and Eastern Europe the notion of a 'Second World' offering an alternative model of development has all but disappeared. True, the Chinese and Cuban models ultimately had most relevance to low-income countries, but with China pursuing a strong market orientation and Cuba experiencing severe political and economic isolation, it is unlikely that either country offers a clear policy direction for others to follow.
3 There is no longer the political unity that was evident during the 1960s and 1970s with the formation of the non-aligned movement and international efforts to secure a New Economic Order. The term 'South' has become part of conventional usage because it avoids the meanings implicit in 'Third World'. At the same time it contrasts with 'North' and conveys the sharp divisions of interests between the two world regions. Some authors have argued that the main differences in national incomes accord to a latitudinal, tropical–temperate divide. However, 'tropical' and 'temperate' simply do not convey the historical and continuing political and economic inequalities that marks the relationship between South and North.

influence on the way in which land resources are utilised. However, there are many other variables which can influence levels of resource exploitation and these may, in turn, be attributed to international financial pressures (e.g. servicing the country's external debt or a deterioration in the terms of trade, i.e. the relative price of the South's mainly raw materials exports as opposed to its imports of manufactured goods). The need to increase export revenues, for example, inevitably encourages the expansion and intensification of production across such economic sectors as commercial agriculture, cattle ranching, mining, forest logging and so on. National and international markets for agricultural and other products clearly influence patterns of resource use, as do government regulations and tax policies. Indeed, in the case of forest resources, national government has often been instrumental in encouraging rapid exploitation, as we shall see in section 4.7.

It should also be noted that there is often a lack of agreement between scientists not only about the causes of environmental change but also about the rates and direction of change. The expansion of the deserts is a case in point, especially the 'Southward march of the Sahara', a widely cited illustration of environmental degradation during the 1970s. It was even claimed in one scientific article that the Sahara was advancing in Sudan at a rate of 90–100 km a year which, as Smil points out, should make any numerate reader suspicious for such an advance would have covered the entire country in less than one generation! But, as he goes on to observe:

> Careful studies show no evidence of this southward march. Satellite monitoring of long-term changes records extensive natural fluctuations, with the Sahara expanding or contracting at a rate of over 600,000 km^2 a year. Detailed studies of the Sudanese situation have not verified any creation of long-lasting desert-like conditions, no major shifts in the Northern cultivation limit, no major changes in vegetation cover and productivity and no major sand-dune formation. Temporary changes of crop yields and green phytomass were caused by severe droughts – and were followed by a significant recovery (Smil, 1993, p.30).

There is no complete agreement, either, about the rate of deforestation, although it is generally held that the current use of this resource is unsustainable. Myers (1993a) uses a figure of 148,000 square kilometres of tropical moist forest lost in 1991 out of a worldwide total of 7.5 million km^2 or around 2%. Yet he identifies 14 major deforestation 'hot spots' which cover 25% of the total area of tropical moist forests but which account for 43% of total deforestation. These areas are undergoing intensive and widespread deforestation at an annual rate of 3.4%, yet demographic criteria cannot be held responsible for more than a part of the pressures being exerted on these forests. In section 4.7 we will examine processes and cases of forest clearance in more detail.

It is, nonetheless, necessary to take heed of global demographic dynamics, for world population reached 5.3 billion by mid-1990 and is growing at a rate of 1.7% per year. Table 4.1 provides a summary of some demographic indicators for the major world regions. Asia accounts for the largest share of world population, with China (1.1 billion) and India (850 million) the most populous countries, although the fastest rate of increase is in Africa which as a continent is growing at an average rate of 3% per year. Meanwhile in the North fertility is generally below replacement levels and the intrinsic rate of population growth (the number of births over deaths) is negative (Alonso, 1987). This divergence in the demographic trajectories of North and South (see Figure 4.1) has led some commentators to speculate on the international security implications of a world where today's most powerful countries comprise a diminishing

Region	Population millions 1990	Average rate growth percentage 1990-1995	Infant mortality rate per 1,000 1990	Urban percentage 1990	Urban growth percentage 1990-1995
World	5,291.2	1.7	63	45	3.0
'North'	1,206.6	0.5	12	73	0.8
'South'	4,084.6	2.1	70	37	4.2
Africa	642.1	3.0	94	34	4.9
North America	275.9	0.7	8	75	1.0
Latin America	448.1	1.9	48	72	2.6
Asia	3,112.7	1.8	64	34	4.2
Europe	498.4	0.2	11	73	0.7
Oceania	26.5	1.4	23	71	1.4
USSR	288.6	0.7	20	66	0.9

Table 4.1 Population indicators for major world regions. Source: World Resources Institute, 1990

proportion of the total global population, although a high proportion of the world's aged population (Eberstadt, 1991).

Indeed, one of the few certainties from which to start is demographic momentum for, irrespective of the efforts directed at reducing fertility, human numbers are set to grow to between 7.6 and 9.4 billion by 2025. In other words, the world will still have to cope with between 44% and 62% more people by that date proving that the greatest policy challenge will be coping with the needs and pressures of the inevitable population rather than attempting to avoid the increment (Overseas Development Administration 1991).

However, this is not the appropriate place to review the main historical-demographic trends and trajectories that characterise the major world regions. Rather, the purpose of the chapter is to explore some of the underlying features and dynamics of population change, relating these to aspects of wealth and poverty and to questions of land use change and environmental degradation. I will concentrate upon land resources and try to understand what lies behind the processes of transformation and destruction of forests, soils, wetlands and biological diversity. This means that we will not be discussing those environmental problems resulting directly from industrial production processes, problems which have arguably had a greater impact on the global commons, for example through the emission of greenhouse gases, the creation of acid rain or the dumping of toxic wastes at sea. Indeed, as the newspapers keep telling us, the environmental consequences of industrialisation are no longer confined to the developed countries of the North.

4.3 Population and environment

Issues and linkages

It is conventional to embark upon an analysis of population–environment relationships by making reference to the positions of Thomas Malthus and Esther Boserup. More than 150 years separate their writings, yet they serve as twin pillars of a debate which seems to have gained or lost little vigour as it has raged between ideological opponents. Although this is not the proper place to summarise the debate from Malthus to the present day, we can note briefly that Malthus was concerned with the relationship between population and food supply under conditions where technology and resources in land remained constant. He postulated that human numbers would outstrip the capacity to produce sufficient food and that 'positive checks' such as poverty, disease, famine and war would impose downward pressure on the rate of population growth in the absence of fertility control. In contrast, Boserup argued that high population densities are in themselves a prerequisite for technological innovation in which agricultural systems continuously evolve into increasingly land-intensive forms. This process, she argues, has given rise historically to five distinct stages stretching from shifting cultivation with long fallow periods to multiple cropping (Boserup, 1981).

It is important to notice that neither author was concerned with the environment other than as a resource for food production. Nevertheless, the central element of change in their respective models – population growth for Malthus, technological change for Boserup – has led many of those involved in the environmental debate to support either a pro- or anti-Malthusian perspective on the cause of the world's ills.

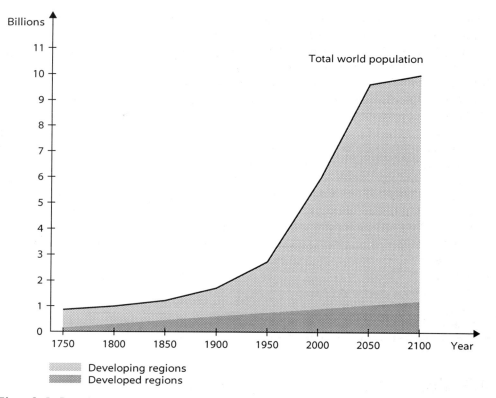

Fig. 4.1 Population growth 1750 – 2100. Source: Thomas W. Merrick (1988) World Population in Transition. In *Population Bulletin*, **41**(2). Washington DC: Population Reference Bureau, Inc.

Thus, on the one side are those such as Paul Ehrlich and Garrett Hardin who favour population control, while on the other side, a range of writers variously attribute environmental problems to inappropriate technology, overconsumption by the afflu-ent, inequality and exploitation: everything, in fact, but population growth (Harrison, 1990). In order to develop a fresh approach toward understanding the linkages between population and environment it is necessary to overcome the apparent dichotomy between the Malthusian and Boserupian models.

One alternative to the simple, if not simplistic, models in which growing population density is either a cause of land degradation or the key to technological innovation is the notion of *Pressure of Population on Resources* (PPR) proposed by Blaikie and Brookfield (1987). It is used to underline the fact that similarly sized populations may make vastly different demands on their resources; or, conversely, by changing learned behaviour and adopting new tools and techniques, humans can use resident ecosystems to support population densities varying in size over many orders of magnitude. Consequently, as Lourdes Arizpe and her co-authors observe, there are many culturally defined sub-species of human society which have different levels of resource use, mediated by technology, values and level of economic development (Arizpe *et al.*, 1992).

103

Blaikie and Brookfield challenge the outcome implicit in Boserup's model that population growth always produces agricultural innovation. They note that in many instances it is not innovation but environmental degradation which results and that one of the weaknesses of Boserup's model is that she isolates population as a single causal variable in a similar way to the present-day followers of Malthus: the neo-Malthusians. Blaikie and Brookfield also draw a necessary distinction between *intensification* – the reduction of fallow and increasing use of inputs to raise output – and *innovation* – the new ways in which the various factors of production are employed. While intensification may act as a block to innovation, for example under conditions where high population densities are supported using simple technology, such conditions usually involve labour-intensive systems maintaining terraces, irrigation canals and other field improvements. If labour is withdrawn from the maintenance of such a system the consequences can be disastrous. Nevertheless, degradation is not an inevitable outcome of population pressure: it can occur, 'under rising PPR, under declining PPR, and without PPR' (Blaikie and Brookfield, 1987, p.34).

A typology of interactions

If we treat population as an independent variable, then, there are four general ways in which it can interact with environment and we will illustrate each of these in turn.

First, population growth may result in the *expansion of the area under cultivation* which leads to resource depletion and ultimately environmental degradation in the absence of institutional and technological change (the *Malthusian scenario*). Such circumstances are to be found in areas of land settlement and frontier expansion. For example, from the mid-1970s the Brazilian government began to support smallholder settlements in the Amazonian states of Rondônia and Acre. In 11 years the population grew tenfold to well over 1 million people by 1986. 'In 1975 only 1,200 km^2 of forest had been cleared, but by 1982 the total had grown to well over 10,000 km^2 and by 1985 to almost 28,000 km^2. During the dry season of 1987 some 50,000 km^2 of forest were burned in these two states alone' (Myers, 1991, p.240). However, a great deal of the destruction attributed to settlers is actually wrought by large-scale landowners, cattle ranchers and logging companies who not only operate more extensively but are often behind the displacement and relocation of settlers.

Second, population growth may result in the *intensification of production*, involving increasing investments of human, natural and financial capital, and in innovation embodying the development of new technical means of production. This technologically optimistic, *Boserupian scenario* represents, historically, the evolution of sophisticated land management systems under increasing population densities. The studies of Michael Mortimore in Northern Nigeria describe an area around Kano where the population density is approximately 350 persons per km^2 and the rate of natural increase is of the order of 2.9% per year. Through the analysis of cropping patterns, soil management practices and demographic change, Mortimore observes that population growth and high density are compatible with sustainable resource management which is promoted by agricultural intensification. He concludes, 'The evidence on soil fertility and farm tree management in the high-density case ...

challenges the view, commonly held, that population growth necessarily puts destructive pressure on smallholder farming systems ...' (Mortimore, 1993, p.65).

Third, population growth may be *scale neutral with respect to the local resource base*, either through the importation of food from elsewhere or as excess population outmigrates, resulting in no demographic pressures for agricultural change. We can again draw upon Mortimore's work in Northern Nigeria to illustrate these circumstances, this time using his observations from an area with a population density of less than 100 persons per km². Here, the rate of net population growth is low, perhaps 1% or less per year. Although the data are not entirely consistent, the general impression given by Mortimore is that the number of households and the cultivated area have barely changed over the period from 1950 to 1986. This is explained by the high level of seasonal, short-term and permanent outmigration from villages of the region. As Mortimore correctly observes, the myth of a full-time farming peasantry, exclusively dependent on the produce of the smallholding, should be discarded. Migration by rural people, whether temporary or permanent, reduces the demand for on-farm food production but generates income. While some of this is used to acquire food produced using resources elsewhere, off-farm income may nevertheless be used to finance investments in agriculture and land improvements for future production.

A fourth form in which population may affect the environment is through *reverse effects* or *feedback loops*. Here changes in the productive potential of the local environment influence the determinants of population: fertility, mortality and migration. It is especially interesting to examine cases where human fertility has been reduced through changes in behaviour. Historically this involved delayed age at marriage, an increase in the proportion of the population which remained unmarried or the limitation of births within marriage by the practice of *coitus interruptus*. Evidence can be found to suggest that all of these practices were common in different parts of Western Europe at different times during the last 300 to 400 years (Grigg, 1980).

A more recent example is found in Mauritius where a sharp reduction in fertility has occurred. Parenthetically, Mauritius has one of the highest population densities in the world (around 590 persons per km², compared to 430 for The Netherlands and 240 in the UK). In the 1950s and 1960s, according to Lutz and Holm, Mauritius experienced very high rates of population growth (peaking at 3.5% per year). Then, in just a few short years, the total fertility rate fell from 6.2 children per woman in 1963 to 3.4 in 1971 and to 1.9 in 1990, one of the steepest declines in fertility in the world. As Lutz and Holm argue, causal effects between changes in population and changes in land use and per capita land availability may go in both directions. On the one hand changes in population size and distribution influence changes in the use of land. On the other hand, a clearly visible shortage of land may induce the population to limit its growth. There is indeed evidence that this factor played a role in the rapid fertility decline in Mauritius (Lutz and Holm, 1993).

4.4 Population, consumption and technology

So, while population is certainly a factor that influences resource use and environmental change, it does so in association with two other variables: *technological capacity* and *levels of consumption*. Thus, a given environmental impact (*I*) is derived from the multiplicative interaction of the three variables – population (*P*), per capita consumption (or *affluence*, *A*) and technology (*T*). This creates a useful shorthand expression, *I = PAT*. Its appeal stems from the way it diffuses the singular responsibility of population, enabling it to be applied equally, whether in the industrialised countries of the North or the rural economies of the South. A UN Population Fund study provides an illustration of how the equation works: Supposing that:

> ... humankind managed to reduce the average per capita consumption of environmental resources (I) by 5 per cent; and to improve its technologies (T) so that they cause an average of 5 per cent less environmental injury. This would reduce the total impact (I) of humanity by roughly 10 per cent. But unless the rate of global population growth (P) – now 1.7 per cent a year – were restrained at the same time, it would bring the total impact back to the previous level within less than 6 years (UNPF, 1991, p.18).

On the other hand Barry Commoner, a critic of inappropriate technology, has used a variant of the *I = PAT* expression to calculate the total environmental impact of industrial pollution and to argue that it is primarily the technological factor rather than population which needs to be controlled. If we wish, however, to understand the relationship between population growth and land use change in the South then we could use another variant of the *I= PAT* expression. For example:

Farmed area = Population × Food consumption per person
× Area per unit of food production

It is clear from this that if technology and food consumption do not change, population growth translates directly into land conversion for agriculture. However, there are other pressures upon land beside its use as a resource for food production.

In the North pressures for land conversion derive from qualitative as well as quantitative increases in consumption. Examples include the continuously increasing aspirations for personal mobility which involve road-building schemes; the ongoing suburbanisation of the countryside; leisure and recreation interests most spectacularly illustrated during recent years by the conversion of farm and other land into golf courses, and so on. These are all processes which are also rapidly underway in most parts of the South. Yet in much of the policy literature one detects more enthusiasm to isolate population as a factor for attention rather than to address either consumption or technology. For example:

> For any given type of technology, for any given level of consumption or waste, for any given level of poverty or inequality, the more people there are, the greater is the impact on the environment (Sadik, 1990, p.10).

While this is strictly correct, it hardly seems fair or meaningful to hold all factors other than population constant. Indeed, if for a moment we widen the terms of environmental impact beyond changes in land use and consider the use of the global commons as waste sinks, it is clear that in the context of the North, it is changes in the factors of consumption (*A*) and technology (*T*) which have the greatest effect:

Excess consumption in the rich countries bears the main blame for damage to global commons. The average person in a developed country emits roughly twenty times more water and climate pollutants than their counterpart in the South. Hence the 57.5 million population growth in the North expected during the 1990s will pollute the globe more than the expected extra 911 million Southerners (Harrison, 1992, p.324).

Consequently, at a global scale population, consumption and technology can be said to be the main driving forces of environmental impact. However, for each of these it is helpful to identify in turn those factors which indirectly determine its size and which encompass the most important social, economic and political factors (see Figure 4. 2).

It is important to consider that irrespective of human numbers, there is a highly inequitable per capita impact on the environment according to the society and economy in which we are born. Ehrlich and Ehrlich (1990) conduct an exercise in which they employ per capita use of commercial energy as a surrogate statistic for A and T. They calculate that each baby born in the United States has an impact on the Earth's ecosystems three times that of one born in Italy, 13 times one born in Brazil, 35 times one in India, 140 times one in Bangladesh and 280 times one born in Chad, Rwanda, Haiti or Nepal. Such a range correlates very well with levels of per capita *GDP*.

While the size of the gross world product – the total of goods and services produced throughout the planet – has been growing at a faster rate than world population (it

Plate 4.1 Rubbish dump on Fanø Island near Esbjerg, Denmark. Silt which is taken from the harbour and which is polluted with heavy metals is tipped here. There is widespread concern that the groundwater is being contaminated. Photo: Mark Edwards/Lineair

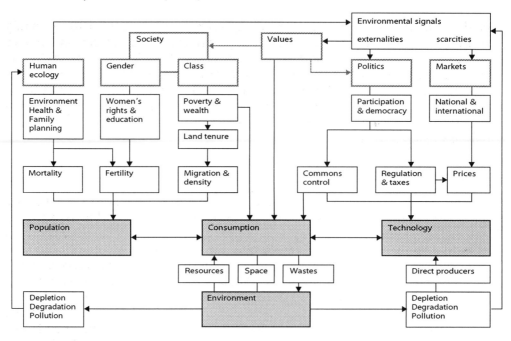

Fig. 4.2 The relationship between population, consumption, technology and environment at a global level. Source: Harrison, 1992

tripled between 1960 and 1989), it has not been divided any more equally. In 1965 the high income countries enjoyed 70% of gross world product, while the South took 19%. By 1989 the 16% of the world's population living in the North accounted for 73% of gross world product, while the 78% living in the South received less than 16% (Harrison, 1992). The rising affluence of a stable population therefore poses as great a threat to the global environment if we consider waste sink services as well as resource use, and the oceans and atmosphere as well as land.

However, while speculating on the relative contributory weight of population, consumption and technology at a global scale is a sobering exercise, it distracts us from examining the linkages between population and land resources in the South. Here, we need a range of regional demographic variables, such as the spatial distribution of population – where people are in relation to the type and resilience of the ecosystem – besides fertility and mortality indicators. We must also understand those factors, or proximate determinants, which give rise to population outcomes. This requires disaggregating the global picture to reveal the regional character of demographic change.

4.5 Regional population trends and dynamics

It is important from the outset to emphasise that the marked national diversity in demographic indicators is unparalleled in human history. Examples of such diversity include: natural growth rates of countries ranging from +4% to –0.2%; average family size from more than eight to around 1.4; age structures that encompass the very youthful (half the population under 15 years) to the aged (less than 20% under 15); and levels of urbanisation that range from 10% to 90% of total national populations. Given this extraordinary national diversity in demographic indicators – which are influenced by the complex interaction of economic activity, historical processes, social structures and cultural traditions – there is consequently an enormous variety of population-environment relationships.

Mortality and fertility

However, it is the rapid growth of world population in the post-war period which has attracted most attention and this is mainly the result of a sharp decline in *mortality levels* owing to interventions in public health and disease control. Crude death rates in the developing regions have fallen from 24 per thousand people in 1950–5 to 11 per thousand people in 1980–5, comparable to rates in the industrial market economies. Life expectancy at birth in the low and middle income countries has risen from 41 to 62 years over this period (World Bank, 1990). The success of public health, sanitation and vaccination programmes is particularly apparent in reducing rates of infant and child mortality which, overall, fell by 36% between 1950–5 and 1975–80 (Hall, 1989). However, infant mortality rates show much the greatest variation of the basic demographic variables, as Table 4.1 demonstrated.

While death rates are approaching their anticipated minimum, birth rates in the South are falling but lagging well behind mortality levels. This 'delayed response' to changes in *fertility* has called into question the applicability of the theory of demographic transition based upon the experiences of 19th century Europe to the developing world today (see Box 2). Unlike mortality, which is highly responsive to improvements in economic development, fertility is a matter of individual and family decision. It therefore is responsive to cultural phenomena – gender relations, marriage contracts, inheritance of wealth and property – and to social and economic influences. Such phenomena – called *proximate determinants* of fertility by demographers – can have complex interactions depending upon the institutional context. It has been suggested, for example, that the currently high fertility rates in sub-Saharan Africa are being maintained by shortened breastfeeding periods, thus reducing the suppression of women's capacity to conceive, and by a reduction in the custom of post-birth sexual abstinence. Consequently, given such complexity, there would appear to be little future in a single, universally applicable theory but rather a recognition that there are many possible demographic transitions, each driven by a combination of forces that are institutionally, culturally and temporally specific (Greenhalgh, 1990).

While fertility levels have generally stabilised at replacement levels throughout the North – the average is now down to 1.9 children per woman, 1.58 in Western Europe (Sadik, 1990) – they have sharply diverged amongst the major regions of the South during the 1970s and 1980s. As Figure 4.3 illustrates, during the period 1960–5 there was little deviation from the mean of 6.1 births per woman, but by 1980–5 large regional differentials had appeared. The largest decline occurred in East Asia where fertility fell to 2.4 births per woman, yet there is no single factor to explain such a

Demographic transition theory

This theory is based on what was observed to occur in the industrialised countries. In the wake of the Industrial Revolution, death rates dropped dramatically, mainly as a result of improved sanitation and public health. Then, after a generation or so of higher population growth, the birth rate also began to fall. In other words, there was a historical shift from a situation of high mortality and high fertility to one of low mortality and low fertility.

Today, in large parts of the South, as previously in Europe, death rates have been reduced. Demographic transition theory expects that after a period of transition (which according to World Bank estimates, may be shorter than in industrialised countries), fertility levels, and thus birth rates, will also fall.

In less developed countries, the experience is much more varied than that of the industrialised countries in the past. The theory would hold that with development and lowering mortality, fertility should follow suit and also reduce. But this has by no means always occurred. This has led some to a discussion of a 'demographic trap' where LDCs become stuck in the transition phase of low mortality/high fertility.

We should note that demographic transition is a model and like any other is open to question. The fact that the model proposes that mortality and fertility rates will take a certain path does not mean that this will happen in practice. In fact the model is one based on a particular view of development which assumes an inevitable progression towards a 'modern' society.

Source: Hewitt and Smyth (1992).

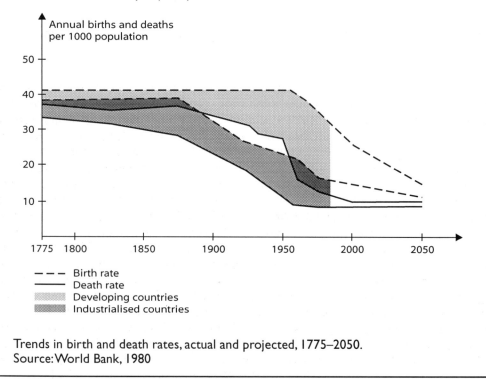

Trends in birth and death rates, actual and projected, 1775–2050.
Source: World Bank, 1980

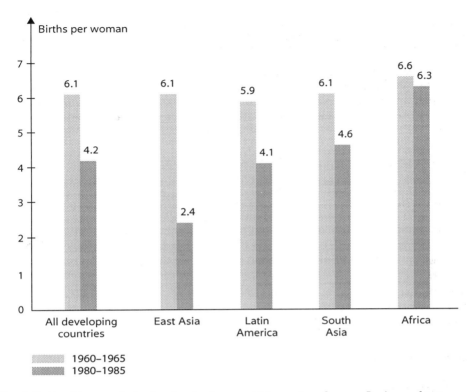

Fig 4.3 Fertility trends in the developing world, by region. Source: Redrawn from Bongaarts *et al.*, 1990

decline. In China a powerful state apparatus assumed the right to impose fertility control, first through the 'later – longer – fewer' (1971–8) programme and then the 'one child' (1979 – present) policy. In South Korea, meanwhile, fertility rates fell by 44% between 1965 and 1982 as women married later and later during a period of rapidly growing economic prosperity and full employment. While fertility rates have continued to fall, the decline has slowed as the average age of women at marriage tends toward a limit (Pearce, 1991). In sharp contrast, however, fertility rates in Africa remain high, having fallen from 6.6 births per woman in 1960–5 to 6.2 in 1985–90. Yet this regional average disguises considerable and growing variation between countries.

A comparison of the *total fertility rate* (TFR, the average number of children born alive to a woman during her lifetime) for 1965-70 and 1985-90 for 49 African states indicates a decline in 22 countries, an unchanged rate in 12 and an increase in the average number of births per woman in 15 countries. Included in this latter group are Tanzania, Malawi and also Rwanda, where the TFR rose from 8.0 to 8.3 in a country which has the highest population density on the continent. Those countries where the TFR remains unchanged include Kenya (8.1) and Cote d'Ivoire with 7.4 births per woman, the two remaining countries in Africa where average annual population growth rates still exceed 4%. In Nigeria, the most populated country in Africa with 113 million people, the TFR fell from 7.1 in 1965–70 to 7.0 in 1985–90 (World Resources Institute, 1990).

Besides a complex raft of factors which underlie a constancy in the birth rate in Africa, population growth averaging 3% per year is also attributable to an infant mortality rate that has been cut by one-third since 1965 and life expectancy that has been raised by seven years. Such improvements derive from the introduction of state-directed health and education services following independence, which have concentrated upon mortality prevention and only recently on fertility reduction. Yet such services have been introduced without reference to traditional systems of education and health care and without regard to the social, environmental and political impact they might have.

With the collapse of economic capacity in Africa during the 1980s, widespread political insecurity and the departure of skilled labour, the ability of the state to deliver health and contraceptive services has been undermined. Indeed, it is questionable whether the state or the poor can have any real commitment to birth control under current circumstances of acute deprivation. For example, in parts of Africa children under the age of five years make up 20–25% of the population yet they account for 50–80% of the deaths. In Europe the mortality rate for the same group is 3%. As long as child mortality remains so high and local survival strategies are ineffective, poor people will maintain high fertility rates to ensure child survival and potential income and labour-generating options.

The status of women and female fertility

The wide variations in fertility levels illustrate the importance of understanding the various proximate determinants. Crucial determinants are marriage age, the status of women, use of contraception, the prevalence of abortion and so on. Clearly, these are themselves fashioned by the socioeconomic and cultural context. Traditional checks on fertility vary across sub-Saharan Africa: some societies practise controls on the starting pattern of fertility (delayed age at marriage, celibacy) while others employ spacing or stopping patterns (extended sexual abstinence, breastfeeding, reduced remarriage). Pathological sterility resulting from the spread of sexually transmitted diseases has also suppressed fertility rates in a broad area of Central Africa (Lesthaeghe, 1986). Consequently, it should be noted that there is a highly uneven distribution of population in sub-Saharan Africa, stretching from the high densities of the cities, along the coast and in the highlands, where population pressures have contributed to environmental degradation, to areas in the interior where low population densities serve as a brake on agricultural development (see Box 3).

It has been suggested that actual family size varies according to the economic position of the household, reflecting differences in infant and child mortality rates as well as the value accorded to children (see below). Here, there is often a striking correlation between wealth and household size. For example, studies in different parts of Northern Nigeria have shown that richer households have more dependents but also meet more of their grain needs than poorer households. Under the system of dryland agriculture in the region larger households (including more wives) means more labour to engage in soil improvement measures, irrigation and tree planting. In other words, improved environmental management is more easily achieved amongst the richer farmers because they can bear the costs and obtain the benefits in terms of enhanced food security (Lockwood, 1991).

Africa: factors in population distribution   **3**

Historically, many areas of Africa actually suffered from *depopulation* as the result of the slave trade, exploitative colonial labour policies and the introduction of new diseases from Europe. In the 18th century, 20% of the world's population lived in Africa; by the year 2000 the figure is expected to be less than 13%, despite recent high rates of growth. Only since the beginning of this century did Africa begin to rebuild its population.

In West Africa the demand for labour is the crucial determinant of population densities and high fertility. There is a very low level of economic development and an undersupply of labour in many parts of the region. This can be traced back to the colonial era when the forced recruitment of labour, forced growing of cash crops, taxation and military reprisals by colonial troops compelled African peoples to produce as many children as possible to increase labour supply and reconstitute as much of their local economy as possible under colonial conditions. Added to this was the large-scale male migration to plantation zones and coastal cities for employment. With husbands absent, women depended even more on children as a source of agricultural labour and security.

Extract of Hartmann drawn from Hewitt and Smyth (1992).

One of the incentives for higher levels of fertility concerns the economic value of children. It has been argued that poor women, in particular, place a high value on children as substitutes for the workload assigned to them under the prevailing gender division of labour. This means that children can, from the age of eight or nine, undertake the care of poultry, small ruminants and even cattle, collect water and fuelwood, look after younger siblings and so on, releasing their mothers to perform more onerous or remunerative activities. Other researchers meanwhile have argued that women express a preference for smaller family size and take measures to limit their number of children. Their ability to do this, however, will depend upon the status of women in a given social and cultural context and on women's control of their fertility not being seen by men as threatening the 'patriarchal' norms of masculinity.

In many societies, the low status of women is strongly linked with high fertility, high maternal mortality and poverty. Given the few resources and opportunities allocated to daughters, which effectively denies them access to education and employment, for many young women the only opportunity for social mobility and personal achievement is to get married early and have large numbers of children as quickly as possible. This is why improving access to education does so much to enhance the quality of women's lives:

> Women with education face expanded opportunities in the labour market; they marry later and have their first birth later. Education gives women greater understanding and access to improved contraceptive practices and information on nutrition, sanitation and child care; … education may (also) help to empower women within their households and communities (Kabeer, 1992, p.27).

Clearly, improving educational opportunities means overcoming deep-rooted gender discrimination which prohibits women from wider social participation. This may appear a difficult task to tackle, but raising the status of women is demonstrably a prerequisite to a more effective population policy that will result in sustained reductions in levels of female fertility. This section thus also illustrates the importance of approaching the issue of population growth through the proximate determinants of fertility at the micro level. At the same time, this wider discussion also highlights the need to consider the range of structural factors (i.e. economic processes) that influence population dynamics, for example as impoverishment influences rates of morbidity and mortality or encourages mobility and migration.

4.6 Incomes in the North and the South

Income, consumption and development

Rising levels of per capita income, as part of a process of economic development, are major variables of land use change, as we have seen in relation to the $I = PAT$ formula. Yet rising income displays a varying *elasticity of demand* (the responsiveness of the quantity of goods and services demanded to changes in income). In the industrialised countries of the North, for example, the income elasticity for food is low and approaching zero (i.e. the demand does not rise in response to increased income), whereas it is high and positive for such functions as recreation and housing. In the South, by contrast, rising per capita incomes stimulate relatively large increases in demand for basic food goods, although as incomes rise this creates a change in the composition of demand (Crosson, 1986). Thus traditional grains and tubers gradually give way to higher protein sources and acquired dietary tastes, such as livestock products, imported cereals and processed foods.

Consequently, it is through the changing effective demand for food that rising levels of income exert different pressures upon the agricultural resource base. For shifts to higher protein diets and the increased demand for livestock products require expanded production of animal feeds. This, in turn, will involve an increase in the indirect per capita consumption of plant energy in a developing country with rising incomes. Given that an estimated 40% of net primary production (NPP) of land-based photosynthesis is currently utilised for food production, this has led some authors to express some real Malthusian concerns: 'For an expanding population with a rising income the demands on the agricultural system (will be) nothing short of monumental' (Pierce, 1990, p.102).

Rising income also creates other far-reaching changes in relation to land use, for example by increasing demand for living space, transport and recreational uses especially amongst urban populations. Rural to urban migration results in a growing share of the total population based in urban areas and this increases aggregate demand as urban dwellers invariably have higher average levels of income and consumption. The consequences are to produce more food for direct consumption by the urban population, as well as cash crops for export to pay for imported food also largely consumed by urban dwellers. The need to engage in export production of land-intensive commodities for high-income countries places a further demand on resources in the South. According to Bilsborrow and Geores (1990), the two main factors responsible for changes in the level of resource depletion are increasing per capita incomes in the North and increasing populations in the South. However:

> (W)ith per capita incomes in low-income countries one-tenth those of developed countries, even with four-fifths of the population residing in low-income countries, the bulk of the growth in effective demand upon resources in low-income countries in recent decades is attributable to *increases in the high levels of consumption of developed countries* (Bilsborrow and Geores, 1990, p.35).

This argument is underpinned by the Ehrlichs who make reference to The Netherlands in developing their case about world-wide overpopulation. They argue that The Netherlands can support a population density of 1031 people per square mile:

> ... only because the rest of the world does not. In 1984–86, The Netherlands imported almost 4 million tons of cereals, 130,000 tons of oils, and 480,000 tons of pulses. It took some of these relatively inexpensive imports and used them to boost their production of expensive exports – 330,000 tons of milk and 1.2 million tons of meat (Ehrlich and Ehrlich, 1990, p.39).

The highly intensive production system which generates the economic surpluses capable of supporting such a population density as in The Netherlands, with its high levels of consumption, creates a large environmental impact (recalling *I = PAT*). Crucially, this impact has both direct, point source, consequences (e.g. the disposal of slurry, described in Chapter 1) and more systemic effects. These include the cumulative processes of atmospheric loading (i.e. methane generated by livestock) and, importantly, the capacity to influence land use in the South for the production of feed grains and export crops.

The functional roles of different groups of countries within the world economic system according to the principles of comparative advantage have led many critics to argue that unequal terms of trade prejudice the prospects of the poorest countries to achieve economic growth. Certainly, the total size of the world economy has grown at a faster rate than population, increasing from 5 trillion US dollars to 17 trillion over the period from 1960 to 1988, at an average annual rate of 3.64%. The relative growth rates of different world regions are, however, quite uneven. While the developed market economies of the North have grown at a rate of 3.5% over the period, rates in the South have been quite divergent, ranging from 2.53% in sub-Saharan Africa to 3.84% in Latin America to just over 6% in South and South-east Asia over the period from 1960 to 1988. Yet it is during the 1980s that these differences have widened, for in Africa and Latin America per capita incomes have fallen while they have continued to rise steadily in Asia. Moreover, the overall gap between the rich North and poorer South continues to widen. Output per capita was 13.42 times greater in the North in 1980 and had increased to 14.7 times higher by 1990 (UN General Assembly Document, 1991).

The relationship between rich and poor countries, as between classes within countries, is ultimately determined by superior economic power expressed in the market place which provides the necessary signals and incentives to the sphere of production. Supported by structural economic reforms to remove 'distortions', the market has heralded a growing trend in many developing countries where basic food staples have given way to export crops and feed grain production for Northern end consumers, resulting in an increasingly segmented structure of agricultural markets in the South (Helwege, 1990).

The role of export crop production as a means of generating economic growth has a long and often controversial history where, since colonial times, it has been suggested that such crops enhance food security through the exploitation of natural comparative advantage. Critics argue, however, that export crops dominate areas of high agricultural potential and enjoy a disproportionate use of natural resources as well as credit and other inputs. The term *ecological footprint* has recently been introduced to describe the environmental and social impacts of Northern consumption patterns in distant places, where the consumers do not observe the consequences of their actions. For example, local food staples are often displaced by export crops onto areas of low agricultural potential subject to greater uncertainty of climate and often lack comparable access to credit and other subsidised inputs. As Leonard observes, the greatest disparities within rural areas of the South are often those between areas of high agricultural potential which have benefited from agricultural modernisation and those areas of low potential which have been neglected (Leonard, 1989). This raises important questions regarding the location of the poor, especially whether there is a clear tendency for many of the poorest people to be found in areas of low potential subject to climatic hazards and resource degradation.

The location of poverty

It is widely assumed that a majority of the poor are located in the most ecologically fragile, low resource areas marked by limited arable land of low potential and subject to the risks of natural hazards and environmental degradation. The livelihoods of the poor in such areas are consequently believed to be highly insecure and exacerbated by the strongly seasonal demand for agricultural labour and the limited opportunities for off-farm employment. But to what degree is there a correlation between social and environmental poverty? Do economically marginal people live in ecologically marginal places?

This certainly appears to be the case in the Sudan, according to a study made by Bilsborrow and DeLargy. They describe developments in the Eastern part of the country where mechanised farming was started in the 1940s by the British, concerned with feeding their troops stationed in East Africa, but continued to grow long after their departure. During the 1960s and 1970s millions of dollars were invested by wealthy Arab states, followed by large World Bank loans, to turn Sudan into the 'breadbasket of the Middle East'. The area under cultivation expanded dramatically as wealthy urban merchants rented lands from the government at low cost, using subsidised machinery and low-interest loans to exploit the soil for maximum profits. The result was rapidly declining yields and land degradation, with entrepreneurs using up one area then renting another rather than implementing conservation measures, a programme which has been described as 'environmental hit-and-run'.

The social implications of this type of mechanised farming, with farmers incessantly vacating old locations and occupying new ones, were negative as well. Family farmers were forced off their land to make way for mechanised farms which also

Plate 4.2 Cattle farming in drought conditions in Gourma, Mali. A delicate balance has to be struck between human activities and environmental protection. Photo: Trond Isaksen/Lineair

blocked traditional nomadic grazing paths and increased conflicts between pastoralists and farmers. The use of savanna land for cultivation meant that herders were forced to intensify grazing in the marginal areas because they had to stay there year-round, leading to patterns of desertification. Finally, the mechanised schemes draw in over 1 million male labour migrants from the West of the country, leaving women and children to eke out survival in a region of drought and environmental degradation (Bilsborrow and DeLargy, 1991).

According to Leonard, a total of 470 million people, or 60% of the developing world's poorest according to his criteria, live in rural or urban areas of high ecological vulnerability – 'areas where they are highly susceptible to the consequences of soil erosion, soil infertility, floods and other ecological disasters' (Leonard, 1989, p.19). Of this total, some 70% live in the squatter settlements and areas of low agricultural potential in Asia, 17% in sub-Saharan Africa and 13% in Latin America. These 63 million people, living in the ecologically vulnerable areas in Latin America, comprise 80% of that region's poorest. Consequently, Leonard believes that poverty in many developing countries is becoming ever more concentrated into definable geographical areas which lack, yet most need, appropriate infrastructure and technology, making increasing numbers of the poorest people vulnerable to environmental hazards and degradation (see Figure 4.4).

117

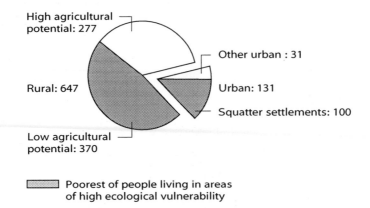

Poorest of people living in areas
of high ecological vulnerability

Fig. 4.4 Where the poorest of the poor live, poorest people in all developing countries (in millions). The poorest of poor are defined as the poorest 20% among the total population of all developing countries. Source: Leonard, 1989

Kates and Haarmann cast doubts on the quality of data employed by Leonard but then observe that, even on his calculations, 43% of the poorest live in areas of high agricultural potential. They argue that it is not appropriate to equate areas of low potential with high ecological vulnerability:

> In many parts of the world, land of low agricultural potential is little used, is appropriately used for pastoralism, or is forested. Although subject to erosion, desertification, and deforestation, these areas are not necessarily more vulnerable than are intensively used lands of high agricultural potential that are also subject to erosion, flooding, and, in the case of valuable irrigated lands, salinisation and waterlogging (Kates and Haarman, 1992, p.7).

While they believe it is difficult to map poor people directly onto threatened environments, Kates and Haarmann do examine whether poor *countries* have more than their share of drylands, highlands and rainforests, three major environments which occupy more than half the world's land area and support one-quarter of its people. They find that low income countries do indeed possess a disproportionate share of savanna grasslands while the very poorest countries, which account for 20% of the land area in the South, possess 63% of its drylands. Moreover, some 71% of tropical moist forests are concentrated in the low income countries, although not in the very poorest, while highland environments are more equally distributed among poorer and wealthier developing countries.

The main thrust of Kates and Haarmann's article, however, is with identifying particular pathways, or spirals, of impoverishment and degradation. Through a review of the literature, they find a remarkable consistency in the analysis of ways poor people lose their entitlements to environmental resources leading to these downward spirals. Driving these spirals are forces acting in combination, two of which are external to the locality (natural hazards, and development and commercialisation) and two which are internal to the community (population growth and poverty) (see Figure 4.5). While all the driving

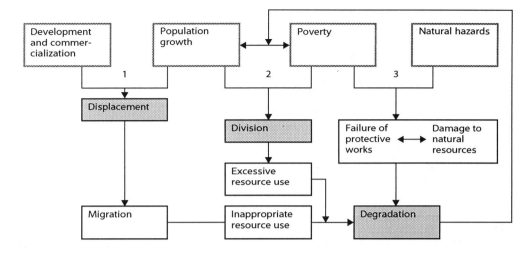

Fig. 4.5 Impoverishment and degradation spirals. Source: Kates and Haarmann, 1992

forces are implicated in the forms that the spiral sequences assume, Kates and Haarmann suggest that two of the driving forces act together in each of the three major spiral sequences which they label *displacement*, *division* and *degradation*. They describe the processes involved in displacement as follows (read in conjunction with Figure 4.5):

> The poor are displaced by activities that, in the name of development or commercialisation, deprive the hungry of their traditional entitlement to the common property resources that are essential to their survival. Large-scale agriculture .. (and many other activities).. dispossess poor people of their resource access directly by expropriation and by destroying or limiting access to small but crucial seasonal resources. The poor are also displaced by wealthier claimants to land who use both legal and illegal means. Finally, the poor are displaced by each other because limited land and employment opportunities often force the young from poor families to migrate in search of land or employment (Kates and Haarmann, 1992, p.8).

Division of land resources, according to Kates and Haarmann again, often comes about in the following way:

> The entitlements of the poor are divided and reduced because of their need to share resources with their children or to sell off portions of their resources to offset extreme losses, such as crop failure, illness or death; to fulfil social requirements, such as marriage dowries; or to provide simple subsistence. Throughout the developing world, the number of landless and land-poor households is increasing (Kates and Haarmann, 1992, p.8).

Degradation of land, they claim, is caused by yet another combination of factors:

> The resources of the poor are degraded by excessive or inappropriate use, by failure to restore or to maintain protective works, and by the loss of productive capacity because of natural hazards. Those who are poor in resources often press what

little they have to levels of production or reproduction – for example by reducing fallow, overgrazing, or excessive fuelwood removal – that cannot be sustained. The degradation of many common property resources, however, occurs because of excessive use, not by the poorest users, but by the wealthier ones, who often have large herds of livestock, require large diversions of water, or use the forest commercially.

The poor may also lack the ability to restore or maintain protective works, such as terraces or drainage canals; lack the means to hire people with specialised skills or to make needed inputs; or lack access to public programmes of resource improvement and renewal. Finally, natural hazards, such as diseases, droughts, floods, landslides and pests also degrade the environment, causing it to lose the capacity to provide particular resources (Kates and Haarmann, 1992, p.8).

This commentary reveals the importance of understanding the different combination of driving forces acting in concert according to specific local circumstances and dynamics. It does not assume the primacy of population growth in causing environmental degradation but rather evaluates demographic factors alongside other driving forces of change. Besides, the extraordinary diversity of regional circumstances should warn us to beware of universal models with singular causal forces of change. This point is illustrated in the next section by the example of tropical deforestation.

4.7 Tropical deforestation: understanding the causes

One of the principal areas where population has been treated as the major driving force of environmental degradation is in relation to tropical deforestation. This is because tropical forests host vital stocks of resources and perform important ecological services. These include: an extraordinary biological diversity in which the forests' canopies alone provide habitats for an estimated 30 million species of insects; the storage of half of all stocks of carbon held in the world's forests which, if released, would increase the concentration of carbon dioxide in the atmosphere and accelerate global warming; and the maintenance of soils capable of supporting the highest biomass productivities (but which decline dramatically when the forests are removed). Yet for countries which possess tropical forests and which aspire to rapid economic development there are strong incentives for their removal. Amongst these are: the extraction and sale of valuable hardwoods; the opportunity to create timber-processing industries; the expansion in the area of arable land for domestic staples, export crops and livestock feeds; and even political considerations. For example, governments have directed forest clearing in order to establish territorial control over areas where national boundaries may be unclear and to strengthen internal security and restrict places of refuge for political opponents (for example, the Zapatistas staged an uprising against the Mexican government in the state of Chiapas in January 1994, then retreated into the Lecandon Forest on the border with Guatamala beyond the reach of the national army). Governments have also encouraged logging in order to assert their rights of national sovereignty over forest resources, rejecting calls for greater conservation as constituting "unwarranted interference in the country's internal affairs ...'.

The variety of circumstances that underlie tropical deforestation demonstrates the need to adopt a regionally specific analysis. For example, in Africa the expansion of export crops has been responsible for much of the deforestation even indirectly, by displacing food crop production and encouraging the encroachment by subsistence farmers onto forest land. Meanwhile, in Central America it is the unequal distribution of land and the expansion of commercial cattle production which have been the major causes of deforestation. In Costa Rica the total area under pasture expanded to occupy almost half of total agricultural land by 1973, so that cattle occupied approximately one-third of the country's total land mass (Annis, 1992); in Mexico, the state of Tabasco lost 90% of its forests during the last four decades to cattle pastures (Barraclough and Ghimire, 1990). We can look in a little more detail at two regions experiencing rapid rates of deforestation but which have different combinations of 'driving forces'.

Central America

A good illustration of the process in Central America is provided by DeWalt and colleagues in their study of Honduras. This country had a population of almost 5 million people in 1989, nearly double the 1970 population of 2.6 million. Over this period Honduras experienced substantial environmental destruction: soil erosion,

Plate 4.3 In the vicinity of Rio Branco in the Amazon basin, Western Brazil. Although trees have grown on this land for an estimated 60 million years, gully erosion has occurred within just a few years of the forest being cut down. The top soil will soon be washed away and the land will remain barren. Photo: Mark Edwards/Lineair

121

watershed deterioration, deforestation and the destruction of coastal resources. At one level it might be understandable to believe that there is a direct link between rapid population increase and the unsustainable use of land and water resources. However, the study demonstrates that behind the facade lie a number of contributory factors:

1 A massive inequality in access to land, where 64% of farms with less than 5 hectares occupy in total only 9% of agricultural land while 4% of rural properties of over 50 hectares own more than 55% of available land.
2 Low incomes (more than 70% of families live on less than $20 per month) and poor nutritional status of the rural population with over 70% of children under five years of age suffering from protein-calorie malnutrition.
3 The expansion of pasture land under World Bank loans. Between 1960 and 1983, 57% of total loan funds allocated by the Bank for agriculture and rural development in Central America supported the production of beef for export and Honduras acquired a disproportionate share of these. It is estimated that almost half of the prime valley land in Honduras is under pasture.
4 Substantial investment in cotton, canteloupe and shrimp production which resulted in the expulsion and exclusion of the poor from agricultural and inter-tidal lands and severe contamination of groundwater and estuaries with DDT and other agrochemicals.

The conclusions of the authors are clear. In Honduras:

> … environmental degradation and social problems often attributed to population pressure arise from glaring inequalities in the distribution of land, the lack of decent employment opportunities, and the stark poverty of many of the inhabitants. It is not the carrying capacity of the land that has failed to keep pace with population growth. Neither is population growth the primary cause of the impoverishment of the Honduran ecology and its human inhabitants. While the destruction caused by the poor in their desperate search for survival is alarming, it pales in comparison with the destruction wrought by large landowners through their reckless search for profit (DeWalt *et al.*, 1993, p.120).

This picture of poverty and resource depletion in Honduras is replicated in the other Central American countries, though each has its distinctive features. It should also be remembered that the region was synonymous with conflict and rural dislocation for many decades, a major cause of environmental destruction. For example:

> Belize, with a 1991 population of about 200,000, has absorbed some 30,000 refugees from El Salvador and Guatemala, – (while) – during the early 1980s, Mexico absorbed as many as 200,000 political refugees from the highlands of Guatemala (and an estimated 42,000 still remain).
> In the late 1980s, tens of thousands of Nicaraguan contras operating in Southern Honduras destroyed much of the forested border zone. As many as 20,000 ex-contras have laid down their arms and, with their dependents, are now seeking land. Some 20,000 'official' refugees and an estimated 100,000 undocumented Nicaraguans are expected to remain in Costa Rica for the forseeable future (Annis, 1992, p.10).

With the consolidation of peace the objective for the region now is to define a new model of development in which the sustainable management of resources is given a high priority. This will mean ensuring that rural people have a stake in a prosperous, secure and democratic Central America, a stake that requires far-reaching agrarian reform to ensure more equity and security of rights to land for the poor. This, together with efforts to increase the participation of local people in the design and implementation of agricultural development strategies, is an indispensable component, alongside macro economic policy reform, for a more sustainable future.

South-east Asia

In South-east Asia there is a different basis to explain tropical deforestation, where six of the 14 main deforestation fronts found world-wide, according to Myers (1993a), account for half the total of 63,400 square kilometres of forest lost in 1991. Here, the strict colonial controls which regulated access to forests were designed to maximise the commercial benefits of teak extraction for the Dutch and British. Following independence, governments asserted their own political control over forests and deforestation became a major component of national development strategies. This has led to state control being extended over the remotest and most peripheral areas in defence of sovereign forest resources and asserting central authority over forest peoples. Yet, if deforestation in South-east Asia is associated with the power of the state, it is also linked to incorporation into the global economy.

In Indonesia the development of a large-scale, export-orientated logging industry made it one of the leading exporters of tropical hardwoods by the 1970s. By 1985, an export ban was imposed on logs by which time more than 100 plywood mills were in operation increasing the added value in the forestry sector. This industrialisation strategy has increased pressure on forest stands as extraction rates are expected to meet the insatiable demand of local mills. For example, at:

> … Riau Andalan, the world's largest single-line pulp mill is being built – in the heart of a 1600 square kilometre natural forest which will be used for raw material. One government official foresees 62,000 square kilometres of forest land under use by the industry by 2005, up from 15,000 currently…

Aside from legal and illegal deforestation and its ecological effects, the consequences so far have included land conflict, forced labour, agricultural watershed damage, ruined fisheries and drinking water supplies, land degradation, destruction of forest commons needed for livelihood, and eviction' (Lohmann, 1994, p.1).

Yet another major dynamic of forest clearance in Indonesia has been the state-directed transmigration programme designed to relieve high population densities in Java and Bali, where more than 60% of Indonesia's 180 million people live on just 7% of the nation's land area. The 'largest land settlement programme in the world' has had enormous consequences for the 'outer islands' of Sumatra, Borneo (Kalimantan) and New Guinea (Irian Jaya) where, since 1950, an estimated 5 million people have been moved. Yet, the transmigration programme has proved extremely controversial for a number of reasons: the consequences for native forest peoples whose lands have been occupied and cleared; the high cost of settlement (up to $10,000 per relocated family);

123

the obvious lack of forest conservation; the failure to achieve sustainable and productive agricultural systems capable of supporting transmigrant households, and so on. Indeed, the management of many of these cleared forest areas has proved extremely difficult for farmers accustomed to rich volcanic soils, as they attempt to maintain productivity on their two hectare allocations in the face of declining fertility, susceptibility to erosion and the dominance of invasive grasses, most notably *Imperata cylindrica*.

Imperata (or *alang-alang* in Indonesian) is estimated to occupy 10% of the former extent of forest in the outer islands. It severely retards natural succession and the replenishment of soil fertility under shifting cultivation, while on small farms it is extremely difficult to work because of its extensive root system. In fieldwork conducted by the author during 1993 in a region of Southern Sumatra, interviews with many transmigrant households revealed lives that were hard, insecure and apparently unsustainable. Most farmers described how they had started to grow rice, cassava, soya and maize on their cleared plots of land, but many found yields went into sharp decline without generous use of chemical fertilisers and *alang-alang* gradually began to take over. Pests are also a major problem: until a few years ago, elephants trampled the fields and monkeys ate the corn, while wild pigs are still a nuisance. But now the main pest is rats – up to 90% of the rice harvest in Isorejo village was lost to rats in 1992 – while there are many kinds of insects, viruses and fungi attacking crops. Perhaps the biggest difficulty facing farmers, however, is their lack of local environmental knowledge, a sufficient understanding of the agro-ecological processes and prevailing climate of their new locality, which presents entirely new management difficulties compared to those with which they were familiar in Java.

In addition, there are continuing conflicts with native farmers who believe they remain the true owners of the land under local customary law; consequently, some transmigrant families have little or no land and await a resolution of the conflict by the authorities. Besides this many villages lack a year-round, clean supply of water, so that gastrointestinal illnesses are common (as well as diseases such as malaria) and problems of food insecurity result from crop failures due to prolonged dry spells. Farmers also have no access to credit, pay high transport costs and receive low prices for agricultural products. Little wonder, therefore, that many transmigrants are forced to work on the agro-industrial estates or for the logging companies in adjacent forests to earn a wage with which to support their families.

4.8 Conclusion

It is clear that in the context of land settlement by small farmers in much of Indonesia and elsewhere, the clearance of tropical forests is not being replaced by stable, productive, sustainable or equitable systems of production, key indicators of agricultural performance (Conway and Barbier, 1988). Rather, forest is giving way to an intermediate and extensive form of land use which is expanding more rapidly by deforestation than it is being reduced by the introduction of successful systems of management. This demonstrates the vital importance of examining the wide range of variables that mediate between population and resource use: decisions over development policy made by governments and financed by international banks; the behaviour of markets in translating demand into production incentives; economic policies that provide differential rewards; the circumstances of poverty which influence household livelihood and demographic strategies, amongst others. Indeed:

> We need to develop a much deeper understanding of the relationships between human populations, their technologies, cultures, and values, and the natural capital (renewable and non-renewable natural resources) they depend on for life support if we are to achieve sustainability (Arizpe *et al.*, 1992, p.61).

This chapter has attempted to expose the dishonesty of blaming the poor for their promiscuity rather than governments and the multilateral agencies for their shortsighted policies and lack of political will to tackle environmental degradation. There is a need for North and South to work together to formulate comprehensive development strategies that reflect the complex interactions of population, consumption, technology and resources, but in a way that will tackle the scourge of poverty, hunger, high childhood mortality and environmental insecurity. In this respect, sustainable development remains nothing more than a slogan until the World Bank statistics on the first page of this chapter are eliminated. This will require a major commitment on the part of the developed North, not just to donate modest amounts of aid but to demonstrate a willingness to work for a more equitable international economic system and more moderate levels of material consumption. As Goodland has asserted, 'One car damages the environment more than one poor person. Control of car populations is even more important than control of human populations' (quoted in Dorner and Thiesenhusen, 1992, p.5).

5

The distribution of environmental costs and benefits: Acid rain

Jan van der Straaten

5.1 Introduction

This chapter discusses the issue of acid rain or, to use the more appropriate term, *acidic atmospheric depositions*, in Europe. Acid rain has become a recurring problem in many European countries over the past couple of decades. It not only causes environmental damage, but also leaves a huge cost in its wake.

The majority of depositions in most European countries come from neighbouring countries. At the same time, most European countries also emit acidic compounds themselves. Consequently, they may be regarded as both the victims and the culprits. Although this may seem to imply an equal sharing of the burden, this is far from the truth. The costs incurred by importing acidifying substances (through deposition) and the benefits reaped from exporting them are unevenly distributed across European countries: some end up as net sufferers, others as net beneficiaries. Solving the acid rain problem therefore demands international co-operation, as no country can solve its acid rain problems without the help of the adjacent producing countries. However, international co-operation is very difficult to pull off, as the interests of the countries involved may well conflict with each other. The present chapter seeks to describe and analyse the negotiation process from a political point of view. Particular attention will be given to the role economic costs and benefits play in this process.

Section 5.2 gives a description of the scientific and historical background of the acid rain problem. After a discussion of the recent history of the problem in various countries, consideration is given to the emissions, the sectors involved and the countries suffering from acid rain. This leads to an analysis of the problem posed by acid rain in political terms. A crucial feature of the analysis is the conception of air as a common property resource. Section 5.3 includes a description of the barriers that hinder the solution of the acid rain problem, placing particular emphasis on European strategies. Attention is also paid to the role of scientific uncertainty and traditional economic theories in the negotiating process. In Section 5.4, the fairly broad analysis as performed thus far is applied to the situation in a specific country, namely The Netherlands. Policies, actual measures taken and their effectiveness are all discussed. The chapter closes with a number of conclusions (section 5.5).

5.2 Atmospheric deposition

What is atmospheric deposition?

The main sources of atmospheric deposition include emissions of *oxidised sulphur compounds* (SO and SO_2, referred to collectively as SO_x), *oxidised nitrogen compounds* (NO and NO_2, referred to collectively as NO_x) and *reduced nitrogen compounds* (NH_3 or ammonia and NH_4^+ or ammonium, referred to collectively as NH_x).

Sulphur compounds are emitted when oil and coal containing sulphur (as they almost invariably do) are used as fuel. In other words, both oil refineries and coal-fired and oil-fired power plants emit sulphur oxides, with the amounts emitted depending on the amount of sulphur present in the fuel. Nitrogen compounds are emitted in various situations, especially when high temperatures are reached in power plants, oil refineries and engines (of motor vehicles in particular). Both these oxidised compounds may result in *acidic atmospheric depositions* (see Box 1) as a result of various chemical conversions. Finally, reduced nitrogen compounds such as ammonia are emitted when

---

1

Why not speak of 'acid rain'?

When it became clear, at the beginning of the 1980s, that forests in Western Germany were dying off on a large scale, it was recognised that the acidity of the rain was to blame. It was then that the term 'acid rain' was coined. The term is, however, unfortunate. Firstly, it covers only a limited set of deposition types, whereas scientists soon discovered forms of deposition other than rain. Some acidic substances are precipitated (*wet deposition*), whilst others come down incessantly in the form of particles (*dry deposition*). Wet deposition includes rain, snow, hail and mist. The majority of the depositions, however, are dry rather than wet.

Secondly, the acidity of the wet deposition is relatively insignificant. In The Netherlands, for instance, rain is neutral rather than acidic, even though it contains oxidised sulphur (SO_x) and oxidised nitrogen compounds (NO_x). Their effect on the acidity of the rain, however, is offset by the alkalinity of the reduced nitrogen compounds (NH_x) that are also present. The neutrality does not prevent the compounds from doing their destructive work. After deposition, each compound undergoes specific chemical conversions that ultimately lead to the damage.

Thirdly, not all depositions are acidic. Some are alkaline and others may have a basically eutrophying (i.e. 'fertilising') effect. It is for these reasons that the term 'acidic atmospheric deposition' rather than 'acid rain' is preferred nowadays, although the less correct term is still in use.

Source: Ivens (1990).

---

manure is produced by intensive cattle farming (see Chapter 1). Ammonia itself is not an acidifying substance. However, acids may be formed either when ammonia is converted into nitric acid (HNO_3) by nitric bacteria in the soil or when it is absorbed by vegetation, which leads to the release of (acidic) H^+ ions. In the latter case, the ammonia has a *eutrophying* effect, i.e. it works as a fertiliser. Maps 5.1, 5.2 and 5.3 show the distribution of SO_2, NO_x and NH_3 emissions over Europe.

Acidic depositions may damage various kinds of valuable environmental resources.

○ *Lakes*, in particular those which are located in regions where the soil does not contain alkaline components, may be easily affected by acidic deposits. The damage is

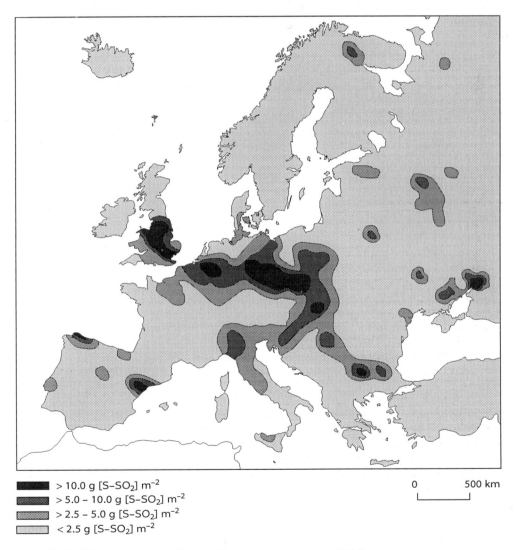

> 10.0 g [S–SO₂] m⁻²
> 5.0 – 10.0 g [S–SO₂] m⁻²
> 2.5 – 5.0 g [S–SO₂] m⁻²
< 2.5 g [S–SO₂] m⁻²

0   500 km

Map 5.1 SO_2 emissions in Europe. Source: Iversen *et al.*, 1989.

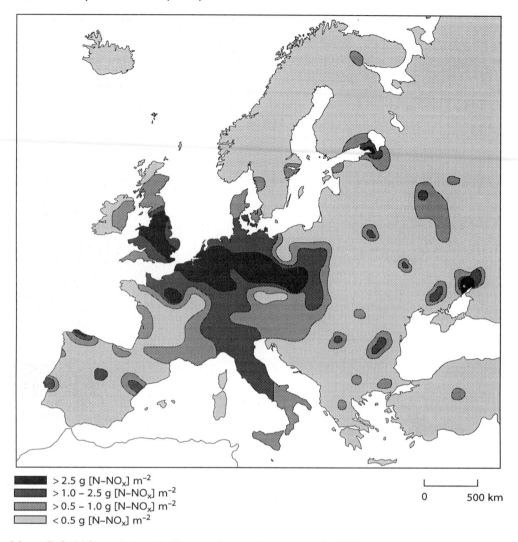

> 2.5 g [N–NO$_x$] m^{-2}
> 1.0 – 2.5 g [N–NO$_x$] m^{-2}
> 0.5 – 1.0 g [N–NO$_x$] m^{-2}
< 0.5 g [N–NO$_x$] m^{-2}

0   500 km

Map 5.2 NO$_x$ emissions in Europe. Source: Iversen *et al.*, 1989.

done because the acid mobilises aluminium in the soil. In the springtime, when layers of snow contaminated with acidic substances melt, the aluminium is washed out into streams and lakes. Fish such as salmon and trout spawn at this time of year; their fertility is severely affected by the influx. Other animals and plants in the lakes are affected when the acidity of the lakes surpasses a certain threshold value. The end result of this acidification process is that the majority of the original organisms are no longer found in these lakes (Johannessen *et al.*, 1980).

○ *Terrestrial ecosystems* are also affected. Although sandy areas in western, central and eastern Europe may be affected, most attention has so far focused on forest ecosystems. They are affected in two different ways. Firstly, they are affected *indirectly* through changes in the acidity of the soil. When a soil becomes more acidic, *cations*

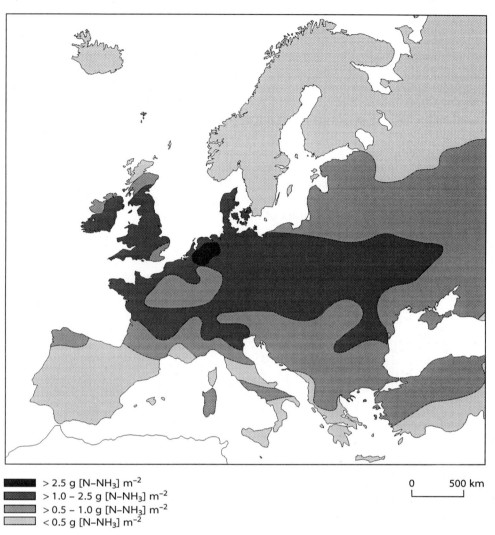

> 2.5 g [N–NH₃] m⁻²
> 1.0 – 2.5 g [N–NH₃] m⁻²
> 0.5 – 1.0 g [N–NH₃] m⁻²
< 0.5 g [N–NH₃] m⁻²

0   500 km

Map 5.3 NH₃ emissions in Europe. Source: Iversen *et al.*, 1989.

(i.e. positively charged ions) that are vital for tree growth, such as Ca^{2+}, Mg^{2+} and K^+, are leached out, resulting in stunted growth. If the soil contains a high percentage of alkalic components, the acidification due to acidic depositions can be neutralised. This is not the case in large parts of the Alps, the mountain ranges of central Europe and the Scandinavian region. Also, the micorrhizas (i.e. vital fungi in the soil associating with the root systems of plants) are damaged by an increase in acidity. Trees can no longer absorb the nutrients they need, again resulting in stunted growth. Secondly, even if the soil is alkaline and the effects of increased acidity are buffered away, trees can still be affected by the *direct* influence of acidic substances on their needles and leaves. This damage hampers the intake of the carbon dioxide and oxygen which the plants need to absorb from the air for their metabolism.

131

○ In most cases, acid rain does not kill trees but simply makes them more vulnerable to various types of disease and insect. Trees become unable to cope with many, otherwise normal, environmental influences (which is why acidic deposition is often referred to as an *environmental stress*). The result is that trees die on a massive scale, as has occurred in the Black Forest and the Harz mountain range in Germany, in many parts of the Northern and Central Alps and in the forests of Slovakia, Poland and former East Germany (MacKenzie and El-Ashry, 1989).

○ It is not only trees that suffer from acidic depositions on the soil. In *nature reserves*, it is also vital that the soil itself is able to function properly. As has already been mentioned, atmospheric deposition may also have a eutrophying effect through the agency of the nutrients it contains. In particular, the ecological value of nature reserves such as peat moors, where the level of the nutrients is normally low, may be affected dramatically by an influx of nutrients.

Plate 5.1 Forest devastated by acid rain in the vicinity of Karlovy Vary in the Czech Republic. Photo: Giri Polacek/Lineair

○ Acid rain affects the surfaces of *historic buildings and monuments* such as ancient churches, houses, statues and bridges. The damage is particularly great in areas where the type of stone used is extremely vulnerable to acidity, such as Vienna. NO_x and NH_x deposits may ultimately increase the nitrogen content of *groundwater bodies* used to produce drinking water. This threat is particularly significant in regions in which there is intensive cattle farming, as the surpluses of manure and artificial fertilisers add to the overall concentration (see Chapter 1). Deposits from traffic only worsen an already dangerous situation. In The Netherlands, for example, an increasing number of wells that are used for the production of drinking water have recently been closed owing to dangerously high levels of nitrogen.

Acid rain has also had a considerable effect on vegetable *crops* in many parts of Europe (MacKenzie and El-Ashry, 1989; Van der Eerden, Tonneijck and Wijnands, 1986).

Reducing NO_x emissions from cars: beating the competition

2

Most of the cars produced in the Federal Republic of Germany have traditionally been (and indeed still are) relatively large and high powered. The UK, France and Italy have concentrated on smaller cars. Germany dominated the market and the position of manufacturers from the other countries was weaker, with the UK car producers being the weakest. All, however, were united in their efforts to ward off competition from the USA and Japan.

It has been Germany which has suffered most from the effects of acid rain and it was Germany which took the initiative within the European Union in proposing an agreement on the reduction of vehicle emissions. All the various proposed measures would, however, have increased the net price of cars. The UK, France, and Italy were afraid that higher prices would result in a loss of market share. They therefore opposed any plan which was aimed at reducing car emissions.

Basically, there were two instruments for reducing emissions: lean-burn engines and catalytic converters. Lean-burn engines emit fewer pollutants as they are more fuel efficient than ordinary engines (they run on a lower petrol-to-oxygen ratio). Catalytic converters had already been introduced in the USA, where they are now mandatory and have resulted in emissions being reduced by 90%. The maximum reduction in emission levels achievable by using lean-burn technology, however, is only 70%. This implies that a reduction of over 70% can be realised only by fitting cars with catalytic converters. After a long period of negotiation on the necessity of strict reduction targets, the European Commission finally decided that a high reduction percentage was vital. This implied a preference for catalytic converters, an approach which gave Germany two advantages. Firstly, it meant better protection of its forests and secondly, it gave the German motor manufacturers a competitive edge. After all, Germany was already experienced in the field of catalytic converters, as it had been exporting its cars to the USA where converters had been obligatory for some time. The lean-burn engine, on the other hand, had been developed in the UK.

Source: (Dietz *et al.*, 1991).

In the early days, when the scientific process of acid rain formation first began to be understood, sulphur dioxide was perceived to be the main culprit. Emissions of NO_x received hardly any attention at that time. However, the situation has since changed rapidly. Not only has scientific understanding of the problem grown steadily, with researchers identifying a more prominent role for NO_x, but the nature of the problem itself has also changed. The rapid increase in the number of motor vehicles has ensured that NO_x takes up a larger share of total emissions. The European Union has given explicit consideration to the problem of reducing NO_x emissions from motor vehicles. It has established a low limit on the permissible level of NO_x emissions from cars, thus effectively forcing car manufacturers to fit their products with catalytic converters (see Box 2).

How did atmospheric deposition come about?

Air pollution has been a normal companion of industrial development ever since the advent of the Industrial Revolution. As early as 1872, in his book entitled *Air and Rain: the Beginnings of a Chemical Climatology*, Robert Smith gave a description of air pollution. He demonstrated that polluting emissions were transported over long distances, causing damage to areas far away from the location of the emitters. The book did not attract much attention at the time. One possible reason for this is that, although the effects of air pollution had been felt in the direct vicinity of industrial plants, it was not perceived as a problem in areas further away.

The situation changed dramatically following the Second World War, when the industrial development of Europe shifted into high gear. In this period, air pollution began to affect public health on a wide scale. Higher than normal mortality rates were registered during periods of smog, for instance, in areas such as Greater London in the UK and the Rijnmond region around Rotterdam in The Netherlands (Jansen *et al.*, 1974). As a result, air pollution became a national health problem. In the 1960s, an attempt was made to solve it by building tall chimneys.

Obviously, the taller chimneys only led to the pollutants being dispersed over an even wider area. Indeed, as early as the beginning of the 1960s, scientists were expressing their concern over the construction of tall chimneys (Baker and Macfarlane, 1961). They felt that such action would only spread pollution over the whole of Europe, as it indeed did (see Map 5.4). Alongside the almost explosive rise in road traffic and the growth in polluting industrial farming practices (see Chapter 1), air pollution has now become a problem of *international* proportions.

The spread of air pollution across national borders has a range of consequences. Ecosystems have been affected, many of which are not capable of coping with the threat. The death of large numbers of fish in Scandinavian lakes is a typical example and it attracted a great deal of attention in the Scandinavian countries in the 1960s (Odèn, 1968). Sweden suffered particularly badly from air pollution and ensured that the issue was placed on the agenda of the United Nations Conference on the Human Environment which was held in Stockholm in 1972. Sweden argued that the damage caused to Swedish lakes was a result of acidic emissions from industrial plants in Poland, Germany, the UK and The Netherlands and asked for the emissions to be reduced. The alleged perpetrators were not prepared to comply, claiming that there was no proof that they were responsible for the damage. The Swedes, however, persisted

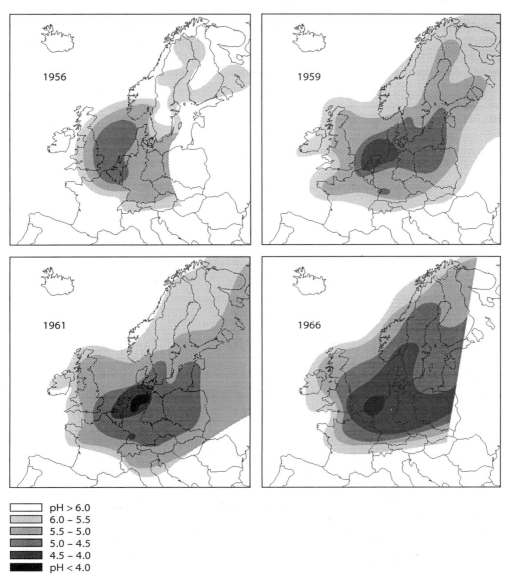

pH > 6.0
6.0 – 5.5
5.5 – 5.0
5.0 – 4.5
4.5 – 4.0
pH < 4.0

Map 5.4 The increasing acidity of precipitation in Europe. Source: Vermeulen, 1977.

and an agreement was reached that international research would be conducted so as to gain more insight into the problem.

The initial results of this research were published by the Organisation for Economic Co-operation and Development in 1977 (OECD, 1977). It became clear that transboundary air pollution was a very common phenomenon. The deposition of acidifying substances from abroad accounted for more than 50% of total depositions in countries such as Norway, Sweden, Finland, Austria and Switzerland. This implied that their problems could be solved only by cutting emissions elsewhere, as the Swedes

135

had already requested. In short, the OECD regarded international co-operation as the only means of finding a solution to the problem (see also Hordijk *et al.*, 1990).

However, there were a number of stumbling blocks in the path towards co-operation. One was that many countries with high levels of emissions, e.g. the former Democratic Republic of Germany, Poland and Czechoslovakia, were not members of the OECD. This meant that other organisations would have to take the lead. And indeed, the United Nations Economic Commission for Europe (ECE), of which all these countries were members, stepped in.

Plate 5.2 Liming by helicopter to neutralise acidification in Lake Bergsjon, near Göteborg, Sweden. Since Sweden started full-scale liming in 1982, 5,500 lakes, as well as 100 streams and rivers, have been treated. The operation costs SKR 100 million a year. Sweden would have to spend three times that amount in order to treat all the acid-effected areas. Photo: Mark Edwards/Lineair

The first conference on the formulation of a European policy for the protection of clean air was convened in Geneva in 1979. Agreement was reached on general principles such as the dissemination of information and technology, the significance of public health and the necessity of reducing emissions. However, it proved impossible to agree on specifics such as the type of action to be taken and the scale and distribution of the costs relating to these measures. The problem of the uneven distribution of benefits and costs among countries formed a major obstacle. It took six years and a succession of conferences before agreement was finally reached at Helsinki in 1985 to aim at a flat 30% reduction on 1980 levels of all transboundary SO_2 emissions. The Helsinki conference was followed by a conference in Sofia in 1988. The ECE again took the initiative for this conference, where the European countries agreed in principle on a standstill with regard to NO_x emissions.

All in all, the negotiations on the question of how to put a lid on air pollution in Europe lasted for many years. There are several reasons for the length of this delay. The first hurdle to be taken was the question of how to set *priorities*. Should priority be given to achieving a reduction in emissions with the strongest adverse effects on European ecosystems, as some argued? This would mean that the worst cases would be tackled first. The Southern European countries in particular supported this standpoint, given that, with their low emission levels, they could afford to stand on the sidelines. Or would it be best to give top priority to those emissions that could be reduced at the lowest cost? In that case, the emphasis would be on obtaining the best value for money, i.e. maximum cost-effectiveness, and an entirely different set of countries would now be required to take action.

Another obstacle related to the *validity of the arguments* used to justify particular measures. For example, some countries argued that they had recently taken rigorous measures. They therefore saw no reason to reduce their emissions by the same percentage as other countries which had hardly reduced emissions at all. Also, there was disagreement over the year of reference. Those countries that had already taken strict measures wanted a year of reference early enough for their recent endeavours to count against the required 30% reduction. Finally, some countries, such as the USSR, were of the opinion that only transboundary pollution (and *not* internal emissions, which they regarded as a domestic problem) should be taken into account.

5.3 Conflicting interests

The previous section briefly discussed the science of acidic atmospheric depositions. It also showed how the depositions came to be recognised as a problem and what political attempts were made to find a solution. This section takes a further look at these efforts, not with an eye on their historical significance but from the perspective of their political relevance. More specifically, there is a need to be aware that attempts to solve the problem of acidic atmospheric depositions met with fierce resistance and that various countries used their political power to stall the negotiations. But why is air pollution such a difficult problem to tackle? What are the barriers to its solution? These are the questions that we shall now be addressing.

Clean air: a common property resource

The key to the answers to these questions lies in the specific characteristics of air when it is viewed as a resource. Since time immemorial, it has been taken for granted that unpolluted air is available for everyone to make use of, much like clean water, ample fish stocks and the biosphere's capacity to process organic waste have been taken for granted. (Of course, there have always been places where the air is unfit for breathing, the water unfit for drinking, fish scarce and wastes hardly decomposed. However this does not detract from the general validity of the statement.) It is a characteristic of such resources that they can all be used by everybody, since nobody in particular owns them. In theory, they can all also be used without diminishing their potential utility for others. Such resources are known as *common property resources*.

It has become obvious, however, that unlimited use does detract from the utility of these resources. Both air and water may be polluted, fish stocks may be depleted and the biosphere's recycling capabilities may be compromised. As the *value* of these resources is beyond doubt, there is a general consensus that someone should speak up on their behalf. Since nobody owns them, however, it cannot be the owner. Moreover, if some individual economic actor stood up and invested in measures to guarantee their quality and quantity, he or she would only stand to lose. After all, while all the costs would be incurred by the one actor alone, the benefits would accrue to all users, both actual and potential. This is hardly an incentive for making the investment. The only solution is collective action, for example at governmental level (see also Van der Straaten and Gordon, 1995, pp.130–58).

While it is possible to see how governmental action could protect, say, inland fish stocks, the same strategy does not work for fish stocks in international waters. So, although the UK may have been successful in re-establishing salmon stocks in the River Thames solely by means of national regulations, The Netherlands would not be able to pull off the same result with respect to the Rhine without international co-operation. In other words, whenever a problem with respect to a common property resource exceeds the boundaries of one nation, international co-operation is imperative. And indeed, this maxim applies to the problem of atmospheric deposition, both in Europe and elsewhere. After all, the prevailing winds carry the pollutants across national borders, from the UK across the North Sea into Scandinavia, from The Netherlands into Denmark and Germany, from Germany into Finland, and so on.

In sum, clean air is a common property resource. Only through collective action can it be preserved. As air pollution crosses national boundaries, collective action implies international co-operation. International co-operation is a far from easy task, however. There are political, scientific, and economic barriers that have to be overcome.

Barriers to international co-operation

Barriers to international co-operation come in many different shapes. There are political barriers, scientific barriers and economic barriers. We shall discuss these in turn.

The main stumbling block on the road to international co-operation on acid rain is of a *political nature* and springs from the *uneven distribution of the costs and benefits*. A situation in which one group of countries is required to pay for the profits made by another group is not conducive to a swift negotiating process. The picture that emerges of the actual distribution of costs and benefits, however, is even more complex than that of one group opposing another.

Firstly, countries such as Switzerland, Austria, Sweden, Germany and The Netherlands suffer significantly from the deposition of acid rain on their territories. The damage may be exacerbated by the specifics of the local situation. Only alkaline soils can neutralise acidity. In countries such as Spain, Greece and Italy, where most soils are alkaline and acidic deposition is relatively low, the damage has been relatively minor. These countries therefore do not have a strong inclination to abate acid rain. The damage caused by acid rain in Northern European countries, on the other hand, is significant. Not only is the soil more vulnerable, the amounts deposited are much larger, too. In other words, it looks as if most costs are incurred by the Northern countries, whereas the Southern countries secure the full benefit of their polluting activities.

Secondly, the costs of abatement are not the same in every country because of the differences in the structures of their economies. For instance, the power plants in the Eastern areas of Germany, Slovakia and Poland use lignite as a fuel. This results in considerably more acidification than the modern power plants operated by most Western European countries or the hydroelectric power plants in Switzerland and Austria. So if the European Commission were to decide that all power plants located in the European Union must reduce their emissions to a certain level, this would lead to a rise in costs in all countries, particularly in those in which lignite-fired power plants are used. And, of course, such a policy would enhance the competitive position of the Western European countries even further.

Lastly, the benefits of the abatement policies, once implemented, differ from country to country. Southern countries with a low level of damage from acid rain will not receive high levels of benefits if measures are taken on a European scale. If, for example, European emissions are reduced to a level that, say, will stop the forests in Germany and The Netherlands from dying off, these countries will collect the benefits of the abatement policies. No benefits will accrue to the erstwhile polluters, who have no doubt been compelled to invest heavily in upgrading their industry and conforming to stringent environmental regulations.

Negotiations to bring down pollution levels will undoubtedly be slowed down by this complex pattern of benefits and costs, as one may expect conflicts to arise over how much should be done by whom. The trick is to find an *optimum point of reduction* at which the costs of environmental measures equal their benefits. Only then is there a chance of an agreement being reached between the parties to the debate. In order to do this, however, one needs to know what the levels of costs and benefits are. Unfortunately, for various reasons, such knowledge is not easy to obtain. Uncertainties and other problems abound, not only at a scientific level but also, and predominantly, at an economic level.

Finding out what damage is done at particular deposition levels presupposes that one has knowledge of so-called *dose-effect relations*. Such relations describe, for example, what damage is done to the forests in western Germany at a variety of deposition levels. There are, however, *scientific barriers* to the investigation of such relations. When it became clear, for example, at the beginning of the 1980s, that the forests in western Germany were dying off, it still took several years before it was generally accepted, based on the results of scientific research, that acid rain was indeed the cause. Even now, not all aspects of the process which causes these woods to die off are fully understood. This provides plenty of opportunities for polluting industries and countries to stress that it is impossible to make reliable calculations of the costs because of the scientific uncertainties that still surround the problem.

An argument that is often used for the same purpose is that environmental countermeasures should not be taken as long as all cause-effect relations are not known. After all, the future might reveal new facts and relations in the light of which the proposed action may prove counter-productive. In other words, the actual costs and benefits may differ from the costs and benefits as currently anticipated. It should be pointed out, however, that, in nearly all cases, these arguments are used by those groups or sectors of society which stand to profit from the present situation.

We shall not go into the validity of these arguments. Suffice it to say that, clearly, they may be effective in stalling negotiations. Other, even more powerful arguments may also be used for the same purpose.

There are also uncertainties ensuing from the difficulty, *economically* speaking, of placing a value on the interests affected. This is clearly a problem where there is a need to calculate the cost. What is, for example, the value of an undisturbed forest ecosystem? Of course, there is a consensus that forests have an economic value resulting from traditional economic activities such as logging. However, forests also have an economic value resulting from their use for recreational purposes. But how is it possible to assess this value? And is there an intrinsic value to Nature, as some indeed argue, which has to be calculated too? These questions are difficult to answer. Nevertheless, it will not do to argue that economic value should therefore be restricted to those elements of value which can easily be calculated (see also Box 3). This problem alone may prevent us from calculating the optimum point of reduction.

Valuing environmental resources

The value which society attaches to natural resources and the environment is not merely the sum total of all the various individual values. Since society has a much longer life expectancy than individuals, society as a whole has values that are likely to deviate from individual values. In addition, an approach based on the summation of individual preferences may imply the extinction of species and ecosystems. All these arguments support the position that the environment is a *merit good*, not merely to be decided upon by the aggregation of individual values and the estimation of willingness to pay at any particular point of time (Opschoor, 1974). This may, at the collective level, lead to the explicit formulation of conservation policies. In this case, economic development must be directed explicitly towards ensuring the sustainability of natural resources and the quality of the environment.

Source: Klaassen and Opschoor (1991).

In order to avoid such a situation, attempts have been made to find a proxy for environmental costs that defy direct economic valuation. In The Netherlands, the ministry responsible has calculated that environmental costs would rise in the short run from 0.35 to 1.1 million guilders (Minister of Public Housing, Physical Planning and the Environment, 1983–4, p.20). These costs may be attributed to agriculture, nature conservation, forestry, drinking water and the protection of ancient buildings and paintings. Recent investigations by scientists at the Agricultural University of Wageningen have made it clear that the costs in the agricultural sector have been underestimated. The costs of acidic depositions have been estimated at 0.87–1.67 billion guilders per year in this sector (Van der Eerden *et al.*, 1986). One should not overlook the fact that the effects of acidic depositions on forestry have been only partly monetarised and that their effects on recreation and tourism and on the value of nature reserves and ecosystems have not been monetarised at all. This implies that the level of the monetarised costs in The Netherlands will be between 1.2 and 2.8 billion guilders. The cost of the disruption of ecosystems is also difficult to indicate, but it seems safe to say that it is substantial. In sum, then, the monetarised and non-monetarised costs are considerable.

Yet another barrier stems from the still widely accepted misconception that environmental problems are not real economic problems. According to this view, economic problems always involve market transactions in one way or another. They are problems of *labour* and *capital*. There is no recognition whatsoever of the close connection between modern environmental problems and market processes. Although, for instance, the economic losses, caused by acidic depositions, to the natural assets of countries such as Switzerland, Sweden, Austria, The Netherlands and Germany are difficult to calculate, it is clear that the economies of these countries incur a loss equivalent to many billions of guilders. The same type of argument can be used when discussing measures aimed at reducing the greenhouse effect, deforestation, the use of pesticides, the pollution of rivers, seas and oceans or nuclear pollution. These environmental phenomena are all associated with a high level of cost. This, indeed, is the very reason why an environmental policy will result in substantial benefits.

Nevertheless, the prevalent opinion in economic literature, and in the public debate for that matter, is that we have 'the economy' on one side and 'the environment' on the other. In other words, the imposition of environmental standards will harm the economy. It is this type of argument that is used primarily by vested economic interests to prevent or put off the implementation of instruments of environmental policy. Where this mode of reasoning is dominant, it is difficult to bring environmental problems to the centre of public debate. This is particularly true where traditional economic problems such as unemployment are relevant. Public debate will then be concentrated on these issues.

There is yet another debate about the foundations of economic theory that impinges upon environmental policy making. Traditional neoclassical (economic) theory is based on an assumption that economic agents behave in a rational way. Major problems arise when dealing with environmental issues, however. This is linked to a fundamental limitation of rational choice theory in the context of environmental issues. In general, the optimisation strategy of rational choice theory implies that production factors are allocated according to the preferences of the economic agents, thereby satisfying as many needs as possible. Put simply, industry produces as much as it can of what consumers want. The same strategy applies to the management of natural resources: resources are used as needed. The present allocation of natural resources is, however, not optimal, as is demonstrated by the degree of undesirable environmental degradation. The neoclassical remedy is to restore optimum resource allocation, for example by means of price manipulation. However, there is considerable doubt as to whether this optimisation philosophy is equally applicable to goal setting in environmental policies (Opschoor, 1987). What is often lacking is essential information on the environmental effects of human actions.

If the effects of so many interventions in Nature are not sufficiently known or are consistently disregarded, an optimum use of natural resources for human production and consumption, as neoclassical analyses and policy recommendations presuppose, becomes problematic. The point is that neoclassical optimisation requires an insight into the effects of alternative behaviour towards Nature with a probability bordering on

Plate 5.3 Port Talbot, in South Wales, United Kingdom. Extremely severe pollution from industrial plants here not only falls on residential areas, causing increased local incidence of illness, but is also carried long distances, thereby contaminating both the land and the sea. Photo: David Hoffman/Environmental Picture Library

certainty or at least with a probability that can be calculated using the theory of probabilities. The former is the familiar assumption of the existence of fully informed agents and simply ignores the problem of inadequate ecological knowledge.

For various reasons ecosystems can change far more capriciously than economists normally assume. Thresholds, synergetic effects and delayed effects cloud the issue of the relations between emissions and the deterioration of Nature (see Box 4). The neoclassical approach to optimising the use of natural resources is therefore pointless, as the quantity of the natural resources available cannot be accurately assessed, at least not at present. In other words, we cannot optimise the use of natural resources as long as we do not know the specific limits beyond which irreversible effects on Nature will occur. Again, we meet with uncertainty, although in this case its importance is less obvious (though no less relevant).

These arguments all influence the political bargaining process. An additional factor is the fact that industries are in a privileged position with respect to governments. If a polluting industry in a certain country has been able to build up a comfortable competitive position by discharging polluting substances into the air free of charge, such an industry will put pressure on the national authorities in order not to have to relinquish this position. Other forms of pressure can also no doubt be exposed. Suffice it to say, however, that negotiations seeking to protect and maintain common pool resources have to align many conflicting interests. They are therefore difficult to conduct and may well take a long time before being completed.

4

Problems of prediction

In general, processes in Nature, and hence human interventions in these processes, are extremely difficult to predict for at least three reasons. Firstly, *synergetic effects* increase the impact of individual emissions on the environment. For example, laboratory experiments have shown that the combined impact on plant growth of the acidifying substances SO_2, NO_x and NH_3, together with ozone, is substantially more severe than the sum total of the impacts of each of these substances separately (Tonneijck, 1981).

Secondly, *thresholds* are very common in ecosystems. Again, acidification serves as an excellent example. As far as most people were concerned, the sudden acceleration in the deterioration of forests and the subsequent death of large tracts of European forest at the beginning of the 1980s came like a bolt from the blue. Apparently, the buffering capacity of the soil had protected trees from serious damage for decades. Once a saturation point was reached, acidifying substances could cause considerable damage to trees, making them vulnerable to many plagues and insects and resulting in so low a resistance to normal conditions that some trees died in just a few years.

Thirdly, many emissions have a *delayed effect* on the environment. It takes decades, for example, before the nitrogen from manure and chemical fertilisers is washed from the top soil into deeper layers, causing severe nitrate pollution of the groundwater, which in most countries is used as a source of drinking water. Even if nitrogen leakages into the groundwater could be stopped, nitrate pollution of groundwater would still continue to increase considerably well into the next century.

In order to gain a better insight into how such negotiations are fed by national policies and how they, in turn, feed into national policies, we will now turn to a discussion of Dutch national policies from the 1980s onwards.

5.4 Dutch acid rain policies

Prior to 1970, air pollution was regarded principally as a threat to public health. In industrialised regions, emissions of SO_2 in particular caused high concentrations of pollutants in residential areas. The aim of the abatement policy was to reduce these concentrations. One so-called solution involved the construction of tall chimneys. However, the total level of emissions increased considerably as a result of constantly increasing production and so pollution spread to all parts of Europe. Measures were taken to clean up the unhealthy residential areas in the London metropolitan region, the Ruhr industrial area in Germany and the Rijnmond region in The Netherlands. In addition, the increased use of natural gas instead of coal and oil and the beginning of the recession in the 1970s lowered emissions of SO_2 (see Zwerver *et al.*, 1984). Yet these measures did not have any positive effect on the acidification of the lakes in Sweden; there was no sound abatement policy.

The massive death of forests in Western Germany led to a sharp reaction in The Netherlands, especially when the same phenomenon became evident in The Netherlands itself at the beginning of the 1980s. The abatement of acid rain became a major political issue. It was recognised that an effective decrease in emissions of acidifying substances would come about only as a result of strict measures. The introduction of such a policy caused many conflicts with vested interests in certain economic sectors. An analysis of these conflicts can provide an insight into the way in which policy on acid rain was effected in The Netherlands. Special attention will be given to the fashion in which polluters tried to influence the format of abatement policies. They used the same type of arguments and mechanisms as were described in the previous section on international negotiations.

As can be seen from Figure 5.1, the deposition of acidifying substances in The Netherlands decreased by approximately 15% between 1980 and 1990. The most important substances were nitrogen oxides (NO_x), sulphur dioxide (SO_2) and ammonia (NH_3). The decrease in the deposition of acidifying substances was chiefly the result of a decrease in the emission of SO_2.

An Air Pollution Act took effect at the end of the 1960s. Under the new act, the Minister of the Environment was made responsible for publishing periodically an Indicative Long-Term Programme for the abatement of air pollution, indicating how government policy on the abatement of air pollution is to be realised.

Until 1984, these programmes followed a strict neoclassical approach. Cost-benefit analyses were undertaken so as to find the optimum pollution level. In 1984, a different point of reference was chosen, i.e. an ecological limiting condition of 1800 acid equivalents per hectare per year. Instead of performing a cost-benefit analysis, an ecological standard was adopted. The idea was that the disruption of ecosystems should be stopped, regardless of the outcome of an analysis of the balance between costs and benefits. The introduction of this standard represented a fundamental change

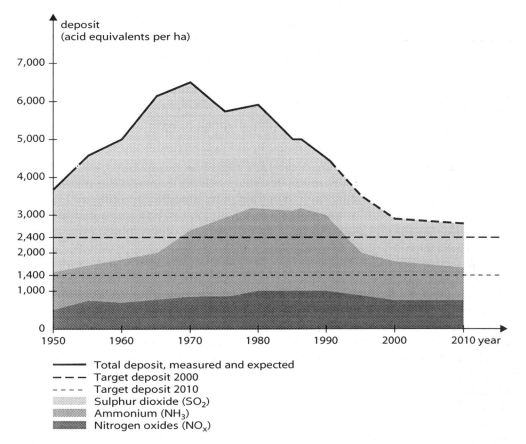

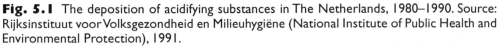

Fig. 5.1 The deposition of acidifying substances in The Netherlands, 1980–1990. Source: Rijksinstituut voor Volksgezondheid en Milieuhygiëne (National Institute of Public Health and Environmental Protection), 1991.

in viewpoint and policy. Meanwhile, the level of total emissions in the course of time was not influenced by this change in paradigm at the Ministry of the Environment. One may conclude that the policy and the measures taken were not effectively influenced by the opinions of the Ministry of the Environment, but that other factors created the actual policy. The question therefore arises as to which factors were dominant in this process of collective decision making. An outline is given below of the most important decisions which were taken on acid rain during the 1980s. This is followed by an evaluation of Dutch abatement policy, focusing on the factors which were dominant in the process of collective decision making.

Summary of policy measures in The Netherlands

The emission of nitrogen oxides by *motor vehicles* is a problem that is virtually global in its extent. If abatement measures are to be successful, international co-ordination is almost always inevitable. An apt example is provided by the introduction of the catalytic converter, a device that reduces nitrogen oxide emissions. Catalytic converters require unleaded fuel, which therefore had to be introduced in all European countries. The problem of its introduction was tackled by the European Union, but a solution was hindered by the divergent nature of the interests of the European countries. The result, after many years of negotiation, was the introduction of a rule that every new car should be fitted with a catalytic converter. The position of The Netherlands was interesting in this respect. On the one hand, the Dutch government posed as a champion of the environment by giving a tax rebate to buyers of cars fitted with catalytic converters. On the other hand, the Volvo plant in The Netherlands, which was unable at the time to produce cars fitted with catalytic converters, was granted a substantial subsidy to protect it against the effects of the various international agreements. This subsidy amounted to donating 400 (Dutch) Guilders to every buyer of a Volvo car (Dietz *et al.*, 1991). High levels of unemployment in the region and previous state support for the Volvo plant were used as arguments to justify this subsidy.

In the *agricultural sector* a Pig and Poultry Farms Act was introduced at the end of 1984. The law was the combined product of the Ministry of the Environment and the Ministry of Agriculture and so included a large number of temporary provisions. Due to the influence of the Minister of Agriculture, these provisions were made so weak that farmers were able to increase production by 30% in the next three years. This act was a piece of interim legislation. It was followed by the Manure Act, which became effective in 1987. This law laid down limits for the total amount of manure which could be spread on the land. Each farmer now has to account for the total quantity of manure produced on his farm. If there is a surplus, it has to be taken to a central agency, which then passes it on to one or more farmers who have a manure shortage (see Chapter 1 for a detailed analysis of this issue).

This law did not have a positive effect on the total amount of ammonia discharged in the agricultural sector. The manure is taken from areas where there is a surplus to areas where there is a shortage yet this does not reduce the total amount of manure, nor does it diminish aggregate ammonia emissions. The idea in the future is for the surplus to be taken to factories where it can be converted into dry compost. Unfortunately, this treatment is very expensive, so much so that such measures are unlikely to solve the problems. In spite of all these measures, programmes, memoranda and laws, every year brings a higher discharge of ammonia than the preceding year. The most important factor in this respect has been the position taken by the Ministry of Agriculture, which has been able to frustrate every measure to reduce the emission of ammonia.

Oil refineries are infamous for their massive discharges of SO_2. The emissions are caused by the sulphur in the crude oil processed by the refineries. In The Netherlands, discharges of sulphur dioxide were lowered by 35% during the period from 1980 to 1989, a rate which was substantially lower than that achieved by power plants, another important producer of sulphur dioxide. Why is this? In order to answer this question, we need to take account of the development of the market for refinery products. The demand for lighter fractions has been increasing for several years and both Shell and Esso have built new refineries in the Rotterdam region to meet this demand.

Esso's Flexicooker refinery started production in 1986. In 1980, Esso was discharging a total of 28,000 tonnes of sulphur dioxide on an annual basis. Esso has stated that the Flexicooker refinery will have the effect of reducing the discharge to just 6000 tonnes. Furthermore, the investment which is needed to reduce these discharges is a profitable one. This means that a considerable reduction in sulphur dioxide emissions can be realised without real cost to the refinery (De Bruin and Van Ooyen, 1986).

Shell's position is completely different. Shell discharged 64,500 tonnes of sulphur dioxide in 1980, 58,000 tonnes in 1981 and 59,000 tonnes in 1982. In 1983, however, the figure shot up to 70,000 tonnes (Rijnmond Region Public Authority, 1983; Fransen, 1985). In 1983, Shell decided to build a new refinery (based on the Hycon process) and requested permission to do so from the local authority for the Rijnmond region (near Rotterdam). Initially, the local authority was willing to grant such permission only if the permit included strict emission limits for sulphur dioxide. Shell replied that such limits would force them to build the new factory elsewhere in Europe, as it would be impossible to comply with the limits. Shell was subsequently granted the relevant permit, but with less stringent emission limits attached to it. In 1985, Shell requested a new permit for all its refineries in the Rijnmond area, which it needed as a result of market developments. Shell now stated that the emission limit for the new Hycon refinery should be 53,000 tonnes of SO_2. Compared with the level of emissions at Esso's Flexicooker refinery, this was still an extremely high level. The local authority in Rijnmond again insisted on a stricter (i.e. lower) limit, but the Minister of the Environment, under pressure from the Minister of Economic Affairs, came to Shell's rescue and agreed to allow the relatively high emission levels (Barmentlo, 1988).

The high level of emissions built into the permit granted to the Shell refinery still has a great influence on the current level of emissions in The Netherlands. Moreover, this information is well known among polluting industries and places them in a comfortable position to use the international competitiveness argument even where there is no real need to do so. The agricultural sector in The Netherlands has been able, for instance, to emit an increasing percentage of the total amount of emissions, as Figure 5.1 demonstrates. The farming sector has frequently used the international competitiveness argument in this debate.

Power plants discharge significant amounts of NO_x and SO_2. It has been the Dutch government's stated policy in recent years to reduce emissions of both nitrogen oxides and sulphur dioxide. As far as nitrogen oxides are concerned, government policy has not had any effect. Why? The price of electricity is the key to the answer here. It affects the competitiveness of Dutch industry in many export markets. By keeping the price of electricity lower than in Germany, where environmental standards are stricter than in The Netherlands (Olthof, 1988), the Dutch were able to secure a competitive edge for their industry. Clearly, competitiveness was given overriding attention when measures to abate the emission of nitrogen oxides were discussed.

The same type of picture can be seen with respect to the reduction of sulphur dioxide emissions, although substantial reductions have been achieved here. In 1980, the Minister of Economic Affairs, who is responsible for electricity distribution, published a paper 'The Coal Memorandum'. This basically outlined the government's decision to diversify the country's energy sources. It argued for the reintroduction of coal-fired power plants. The environmental movement was successful in its campaign to have strict emission limits laid down in the memorandum, leading not only to low levels of sulphur dioxide emissions but also to higher electricity prices. However, it was not industry that had to foot the bill, but households. Indeed, industries got a substantial rebate so that, effectively, electricity prices remained unaltered for them. The government argued that it was this that allowed industry to stay competitive internationally. Clearly, traditional economic arguments were given a higher priority than environmental interests.

An evaluation of Dutch acid rain policy

The abatement policy on acid rain has been largely ineffective. Without exception, the Dutch government has protected polluting industries, i.e. exporters, motor manufacturers, refineries, particularly Shell, and the agricultural sector. This has resulted in significant damage being caused to ecosystems, damage which cannot be monetarised. Additionally, a cost of many billions of guilders has been imposed every year on non-polluting sectors of the Dutch economy.

The level of this damage justifies strict measures. The introduction of the ecological limit of 1800 acid equivalents in 1984 did not have any effect at all. The dominance of traditional economic interests was so great that such standards were relegated to the sidelines.

These examples clearly demonstrate that, although sound plans for abating environmental disruption may be proposed, other factors become more important when actual decisions need to be taken. This is not surprising. A mixture of theoretical economic insights and institutional factors form the basis for this behaviour. On the one hand, the production factors of labour and capital occupy such a strong position in the state machinery that a sound environmental policy can be implemented only once the representatives of both labour and capital are convinced that such a policy will benefit them. On the other hand, the ideas about theoretical economic issues which are promulgated by opinion makers representing labour and capital are not generally in line with the needs of environmental protection. Economics deals with factors such as the growth of production, the mobility of production factors, the government budget, the level of profits, employment, interest rates, etc. Nature and the environment are not seen as important economic production factors that are comparable with labour and capital. In some cases, Nature and the environment are even viewed as limiting factors, which can be put aside when more 'real' economic variables become relevant.

The level of Dutch emissions is substantially higher than the level of depositions in The Netherlands (Van der Straaten, 1990). This implies that The Netherlands is a net exporter of acid rain, a point which has not received any proper attention in Dutch politics. This demonstrates that international complications are given a low profile by the Dutch government, thus enabling it to adopt a more comfortable position in the international arena than its record really merits.

5.5 Conclusion

It is obvious from the previous sections that there is a problem in the distribution of costs and benefits among different groups of society. If the intensive cattle-farming sector, for instance, is able to maintain the same level of emissions while other sectors such as oil refineries and power plants are forced to reduce considerably their emissions, this will impose relatively high costs on the latter sectors. In the intensive cattle-farming sector, the production costs are passed on to other sectors or to other countries. In most situations, this would be a domestic problem as national authorities are traditionally responsible, from a political point of view, for the distribution of costs and benefits in society.

However, this problem has become more and more of an international one due to the transboundary nature of acid rain. International bargaining and co-operation are necessary if environmental problems are to be solved. This opens up the possibility of the national authorities, which are the negotiators in an international bargaining process, being pressured in order to ensure that they secure good results that favour their own polluting industries. One should not forget that the polluting sectors are not the same in all European countries. In The Netherlands, for instance, intensive cattle farming is a more important factor than in other European countries. The percentage of nuclear power plants is relatively high in France, while lignite-fired power plants are more common in Germany. This implies that strategies to reduce emissions by lignite-fired power plants will influence the German economy more than the French one. Additionally, some countries are more advanced in terms of technology and this may place them in a better starting position if certain reductions have to be achieved.

The difference in the vulnerability of national ecosystems to acidification means that some countries suffer more from acid rain than others. The soil in countries, such as Germany, The Netherlands, Sweden, Austria and Switzerland, is such that it does not neutralise acid precipitation. Alkaline soils are better equipped to do this. In other words, the countries which suffer most from acid rain do their utmost to place the acidification problem on the international agenda, whilst others which are less affected tend to play down the problem.

In this debate, traditional economic arguments are used to neutralise the relevance of natural resources (such as forests, ecosystems and nature reserves) as production factors in favour of labour and capital. The recommendations made by economic theories for calculating the social cost of external effects and incorporating them in the burden of polluting industries completely overlooks the difficulties associated with a situation in which there are no markets. Thus, the interests of polluting industries are generally given too much weight compared with the unpriced natural resources.

The uncertainties which are normal in ecosystems are completely different from the uncertainties in traditional economic theories. In many cases, it is not clear what the effects of a certain type of pollution will be in the long run. These uncertainties are often used by polluters to neutralise environmental policies. They claim, for instance, that more research is needed to gain greater insight into the complexity of the ecosystem. In the meantime, however, the polluting activities continue or increase and cause ever more damage to the ecosystem. As has already been argued, acid rain is an international problem which cannot be solved without international co-operation. However, even the plea for international co-operation leads, in most cases, to long delays in the implementation of strict limits.

Traditional conflicts in modern societies are generally focused on income levels among different groups of society, the level of unemployment and public spending on certain public goods. Certain social mechanisms have been constructed over a long period for debating these problems and for finding political solutions based on the

149

power of interest groups in society. However, the distribution of the costs and benefits of an abatement policy on acid rain is such a relatively new phenomenon that there is no institutional framework for solving the problem. International problems are more difficult to discuss and to tackle than national problems and institutional mechanisms for solving acid rain problems are very scarce in the international arena. This means that international negotiations are particularly difficult. New arrangements and institutional frameworks have to be constructed. As long as the economic interests of the European countries remain divergent, this task will be far from easy.

This process of shifting the burden of the abatement policy to other groups in the same state, to other nations by exporting acid rain and refusing to reduce emissions, or to other generations by neglecting the problem, is a normal political issue. The aim of politics is, after all, to maximise the gains to individuals and groups from the national wealth and income and to minimise the costs which have to be incurred in order to obtain these results. This is exactly what happens when acid rain comes up for discussion. All the groups in one country and all countries use the same approach and this results in long processes of negotiation in which reductions in emission levels are difficult to achieve.

6

Transboundary transfers of hazardous and radioactive wastes

Andrew Blowers

6.1 The creation of the problem

At the end of the 1980s a number of incidents drew international attention to the problem of the transportation, management and disposal of hazardous and radioactive wastes. I shall begin with a discussion of three notorious examples of the problem. These examples primarily serve the purpose of identifying some of the issues that arise from the deliberate (legal or illegal) physical international transfers of hazardous and radioactive wastes. They provide an empirical background to the analysis that follows.

Case 1 The Khian Sea

In August 1986 the *Khian Sea,* which came to be called the 'leper of the oceans', left Philadelphia laden with 15,000 tonnes of municipal incinerator ash. Its voyage resembled that of the Flying Dutchman doomed to range the seas in search of a haven to land its cargo. Its various stops included Fort Lauderdale (Florida, USA) Puerto Rico, the Antilles, the Dominican Republic, Jamaica, Panama and the Cayman Islands before it dumped 2000 tonnes on the shore in Haiti in January 1988. The description of the cargo had changed during the voyage from non-hazardous ash to 'general cargo' to 'bulk construction material' and finally to 'top soil ash fertiliser'. This created a strong reaction and led to studies recommending the removal of the dumped material (Hilz, 1992, p. 26). It appears that subsequently the *Khian Sea* wandered the oceans, changed its name twice and dumped the remainder of its cargo presumably in the ocean and eventually arrived off Singapore, unladen and with a new name (*Pelicano*) in November 1988.

This case raises three issues. One is the failure to describe the wastes as hazardous though they may contain hazardous materials. Second is the unclear and false descriptions of the cargo that were given at different times. And third is the problem of ultimately preventing such cargoes from being dumped either on land or at sea. These issues of *falsification* and *dumping* are also clear in the second case.

Case 2 Toxic wastes to Koko, Nigeria

Between 1987 and 1988 shipments amounting to about 4000 tonnes of mixed chemical wastes, including about 150 tonnes of highly toxic PCBs, had been exported to Nigeria from Italy and were stored in drums on a site near the river port of Koko. An Italian businessman had persuaded a local landowner to store them at a cost of US$100 a month. In collaboration with a local firm, health inspectors and customs officers, he was able to gain the necessary documents. Once on site some of the drums began to smell and leak; reports of premature births and deaths from contaminated rice followed. A major risk to health and the environment had been introduced as a result of collusion and corruption involving businessmen and officials.

Nigerian students in Italy revealed the dumping, much to the embarrassment of the Nigerian government which had been prominent in condemning dumping in neighbouring countries and had promoted a resolution against dumping passed by the Organisation of African Unity (OAU). In the wake of a potential political backlash Nigeria announced the evacuation of Koko, imposed the death penalty for importers of toxic wastes, arrested 40 people for conspiring to bring the waste into the country, recalled her ambassador to Italy and seized a Danish ship that had conveyed some of the wastes and an Italian ship in harbour in Lagos. After negotiations conducted against the backcloth of international media attention the mixed and dangerous cargo was transferred from Koko to two ships (causing severe symptoms to some of the dock workers) bound for Italy.

The story did not end there. One of the ships, the *Karin B* (see Plate 6.1) was initially refused entry to Ravenna as a result of strong local opposition. The ship tried

Plate 6.1 Toxic waste carrier Karin B. Photo: Miguel Greino, Environmental Picture Library

unsuccessfully to land the cargo in the Canary Islands and Cadiz, was banned from British ports, prevented from entering French territorial waters before eventually being allowed, with the other ship, the *Deep Sea Carrier*, to unload in Ravenna in December 1988. The wastes were ultimately incinerated in the UK.

Apart from demonstrating the problems of illegal transfer of wastes, this case highlights two other features of the politics of hazardous wastes. One is the *opposition* aroused by such transfers which is both local and fuelled by the media and publicity by NGOs. This has the effect of severely limiting the legal options for disposal of wastes. The other feature is the tendency for wastes to be dumped on poor or powerless communities or countries. In this case the conflict was aroused between the advanced industrial nations (represented by Italy), which produce the bulk of such wastes, and the developing countries which, intentionally or illegally, become the dumping grounds for such wastes (if the price is high enough). The trade in hazardous wastes is a case of *externalities* being exported from richer to poorer countries and it has led to the establishment of international agreements to regulate and control the trade.

Case 3 Radioactive wastes from Sellafield, UK

The international trade in radioactive materials has also had major political implications as the following example demonstrates.

Sellafield, on the coast of West Cumbria in England, is the centre for the UK's main nuclear reprocessing operations. At this complex spent fuel is brought in from power stations mainly in the UK but increasingly from overseas countries, particularly Germany and Japan. Here it is stored and then chemically processed to extract out the plutonium and uranium it contains. The plutonium was initially needed for the weapons programme but subsequently it was envisaged as the fuel input for the new fast breeder reactor programme. With the ending of the Cold War and demilitarisation the military demands have been reduced; with the abandonment of the breeder reactor programme there is no obvious civil market for these products (apart from possible use in mixed oxide fuels, MOX, which in the early 1990s was more expensive than natural uranium fuel). Consequently there is a surplus of plutonium which, along with the continuing production from reprocessing, must be managed in some way. In addition, substantial volumes of radioactive wastes (some of them plutonium contaminated) which arise from reprocessing must also be managed. These problems of managing radioactive materials and wastes have been a major source of political debate and conflict in the UK since the early 1980s.

Moreover, the problem is not confined to the UK. With the need for plutonium and enriched uranium vanished, the main justification for reprocessing has been as a method for managing nuclear waste and attracting foreign customers and income. Thus the £2.5 billion thermal oxide reprocessing plant (THORP) was approved in 1978 at a time when a continuing and increasing demand for plutonium was foreseen. By 1994, when it was finally commissioned, British Nuclear Fuels (BNFL) emphasised the £500 million profits already secured and the potential future earnings that could be achieved through gaining foreign contracts. Sellafield (along with Cap de La Hague, near Cherbourg in France) had become the focus for an increasing foreign trade in plutonium and radioactive wastes.

The transboundary movement of radioactive wastes identifies several issues for international environmental policy making. First, the trade is determined by the

Plate 6.2 Vacated housing at Love Canal

policies of individual nation states and not subject to international agreement or supervision. Secondly, the trade identifies conflicts between environmental interests as expressed by local groups or NGOs and the economic (and, to an extent, military) interests of certain countries. Third, the trade is restricted to a very few industrialised countries (trade from reprocessing is at present only generated in the UK, France and Russia) but its environmental impacts can be far reaching. Fourth, plutonium is now in oversupply and could be regarded as a waste rather than a product. Its existence potentially poses the threat of nuclear proliferation which could lead to greater global political instability. The break-up of the Soviet Union has led to a nefarious trade in plutonium and uranium which may contribute to the nuclear weapon-making capacity of several states or add to the threats of international terrorism. Finally, the problem of managing radioactive wastes may impose risks and costs that are borne by specific communities but which also extend down to future generations. Inequalities in risks raise major policy issues of equity in the management of radioactive materials.

Issues

These examples point to a number of issues. First, they show *trade* in its capacity of a means of transferring environmental problems between countries; and they identify *wastes* as a cause of such problems. Second, they raise questions of *equity* which, in the case of hazardous wastes, have a geographical dimension between North and South or, in the case of radioactive wastes, an additional temporal dimension between present and future generations. Trade and equity issues create conflicts between environmental and economic interests. The outcome of these conflicts in terms of policy reflects the relative power commanded by different interests.

In this chapter I attempt to throw further light on the key question for this book: *What are the causes of international environmental problems, and what are the conflicts surrounding their definition and potential solution?* To that end I shall analyse the causes of political conflicts over the trade in wastes, the power of the interests involved and the policy outcomes. There are three parts to this analysis. In the first part (section 6.2) I shall define the nature of hazardous and radioactive wastes and distinguish the environmental problems caused by them. In the second part (section 6.3) I shall consider the sources of conflict over the management of hazardous wastes and the interests that are involved. In the third part (section 6.4), the outcomes of conflicts will be evaluated in terms of international agreements that have been reached. The concluding portion of the chapter (section 6.5) returns to the key question for the book and focuses on conflicts of interest and the exercise of political power.

6.2 The anatomy of the problem

An immediate difficulty with wastes is defining the problem. Waste is usually defined by exclusion, by what it is not. In this definition waste is any material in liquid, gaseous or solid form that is unwanted and unused in the production process. The OECD has defined wastes quite simply as 'materials … intended for disposal for specified reasons'(OECD, 1988).

Wastes are, therefore, the back-end of the cycle of production whereby energy is applied to transform natural resources into food or into material or non-material (e.g. electricity) products for human consumption. But the definition is not so straightforward as it seems. The distinction between wastes and products is not always clear. This is especially so when it is not clear whether the discarded materials may, at some stage, be reused or recycled. The distinction is often made between wastes for disposal and wastes for recovery. The latter are excluded from international agreements even though there may be little prospect of them being returned to the production process. The ambiguity surrounding definitions of waste makes effective regulation and control very difficult.

The definition of hazardous wastes

The problem is compounded when it comes to attempting to classify wastes. Wastes become a problem when they are harmful to the environment or to human health. They become *hazardous* wastes. These are defined as 'waste that has physical, chemical or biological characteristics that cause or contribute to threats to human health (leading to serious illness or death), or adversely affect the environment when improperly managed' (Cutter, 1993, p.114). There is considerable confusion in vocabulary since hazardous wastes may embrace a range of definitions relating to their nature (e.g. toxic wastes, dangerous wastes, special wastes), their legal category (e.g. controlled waste) or the problems of managing them (e.g. difficult wastes)(see Box 1). This chapter is concerned

---

Hazardous wastes – definitions and categories

In the UK, *controlled wastes* are so-called because they are subject to control as household, industrial or commercial waste under the Environmental Protection Act of 1990. These wastes are now known as *directive wastes* since the definition of waste under the European Directive 91/156/EEC has been applied to ensure a single definition of waste throughout the EU. This directive defines wastes as 'any substance or object – which the producer or the person in possession of it discards or intends or is required to discard'. The substances included and the exceptions are defined in schedules to the regulations.

It is clear that the directive perceives waste as posing a threat to human health or the environment arising 'from the fact that the producers of the substances or objects concerned will normally no longer have the self interest necessary to ensure the provision of appropriate safeguards'.

○ *Special wastes* is a category of controlled waste statutorily defined as waste which 'is or may be so dangerous or difficult to dispose of that special provision is required for its disposal'. Such wastes may be defined by reference to certain properties such as flammability, carcinogenicity, corrrosivity and toxicity. They are wastes that contain substances that are dangerous to life or have a flashpoint of 21°C or less or are medicinal products available only on prescription.

○ *Toxic wastes* is a loose definition referring to those wastes which have toxic properties.

○ *Hazardous wastes* are defined under EEC directives as wastes which are hazardous because of their physical or chemical characteristics, the process by which they were produced or their effects on human health and the environment. Among the categories of wastes defined in the directive are contaminated materials, unusable parts, residues of various kinds, adulterated materials, products for which the holder has no further use, ending with the all-encompassing 'any materials, substances or products which are not contained in the above categories' (Directive 91/156/EEC).

Other terms such as *difficult wastes* or *clinical wastes* are also sometimes used but they have largely been subsumed under the more precisely defined regulations and lists presented by the Department of the Environment and the EEC.

Source: BMA (1991).

---

with hazardous wastes rather than wastes in general or toxic substances used in production, though there is some common ground in dealing with the problems.

Hazardous wastes arise from the manufacture of chemical substances used in a variety of industries. Hazardous wastes may be defined by listing of specific substances. The UK Department of the Environment provides a 'Red List' of substances defined by toxicity, persistence in the environment and bio-accumulation (potential for concentration in the food chain). The EC similarly defines 'hazardous waste' as wastes on a list which takes into account various properties. The OECD gave a rough estimate that in the late 1980s there were 338 million tonnes of hazardous wastes produced, of which 275 million came from the United States and 24 million from western Europe.

Over 50% were chemicals. The major categories of hazardous wastes in Europe were solvents, waste paint, heavy metals, acids and oily wastes.

Various international agreements have attempted to specify the categories and characteristics of hazardous wastes. Nevertheless there remain inherent problems of definition and classification which have the following consequences. First, it is difficult to distinguish between substances which are waste and those which have potential use. Thus, some substances which should be treated as wastes may, instead, be treated as products. In particular under international agreements it is possible to export waste for recycling. Second, there can be inconsistencies in classification leading to incorrect or imprecise labelling of wastes. Third, in order to be inclusive, definitions may become excessively vague. For instance, under the Basel Convention (which will be considered in Section 6.4) hazardous wastes can include any wastes considered hazardous by the domestic legislation of the party of export, import or transit. Again, this can lead to inconsistent approaches to hazardous waste management. Fourth, there may be deliberate false labelling of wastes as in the case of the *Khian Sea* (see case 1 above).

The classification of radioactive wastes

Radioactive wastes are in a category of their own in terms of definition, classification and management. Although hazardous, dangerous and sometimes toxic, these wastes are treated quite separately from all other hazardous wastes. Radioactive wastes arise from the various stages of the nuclear cycle (in particular as tailings from uranium mining, as spent fuel from nuclear reactors and as various waste streams from reprocessing operations). Radioactive wastes can occur in liquid, gaseous or solid forms. There is no common international classification of radioactive wastes; instead there are different national classifications based on sources, disposal routes and levels of radioactivity. However, the classification systems are broadly comparable (see Box 2).

Radioactive wastes are a source of radioactivity which arises from the radionuclides contained in the waste stream. These radionuclides vary in terms of their *longevity* (defined as half-lives to measure the rate of radioactive decay), their *activity* (the number of radioactive emissions per second measured in terms of becquerels – 1 Bq is one spontaneous transformation per second – which have replaced curies as the commonly accepted measurement), their *type* (alpha, beta or gamma) and their *biochemical properties*. For example, one of the most dangerous radionuclides is plutonium-239 which has a half-life of 24,000 years and is an alpha emitter. It is also highly toxic with a propensity to accumulate in the lungs and bone marrow. 'It has been said that it would be fairly safe to sit on a lump of plutonium wearing only a stout pair of jeans. On the other hand, it could be fatal to inhale even a very small particle of it' (HMSO, 1986, p.xvi).

As with hazardous wastes there is a problem in distinguishing radioactive substances which are wastes from those which are potential products. In the UK and France spent fuel is reprocessed as an integral part of the fuel cycle to extract uranium and plutonium. In these countries spent fuel is a resource whereas in the United States and other countries it is regarded as a waste to be disposed of. The same might now be said of plutonium, once a product in high demand. The ending of the

---

Classification of radioactive wastes

2

Radioactive wastes are defined by the International Atomic Energy Agency (IAEA) as 'any material that contains or is contaminated with radionuclides at concentrations or radioactivity levels greater than the "exempt quantities" established by the competent regulatory authorities and for which no use is foreseen'. The exempt wastes, below regulatory concern (brc), are deemed to represent an insignificant hazard to the environment and health and therefore can be managed as non-radioactive wastes. Radioactive wastes are classified according to:

○ *Source* – uranium mining, milling, fuel enrichment and fabrication, power production and reprocessing.
○ *Half-life* of the radioisotopes contained in the waste. This is a measure of radioactive decay, the length of time taken for a radionuclide to lose half its radioactivity. The basic distinction is between long-lived with half-lives of over 30 years and short-lived with under 30 years.
○ *Concentration* of radioisotopes. This leads to a classification based on activity level giving three categories – high, intermediate or low level wastes.
○ *Type of ionising radiation*. The three types are alpha radiation which is the least penetrating but very damaging to living cells, beta and gamma radiation which are very penetrating and which require heavy shielding to prevent them affecting external body surfaces.

The USA classifies wastes according to a combination of source, type and concentration. Most other Western countries use the following broad classification:

○ *High-level wastes (HLW)* are heat-generating wastes arising from spent fuel reprocessing in liquid or vitrified form or as solid spent fuel from nuclear reactors. They are long-lived with significant alpha radiation and are highly dangerous. They are low in volume (about 1.5% of the total) and high in radioactivity (around 99% of the total). The proposed method of ultimate management is deep geological disposal.
○ *Intermediate-level wastes (ILW)* are created during the process of energy production and reprocessing and include fuel cladding, control rods, filters, sludges and resins. They are subdivided into *long-lived ILW* with half-lives of over 30 years and mainly alpha emitters (requiring deep geological disposal) and *short-lived* (under 30 years half-life and mainly beta and gamma emitters).
○ *Low-level wastes (LLW)* are short-lived, high volume wastes arising from contamination of clothing, plastics, paper, debris and other materials during nuclear processes. In the UK it is estimated they account for about 84% of the volume but only around 0.1% of the total radioactivity.

Sources: IAEA (1992); Blowers *et al.* (1991).

Cold War and subsequent disarmament has left a surplus of nuclear warheads. Plutonium is no longer in demand for the fast breeder reactor programmes which have been abandoned in many countries. And, with low prices for natural uranium there is little demand for mixed oxide fuel (MOX) which uses plutonium. Plutonium is now in surplus. Stockpiles, estimated in 1992 at around 300 tonnes in the civil programme and as much as 1000 tonnes in the military sector, were still being added to by continuing reprocessing. With such a substantial overhang plutonium might be regarded as a waste product. But it remains a product in potential, if clandestine, demand for military purposes. The possibility of the proliferation of nuclear armaments poses a threat to world security and therefore the plutonium surplus must be carefully recorded and securely managed. An underground traffic in plutonium and uranium exists and quantities have disappeared from various stockpiles, notably in the former USSR.

From an international perspective the three key issues which arise from the problems of classifying radioactive wastes can be summarised as follows:

1 the difficulty of securing compatibility among diverse national systems of classification
2 the problem of distinguishing radioactive waste from radioactive resources
3 the danger that, as a result of miscalculation or corruption, radioactive wastes or plutonium may be unaccounted for and diverted for military purposes.

The environmental problems of hazardous wastes

Wastes are harmful when they become pollution. Pollution has been defined as 'The introduction ... into the environment of substances or energy liable to cause hazards to human health and harm to living resources and ecological systems, damage to structures or amenity, or interference with legitimate uses of the environment' (Holdgate, 1979, p.17). There are certain basic differences between the environmental risks from hazardous wastes and those from radioactive wastes.

Hazardous wastes are conveyed through environmental pathways of atmosphere and water or are transported in solid form on land or sea. They have a variety of environmental impacts. They can damage *amenity* through, for example, unpleasant odour or discoloration of watercourses or the dereliction caused by spoil heaps. They may also cause *ecological* damage through the pollution of the air and groundwater and the contamination of soil, rivers and oceans. This poses threats to *resources* and *biodiversity*. Some wastes may have a major impact on ecosystems. CFCs are a good example; they can deplete atmospheric ozone and contribute to the greenhouse effect thus having a major deleterious impact on global ecosystems.

Hazardous wastes also pose threats to human health either directly through contact and ingestion or indirectly through environmental impacts on the food chain. They can cause acute reactions (from mild symptoms such as nausea, dizziness or headache to severe conditions like paralysis and burns) and may, ultimately, lead to death. Some hazardous wastes may have carcinogenic effects or have long-term genetic impacts. But it is extraordinarily difficult to identify the precise causes and effects of hazardous wastes on human health; it is an area of great scientific uncertainty. Among the problems are that hazardous wastes are complex mixtures so that it is difficult to single out the impact of specific compounds; the level of hazard varies over time and place; individual exposures vary widely; the relationship between dose and response is difficult to evaluate and the toxicology is imperfectly understood for many chemicals entering the body.

159

The risks to human health from hazardous wastes have been underlined by a number of incidents. Two of the most well-known are outlined below.

Minamata Bay, Kyushu, Japan

For several years during the 1950s uncommonly large numbers of patients with neurological disorders (blindness, brain damage) were diagnosed; also by 1974 about 800 cases of poisoning and over 100 deaths had been recorded. In 1959 these cases were traced to fish and shellfish, common in the local diet, which had been contaminated by methyl mercury discharged from a fertiliser plant. The problem was initially brought to light by evidence collected by local doctors.

Love Canal, Niagara Falls, USA

For over two decades from 1930 the Hooker Chemical Company dumped about 21,000 tonnes of hazardous wastes (including benzene, toluene, chloroform, trichloroethylene) into an unfinished canal. The site was 'sealed' and 'reclaimed' and sold to the local school board who sold it in parcels and a new residential development was completed in the 1970s. Toxic fumes from the wastes began to seep up through the soil into the basements of homes, the soil became contaminated and there was great anxiety about the health effects as a variety of complaints, including various cancers, chromosome damage and low birthweight, were attributed to the wastes. The incidence and causes of these various health effects proved very difficult to determine. Nevertheless a vigorous local campaign by residents drew national attention to the issue, the site was evacuated and boarded up and for long remained a silent symbol of the problem of hazardous wastes. By 1990 the homes were being sold off as the area was declared clean and habitable again.

To these cases could be added other examples such as the explosion at Flixborough, UK, 1974 that killed 28 people and caused 3000 to be evacuated; dioxins in the air (Seveso, Italy, 1976) killing over 100,000 grazing animals and forcing 1000 people to flee; Cubatao, Brazil, in 1984 where a pipeline exploded killing at least 500; or methyl isocyanate escaping from the Union Carbide plant in Bhopal, India, in 1984, the biggest industrial disaster of all resulting in about 2500 deaths and thousands of injuries.

These incidents have served to draw international attention to the problems associated with hazardous substances whether from routine dumping as waste or from accidents during production. Some incidents are restricted to one country but others involve neighbouring countries, too. Together with the evidence of illegal and routine dumping of unwanted hazards on Third World countries (described at the beginning of the chapter) they have ensured that the issue of hazardous wastes has been politicised to the point where action both national and international is demanded.

The environmental problems of radioactive wastes

In certain respects radioactive wastes are uniquely hazardous. Radioactivity is invisible, pervasive and can be dangerous through proximity as well as through inhalation or ingestion. The risk varies according to type of radionuclide but some of the most dangerous have exceedingly long half-lives, to all intents and purposes remaining dangerous in perpetuity. Moreover, once radioactivity reaches the accessible environment (i.e. where it comes into contact with people through the food chain or in the air or water) its impacts are inevitable and irreversible.

The links between radioactivity and certain cancers and genetic effects are established though not fully understood. Indeed, the problem of confirming specific cause and effect is beset by a range of seemingly intractable problems. It is difficult to provide studies over sufficient time-scales, to create effective monitoring systems, to identify and isolate potential causes, to comprehend the pathology or to predict the impacts of particular doses on specific populations. An extensive study into the links between Sellafield and the incidence of local leukaemia clusters could only conclude that the link was 'not one which can be categorically dismissed, nor on the other hand, is it easy to prove' (Black, 1984).

Radioactivity occurs naturally as well as from nuclear facilities and weapons. Indeed, it is frequently pointed out (especially, it must be said, by the nuclear industry) that a very small proportion arises from the nuclear industry (just over 1%) with about a fifth coming from medical sources, especially X-rays. Natural background radiation accounts for most of the rest (apart from that occurring naturally within the body) coming from radon gas, cosmic rays and rocks and soils. However, nuclear facilities present a concentration of radioactive risk which is, in principle, avoidable.

It is the public anxiety surrounding radioactivity which places it in a unique category of hazardous activity. Opinion polls of public attitudes to nuclear issues require very careful interpretation. For example, nuclear waste was selected as the most important national environmental problem in Britain in two surveys taken in 1986 by the Department of the Environment (52% of respondents) and 1989 (18%)(HMSO, 1992, p.227). But, in another case, when people were asked to identify major problems, only 11% indicated environmental problems and when asked which kinds of pollution were of concern, only one in five of these mentioned nuclear power or waste (British Nuclear Forum poll, 1992).

How are we to interpret such figures? Obviously much depends on the nature of the questions asked and the context in which the enquiry is set. But, even allowing for this, we need to consider the following factors at least before reaching any conclusion. One is that environmental issues themselves are competing with other problems for attention and, though interest in them rises and falls, the state of the economy or health services tend to claim more consistent public attention. A second factor is that the problem of nuclear waste is very complex and quantitative polls cannot register the range of feelings and attitudes it engenders. They fail to 'capture the more subtle forming influences ... in the public perception of risk and risk-generating institutions' (Wynne *et al.*, 1993, p.24). Thirdly, another aspect of complexity is that both polls and the public fail to distinguish between different aspects of the nuclear industry or between different levels of risk. Thus, public anxiety is aroused by any nuclear facility (reactor, waste facility, reprocessing plant) whatever the level of risk involved. Fourthly, polls are inevitably selective and the information they yield can be used to support particular viewpoints. This is especially so in such a controversial area as the nuclear industry. In support of its case the nuclear industry points out that public support increases with greater familiarity with nuclear processes. On the other hand, opponents might argue that communities which are most familiar with nuclear power are likely to support it because they are economically dependent upon it.

As with hazardous wastes, anxiety about the nuclear industry has been fanned by a number of incidents. Among the most celebrated have been those outlined below.

Three Mile Island, Harrisburg, USA, 1979

Technicians were working on reactor 2 of the Three Mile Island plant during the night while it was on full power when vital cooling water supplies were cut off and began to drain out through a valve that had opened without being indicated in the control room. Since operators believed the cooling water system was functioning they shut off the emergency pumps, causing the reactor to overheat, coming close to meltdown. Although it was eventually brought under control the accident had caused over 100,000 people to flee from the surrounding area. It was a critical turning-point, undermining confidence in nuclear power and provoking adverse reactions to nuclear power in the USA and Europe.

Windscale/Sellafield, UK

There was a major fire at the Windscale plutonium production plant in 1957 causing considerable radioactive contamination in vegetation and milk supplies in the surrounding area. A catastrophe was averted by most of the radioactivity being trapped in the filter

Plate 6.3 Seascale village, with Sellafield nuclear reprocessing plant in the background. Photo: Morgan/Greenpeace

of the chimney at the plant; even so the full scale of the accident was kept from the public and not finally revealed until 30 years later. Since then there have been a number of incidents at the Sellafield complex, notably in 1973 when an old reprocessing plant caused contamination of workers and was shut down. A decade later the accidental discharge of radioactive 'crud' into the Irish Sea was discovered by Greenpeace and led to the closure of a local beach for 24 hours and warnings to the public not to use the beaches 20 miles in each direction for several months. These and other incidents, aside from authorised and routine discharges, were highlighted by the media and anti-nuclear groups, increasing public concern about nuclear operations at Sellafield and drawing international attention to the site.

Chernobyl, Ukraine, 1986

During the night shift on 26 April control rods were pulled out of the fourth reactor as part of a deliberate but unauthorised experiment and efforts to get the situation under control aggravated the problem, causing the reactor to go critical. The top of the reactor core heated up and as the pressure of hydrogen built up the ceiling cracked and the roof of the reactor building lifted off. The graphite in the core had caught fire and melted part of the fuel, propelling radioactive materials 5000 feet into the atmosphere. The radioactive cloud spread rapidly north-westwards, affecting a wide area of the Ukraine, Byelorussia, Russia and Northern Europe. The disaster was not publicised until high levels of radioactivity were recorded in Sweden. It was two days before the local town of Pripyat was evacuated and six before evacuation began at Chernobyl (population 40,000) ten miles away. Altogether nearly 100,000 people were evacuated and a large area was contaminated. The death and sickness toll resulting from the accident is gradually being revealed but the full dimensions cannot be calculated since the impact will extend over a wide area and over many generations. But Chernobyl was a defining moment for the nuclear industry, providing a demonstration of the catastrophic potential of a nuclear accident and also revealing 'the limitations of international policy for containing catastrophic risks, and some of the true costs of nuclear power' (Birnie and Boyle, 1992, p.348).

These (and to some extent other less publicised) incidents have helped to create the international political context for the nuclear industry. There is a recognition that, while the risks of a major accident may be statistically low, an accident, should it occur, can be catastrophic, a threat to health and possibly even survival over wide areas and many generations. Since the impact of such accidents can cross frontiers the safety of nuclear reactors constitutes an international problem.

The incidents have occurred as a result of the production of nuclear energy or reprocessing operations. They illustrate why nuclear risk is regarded with such alarm. They are intrinsically connected to radioactive waste, either as deliberate discharges into the environment (as at Sellafield) or as highly radioactive materials from the reactor core which are unusable and which must be managed (as at Three Mile Island and Chernobyl). The routine transport of nuclear wastes is also an integral part of the nuclear cycle. In some countries, particularly where spent fuel is destined for direct disposal, the complete cycle is contained within national territory (India, USA, Canada). But, in those countries which engage in reprocessing, international trade in spent fuel is encouraged.

163

The risks of accident, proliferation or routine impact on the environment or human health arising from this trade constitute an international problem.

So far I have examined the environmental problems created by hazardous and radioactive wastes and their international implications. In the next section I shall examine the various methods of dealing with these problems and the conflicting interests that result.

6.3 The management of wastes – conflicting interests

Hazardous wastes – the problem of management

Hazardous wastes are overwhelmingly produced in the advanced industrial countries. OECD estimates indicate that only 16 million tonnes out of a total of 338 million tonnes originated outside the OECD countries and Eastern Europe (OECD, 1991, p.146). Much of this waste is handled within the countries of origin and is either discharged to the atmosphere (through incineration) or the marine environment through pipelines, or landfilled. But these methods of managing wastes have become increasingly difficult.

In the first place, the siting of waste management facilities is almost always a source of local conflict. Opposition from environmental groups and local communities has made it increasingly difficult for existing facilities to remain open and almost impossible for new sites to be achieved for managing hazardous wastes. In the UK there has been continuing controversy over incineration of toxic waste which contributed to the shutdown of Rechem's plant at Bonnybridge in Central Scotland in 1984, prevented the development of Leigh International's proposed plants near Doncaster and at Trafford in England and continues to beset existing plants, notably the Rechem incinerator at Pontypool in Wales.

The UK has typically used landfills to dispose of much of the hazardous waste with the most toxic wastes being handled at a few sites such as Pitsea in Essex. Public concern has been developing over the dangers lurking in abandoned landfills. In 1990 a report drew attention to the 1300 sites from which toxic materials could be leaking into groundwater and identified 59 from which there was a serious risk of contamination (Friends of the Earth, 1990). Another report suggested there were 50,000–100,000 sites potentially contaminated and observed that there was no reason 'to be complacent about the quality of waste management in this country' (House of Commons Environment Committee, 1989–90, para 25).

Public concern has also contributed to a progressive tightening of legislation. In Germany, Sweden and the UK, for example, legislation to control hazardous wastes was initiated during the 1970s. In the UK the Environmental Protection Act of 1990 was a comprehensive (part consolidation and part initiation) piece of legislation which, among other things, embraced the concept of *integrated pollution control* (IPC). This introduces a cross-media approach bringing together the hitherto separate inspectorates for air pollution, radioactive substances, hazardous wastes and water quality. It inaugurates a much tougher regime of waste disposal including a 'duty of care' from cradle to grave binding all holders of waste to take all reasonable measures 'for ensuring that it does not escape from control, that it is transferred only to an authorised person and that it is adequately described to enable proper handling and treatment' (Department of the Environment, 1990). Meanwhile the EC had introduced a range of directives on waste from the early 1980s covering the reduction, recycling and safe disposal of wastes, asserting the polluter pays principle and ensuring adequate control of wastes during both transit and disposal. The EC was also intent on eliminating the co-disposal of liquid and hazardous wastes with domestic wastes in landfills, a common practice in the UK. Local, national and international pressures were combining to place a premium on hazardous waste disposal facilities.

These pressures inevitably helped to increase the costs of disposal. Costs have been increasing as a result of more rigorous monitoring and control and the costs of clean-up, as well as the shortage of suitable landfill sites and other disposal facilities. In the late 1980s it was estimated that the cost of disposing of domestic waste in New York was £80 per tonne, in Philadelphia £26.50 but in England and Wales with greater landfill availability the cost was only £5. The differences between industrialised and developing countries were even greater. For example, one estimate for the treatment of hazardous wastes, including PCBs, gives costs of up to US$3000 per tonne in the industrial countries but as little as US$2.50 per tonne when exported to developing countries. Such enormous differentials combined with diminishing availability of disposal facilities provide a singular incentive for waste producers in industrial countries to seek solutions elsewhere. Despite this, most hazardous waste is still handled within the industrialised world, the majority of it within the countries of origin (see Box 3).

Of the total trade one estimate suggests that as much as 80% is within the OECD countries. As much as 90% of the US export is estimated to go to Canada and 80% of West European trade is within Western Europe. For example, the UK with its sophisticated incineration plant and landfill capacity is a net importer of hazardous wastes coming from Switzerland, Belgium, Ireland, The Netherlands, Italy, Austria and other West European countries.

This trade among industrialised countries is justified on the grounds that it makes common sense for those countries (like the UK) with appropriate facilities to deal with hazardous wastes, especially from smaller countries which do not have the volumes to justify investment in appropriate facilities. But the trends are towards the reduction of such trade. One reason for this is public concern. This was demonstrated, for example, in 1989 when the attempted export of PCBs from Canada to Britain in Russian freighters was blocked after protests from Greenpeace. Another reason is the possibility of accidental releases. In Europe three such releases have had a significant impact on legislation. The Flixborough accident in 1974, mentioned earlier, led to reports that influenced the control of manufacture of dangerous chemicals. The 1978 accident at Seveso in Italy, when a cloud of poisonous chemicals was released and drums of waste disappeared, led to the EC's so-called Seveso Directive which laid down the controls necessary to prevent such accidents and to control the movement of wastes across borders. A decade later a fire at a chemicals plant in Basel caused 30 tonnes of poisonous chemicals to flow down the River Rhine and led to tighter controls on the storage of chemicals.

As concern about the implications of transboundary hazards has grown so the EC has moved towards asserting the *proximity principle* whereby 'waste must be disposed

Trade in hazardous wastes

According to OECD figures, in the late 1980s the largest exporters of hazardous waste were as follows:

	in tonnes	% of total produced in country
Germany	1,058,000	18
Netherlands	189,000	13
USA	127,000	n/a
Switzerland	108,000	27
Canada	101,000	3

Within the OECD the UK, France and Canada were among the net importers of hazardous wastes. The high German total of exports reflects trade to the neighbouring former GDR. Since reunification this trade is, of course, all within Germany. The major sources of UK imports in 1990/91 were as follows:

	in tonnes
Switzerland	13,550
Belgium	9,229
Ireland	3,986
Netherlands	3,949
Italy	3,583
Austria	2,912
Others (including Sweden, Spain, Portugal, Germany)	6,746
Total	43,955

Sources: OECD (1991); Environmental Data Services, June 1992.

of in the nearest suitable facility while making use of the most appropriate technologies to guarantee a high level of protection for the environment and public health' (European Parliament, 1990). However, this appears to conflict with the principle of the internal market which asserts the free movement of goods within the common market. The emphasis would therefore be on the prevention of waste, maximum recycling and the creation of an EC-wide infrastructure for safe disposal.

Hazardous waste – political conflicts

Despite these efforts there remains a volume of hazardous wastes that is not managed within the advanced industrial countries but which has been disposed of in one of two ways. One is by discharging wastes into the marine environment either from land-based sources by pipeline or by incinerating or dumping by ship in the ocean. This pollution of the global commons has provoked considerable international attention leading to the development of international policies. The interests of a few industrial-ised nations (and the companies which produce the wastes) in discharging unwanted wastes into the ocean directly conflicts with the common interest in preventing risks to the marine environment to present and future generations. This conflict of interests provides the motivation for attempts at international action to regulate, and possibly eliminate, the disposal of hazardous wastes in the marine environment which is the subject of section 6.4 of this chapter.

The second disposal route for hazardous wastes that are not managed within the advanced industrial countries, has been to export it for land disposal elsewhere. Reference was made earlier to this trade and examples were given at the beginning of this chapter. There have been basically two major trading flows of hazardous wastes. One has been from West to East and the extent of this trade has only recently been revealed with the collapse of the centrally planned regimes of Eastern Europe. According to one estimate, around 10–15% of West European export finds its way to Eastern Europe. Since the major recipient was East Germany, now incorporated into Western Europe, reunited Germany has inherited a substantial problem of toxic waste contamination.

The developing countries receive the remainder of the exported waste. The need for the rich countries to get rid of a problem matches the desire for profit by waste handlers

Plate 6.4 German pesticide waste on a train in Bazje, Albania. An example of waste dumped as 'humanitarian aid'. Photo: Vielmo/Greenpeace

and the need for economic investment in the poor countries. Estimates of total quantities vary and there are, of course, hazardous waste imports that go unrecorded. This export trade has been vilified as 'garbage imperialism' and is a clear example of the process of uneven development. Box 4 gives some examples of the export trade to developing countries.

The disposal of hazardous wastes into the marine environment or on land in developing countries have become matters of international conflict of interests. There

---

Exporting hazardous wastes   4

The case of dumping of toxic wastes in Nigeria from Italy carried by the *Karin B* is described at the beginning of the chapter. Some other cases include the following countries:

○ *Benin*. In late 1980s shipments of up to 5 million tons of toxic and mixed wastes were proposed at $2.50 per ton with a total value of $12.5 million to the economy. Radioactive wastes from the former USSR were discovered illegally buried below an airfield. Agreement was reached with France to undertake nuclear waste burial in exchange for cash and assistance.
○ *Guinea*. In 1988 15,000 tonnes of toxic incinerator ash were received from the USA but returned after international protest.
○ *Guinea-Bissau*. A $120 million contract (more than the country's annual budget) to store industrial wastes was rescinded after public outcry. A deal to take wastes from the USA and some European countries worth $600 million was also postponed.
○ *Djibouti* was the initial destination of 2400 tonnes of toxic waste from Italy in 1988. After refusal the cargo was transported to Venezuela and Syria, thence back to Italy and was finally incinerated in the UK.
○ *Gabon* has received nuclear wastes from Canada and the USA.
○ *Johnson Atoll* in the Pacific has become the site for the incineration of chemical weapons from the USA.

There are many other examples of such trade. Dumping by West European countries on their less developed East European neighbours is also commonplace. For example:

○ *Rumania, 1988*. Over 4000 tonnes of hazardous wastes containing PCBs from Italy, The Netherlands and West Germany were illegally dumped and leached into the Danube delta.
○ *Poland, 1988–9*. Incorrectly labelled barrels containing cyanamide, chlorinated solvents and PCBs were dumped by Austria.
○ *Germany*. The Schoenberg dump in former East Germany has received over a million tonnes of hazardous wastes each year since 1979 from West Germany, Austria, Italy and other European countries.

Dumping in Western countries is not unknown, as the following example indicates:

○ *Belgium, 1983*. 27,000 tonnes of toxic wastes were illegally dumped by a West German firm into an abandoned quarry at a considerable saving over disposal costs in Germany or France.

Sources: Blowers (1993), p.76; Cutter (1993), pp.137–8.

---

are various dimensions of conflict. The use of the oceans for dumping involves the global commons and a conflict between private, commercial or national interests in profit against the common interest in a healthy environment. It is a problem of global significance requiring international action in which conflicting interests must be reconciled. The dumping of wastes on developing countries also involves a variety of interests – private, national, local, global – in conflict. It also raises issues of development and distribution. While the environmental problems may be localised they have global ramifications, bringing the interests of the wealthy North into conflict with the poorer nations of the South. They may be seen as part of a broader, structural conflict that both reflects and reinforces patterns of uneven development. I shall return to these issues in concluding section of this chapter. By contrast, conflicts over radioactive waste are, to a large extent, still confined to the advanced industrial countries.

Radioactive wastes – the problem of management

Radioactive wastes pose somewhat different management problems. Once nuclear fission occurs, radioactivity is inevitable and constitutes a hazard in operating power stations, through the possibility of accidental emission and through the waste that is produced. Moreover, when a nuclear power station, reprocessing plant or other facility ends its useful life it must at some point be decommissioned and then itself adds to the accumulated burden of radioactive waste. After shutdown the spent fuel may be removed but the rest of the plant may be left to allow some radioactive decay so that dismantling may be safer. In the case of British nuclear power stations a period of up to 135 years has been considered before final decommissioning. Given the long time-scales involved in developing, operating and decommissioning nuclear plant, nuclear waste management raises questions of how we should deal with the problem of consigning present problems to future generations. Once we take into account the extremely long time periods over which radioactive decay takes place (in the case of some radionuclides sometimes stretching into many thousands, even millions of years) we are dealing with risks that are, to all intents and purposes, permanent. It is necessary, in the interests of sustainable development, to safeguard against such risks as far as possible. In short, these wastes pose a critical problem of how present society deals with the future. This is often called the problem of *intergenerational equity.*

Conventionally this problem is approached through the process of *discounting.* Discounting is both an accounting and an ethical issue and a subject of much debate. In accountancy terms it is a method of calculating investment preferences over time: it is a means of evaluating the opportunity costs of alternative investments. It does so by providing a measure of the present value of an investment needed in the future. In other words, it estimates what would have to be invested now to achieve a specified amount at a specified future date. The calculation is based on the recognition that present money values depreciate through inflation, so will be less in the future. To account for this a *discount rate* is applied. If an investment achieves a higher rate of return than the discount rate it will be deemed profitable and hence financially efficient.

The calculation will, of course, depend upon two judgements: one on the *time period* for the investment and the other the *discount rate* chosen. For example, at a 10% discount rate the present value of £1000 worth of costs or benefits three years ahead will be £729 (£1000 × 0.9³), whereas at a lower discount rate, say 5%, it will be higher (£1000 × 0.95³ = £857). If a longer time period is chosen the present value will also be lower. Using our example, over six years at a discount rate of 10% the value will be £478 (£1000 × 0.9⁶) and at 5% it will be £698 (£1000 × 0.95⁶). So, the higher the discount rate or the longer the time span, the less the future investment or cost is worth in present values. Thus for very long-term projects such as decommissioning a nuclear power station the present values are very low. If a typical power station in the UK is decommissioned after 135 years after shutdown (to allow for cooling, demolition of plant and removal of the reactor core prior to site restoration) the undiscounted costs of £370 million would be reduced to only £25 million if a 2% discount rate were used (working backwards, that is £25 million × 1.02^{135} = £370 million). The idea behind discounting the cost of decommissioning is to ensure that the present generation puts in place sufficient resources for the future generation to pay for the decommissioning when it falls due.

Over such long time-scales it seems clear that the future is literally discounted, i.e. valued much less than the present. This introduces ethical considerations. Long-term discounting could be justified on the basis that the future generations will be wealthier and have the technology able to cope with the problem more easily. They will gain the benefit of a technology whose research and development costs have been borne by the present generation. Conversely, it can be argued that there is no certainty that economic growth will be sustained even at the level of 2% necessary to ensure the funds will accumulate. Over such a long time span political stability cannot be assumed; in any case it is likely that the present institutional structure responsible for the nuclear industry will have changed or disappeared. Moreover, it is quite possible that nuclear technology will have been abandoned and thus the expertise involved in dealing with the problem will have been lost. In terms of sustainable development it would seem preferable, as far as possible, to avoid bequeathing incalculable risks to future generations. Over long time-scales it can be argued that the rational economic calculations involved in discounting procedures should surrender to the observation of ethical principles based on considerations of environmental safety and social equity.

Ethical considerations are also raised when it comes to the question of how to manage the total volumes of radioactive wastes arising. Certain management routes have already been effectively ruled out for environmental reasons. For a long time during the years when the nuclear industry was rapidly developing in advanced countries as a means of providing cheap, clean and safe electricity, the management of radioactive wastes was not an issue and, if it was considered at all, it was regarded as a technical matter. For many years nuclear wastes were left *in situ* or dumped in the oceans. The environmental legacy of inadequate storage on land is now evident in the risks of land contamination or threats to aquifers on the major military installations in the United States, at Hanford in Washington State and the Savannah River in South Carolina. Similar problems may be found in other countries and the extent of radioactive contamination of areas in the former Soviet Union has only recently come to light (see Box 5).

As the volumes of radioactive wastes accumulated and as environmental concerns began to develop so the issue of radioactive waste management became politicised and, one by one, options were cut off. First, *sea disposal* was abandoned. The United States,

Some radioactive waste problems **5**

Problems with nuclear power or reprocessing plants such as at Sellafield, UK, Three Mile Island, USA, and notably at Chernobyl, Ukraine, have been well publicised. But there have also been problems involving nuclear waste.

○ *Hanford, Washington State, USA.* Hanford is a large complex and the major centre for the production of nuclear weapons in the USA. There have been several incidents here. In the 1940s and 1950s Hanford routinely released radioactive iodine substantially above levels considered to be safe. In 1949 the 'Green Run' experiment caused the deliberate release of 5500 curies of iodine and other fission products creating a 200 x 40 mile plume over the area, hundreds of times above the accepted tolerance levels. There have been many other incidents and there are fears of leakage of high-level wastes finding their way into the Columbia River.

○ *Chalk River, Canada.* A reactor accident in 1952 led to a major clean-up problem and the danger of radioactive ash and dust being dispersed from the site.

○ *Windscale, Sellafield, UK.* There have been a series of incidents at this site. Two of the most well known were described earlier.

○ *Chelyabinsk, USSR.* A major incident, kept secret for two decades, involving an explosion at a reprocessing plant killed an unknown number of people and contaminated an extensive area around Kyshtym in the Urals.

○ *Goiania, Brazil.* Medical radioactive waste was abandoned, causing four deaths.

Sources: Blowers *et al.* (1991); Cutter (1993).

acknowledging environmental objections, ceased ocean dumping (mainly in the North Atlantic) in 1970. By the late 1970s the UK, which conducted annual sea dumps in the North East Atlantic for its own wastes and those from The Netherlands, Belgium and Switzerland, also ran into concerted opposition from scientists, national governments, non-government organisations, the media and trade unions. Scientific opinion was divided on the level of risk. It has been argued that 'the strongest defenders of the pro-dumping lobby have been not government regulators or industrialists intent on cheap options, but marine scientists with a lifelong record of involvement in dumping programmes' (Stairs and Taylor, 1992, p.123).

Some scientists, however, were maintaining that radioactivity could be concentrated in marine organisms and particles and eventually enter the food chain. The direct action campaign begun by Greenpeace in 1978 included a celebrated film of their inflatable dinghies trying to halt the dump, which drew considerable media attention. But they also lobbied the London Dumping Convention (LDC), which was a global treaty established in 1972 to regulate the disposal of wastes, including radioactive wastes, at sea. Granted observer status on the Convention in 1981 Greenpeace was in a good position to deploy its lobbying and scientific expertise to influence national government delegations to the LDC. In particular two small Pacific island states, Kiribati and Nauru, stimulated action which led to a moratorium on dumping radioactive wastes at sea being carried against the objections of the US, UK, Japan, Netherlands, South Africa and Switzerland. Finally, by 1983, as protests and demonstrations reached a crescendo, the transport trade unions took the decisive action of refusing to sanction the annual British sea dump. Although the UK has not formally abandoned sea dumping, the LDC moratorium has been observed and renewed.

The ending of sea dumping demonstrates the success of an alliance between threatened nation states, an environmental NGO and trade unions. These organisations were able to deploy sufficient expertise, influence and effective power to defeat a combination of scientific experts, nuclear interests and nation states with a high stake in sea dumping. The outcome was a ban on sea dumping reflecting the assertion of the common interest in the protection of the global commons against more narrow commercial and national interests.

On *land*, too, it has become increasingly difficult to secure politically acceptable management options. In the UK, for example, efforts to identify sites for a possible deep repository for the disposal of high-level wastes (HLW) were abandoned in 1981 after protests from local groups at the proposed sites. Similarly, plans to use an abandoned anhydrite mine at Billingham on Teesside for intermediate-level wastes (ILW) were defeated by the strength of local protest in 1985. Shortly afterwards four sites in Eastern England were selected for comparative analysis as prospective shallow burial facilities for low-level wastes (LLW) and short-lived ILW. Again, a co-ordinated campaign of lobbying, protests and scientific expertise forced a government with-drawal in 1987. As all these options became eliminated there was a retreat to Sellafield as the prospective site for a deep repository for ILW and LLW. The decision was essentially a pragmatic response to political conflict.

In other countries, too, the search for management options for radioactive wastes has demonstrated the need to secure political acceptability. In the United States a whole series of potential sites for a deep repository for HLW have been abandoned since the mid-1970s. It has proved so far politically impossible even to nominate potential sites in the Eastern states and in the West a rigorous process of comparative site characterisation was jettisoned in favour of selecting Yucca Mountain in the Nevada desert in order to minimise costs and opposition. Meanwhile, in another desert location an underground repository for military nuclear wastes has been excavated at Carlsbad, New Mexico, but has endured continuing opposition to prevent its opening. Elsewhere the determination of three states (South Carolina, Nevada and Washington) to close their LLW disposal facilities led to a policy whereby groups of states must form compacts and identify a LLW site to receive their wastes. Not surprisingly the search for new sites has frequently met with determined local resistance.

In Canada a protracted period of research is being undertaken before the search for disposal sites for HLW begins. In Germany, sites in Lower Saxony for radioactive waste disposal have met with determined opposition. In Sweden, where a phasing out of the nuclear industry was agreed, it was politically possible to excavate a sub-Baltic repository in crystalline rock, but there remains the problem of finding an acceptable deep repository for HLW. In France, the most pro-nuclear of Western countries, opposition at four rural locations selected as potential sites for a deep repository precipitated a major shift in policy with the announcement in 1991 that two sites would be selected for a 15-year period of research into the management of HLW. Selection would take place on the basis of discussion with potentially interested areas. This mediative approach has slowed down the programme.

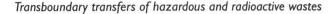

Plate 6.5 Crew on board the Greenpeace boat *MV Greenpeace* tracked down the Russian dump ship *TNT 27* and documented its activities as it dumped nuclear waste into the Sea of Japan. Photo: Hiroto/Greenpeace

Proposals for land disposal have, in almost every case, provoked conflicts between environmental interests and the nuclear industry which have local and national dimensions. So far there has not been a markedly international dimension to these conflicts. But, as the transfer of nuclear materials between countries increases, and as networks of protest are built up by organisations spanning several countries, so wider, international interests will impinge on national policy and local siting proposals.

In nearly every country with a nuclear industry the options for disposal have narrowed. With sea dumping effectively ruled out and new greenfield locations almost impossible to secure against intense opposition, the nuclear industry has had to undertake a pragmatic retreat to those locations where least political opposition and greatest public acceptability can be anticipated. But, even in these locations – Sellafield, Nevada, Carlsbad and the rest – there is neither undivided political support nor unequivocal scientific and technical agreement that the appropriate solution has been found.

Even if agreement could be reached on appropriate sites, there is considerable disagreement as to whether the disposal of wastes is the appropriate solution at the present time. The debate has political, economic and ethical dimensions. Politically the difficulty of securing disposal sites leads to consideration as to whether continued storage above ground is a desirable option. Surface storage may be favoured on other grounds, too. Environmental groups have long argued that disposal is a final solution that may consign major problems to future generations (perhaps thousands of years hence) if radionuclides should find their way through engineered and geological barriers and into the accessible environment. Furthermore, they argue that storage, surveillance and monitoring is a better guarantee against the risk of proliferation. They have for example in Germany found unlikely allies in some nuclear generators, like Scottish Nuclear, who favour dry surface storage for commercial reasons.

All these arguments are countered by those interests favouring deep geological disposal. They claim that the present generation should deal with the problems it has created; that routine monitoring cannot be carried on indefinitely; that deep disposal in engineered repositories in suitable geological formations represents the safest option; that surface storage increases risks to workers; and that the dangers of proliferation will be multiplied by a large number of dispersed storage sites.

Radioactive wastes – political conflicts

The specific conflicts over sites and over storage or disposal are not simply conflicts within the nation state. Quite aside from land-based discharges to water or atmosphere that may be transboundary, the problem of nuclear waste management has become international in two particular respects. One is through international co-operation in seeking solutions to the problems of management. There is considerable international discussion, research and development of options. For example, the deep underground research facilities at Stripa in Sweden and at Lac du Bonnet in Manitoba, Canada, are international scientific projects designed to investigate suitable hydrogeological formations, conduct experiments on engineered barriers and examine methods of waste emplacement. Although there is as yet an absence of internationally agreed criteria and standards for radioactive waste management, individual national governments will draw on this research experience. The second reason why radioactive waste management has become a major international environmental and political issue is the increasing transboundary movement of radioactive materials. This has been largely a result of the reprocessing industry.

Reprocessing

The main reasons for conflict over reprocessing were outlined in section 6.1 using the example of the THORP plant at Sellafield. Two Western countries (Britain and France) are committed to commercial reprocessing, Japan is developing facilities and reprocessing is an integral part of the fuel cycle in Russia and India. The United States maintains separate reprocessing facilities for military purposes (though much run down following the end of the Cold War) but since the mid-1970s commercial reprocessing has been abandoned there on grounds of cost and proliferation risks.

In the case of Britain and France, reprocessing is undertaken both to complete the domestic fuel cycle but also to win foreign contracts. (Russia's reprocessing facilities are an integral part of the fuel cycle which previously processed spent fuel from within the USSR and its East European allies.) The case for reprocessing has changed with more emphasis on it as a means of dealing with wastes and less as a source of plutonium and fuel. In the case of THORP it was emphasised that the project would support over

5000 jobs with over 3000 locally in an area of high unemployment. It was also justified in terms of foreign earnings with profits from THORP estimated by the operating company, British Nuclear Fuels, to be about £500 million during the first ten years of the plant's operation.

It is this foreign trade that causes an international political problem. Since under the contracts all wastes arising from reprocessing must be returned to the country of origin, there is a potential trade in radioactive wastes as well as in the reprocessed plutonium. This contradicts the proximity principle that countries should move towards self-sufficiency in the final disposal of their wastes. The problem that must be faced was indicated at the end of 1992 when a shipment of 1 tonne of plutonium from the French reprocessing plant at Cherbourg to Japan attracted significant publicity and several countries barred it from their waters. Two years later, amid protests, a shipment of radioactive waste was successfully sent from France to Japan thereby inaugurating a continuing international trade in hazardous materials.

Under substitution arrangements foreign governments may have an interest in receiving back smaller volumes of substituted HLW leaving in the UK ILW and LLW of equivalent radioactivity but of much higher volume. Although substitution is neutral in terms of radioactivity it would mean the UK would become the final resting place for the bulk of the wastes arising from foreign contracts.

Reprocessing has become controversial for several reasons. One is that it allegedly creates greater volumes of waste. One calculation suggests that the volumes of ILW and LLW (if decommissioning wastes are included) amount to 189 times the volume of the original fuel assembly (Large *et al.*, 1992). On the other hand reprocessing reduces and concentrates the volumes of HLW. And it can be argued that the alternative to reprocessing, using natural fuel, would create much larger volumes of uranium mill tailings. A second problem is that the facilities for dealing with the volumes of wastes from reprocessing are not always available. If substitution goes ahead the UK may need extra capacity to manage foreign wastes in perpetuity. The proposed repository at Sellafield is unlikely to be ready (if it is eventually approved) until well into the next century.

The third problem is the changing pattern of reprocessing. The major customers for Sellafield, Germany (where reprocessing has been vigorously opposed and which is likely to cease exporting for reprocessing when current contracts are fulfilled) and Japan (which is constructing its own reprocessing facilities) are likely to disappear, leaving France and the UK to seek alternatives. The possibilities of new markets in countries like South Korea, which are in politically unstable parts of the world, would increase the risks of proliferation. Opponents of reprocessing argue that the dangers of accidents, sabotage, theft or diversion of shipments of plutonium and wastes are likely to increase with the long routes to dispersed markets. Although reprocessing remains a matter of national policy it gives rise to trade in hazardous materials which constitutes an international problem.

Management of radioactive wastes – some conclusions

Radioactive wastes pose environmental hazards that can affect large areas and extend down the generations. There are, perhaps, three levels of conflict that arise over radioactive wastes. First is the conflict over the global commons, the fear that radioactivity may enter the marine environment and pose widespread risks. This has already led to the cessation of sea dumping but seaward discharges and seaborne trade in radioactive materials still continue.

The second level of conflict is over the management of wastes on land. Where the waste is in the form of spent fuel the question is whether to continue storage or to seek disposal facilities. The intense local conflicts over siting of proposed repositories in all countries have had two effects. One is to deny, delay or defer decisions over specific sites. The other is to ensure that the nuclear industry seeks out politically acceptable solutions which nearly always are found in existing nuclear locations, the so-called 'nuclear oases' (Blowers *et al.*, 1991). These are frequently remote, economically marginal communities which bear a disproportionate share of environmental risks (an aspect of uneven development we shall return to at the end of the third book in the series.) The search for acceptable sites has led to discussion (at present little more than speculation) of the possibilities of developing remote international repositories, possibly in Eastern Europe or developing countries.

The international context of radioactive waste management is clear in the case of commercial reprocessing which produces plutonium and generates large volumes of wastes which must be repatriated (possibly in substituted form). This creates conflicts over the transportation and trade in dangerous substances, involving environmental groups and governments concerned about environmental risks and nuclear proliferation.

The third level of conflict is between present and future. The problem here is to prevent irreversible damage to the environment and to avoid risks to future populations. The requirement of avoiding future burdens invokes the precautionary principle but this is difficult to interpret. One view might be that it is better to take action now (by building repositories, etc.) and thus remove the burden from the future. The opposite view is that it is better to wait until there is greater scientific certainty about the technology and safety measures, thus avoiding placing a burden of risk on the future. These are ethical as well as practical questions.

These conflicts, and those over hazardous wastes too, can also be viewed in terms of different dimensions of power. At one level they can be interpreted as bringing into opposition a range of actors representing a variety of interests who derive their power from different sources. Thus the scientific community deploys expertise to influence the course of conflict; environmental groups use their ability to lobby, to influence the media and to build up coalitions; the nuclear industry provides jobs and wealth and its military connections provide it with close, often secretive, ties with government. Essentially each interest seeks to influence policy makers by exerting its power in critical ways at critical times. The outcome of conflict is not predestined but reflects the varying capacities of the different actors to influence events which vary over time and space. This analysis is applicable to individual conflicts.

At a more general level it may be argued that power relations are structured in such a way that certain powerful forces – countries, classes – exert such economic and political dominion that the outcomes of conflicts inevitably reflect their interests. Such an explanation is helpful (to some extent) in the case of hazardous wastes where there is a clear North-South conflict and evidence of dominance and dependence, but it is less useful for radioactive wastes, which are largely confined to the developed countries. However, with the break-up of the former Soviet Union there are signs that Western interests will assert their economic power to shape global nuclear policy both at a military and commercial level.

Radioactive waste management is a subject of considerable scientific uncertainty and political conflict. Although international action has been taken to suspend ocean dumping, nuclear waste is, by and large, an issue that is left to national governments. Countries are relatively free to pursue their own policies on the nuclear fuel cycle, on the methods of storage and disposal and on the transport of wastes. Nuclear waste has remained relatively low on the agenda for international governmental action but it is an issue that has attracted considerable attention from environmentalists and peace campaigners. Given its indivisible links with the military and the problems of proliferation radioactive waste is now a key element in a much wider international issue.

6.4 The search for solutions

I now turn to examine the principles that have influenced international action to prevent or control the environmental risks arising from transboundary movements of hazardous and radioactive wastes. So far we have looked at the international problems that are created by these wastes and at the nature of the conflicts to which they give rise. Now I shall focus on potential solutions and the problems of achieving them. As before I shall deal with hazardous and radioactive wastes in turn.

Hazardous wastes – from problem to policy

The various international attempts to control the dumping and trade in hazardous wastes have certain features in common. They combine:

> ... an increasingly strong preference for elimination or disposal at source of toxic, persistent, or bio-accumulative waste wherever possible, with, in other cases, a regime of regulation, monitoring, prior environmental impact assessment, or prior consent designed to minimize the risks of disposal and provide for the protection of other states and the environment of common spaces (Birnie and Boyle, 1992, p.302).

But the degree to which international agreements have achieved these principles varies according to the types of transboundary problem.

There are three types of transboundary problem that arise. These are discharges into the marine environment from *land-based sources* which account for the bulk of wastes; *dumping at sea*; and *international trade* in wastes. The first two affect the global commons while the third involves the transfer of the problem of managing wastes from one country to another.

Land-based discharges constitute by far the biggest volumes of waste products entering the marine environment and include bulky materials (sewage sludge, inert materials, etc.) which may be harmful but are not strictly speaking hazardous wastes. Regulation of these discharges has depended upon regional agreements which have tended to be voluntary and depend heavily on the willingness of national governments to take action. There has naturally been resistance on the part of some governments to controls since these would affect industrial policy and could be seen as an infringement on sovereignty. Conversely, there has also been pressure to clean up discharges which have a detrimental environmental and economic effect on neighbours. For instance, Sweden pressed for controls over chlorine discharges into the Baltic because Finnish pulp and paper plants were not only creating an environmental problem but were also enjoying a competitive advantage through less stringent regulation. Economic interests tend to be prominent in agreements on land-based sources.

There is no global treaty on land-based sources. Although the UN Convention on the Law of the Sea (UNCLOS) provides a general framework, it tends to respect economic considerations and hence to rely on regional co-operation as a means of achieving ecological protection. Major regional agreements have emerged in the Mediterranean, Baltic and the North Sea with others covering the south-east Pacific and the Persian Gulf. The North Sea is protected by a number of institutions including the Paris Commission and the International North Sea Conference. These have had some impact (for example, the agreement to end dumping of sewage sludge in the North Sea by the end of the century or the reduction in the disposal of lead and cadmium), but in general the pace of progress is determined by national interests. These regional agreements, though often general in character, have generated a number of specific commitments with mechanisms designed to ensure clean-up.

Coastal and near-shore areas are highly vulnerable. It is here that human populations are most thickly concentrated. Coastal environments 'are often the most complex and sensitive to pollution because of slow water renewal and generally limited depth ... . It is in these regions that the most detrimental ecological effects have been observed' (OECD, 1991, p.81). But it is in coastal areas that the conflicts between national and common interests are most acute.

However, when it comes to *dumping of wastes at sea* international action has been more vigorous and effective. The third UN Convention on the Law of the Sea (UNCLOS III), which concluded in 1982 and came into legal effect in November 1994 following ratification by 60 countries, establishes a whole range of hortatory restrictions, including dumping of wastes on the high seas and urging co-operation among states to prevent pollution and to clean up damage. While this convention provides an overall set of principles, of more significance have been those treaties which address specific issues and which are binding on the participants. These include the International Convention for the Prevention of Pollution from Ships (MARPOL) which covers marine pollution from ships which are responsible for about 10% of the total pollution discharged into the oceans. MARPOL sets limits to operational discharges, refuse and noxious substances and applies stowage standards to prevent accidental releases.

The London Dumping Convention (LDC, officially the Convention on the Prevention of Marine Pollution by Dumping of Wastes and Other Materials), established in 1972, has proved generally effective though it has obvious weaknesses. Resolutions are not binding on non-concurring parties so that, if it decided to do so, the UK could resume dumping of radioactive waste with impunity. The 'only effective forces for compliance at present are reasoned argument and the embarrassment factor' (Stairs and Taylor, 1992, p.117). The strength of the LDC lies in the fact that it is a global treaty which has been widely ratified. It applies minimum standards and bans certain activities altogether. For example, as we saw earlier, radioactive waste dumping at sea is effectively ruled out and incineration is severely restricted. The LDC has asserted the principle 'that dumping should be eliminated unless there are no alternatives and it can be proven harmless, a significant reversal of the burden of proof' (Birnie and Boyle, 1992, p.322). It also has a consultative supranational supervisory body, composed equally of industrial and developing nations, which meets regularly to review and develop its regime. Its success can be measured in the reduction of industrial waste dumped at sea, down from 17 million tonnes in 1979 to 6 million in 1987.

The relative success of the LDC in developing an anti-dumping regime can be attributed to two factors in particular. One is that the composition of the LDC means that it is difficult for a few industrial nations to impose their interests against a general presumption that the global commons should be protected in the general interest and for future generations. A second is that the LDC has been strongly influenced by the lobbying, scientific advice and publicity generated by NGOs, notably Greenpeace. This has opened up the process of negotiation, providing counter-expertise and mobilising opposition to pro-dumping lobbies and arguments. The success of the LDC could lead to unintended consequences that might be environmentally detrimental such as greater pressure for on-land dumping, illegal dumping at sea or blanket policies (e.g. bans of sewage dumping at sea) which may benefit some areas (e.g. North Sea) while causing problems elsewhere (e.g. encouraging offshore disposal by pipelines in developing countries).

International trade in toxic and hazardous wastes is covered by treaties that attempt to reconcile conflicts and deal with problems of monitoring and compliance. International action is in a period of transition as the movement to secure a ban on all forms of trade in such wastes gathers momentum but is resisted by powerful national interests. Both sides of the argument claim scientific support and environmental justification for their position. At the heart of the conflicts are issues of inequality as wealthy nations seek to find ways of dealing with the problems which may ultimately mean imposing them on poor developing countries.

There are various bilateral, regional, interregional and global agreements designed to control and regulate the trade. Among bilateral treaties are those between the United States and Mexico and Canada whereby shipments must be notified and approved by the importing state. The OECD has played a significant role in creating an international framework of law and legislation on hazardous wastes. At the regional level the EC has derived its own legislation from OECD directives (see Box 6).

The intention of the EC legislation is to minimise waste volumes, to emphasise the proximity principle and to ensure that any residual trade between member countries is fully documented. Thus it does not ban trade altogether. While this may encourage management in appropriate facilities it may also lead to dumping in the least developed parts of the EU. Other weaknesses of the directives lie in the problems of classification which omit certain important categories (e.g. radioactive wastes) and in definitions of safe management which leave the determination of methods to the individual countries.

Regional and bilateral treaties among industrialised countries may encourage export to developing countries. The dumping of wastes in African countries (described at the beginning of the chapter) provoked retaliatory action in the late 1980s in the form of an outright ban on the trade. The 1991 African Convention on Transboundary

EC Directives on hazardous wastes

1978 Directive on Toxic and Dangerous Wastes replaced by *1993 Hazardous Wastes Directive.* These provide definitions, introduce the preventative principle (i.e. that waste generation should be minimised and wastes disposed of safely) and apply the polluter pays principle.

1984 Directive on the Transfrontier Shipment of Hazardous Wastes. This introduced control of movement between member states and between the EC and other countries. It applied the principles of notification and consent and provided a core list of hazardous substances to which individual member states could add those they considered hazardous. It will eventually be replaced by a regulation implementing the Basel Convention (see below).

Movements of Hazardous Wastes (the Bamako Convention) prohibits imports and regulates trade among African countries. An interregional agreement between the EEC and 68 African, Caribbean and Pacific states, known as the Lomé IV Convention and signed in 1989, bans exports and imports of hazardous wastes, including radioactive wastes, between the signatories.

These agreements go further than the global Convention on the Control of Transboundary Movements of Hazardous Wastes and Their Disposal (the Basel Convention) adopted by 116 countries and the EEC in 1989. This emerged from work undertaken by the OECD in the early and mid-1980s. While not banning trade, once ratified it will recognise bans imposed by other agreements and permit trade only where this enables safe management to be undertaken in appropriate facilities. Prior informed consent is required before trade occurs and environmentally sound management must be undertaken. Illegal exports must be repatriated. The Basel Convention has a number of weaknesses. It is limited to wastes for disposal and does not therefore include materials for reuse or recycling. Environmentally sound management is vaguely defined as 'taking all practicable steps to ensure that hazardous waste or other wastes are managed in a manner which will protect human health and the environment against the adverse effects which may result from such wastes'.

At a global level a compromise has been struck. If the regime proves too tough it will offend the interests of certain countries and so delay the chances of ratification. Further, it may stimulate illegal trade and poor management practices on land. The need for proper enforcement, adequate financial resources and stronger institutional capacities to deal with problems is recognised in Chapter 20 of Agenda 21 (United Nations, 1992a).

Hazardous wastes – the principles of policy

Although policy making for the international control of hazardous wastes is slow to evolve, certain principles have been established. The key one is the *precautionary principle*, which is both vague and all-embracing but covers the need to minimise production of waste in the first place and to manage it so that, so far as possible, it does not offend the environment for present or future generations. It embraces the principle of *environmentally sound management* which places emphasis on care in handling the transportation, storage and disposal of wastes. To achieve this two further principles must be observed. One is the principle of *prior informed consent* so that all trade is based on open declaration and agreement. The other is the *proximity principle* which urges that wastes should be managed as close to their source as is possible, consistent with environmentally sound management.

These principles have led to the progressive banning of sea dumping of wastes and bans to trade in various parts of the world. It has not eliminated trade altogether and the illegal trade may cause 'serious threats to human health and the environment and impose a special and abnormal burden on the countries that receive such shipments' (United Nations, 1992, p.205). Where the national economic interests of the industrial countries are most threatened, as in the case of land-based disposal which covers the bulk of hazardous wastes, progress in reaching binding agreements has been feeble. Conversely, import bans have been introduced by African countries which are no longer prepared to secure economic advantages at the price of environmental contamination and threats to health. The bans are part of a much wider conflict over environment and development and between national and global interests which surfaced prominently at the UN Rio Conference. Most progress has been made where national economic interests are least threatened. The banning of sea dumping covers a relatively small volume of hazardous wastes (about 10% of the total) and covers the high seas where international jurisdiction is paramount.

In the case of hazardous wastes international regulation has been consistently developed. In contrast radioactive waste regulation and control remains substantially in the hands of the nuclear nations.

Radioactive wastes – the limits of international action

Given the potential scale of disaster that could result from an accident involving nuclear materials, including wastes and plutonium, the weakness of international safeguarding regimes may seem surprising. For instance, when the Chernobyl accident occurred there was no obligation of notification and it was not until Swedish authorities registered the fall-out nearly two days later that the scale of the disaster was first realised. Throughout the history of the nuclear industry states have been unwilling to accept international controls over their activities.

It is the weakness of international regimes over the nuclear industry rather than their absence that is most evident. As we saw earlier, an indefinite ban on the dumping of nuclear materials at sea has been agreed. The Bamako and Lomé Conventions include the banning of the import of radioactive wastes. At the strategic level since 1963 tests of nuclear weapons have been periodically observed by some nuclear powers and the 1968 Nuclear Non-Proliferation Treaty provides for an inspection system to ensure compliance among signatories.

There are also advisory standards produced by the International Atomic Energy Agency (IAEA). Established in 1956, its original purpose sought to stress the peaceful rather than military purposes of nuclear power. Its objective was 'to accelerate and enlarge the contribution of atomic energy to peace, health and prosperity throughout the world'. Radioactive waste was initially almost an incidental concern but attention to the problem gradually increased and accelerated after Chernobyl. The IAEA has published a whole series of standards covering installation, transportation, handling, conditioning and disposal of radioactive wastes and codes of practice, including one for transfrontier transport. The standards are set to conform to the radiological protection limits recommended by another international body, the International Commission for Radiological Protection (ICRP). Within the OECD countries the Nuclear Energy Agency also fulfils an advisory role, disseminating information and sponsoring research. At the EU level the nuclear agency Euratom does provide legal obligations over nuclear safety and oversight of radioactive waste plans but has tended to focus more on the research and development of nuclear energy. Birnie and Boyle conclude that 'It is not a good advertisement for the performance of the European Community in environmental matters' (1992, p.357).

The international regimes covering nuclear facilities are advisory and therefore states are relatively free to develop their own standards, to locate nuclear facilities where they please and to decide on levels of discharge of radioactive materials on their territory and into the neighbouring coastal areas. They are also free to determine the methods of radioactive waste management and to decide whether or not to reprocess spent fuel. They may also engage in trade in nuclear materials and wastes provided that they abide by non-proliferation requirements.

This paradox of a high potential risk and a liberal international regime may be explained in several ways. In the first place the nuclear industry is relatively restricted to about 25 countries mainly in North America, Western and Eastern Europe and Japan. The movement of nuclear materials between them has been mutually acceptable. A second reason is a general presumption among these nuclear states that each is competent and willing to ensure high safety standards and to accept at least the minimum standards recommended by international bodies. Thirdly, the nuclear industry is shrouded in secrecy arising from its military origins and continuing links to nuclear weapons. Except in the case of inspection to prevent proliferation, national security serves to justify unilateral nuclear policy making.

This national approach to nuclear policy is open to challenge on several fronts. Within most nuclear nations there is growing concern about the risks of accidents from nuclear facilities and anxiety about the health risks to present and future generations. It is becoming increasingly difficult to secure sites for nuclear projects, including waste repositories, and more and more the nuclear industry is forced back to sites where it already has a significant presence. At an international level opposition is also developing to the trade in nuclear materials, notably plutonium, but it is likely to affect nuclear waste once shipments begin. Opposition to the nuclear industry brings together a diverse assortment of interests including local communities (against nuclear facilities in their own area though not necessarily against nuclear energy), peace campaigners and environmental groups intent on closing down the nuclear industry worldwide. It is further complicated by the different stages in the nuclear cycle. Thus reprocessing may be opposed by countries such as the United States which are concerned about proliferation risks or by those (including some nuclear utilities and governments) who consider reprocessing to be more expensive than alternatives such as dry storage.

It is because nuclear energy (and the risks to which it gives rise) is so contentious and divisive that international agreements are unlikely to develop. Radioactive waste management has had a low priority on the international agenda for action. The convoluted and timid pronouncements in Agenda 21 make this much clear, as the extract in Box 7 shows. Unlike all other hazardous wastes, radioactive wastes are dangerous through proximity and, if not properly managed, can inflict serious harm on substantial areas, harm that may not transpire for thousands of years. Moreover, they are indivisibly linked to an industry that has the potential to cause widespread and catastrophic destruction, as Chernobyl has shown. They are also linked to the production of plutonium through reprocessing which has the capability of global destruction. With the ending of the Cold War proliferation has become increasingly difficult to control.

7

Extract from Agenda 21 on safe and environmentally sound management of radioactive wastes

States, in co-operation with relevant international organisations, should:

> ... not promote or allow the storage or disposal of high-level, intermediate-level and low-level radioactive wastes near the marine environment unless they determine that scientific evidence, consistent with the applicable internationally agreed principles and guidelines, shows that such storage or disposal poses no unacceptable risk to people and the marine environment or does not interfere with other legitimate uses of the sea, making, in the process of consideration, appropriate use of the concept of the precautionary approach.

Source: United Nations (1992), p.216.

Thus the stakes are high. For the opponents of the nuclear industry it is not a matter of securing better international management regimes. It is a matter of destroying the industry itself. For the nuclear industry and its supporters a solution to the problems of nuclear waste has become a necessary condition of legitimating continued expansion. In this respect the conflict over radioactive waste management is literally a part of the conflict over the survival of the nuclear industry.

6.5 Conclusion

In this chapter I have used the example of hazardous and radioactive wastes to explore the main question for this book, *What are the causes of international environmental problems, and what are the conflicts surrounding their definition and potential solution?* Some of the major differences between conflicts over hazardous and radioactive wastes have been identified. In particular trade in hazardous wastes has underlined problems of uneven development in terms of North-South conflicts whereas radioactive wastes are still largely a problem confined to Northern nuclear nations (though inequalities between the West and the former Soviet bloc in the East are beginning to emerge). The existence and the threat of dumping hazardous wastes in the oceans or on the territory of developing countries has provoked conflicts which have led to significant international agreements, some of them of global dimensions. By contrast, although the trade in radioactive materials and the problem of disposing of wastes pose increasing international problems, so far policy making has been firmly controlled by individual nation states and international action, in so far as it exists at all, has tended to be advisory.

Aside from these differences both hazardous and radioactive wastes provide evidence for some brief general conclusions on the nature of the conflicts, the interests involved, the sources of power to determine outcomes and the policy implications.

Conflicts

As with many other transboundary problems the basic cause of international conflict over hazardous and radioactive wastes is the externality effects brought about by transboundary transfers. These wastes can be detrimental both to the environment and to health and are, therefore, unwanted. Indeed, proposals to dump or manage wastes arouse local opposition and, as we have seen, dumping on developing countries has been much resented. Wastes may also infiltrate the global commons of the oceans and seas and, here again, the potential dangers have led to bans on sea dumping and control over land-based discharges.

The conflicts occur at different levels. At one level they are intensely *local* as the campaigns to prevent radioactive waste facilities, hazardous waste incinerators or other processing plant amply demonstrate. It is difficult to find sites since such facilities deal with wastes from far afield and bring few benefits to the locality. This concentration of risk and dispersal of benefits relates the problem of site selection to national and even international policy making. Here we see once again the relationship between the local and the global.

Conflict also occurs *over time* between generations. The notion of sustainable development and its related precautionary principle suggest that the present generation should not pass down risks greater than those accepted today nor should we bequeath a degraded environment or depleted resource base. Action must be taken now to prevent unacceptable burdens on the future. This responsibility has been embodied in agreements to protect the global commons such as the ban on sea dumping of nuclear and other hazardous wastes. Discounting has been used as a means of ensuring that future generations have the necessary resources to deal with any problems arising from the present, for example, decommissioning nuclear facilities. But, discounting depends on continuing technology and on institutional, economic and political stability, conditions that becomes less plausible the further we look into the future. Over much longer time spans we cannot even assume climatic or geological stability and yet some of the most persistent substances will remain dangerous over thousands, in some cases millions, of years. Looked at in this way, assumptions about the safety of nuclear repositories have a heroic, not to say fantastic, quality about them.

Interests

Conflicts represent a clash of opposing interests. These interests have both an ideological content and an organisational context. Ideologically the opposing interests can be broadly categorised as environment versus development, private versus public, national versus global and so on. They are not necessarily mutually incompatible. For instance, the whole point about sustainable development is to try to reconcile the disparate goals of environmental sustainability and economic development. In the longer term private interest in economic gain is best satisfied by protecting the environment in the public interest. Similarly, national ideologies of sovereignty and economic growth may increasingly contradict the need for agreement to protect resources and conserve the environment. In short, interests are not always discrete and single-minded but diverse, overlapping, interconnected and varying over time.

Interests are usually advanced through organisations though organisations vary markedly in their degree of coherence, longevity or formal structure. Environmental interests have been advanced by communities of scientists, by NGOs and by environmental movements of local communities and networks of interest groups. Typically they find themselves in conflict with business organisations which produce, trade and manage hazardous materials. But, it is not always a simple contest between single-minded opposing organisations. Scientific communities, often very loosely organised if organised at all, provide conflicting evidence and, in the face of the empirical and theoretical problems posed by environmental factors, maintain what Yearley (1991) analyses as a case of *pragmatic uncertainty* in which knowledge is provisional and depends on judgement and so may offer comfort to both sides in a dispute. Protest groups often hold together as uneasy alliances, dissolving quickly once their objective is achieved. For instance, local nuclear protest groups include both supporters and opponents of nuclear power and bring together people of widely differing ideologies united only in their determination to prevent nuclear facilities being developed in their locality. Nor is the business community unilaterally hostile to environmental movements, as the so-called greening of many companies testifies.

Power and policy

The success of interests in securing objectives depends on the effective power they are able to deploy. There are different views on the question of power (Lukes, 1974; Blowers, 1984). One view (known in social science as a *pluralist view*) holds that there are many interests that are in competition, each seeking to influence relevant decision makers. The resulting conflicts are settled usually by negotiation, consensus and compromise. This view assumes that government is responsive, open and capable of resolving conflicts of this kind. A variant of this view (known as *elitism*) argues that competition among interests is unequal since some have greater access to decision makers than others and are able to achieve their objectives through suppression, control or manipulation of information.

These approaches may be broadly applied to international decision making on hazardous and radioactive wastes. A pluralist approach perhaps best serves the case of hazardous wastes where environmental NGOs have used scientific evidence, publicity through the media, organisation of local protests and lobbying of governments to draw attention to the dangers of trade. Governments have responded by banning dumping and establishing control regimes. Nuclear waste, with its connections to the military, close relationships between the nuclear industry and government and tendency towards secrecy, evinces a more elitist interpretation of power. Yet the ability of NGOs and other protest groups to force the issues into the open, to orchestrate alliances and coalitions, to lobby opinion and governments and, on occasion, to succeed in their objectives (as over sea dumping or repository siting) suggests that access is not one-sided and that deployment of pluralist politics can prove successful. At the same time, some environmental NGOs are gaining privileged access to government while the nuclear industry must increasingly look for public support.

Against this type of analysis there is the view that power is not distributed among a range of interests competing for influence over policy makers, not even unequally, but rather that power is deeply embedded in the economic and political structure. Economic power is reflected in political power. The powerful – social groups, nations – are able to exploit their position and dominate the powerless. As Gaventa puts it, 'Power seems to create power. Powerlessness serves to reinforce powerlessness. Power relations, once established, are self-sustaining' (1980, p.256). This view would explain the tendency for environmental risks to be concentrated in remote, often economically dependent 'peripheral' locations (Blowers and Leroy, 1994). Sites for radioactive wastes are usually associated with remote areas dependent on the nuclear industry. In a similar way the dumping of hazardous wastes in developing countries reflects the pattern of economic domination and dependence that is a structural feature of the contemporary world.

The different views of power each shed light on aspects of contemporary conflicts over hazardous and radioactive wastes. They suggest that policies will need to incorporate concepts of equity and methods of compensation if they are to be successfully implemented. The constraints and opportunities for policy making will be a major theme of the third book in this series (Blowers and Glasbergen, 1996).

7

Climate change: From science to global policies

Pieter van Beukering and Pier Vellinga

7.1 Introduction

It has become evident over the past few decades that human activities are significantly altering the atmosphere's composition and its radiative properties. This has resulted in global environmental problems such as climate change and ozone depletion, which have potentially far-reaching effects on society. The focus in this chapter is on global climate change and the process that eventually led to the United Nations Framework Convention on Climate Change (FCCC).

Before the Convention was signed at the United Nations Conference on Environment and Development (UNCED) in Rio in June 1992, various scientific trends and political mechanisms could be discerned interacting in an evolutionary process which is still far from being concluded today. Scientific progress is gradually improving our understanding of the impact of the atmospheric changes. At the same time, international consultation mechanisms have come into being which have facilitated the development of a global climate policy. Climate change affects the private sector, governments, non-governmental organisations, the scientific community and many other societal actors. It can probably be considered as the most complex public policy issue ever to have confronted the international community. The formulation and adoption of the Climate Change Convention has been a major exercise in conciliating an immense diversity of conflicting interests. By providing an overview of the numerous scientific and political dimensions of the climate change issue, this chapter seeks to explore how divergent interests were reconciled in the policy-making process.

Several developments will be discussed separately. First, section 7.2 elaborates on the causes of climate change and the related scientific and policy issues. Section 7.3 gives a historical discussion of how climate change came to be a topic of debate in the international scientific and political community and how it resulted in the Framework Convention on Climate Change. The development of a global treaty involving so many different parties has been a highly complex process. This is clearly understood if one concentrates on the differing and often conflicting starting points and interests of the major countries. In section 7.4 the contrasts between the major world regions in developing and implementing climate policies will be emphasised. Finally, section 7.5 draws some conclusions.

7.2 Science and policies

Any examination of the political process surrounding global warming must begin by looking at the scientific aspects of climate change. In turn, we shall look at physical causes, effects and the scientific uncertainties regarding climate change. Then we shall analyse climate policies, revisiting the causes, the impacts and the uncertainties of climate change.

Science: causes of climate change

The greenhouse effect is a natural phenomenon that keeps the Earth warmer than it would otherwise be. It is caused by so-called greenhouse gases. One distinguishes natural greenhouse gases, the main ones being water vapour (H_2O), carbon dioxide (CO_2), methane (CH_4), nitrous oxide (N_2O) and ozone (O_3), and human made greenhouse gases such as chlorofluorocarbons (CFCs) and variants. Because of their physical properties, greenhouse gases permit short-wave radiation emitted by the Sun to pass through them, but absorb the long-wave infra-red radiation that is in turn emitted by the Earth. The Earth would be 33°C colder without this naturally occurring greenhouse effect (Watson *et al.*, 1990). Tropospheric water vapour (H_2O) is the single most important greenhouse gas yet its atmospheric concentration is not directly influenced by anthropogenic emissions (emissions originating from human activities). Instead it is influenced indirectly by temperature. Similarly, ozone (O_3) formation and degradation is not a direct but an indirect result of anthropogenic emissions. For this reason, H_2O and O_3 are not usually included in an analysis of climate change.

As is evidenced by Table 7.1, the chemical composition of the Earth's atmosphere is changing. This is mainly due to human activities. Since the Industrial Revolution,

Atmospheric concentrations[1]	CO_2	CH_4	N_2O	CFC-11	CFC-12
Units[2]	ppmv	ppmv	ppbv	pptv	pptv
Pre-industrial (1750–1800)	280	0.8	288	0	0
Present day (1990)[3]	353	1.72	310	280	484
Current rate of change per year	1.8 (0.5%)	0.015 (0.9%)	0.8 (0.25%)	9.5 (4%)	17 (4%)
Atmospheric lifetime (years)[4]	50–100	10	150	65	130

Explanation of notes: 1. Ozone has not been included in the table because of a lack of precise data. 2. ppmv = parts per million by volume; ppbv = parts per billion by volume; pptv = parts per trillion by volume. 3. The current (1990) concentrations have been estimated by an extrapolation of measurements reported for earlier years, assuming that the recent trends remain more or less constant. 4. For each gas in the table except CO_2, the 'lifetime' is defined here as the ratio of the atmospheric content to the total rate of removal. This time-scale also characterises the rate of adjustment of the atmospheric concentrations if the emission rates are changed abruptly. CO_2 is a special case since it has no real sinks but is merely circulated between various reservoirs (the atmosphere, ocean and biota). The 'lifetime' of CO_2 given in the table is a rough indication of the time it would take for CO_2 concentrations to adjust to changes in the emissions·

Table 7.1 Summary of key greenhouse gases influenced by human activities (Source: Watson *et al.*, 1990.)

atmospheric CO_2 concentrations have risen by 25%, from 280 to over 350 parts per million. This anthropogenic influence has increased in significance during the period since 1960. The sources of greenhouse gases are very diverse. The anthropogenic increase in CO_2 is principally the result of the burning of fossil fuels such as coal, oil and gas and changes in land use (e.g. deforestation). CH_4 originates from cattle, sheep, landfills and wet rice production. N_2O is emitted primarily by chemical processes in the soil and water surface as a result of, for instance, fertiliser use. Finally, CFCs and HCFCs are industrially manufactured gases, used in refrigerators, foam blowing and solvents. An examination of Table 7.1 demonstrates that the anthropogenic influence on the radiative balance, and thus on the climate system, is already significant and, as stated by the Intergovernmental Panel on Climate Change (IPCC), will ultimately lead to perceptible climate changes (see also section 7.3).

Science: impacts of climate change

If the emissions of greenhouse gases in the atmosphere are not reduced (the *business as usual* emission scenario), the IPCC forecasts that the mean global temperature will rise over the next 100 years at a rate of approximately 0.3°C per decade (with an uncertainty range of 0.2°C to 0.5°C per decade) (Houghton *et al.*, 1990; see also section 7.3).

Plate 7.1 Smog hanging over Mexico City due to extensive traffic. Photo: Ron Giling/Lineair

The impacts of climate change vary significantly from region to region and from season to season. The degree of warming is predicted to be 50–100% above the global mean in high Northern latitudes in winter. Land surfaces will warm up more rapidly than the ocean. Precipitation is expected to increase in middle and high latitudes, especially in winter. Increased precipitation is also expected in the tropics (Mitchell *et al.*, 1990). Consequently, global warming will initiate a shift in climate zones. Estimates show that a temperature increase of 1° would cause the climatic boundaries of agriculture in the Northern hemisphere to shift to the north by 200–300 kilometres (Izrael, 1991). Adaptation (probably through trial and error due to the inevitable uncertainties) to the new conditions will be required, creating considerable ecological and economic costs.

The impact on society may well be felt particularly keenly in the form of a rise in the sea level, caused by the thermal expansion of the water as well as the more rapid melting of glaciers and polar ice sheets. Warrick and Oerlemans (1990) estimate that the predicted increase in temperature will lead to a rise of 3–10 centimetres per decade. Even if action is taken to reduce global emissions, the sea level is still likely to rise significantly during the next century on account of the greenhouse gases which are already present in the atmosphere. Low-lying coastal areas, where both population and agriculture are often concentrated, are directly threatened and the long-term existence of the small island states is at stake (Gilbert and Vellinga, 1990).

A costly impact of climate change on society is the change in the patterns, frequencies and intensities of extreme weather events. Although science is not able to explain this phenomenon adequately, the recent increase in the scale of damage caused by extreme weather events may be an indication of the predicted relation between temperature rises and more severe weather. A northward shift in the pattern of gales and hurricanes, exposing unprepared and more vulnerable areas, would have a particularly severe social impact. In addition, other types of climate extremes such as high-temperature events (over 35°C) are expected to occur more often, causing increased droughts. At the same time, cold waves will be less frequent and less intense. Such effects could be damaging to agricultural productivity. Milder winters will increase crop damage caused by insects and pests during the summer. Also, certain trees need a period of frost in order to bear fruit. The IPCC (1990) also predicts a shift from gradual precipitation to heavy local rainfall. Consequently, there will be a greater risk of river flooding.

The climate change, however, will also have a positive impact on agriculture in the form of the so-called *fertiliser effect* exerted on plant growth by a higher atmospheric CO_2 concentration. So far, however, experiments have not been able to give conclusive proof of the nature of the overall effect of climate change on agricultural productivity. If anything, research suggests that an increased CO_2 concentration may indirectly limit, rather than enhance, plant growth. The mineral nutrient uptake by microflora supposedly becomes enhanced, resulting in a lack of nutrients for plants (Diaz, 1991). Also, climatic change will have effects besides CO_2 fertilisation, such as temperature changes, extreme weather events, soil moisture changes, changes in precipitation, pests, etc., all of which will have an impact on agriculture. Regional computer models which attempt to take account of the full range of these impacts point to a decrease of 10–15% in agricultural output in Africa, Latin America and certain parts of India and South-east Asia (Fischer *et al.*, 1993).

Global warming is also projected to have far-reaching effects on health. Although winters will be less severe and consequently cause less illness and fewer deaths, the negative impact of milder winters is likely to overshadow these benefits. Temperature rises and precipitation changes will affect vector (disease-transmitting) species such as mosquitoes, as well as the quality of the water and air and stress conditions. Morbidity and mortality will probably increase as a result of an increased incidence of respiratory, vector-borne and water-related diseases. In addition, heat waves will occur more often, causing increased stress, especially in urban areas. At the same time, local food shortages should be expected as a result of poor harvests (Rouviere *et al.*, 1990). The less resilient members of the population will be most vulnerable and will consequently suffer most.

In addition to a gradual change in the climate system, sudden instabilities cannot be ruled out. Palaeo-records indicate that some 10,000 years ago the temperature probably increased by 7°C over a period of only 50 years. During that period, the sea level rose at a rate of several metres per century. A sudden change in ocean currents from one quasi-equilibrium pattern to another equilibrium pattern is the most plausible explanation. Model experiments have confirmed that such a type of shift may also be triggered by increasing greenhouse gas concentrations in the atmosphere. A most intriguing aspect of such 'flip-flop' climate changes is that they seem to be irreversible.

Yet another threat posed by human-induced climate change is the so-called *runaway greenhouse effect*. Global warming may lead to the release of additional greenhouse gases by vegetation, the ocean and the soil. In this way, the greenhouse effect would be a self-accelerating phenomenon fed by positive feedbacks. This could happen, for instance, if large quantities of methane were released as a result of the thawing of tundra soils, which would in turn exacerbate the greenhouse effect. Similarly, the Earth may respond by absorbing more greenhouse gases through ocean current shifts and/or plant growth. Such effects are still highly uncertain. Current observations, however, suggest that positive feedbacks may dominate (Houghton *et al.*, 1992).

Scientific uncertainties

A major constraint restricting the action which can be taken to curb climate change is the various uncertainties we are faced with. At present, uncertainties exist with regard to almost every aspect of the greenhouse effect: the sensitivity of the average global temperature and mean sea level to the increase in greenhouse gases, the timing of the expected climate change, the natural variations in the climate, and the regional climatic impacts. This may well produce a state of paralysis among stakeholders, who may hence postpone decisions or the implementation of emission-reducing measures (De Freitas, 1991). Substantial scientific progress would need to be made in order to overcome these uncertainties. However, there is only a slight chance of such uncertainties being resolved quickly. It is indeed likely that the effects of climate change will actually be felt before any full scientific consensus is achieved on the subject. Given the largely irreversible nature of climate change and its long-term nature, postponing action in the hope that new information will resolve or at least reduce present uncertainties is a dangerous strategy.

How should scientific uncertainties be dealt with? Current options include the development of new production and consumption technologies in order to limit the costs of reduction and the accomplishment of immediate reductions in emissions with the aim of curbing the global warming process. Each of these options is essential for a timely response (Manne & Richels, 1991).

Above all, one must be aware of the relationship between uncertainty about the consequences of accelerated climate change and the effectiveness of response options, especially as to how this relationship changes over time. Figure 7.1 illustrates the trade-off between effectiveness and certainty. Measures to reduce emissions taken today will have a lasting and immediate effect on the future emission level of greenhouse gases. Similar limitation measures taken in 2050 (rather than now) will obviously be insufficient to obtain the same emission reductions which could have been achieved by then if action had been taken now. The present effectiveness of emission limitation is therefore high. At the same time, the present degree of certainty with regard to the greenhouse effect is low. Certainty is likely to increase in the future as a result of scientific research and monitoring; then policy makers will be more confident about the measures to take. However, as has already been argued, these measures will be less effective (Vellinga & Swart, 1991).

There are basically two types of policy which can be used as a means of responding to the possible impacts of climate change. First, *emission reduction measures* or *carbon sequestration* can be initiated in order to minimise the causes of global warming. This response is called a *limitation policy*. Second, one can focus on the effects of climate change and apply *adaptation policies*, such as building higher dykes as protection against rises in the sea level. The two policies are closely related: the less one limits climate change, the greater the costs of adaptation are likely to be. Yet, even if the focus is entirely on limitation, adaptation measures will still be indispensable, since limitation measures can never fully eliminate climate change. The climate scenario studies published by

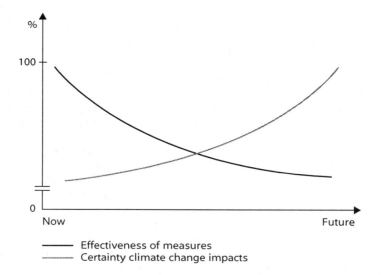

Fig. 7.1 The policy dilemma: the trade-off between the effectiveness of measures and scientific uncertainty. Source: Vellinga and Swart, 1991

Working Group I of the IPCC suggest that control policies on emissions can slow global warming, perhaps from 0.3°C/decade to 0.1°C/decade (IPCC-RSWG, 1990). An appropriate climate policy will therefore not focus on either one of these policy options, but will use a combination. In what follows we will discuss both limitation and adaptation strategies. However, both policies are constrained by the existence of scientific uncertainties. How to deal with them will conclude this section of the chapter.

Policies addressing causes

At present, most limitation policies focus on the reduction of greenhouse gas emissions and follow a 'gas by gas' approach (see Box 1). The reasoning behind this is that, as the exact *greenhouse warming equivalents* for all the various greenhouse gases are not yet known with any degree of certainty, it is more sensible to tackle the gases separately in the first phase of policy making. Once the exact global warming potentials are known, a 'comprehensive' gas policy can be applied, with trade-offs between gases. With such a comprehensive approach, a combination of the most effective measures is chosen irrespective of the greenhouse gas on which they are focused (Rijsberman *et al.*, 1993).

A policy designed to tackle the causes of climate change generates both short-term and long-term positive side effects. Such measures can be justified even in the face of scientific uncertainties because they make sense for reasons other than climate change. They may therefore be characterised as *no-regrets policies* (Bodansky, 1993). Limitation measures such as the improvement of energy efficiency will, for example, also enhance economic performance, reduce other pollutant emissions and increase energy security, besides reducing CO_2 emissions. Similar positive side effects can be realised with other limitation measures such as the use of cleaner energy sources and technologies, improved forest management and the expansion of forest areas, the phasing out of CFCs, improved livestock waste management and changes in fertiliser use.

Global warming potentials and equivalents

1

By definition, each greenhouse gas is able to make a specific contribution to global warming. This potential contribution of a greenhouse gas is called its *global warming potential*. The global warming potential of a greenhouse gas depends on its capacity to absorb radiation and on its atmospheric concentration. The more it is able to absorb and the higher its concentration, the larger its contribution.

Suppose we know that gas A has an absorption capacity twice that of gas B. With identical amounts of A and B, A's contribution to global warming is twice B's. Conversely, for a given contribution, the allowable concentration of gas A is half that of gas B. One may thus exchange gas A for gas B, provided one keeps in mind that per unit A's contribution is twice B's. This is what is meant by the *greenhouse warming equivalents* of A and B, the extent to which A can be exchanged for B.

At present, although we know much about the concentrations of the various greenhouse gases, we know relatively little about their absorption capacities. Therefore, it is impossible to calculate greenhouse warming equivalents and one is forced to follow a gas by gas approach.

In the longer term, limitation policies will go hand in hand with the achievement of sustainable development. Sustainable development in this respect implies both increasing the efficiency of resource use and striving for renewable resources and thus lower greenhouse gas emissions. Long-term measures should be implemented at both national and international levels. Examples of long-term limitation measures are accelerated and co-ordinated research programmes, the development of new technologies (in particular renewable ones such as in relation to solar and biomass energy), review planning, the encouragement of beneficial behavioural and structural changes and the expansion of global observation and monitoring systems (IPCC-RSWG, 1990).

The international dimension of limitation policies is of great significance. Climate change is probably the most prominent cross-border environmental problem on Earth. The global weather and climate system has the effect of continuously mixing the greenhouse gases around the Earth. Emissions of greenhouse gases in one location will thus eventually cause damage on the other side of the planet; indeed, every nation will be affected by them one way or another. Emissions originate from all parts of the world so only a worldwide limitation strategy can be effective.

Limitation measures should be initiated by the developed or industrialised countries. Such an argument is legitimate for historical reasons, given the present emission situation and the current capacities of these countries to limit emissions. At present, the developed countries, which account for only 20% of the world's population, are responsible for approximately 75% of global CO_2 emissions. Projections suggest that business as usual conditions will lead to modest but constant growth in the level of emissions in the developed countries. The developed countries may therefore be expected to take the lead in addressing the climate change problem. It is very likely that emission reductions of 1–2% per year in these countries will be necessary to keep climate change within 'acceptable limits'. At the same time, CO_2 emissions from developing countries are growing fast, in keeping with their need to meet their development requirements. Over time, these are likely to represent an increasingly significant percentage of global emissions. Estimates show that CO_2 emissions in developing countries, which are currently growing by 4% per annum, will equal those in developed countries by the year 2030 and will exceed them thereafter (Vellinga and Swart, 1991).

A global strategy is required in order to achieve a situation in which the developed countries reduce greenhouse gas emissions and the developing countries simultaneously redirect their economic development into a low-emission growth track. Figure 7.2 depicts a conceivable scenario in which the developed countries take the lead in short-term emission reductions and the developing countries moderate the average growth in emissions (i.e. 2% annual growth instead of the present 4% per year) for the next 40 years, after which they actually succeed in reducing the level of emissions. The newly industrialised countries (Hong Kong, Singapore, South Korea, Taiwan), where CO_2 emission rates are currently growing at 4–6% per year, will need to follow the reduction rates of the already industrialised countries considerably earlier.

International political consensus on a global strategy is essential for such a development to take place. Unfortunately, there are several obstacles blocking such an agreement (Bodansky, 1993). First, because the causes of the greenhouse problem are deeply embedded in the world economy, stakes in the negotiations are very high. Many

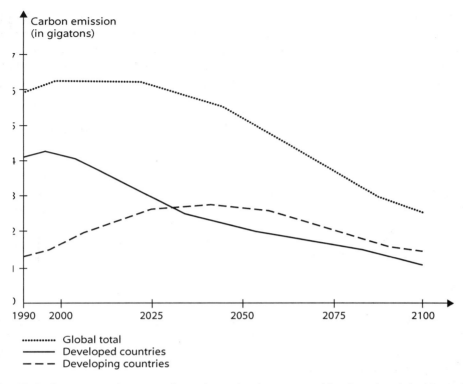

Fig. 7.2 A conceptual strategy for industrialised countries (developed and developing) for limiting and reducing global fossil fuel carbon emissions. Source: Vellinga and Swart, 1991

different sectors, such as transportation, industry, agriculture and forestry, are involved. Consequently, as a result of the diverse economic and social characteristics of the various countries, the interests involved are also highly divergent. For instance, as will be explained below, the stakes of the so-called small island states are completely unlike those of OPEC members. Another obstacle is the large number of parties participating in the political process. While there is a need for involving every nation in the world (more than 150 states participated in the UNCED Conference in Rio de Janeiro), this tends to slow down the negotiations. The process is further complicated by its multidimensional character. Not only do negotiations take place among the developed countries, the negotiations also redefine the North-South dialogue and the debate among developing countries. A final constraint, and one which has been continuously dominant during the climate negotiations, is the existence of scientific uncertainties with regard to almost every aspect of climate change. To this we will give attention after having discussed the second coping strategy – adapting.

Policies addressing impacts

Unlike limitation policies, *adaptation policies* do not focus on the causes of climate change. Rather, they concentrate on the impacts. For example, crop planning in the agricultural sector can be adjusted to changing climatic conditions. Adaptation policies are critically important for a number of reasons which are independent of limitation policies. Because it is believed that there is likely to be a time lag between emissions and subsequent climate change (owing to the greenhouse gases which have already accumulated), the global climate is already bound to change. Adaptation measures will therefore be inevitable, regardless of any limitation actions that are taken.

As is the case with limitation policies, adaptation policies may generate beneficial side effects. For instance, coastal vulnerability research helps to identify areas which are potentially at risk of suffering damage from a sea level rise or extreme weather events. At the same time, the findings of such research can lead to better protection against normal weather extremes and climate variability. Similarly, beneficial effects can be generated through adaptation strategies in the field of resource use and management, addressing the potential impacts of global climate change on food security, water availability, natural and managed ecosystems, land and biodiversity. In other words, adaptation policies also encompass numerous no regrets options.

The precise impact of climate change on natural resources and human activities is poorly understood, although our level of understanding is gradually improving. There are two basic types of adaptation strategy. On the one hand, specific measures can be aimed directly at specific effects on specific sectors. This *effect by effect* approach takes no account of the fact that one sectoral measure may affect other sectors. On the other hand, an *integrated approach* can be applied which includes the integration of programmes and plans for economic development and environmental quality management.

Policies addressing uncertainties

Scientific uncertainties can never be fully eliminated and will therefore continue to confront policy makers and other economic participants (Sloep and Van Dam, 1995). If an experiment does not confirm or disprove a certain theory or hypothesis, scientists can afford to continue and gather more information; but policy actors cannot afford to wait, they must choose a course of action. Many policy makers have adopted the *precautionary principle* as a means of dealing with uncertainties (see Box 2). This principle says that, rather than await certainty, governments should act in anticipation of environmental harm to prevent harm from occurring. Its essence is encapsulated in the old saying 'an ounce of prevention is worth a pound of cure' (Bodansky, 1991).

The precautionary principle   **2**

The precautionary principle originates from marine pollution issues. It is mentioned in Article 3 of the Framework Convention on Climate Change. The article reads as follows:

> The parties should take precautionary measures to anticipate, prevent or minimise the causes of climate change and mitigate its adverse effects. Where there are threats of serious or irreversible damage, lack of full scientific certainty should not be used as a reason for postponing such measures ...

Carried over to the climate problem, this means that the risks associated with a rapid increase in the anthropogenic greenhouse gas concentration and its related influence on the global climate form adequate grounds for initiating greenhouse gas emission reduction measures; the uncertainties currently surrounding climate model simulations should not be used as an argument for not taking precautionary measures (Jansen *et al.*, 1993). The IPCC explains that an immediate emission reduction of over 60% would be required in order to stabilise atmospheric greenhouse gas concentrations at today's levels (Houghton *et al.*, 1990). The human race has only one planet at its disposal; 'experiments' such as accelerated climate change, with their potentially far-reaching consequences for future generations, have moral implications of an unprecedented nature.

However, although the precautionary principle is useful as a general goal, it is unsuitable as the ultimate solution to climate change. As it does not specify how much caution should be used, it is too vague to serve as a regulatory standard. In order to know how and when to apply the precautionary principle, one needs to know the risks and uncertainties associated with particular activities.

In order to get a better notion of the risks involved, decision models should be applied to understand, for instance, the consequences of an *act then learn* scenario versus a *learn then act* scenario. In fact, a *learn* and *act* scenario is often regarded as the optimum strategy (Manne & Richels, 1993). In addition, precautionary measures would have a sounder basis if scientists were more often prepared to quantify the extent of certainty or uncertainty in terms of probabilities (Tol & De Vos, 1993). Only then could decision makers comprehend the costs and benefits of taking, or not taking, a measure with regard to the complex climate problem. One way of avoiding the consideration of uncertainties is by limiting climate policy to no-regrets measures. Within this option, priority is given to instruments that serve a number of objectives (e.g. social, employment and environmental) and simultaneously result in a reduction in greenhouse gas emissions. In fact, such policy cannot be viewed as a true climate policy, since these measures already make sense for reasons other than climate change.

There are several halfway houses in between the two extremes of no-regrets and the measures that follow from the precautionary principle. Traditionally, uncertainties have been excluded by instituting insurance premiums to compensate for unforeseen events. The halfway house policies thus initiate no-regrets measures plus additional investments in emission limitation as an insurance premium. Such an insurance premium is paid in order to compensate partly for the damage which will be caused if climate change is found to be taking place, as well as to avoid having to implement drastic action at short notice.

Policy making to deal with climate change, then, must face two major problems. One is the fact that, in the face of uncertainty about the causes and impacts, there is relative uncertainty about the effectiveness of possible strategies. Related to this problem of uncertainty and compounding it is the fact that there are many conflicting interests both now and in the future. Each will have a particular perception of relative priorities of economic development and environmental protection which will influence the nature, timing and extent of the strategies adopted.

Whatever strategy is adopted by policy makers, there is no guarantee that serious environmental damage will be prevented. Many of today's most serious problems were not anticipated at the time when they arose and would probably not have been prevented even if the then decision makers had adopted the most cautious approach (Bodansky, 1991). Nevertheless, there is no justification for ignoring accelerated climate change while scientists point to the possible dangers. It is for this reason that the problem of climate change has been recognised by the international community and has evolved into probably one of the most complex public policy issues ever to confront decision makers, involving a wide range of participants varying from heads of state to local officials and multinational industries to environmental organisations throughout the world (Reinstein, 1993a).

7.3 Historical developments

The international negotiations on the Framework Convention on Climate Change took place between February 1991 and May 1992, under the auspices of the Intergovernmental Negotiating Committee (INC) created by the United Nations General Assembly in its Resolution 45/212 passed on 21 December 1990. Unofficially, the negotiations began earlier and, no doubt, will continue for many years to come. In this section, the historical development of the negotiations will be described from three different angles: the scientific, the national political, and the UN political in order to draw out the interests involved and the conflicts that had to be solved.

The scientific angle

Climate change was signalled in the 1970s. The first global debate on climate change was launched by the World Climate Conference in 1979, which was organised by the World Meteorological Organisation. There, Climate change was recognised as a serious problem. The Conference ended with the formulation of the following declaration:

> The Conference finds that it is now urgently necessary for the nations of the world: […] to foresee and to prevent potential man-made changes in climate that might be adverse to the well-being of humanity.

Six years later, the World Meteorological Organisation organised a meeting with the United Nations Environment Programme (UNEP) and the International Council of Scientific Unions at Villach, Austria, with the aim of discussing the role played by greenhouse gases in causing climate variations. Scientists from both developed and developing countries concluded that:

> ... increasing concentrations of greenhouse gases are expected to cause a significant warming of the global climate in the next century.

In 1987 the report *Our Common Future*, commonly known as the Brundtland Report, was published by the World Commission on Environment and Development. It pays considerable attention to the risks associated with anthropogenic climate change:

> How much certainty should governments require before agreeing to take action? If they wait until significant climate change is demonstrated, it may be too late for any counter-measures to be effective against the inertia by then stored in this massive global system.

In response to the call for action by the World Commission, the government of Canada invited 300 world experts to the Toronto Conference on the Changing Atmosphere, held in 1988 in Toronto, Canada. For the first time, scientists and policy makers convened to discuss climate change. The Toronto Conference concluded with the recommendation that countries should '[...] reduce CO_2 emissions by approximately 20% of 1988 levels by the year 2005 as an initial global goal'. This historical target is referred to by the international community as the *Toronto Target* and has had a great impact on the debate on climate change. Its influence is now waning, however, as fewer and fewer countries regard its attainment as feasible.

Later in the same year, the Intergovernmental Panel on Climate Change, to which we already have referred, was established under the joint auspices of the World Meteorological Organisation and UNEP. This panel was charged with assessing the scientific information relating to the various components of the climate change issue and formulating realistic response strategies for the management of this problem. Three working groups were formed for this purpose to study the scientific aspects, the impacts and the response strategies, respectively. A special group was also set up in order to facilitate the participation of developing countries in the IPCC process.

Each working group took two years to complete a detailed review of the state of knowledge in its area of expertise. At its fourth Plenary Meeting in Sundsvall, Sweden, in August 1990, the IPCC approved this First Assessment Report. It concluded that, under a business as usual scenario, there would be an average increase of 0.3°C per decade in mean global temperatures, which would result in a rise of six centimetres per decade in the sea level, and that policy measures could be taken to limit this to 0.1°C per decade. The IPCC discussed various limitation and adaptation strategies such as improved energy efficiency, promoting the use of clean energy sources, improved forest management, phasing out the use of CFCs, improved waste management, developing emergency plans especially for risk-prone areas, etc. In addition, the IPCC recommended that countries should start to negotiate a convention (Rochon *et al.*, 1990).

In February 1992, the IPCC issued a supplement to its 1990 report, incorporating the work done in the intervening year and a half and essentially reaffirming the conclusions drawn in 1990. This supplement was intended to assist the INC negotiations, which were at that point approaching their final phase. The negotiations were motivated, however, almost entirely by political forces rather than by scientific analysis and as the IPCC supplement simply confirmed earlier scientific findings, it had little impact on the outcome of the negotiations. (This section is based mainly on Wolters *et al.*, 1991.)

The political angle

In the meantime, political momentum was building up. The year 1989 was one of great political debates on climate change. The first international political agreement dealing explicitly with the issue of climate change was a resolution adopted at the 43rd session of the UN General Assembly on 27 January 1989. This resolution was formulated as a direct response to a proposal put forward by the government of Malta and as an indirect response to the growing international consensus reflected in meetings beginning with the first World

Climate Conference in 1979, and including the conference held at Villach, Austria, in October 1985, to which we have already referred, and the Toronto Conference in 1988.

In March 1989, at the invitation of France, Norway and The Netherlands, representatives of 24 countries, including 17 heads of state or government, were invited to a summit meeting in The Hague to consider the issue. Here, they declared their commitment to addressing the problem of climate change (The Hague Declaration). The original goal of the meeting was to develop a new regime (along the lines of the UN Security Council) on global environmental issues. In the event, this goal proved to be beyond the reach of consensus. Nevertheless, the fact that heads of state were discussing climate change reflected the increasing importance of the issue.

Another political meeting was held in Dakar, Senegal, where the heads of French speaking countries met in May 1989 to endorse The Hague Declaration and to set an agenda for action. A number of other political initiatives were taken in that same year and these paved the way for a focused debate on various aspects of the issue of climate change in Noordwijk in The Netherlands. This led to the adoption of the Noordwijk Declaration on Climate Change by 67 countries in November 1989; the declaration proposed, *inter alia*, the following long-term target:

> Stabilising the atmospheric concentrations of greenhouse gases is an imperative goal. The IPCC will need to report the best scientific knowledge as to the options for containing climate change within tolerable limits. Some currently available estimates indicate that this could require a reduction of global anthropogenic greenhouse gas emissions by more than 50%.

Clearly, the trend of increasing emissions needed to be reversed in order to stabilise the atmospheric concentration of greenhouse gases. This is why the initial goal was to stabilise emissions in the short term. Simultaneously, it was agreed that sink management (i.e. forest preservation and replanting) should be improved. The following step was to be a reduction in greenhouse gas emissions. Consequently, the following short-term targets were formulated in Noordwijk:

> CO_2 *Target*: In the view of many industrialised nations, such stabilisation of CO_2 emissions [at 1990 levels] should be achieved as a first step at the latest by the year 2000.
> *Forestry Target*: Agrees to pursue a global balance between deforestation on the one hand and sound forest management and afforestation on the other. A world net forest growth of 12 million hectares a year at the beginning of the next century should be considered as a provisional aim.

This meeting had considerable political impact internationally and later that month the Maldives hosted the Small States Conference on Sea Level Rise (at Malé), where climate change was discussed for the first time by the vulnerable small island states. By the end of 1989, climate change was very high on the international agendas of both developing and industrialised countries.

In April 1990, the then US president George Bush invited policy makers from several countries to the White House Conference on Science and Economics Research related to Climate Change. The Conference strongly supported the need to integrate scientific and economic research on global change as an alternative to the more difficult measures of emission control. Later that year (in May), the ministers of the

Economic Commission of Europe (ECE), a United Nations regional grouping of Western Europe, Eastern Europe and North America, met in Bergen, Norway, in order to prepare for the forthcoming UNCED, scheduled for June 1992 in Rio de Janeiro, Brazil. The ministers formulated an explicit definition of the precautionary principle, which they felt should guide the action and policies which were required to address the problem of climate change. The first regional target on this issue was set when the European Council met in October 1990 to establish a CO_2 target for EU countries as a whole.

This was clearly a political signal intended for the Second World Climate Conference, which was due to be held the following month in Geneva (November 1990). This conference was attended by 137 countries and can perhaps be described as the biggest governmental meeting focusing on environmental issues prior to UNCED. Several questions which had arisen in the previous conferences were addressed. The precautionary principle was accepted as an integral part of any global strategy:

> In order to achieve sustainable development in all countries and to meet the needs of present and future generations, precautionary measures to meet the climate challenge must anticipate, prevent, attack, or minimise the causes of, and mitigate the adverse consequences of, environmental degradation that might result from climate change. Where there are threats of serious or irreversible damage, lack of full scientific certainty should not be used as a reason for postponing cost-effective measures to prevent such environmental degradation.

In determining who must take the initiative, the conference declaration furthermore stated:

> Recognising further that the principle of equity and the common but differentiated responsibility of countries should be the basis of any global response to climate change, developed countries must take the lead.

Prior to the Second World Climate Conference, the members of the EU had committed themselves to stabilising CO_2 emissions at 1990 levels by the year 2000. They were joined shortly before the conference by the members of the European Free Trade Association. Canada, Australia, and New Zealand independently adopted similar political commitments, in some cases including other greenhouse gases. Japan, which had been cautious to that point about commitments which could seriously affect its energy costs and hence its industrial competitiveness, also joined the EU and the OECD countries mentioned. Among developed countries, only the United States was without any kind of emissions target. In the end, the conference's ministerial declaration basically finessed the issue by calling on the developed countries to:

> ... establish targets and/or feasible national programmes or strategies which will have significant effects on limiting emissions of greenhouse gases not controlled by the Montreal Protocol on Substances that Deplete the Ozone Layer.

Since most countries already had either a target or a national strategy, this appeal had little impact on those countries attending. Nevertheless, the conference was an important event because, for the first time, developing countries participated as equal partners in the discussions and made clear that North-South issues would play a prominent role in the coming negotiations. (This section is based mainly on Reinstein, 1993a.)

The UN policy development angle

For many years, the issue of the transfer of money and technology from the developed countries to developing countries has been the subject of considerable debate. The climate issue provided a new opportunity to revisit these old concerns.

Against this background, the UN General Assembly met in the autumn of 1990 and began a debate that resulted in Resolution 45/212. Two themes emerged during the discussions. One was the question of *form and process*, namely the relationship between the Intergovernmental Negotiating Committee (INC) established by the resolution and other UN bodies, including the General Assembly itself. The other was the *substantive nature of the commitments* which were to be negotiated: would there be separate protocols on CO_2 emissions by the energy sector, the forestry sector and so on and, in view of earlier resolutions passed by the General Assembly, to what transfer of money and technology would the developed countries be willing to commit themselves?

With regard to the first question, it was decided that no parallel negotiations outside the INC would be held on the protocol. The question of the financial and technological wishes of developing countries was more difficult to resolve and continued to be a major issue throughout the negotiations. In the end, Resolution 45/212 simply considered that the climate negotiations 'should be completed prior to the UNCED conference in June 1992 and opened for signature during the Conference'. The resolution also reaffirmed the concerns of all states about climate change and the specific needs of developing countries.

In the two years still left until the Rio conference, several meetings of the INC were held and various issues were discussed. The participating groups took divergent positions. Countries whose economies were in a state of transition (mostly in Central and Eastern Europe) had trouble reaching and adhering to the proposed targets, while developing countries wanted to discuss the provision of fresh financial support and the transfer of technology. As a first step, the negotiating process was distributed over two working groups, which were chaired by different countries providing the best possible representation of the many interests that would have to be reflected in the negotiations.

Once this had been done, various strategies for tackling the climate problem were discussed. From the outset, the United States argued for a *bottom-up* or no-regrets approach. Such an approach would start with taking actions that were already justified for reasons other than climate change. However, it could not be guaranteed to produce a specific result. Other countries were in favour of a *top-down* approach. This would involve laying down targets and timetables for greenhouse gas reductions. A compromise was introduced by Japan: the concept of *pledge and review*. Each country would 'pledge' either targets and timetables or a national programme or strategy (or both). Other countries could then formally 'review' or comment on these efforts and, as appropriate, make suggestions for improving them in the next 'pledge' cycle. Although formal agreement was far from being achieved, the deadlock was finally broken at the end of the fifth session of the Committee, when the US and the UK worked out the wording of the compromise deal that shows great similarity to Article 4(2) described below.

The last negotiating session before the Rio conference took place in New York in May 1992 (INC-5, second part). The final text was very carefully drafted so as to satisfy as many countries as possible, including all the developed countries. On the evening of 9 May 1992, the world's first truly global environmental agreement, providing a dynamic link between environmental protection and economic considerations, was finally signed by 155 States and the EU. 'It is a package which contains something for almost all of the negotiating States, but leaves none entirely satisfied' (Sands, 1992)

The relationship between scientific evidence and policy strategies was shaped by the conflicting interests of the different parties. At the international level it is possible to distinguish broad contrasts in the interests of the major world economic realms; that is, the industrialised North, the economies in transition in the former communist bloc and the developing countries of the South.

7.4 Climate change: regional aspects

During the course of the negotiations leading up to the Convention the diversity of conflicting interests both within and between the major world groupings became apparent. These interests manifested four dimensions.

Firstly, and most importantly, the interests were based on the *economic features* of certain countries. Broadly speaking, three economic clusters were formed: the developing countries, the countries with economies in transition and the developed countries. Secondly, *physical conditions* also played a significant role. A country such as Switzerland has less to fear from a sea level rise than Bangladesh. The *energy dependency* and CO_2 emission conditions of the various parties provided a third dimension. Table 7.2 depicts the differences in CO_2 emissions in the major countries. Finally, *political factors* influenced the final draft of the Convention. For instance, the differing power and impact of environmental lobbies in the political systems had a concomitant impact on the attitudes adopted in the climate negotiations. Several cases will now be described based on these dimensions.

Country	Total (1,000 ton)	Percentage of world total	Per capita (ton/inhabitant)	Per GDP (kg/$)
World	21,863,088	–	4.21	1.0
US	4,869,005	22.3	19.68	0.9
USSR	3,804,001	17.4	13.26	1.4
China/India	3,040,549	13.9	1.47	4.5
EC	2,562,318	11.7	9.17	0.5
Eastern Europe	1,193,167	5.5	8.82	3.1
Japan	1,040,554	4.8	8.46	0.4

Table 7.2 Total and per capita CO_2 emissions from industrial processes in 1989. Source: The World Resources Institute (1992)

The industrialised countries

The developed countries have been responsible for most of the global greenhouse gas emissions so far and will thus have to play the leading part in solving the issue of global warming. Besides the fact that developed countries are the largest emitters, they also have the best available technologies for reducing emissions. In spite of this, this group was far from united during the negotiations and their positions were extremely diverse. This is reflected in Article 4(2) (see previous page) of the Convention, which states that each industrialised country is required to take those actions it has identified as being appropriate and feasible in its national circumstances. The following discussion of the positions adopted by certain countries, focusing on the major parties (United States, the European Union and Japan), elucidates the way in which these individual parties interpreted their situations and the impacts which they had on the process.

Responsible for 22% of total global CO_2 emissions, the United States of America (US) is the world's largest greenhouse gas emitter. Its CO_2 emissions are also the world's highest on a per capita basis. These points are often cited by representatives of developing countries in order to emphasise the historical responsibilities of the US for global warming. The US approached the climate issue in a way very different from Europe, Japan and other OECD countries. On the one hand, its scientific awareness and knowledge of climate change was advanced due to high research budgets and well-established scientific institutes for climate science. On the other hand, the US was the most timid of all OECD countries in endorsing ambitious policies on climate. This was due in part to questions and concerns arising from a preliminary economic analysis conducted by US experts and in part to the conservative ideology of top White House officials. Because of its large size, its geographic separation by two oceans from Europe and Japan and its very different constitutional, legal and political system, the United States often has a tendency to see things differently and go its own way. The climate change issue was no exception.

The United States' rationale was based on the premise that, as long as there was still any scientific uncertainty about the impact of global warming, it would be premature to agree on targets and timetables. The US therefore stressed the scientific uncertainties and sought to go slow on responding to climate change, thereby protecting its domestic industrial sectors which were most closely tied to energy production and consumption (i.e. coal and oil production, the automotive industry, chemicals and primary metals). This strategy was opposed by the majority of other OECD countries, which had all adopted emission targets.

During the negotiating process, the US provided the only counterbalance offsetting the momentum of most OECD countries, whose desire was to move forward quickly. If the rest could be accused of an excess of idealism over pragmatism, the US was certainly guilty of an excess of pragmatism over idealism. At the same time, the difference between the US position and that adopted by the other OECD countries could also be described as a practical versus a political standpoint. The US was simply not convinced that a climate policy with targets and timetables could accomplish the projected emission reductions. The EU, on the other hand, believed that the strength of a climate policy would be adequate. In the end, the combination of American arguments and its enormous influence as the world's largest economy and emitter of greenhouse gases caused the rest of the world to agree to a compromise text in the climate treaty that balanced concerns on both sides.

After the US presidential elections in November 1992, the new US President, Bill Clinton, announced a new US policy on climate. On 19 October 1993, President Clinton unveiled what he called a 'detailed, realistic and achievable' plan to return national greenhouse gas emissions to their 1990 levels by the year 2000. The strategy emphasised measures that could be implemented rapidly and without congressional approval. The programme's success or failure fully depended on the response of US society in showing that it was capable of controlling its emissions through voluntary measures and a minimum of government intervention. The administration warned, however, that it would propose 'additional administrative, regulatory or legislative actions' if the 'voluntary' approach were to fail.

The European Union (or the European Community, EC, as it was then still called) played an important role as a collective actor in the international debate on climate change. The EU is responsible for about 12% of the world's total annual CO_2 emissions. Unlike the US, the EU took a very progressive stand during the climate negotiations and was prepared to endorse a convention that included specific targets and timetables aimed at stabilising CO_2 and other greenhouse gas emissions. One reason for this radical stance was the rapidly growing environmental awareness in all sectors of society in the EU. A second reason was the new challenge faced by the member states to build a European partnership. In October 1990, therefore, the EU agreed to stabilise total CO_2 emissions by the year 2000 at the 1990 level for the Union as a whole. In addition, EU members acknowledged the need to reduce the rate of deforestation and thereby achieve an increase in the sink capacity of the world's forest reserves.

The EU's decision to stabilise carbon dioxide emissions at a Union level created some flexibility among the member states. The more industrialised nations, such as Germany, The Netherlands and Denmark, would make a greater effort to cut emissions, creating the margin necessary for the less developed countries, such as Spain, Portugal, Greece and Ireland, to increase economic growth (and the emissions of CO_2 that are to some extent related to economic growth). Such a flexible approach, which is called *burden sharing*, was necessary to bring all EU parties into the game (Vellinga and Grubb, 1993). For example, total carbon dioxide emission per capita in Portugal is about 1 tonne at present, whereas this figure is more than three times higher in Germany.

The member states have consequently made different commitments with respect to the stabilisation target. Belgium, France, Luxembourg and Italy have unconditionally adopted the EU target. Spain, Portugal, Ireland and Greece have adopted the EU target on condition that their present CO_2 emissions are allowed to grow. Germany, Denmark and The Netherlands have committed themselves to targets which are more stringent than the overall EU target. The UK was the only member state which originally planned to set 1990–2005 instead of 1990–2000 as its target period. Eventually, however, even the UK joined the EU regime in October 1990 (Schepers, 1991).

The EU strategy is based on a combination of the principle of no regrets and the search for a minimal cost solution. In this regard, the Commission has suggested using a wide variety of instruments such as voluntary agreements, research and development efforts and, most important of all, an energy and carbon tax. However, as a strong

205

Plate 7.2 Coal-fired power plant at Nijmegen, The Netherlands. A source of greenhouse gases emissions. Photo: Ron Giling/Lineair

collective agreement has not yet been reached at EU level, the actual implementation of the measures has been left to individual member states. So far, this approach has not proved very successful (Vellinga and Grubb, 1993). In the environmental field, the complex constitutional structure of the EU is still evolving, as it is in other fields such as foreign policy. The establishment and implementation of EU greenhouse gas policies have hence been constrained by various political frictions, which both complicate the EU's role in international negotiations and hamper internal implementation. Attempts to adopt EU policies on global warming have coincided with the intensifying conflict over formal moves towards greater monetary and political union.

A good example of this friction (between environmental and economic interests on the one hand and between individual and community interests on the other) is the recent attempt to introduce a community-wide carbon tax. The UK opposed the proposal because it could see no reason why it should overachieve in order to compensate for the underachievement of others. At the same time, six other EU countries (Belgium, Denmark, Germany, Italy, Luxembourg and The Netherlands) said that the EU could not possibly meet its obligations unless the energy and carbon tax was adopted in due course throughout the Union. This incident emphasises the difficulty of imposing a common target on such a wide diversity of countries (Wynne, 1993).

Japan's share in the world's CO_2 emissions is less than 5%. However, beyond this relatively modest share lie the more significant, technological aspects of its global role. As far as the limitation of CO_2 emissions is concerned, Japan has achieved one of the highest levels of energy conservation among the developed countries. Despite the fact that the gross national product began to grow sharply in the 1970s, CO_2 emissions increased only slightly until the end of the 1980s. This tendency owes much to the technological progress achieved in relation to energy conservation (although the result is slightly distorted because a large number of primary energy-intensive manufacturing industries have moved to other countries in South-east Asia). Thus, Japan is ahead of the

206

EU and far ahead of the US (see again Table 7.2), especially on a CO_2 emission per capita basis. It is therefore not surprising that Japan has followed the EU in promoting targets and timetables (albeit on a per capita basis). Japan and the EU jointly opposed the more hesitant attitude taken by the US and the OPEC countries (Bodansky, 1993).

The high population densities on Japan's main islands and the spectacular growth of its industrial facilities in the 1950s and 1960s led to Japan being one of the first industrialised market economies to react to some of the acute effects of modern industrial pollution (Vernon, 1993). As a result of this relatively early initiation of an environmental policy in Japan, it is less easy to compare Japan's current environmental improvements with those of other countries. Japan is one of the countries which have achieved the most remarkable fuel switching results during the period since the first oil crisis. Due to its already high level of energy conservation, further limiting of CO_2 emissions by saving energy will be difficult. Technologically more advanced measures are needed. The costs of CO_2 limiting measures will therefore be higher in Japan than in any other country.

Japan (together with Germany) was at the forefront of those countries which also viewed the convention as an instrument for gaining longer-term competitive advantage by requiring the further development, production, use and dissemination of innovative new technologies. In addition, Japan has supported the idea of transferring some finance and technologies to other countries, especially developing countries.

In contrast with the US and Europe, Japanese policies tend to move forward rather like a supertanker at sea. It is highly unusual for any entity in the government structure to take an independent line and disregard or override an existing international agreement. Unlike the significant influence exerted by environmental and green NGOs in other OECD countries, informal forces in Japan have had relatively little impact on Japan's contribution to international environmental policy making (despite the domestic activism which has been seen in Japan in relation to a number of environmental matters). Programmes are shaped much more by expert opinion than by political pressure (Vernon, 1993). The crusading elements so evident in European and US environmental movements are scarce, though growing, in Japan's policy-making establishment.

With the Japanese economy continuing to grow, Japan's energy consumption has also expanded since 1987 at a much higher rate than had been predicted. This has made it harder for Japan to attain the CO_2 stabilisation targets. Over the two years from 1988 to 1990, the GNP grew at an average of 5.3% per annum and energy consumption increased by an average of 4.5% annually, pushing CO_2 emissions up to 7.2% of the world total in two years. At that time, the Japanese Ministry of International Trade and Industry (MITI) remarked that Japan might be urged to make drastic reviews (i.e. downward revisions) of its economic growth and energy policies if it faced international demands for short run stabilisation of CO_2 (Matsuo, 1992). MITI had actually planned a large-scale investment in nuclear energy to allow for higher electricity demand and to ensure, at the same time, that the CO_2 stabilisation target could be met. Public pressure has brought the proposed nuclear expansion into question. In MITI's view, without an increase in nuclear energy, drastic changes in the future shape and management of the Japanese energy economy will be required in order to reach the CO_2 target. On the other hand, Japan's Environment Agency takes a more optimistic view on these matters, stressing the opportunities for energy efficiency.

In the field of diplomacy and active international policy development, Japan, like Germany, has played a modest role since the Second World War. In the area of global policy making, Japan has often followed the US. The climate negotiations were one of the first occasions on which Japan took a position different from the US by following the EU. This should be attributed to a number of factors. Firstly, the EU was a rapidly growing economic and political factor in the late 1980s. Secondly, Japan was becoming more self-conscious *vis-à-vis* the US; it was keen to take a leading role in the global climate issue (perhaps to compensate for its environmentally unfriendly positions on other issues such as drift net fishing and whaling). Thirdly, Japan recognised the technological challenge of the climate change issue.

Countries with economies in transition

The problems faced by the former socialist countries of Central and Eastern Europe led to a novel distinction being drawn in the convention. In order to differentiate between the specific commitments relating to sources and sinks of CO_2, a distinction was made between developed countries and developed countries undergoing the process of transition to a market economy. The Central and Eastern European countries are showing falls in emissions due to the process of economic restructuring. So, while they were hesitant about committing themselves, they appeared to be more advanced than any other group of countries in terms of CO_2 emission reduction. On the other hand, as soon as the process of transition has been completed, emission trends may well increase again.

In *Eastern Europe*, a process of rationalising energy consumption has not yet taken place. While Western Europe dominated Eastern European countries in the 1950s in terms of CO_2 emissions, in the 1980s overall energy-related CO_2 emissions in Eastern Europe were almost twice as high as those observed in Western Europe. On a per capita basis, CO_2 emissions in Eastern European countries were also higher than in Western Europe. On the one hand, this contrast can be attributed to efficiency improvements in Western Europe. On the other hand, it also is a result of the inefficient utilisation of energy in Eastern Europe during the past 30 years.

In 1985, the average energy intensity of industry, in terms of quantities of energy per unit of GDP, was much higher in Eastern Europe than in Western Europe. This implies that, in a no-regrets scenario, Eastern Europe holds great potential for improvements in energy intensity. Limitation measures can reduce production costs, lower energy consumption and reduce CO_2 emissions both per unit of GDP and per capita. Theoretically, this means that Eastern European countries can continue to increase production without necessarily increasing CO_2 emissions. Its international energy dependency is another good reason for Eastern Europe to increase its energy efficiency.

As a result of the process of political transition, the Eastern European countries are now in an unusual position. Although the level of energy efficiency remains unchanged, total energy demand is decreasing. This decrease is, however, only temporary. The transitional process will eventually be completed and the economy will recover. Without efficiency measures, energy consumption will return to its previous level, leading to both adverse economic effects and environmental damage (see also Chapter 3).

Several measures have been proposed to ensure that the transition is accompanied by efficiency improvements. Price reforms could play a major role in this regard. In addition, and in conjunction with price reforms, best available technologies will be very effective in meeting these goals. In this context, technology transfer from the other developed countries, as mentioned in the convention, could play a significant role. In fact, many Western European energy utilities are extremely interested in initiating projects and joint ventures in order to receive emission reduction credits. Whether such an approach – known as *joint implementation* – will get off the ground, however, is something which remains to be seen (for a critical note, see Jones, 1993).

The Eastern European countries played a receptive and sometimes constructive role in the negotiations. During the preparations for the Second World Climate Conference and for UNCED, there were regular contacts between the EU and its member countries on the one hand and Eastern European countries on the other. The EU countries assisted the Eastern European countries with their CO_2 assessments and, in view of the political situation in Europe, it is not surprising that Eastern European countries such as Poland, the Czech Republic, Slovakia and Hungary have adopted (or agreed to) similar CO_2 targets as has the EU as a whole. The Eastern Europeans' position in the negotiations was dominated by a basic concern about climate change and by an eagerness to join the EU countries.

Russia's power and role changed considerably during the process of global policy development. Russian scientists were among the first to recognise the importance of the greenhouse effect and climate change. Much Russian scientific work has been based on an analysis of climate changes in the past (a discipline known as *palaeoclimatology*). Whilst Russian scientists recognised the potential for catastrophe, they also recognised the potential gains for Russia in a warmer climate. The Russian government has always stressed the benefits of climate change. During the negotiations, the Russian delegates took the position that it would be very premature to take any action to limit emissions. The degree of influence which the Russians exerted on the process decreased during the negotiations to almost nil as it was not even clear on some occasions how the Russian Federation was represented and what the mandate of the delegation was. In fact, because of its national and international policy priorities, Russia was left with no room for any strong role in the climate issue.

With respect to emissions of greenhouse gases, Russia is in a position very similar to that of the Eastern European countries. Following the dissolution of the former USSR, which was initiated by the transformation process of its centrally planned economy, there was a significant decline in the level of greenhouse gas emissions. However, this emission reduction is not the result of an improvement in energy efficiency and is likely to be eliminated as soon as the Russian economy recovers from its transitional situation (see Chapter 3). At present, by accounting for 17% of global CO_2 emissions, the former USSR – of which Russia is by far the biggest source – occupies the second place in the list of major CO_2 emitters in the world and consequently still plays an important role. However, besides being a large consumer of energy, Russia also plays a particularly significant international role as an energy producer. More than 20% of world oil production and almost 40% of world gas production originates from Russia (Makarov and Bashmakov, 1990).

At the same time as it consumed oil, gas and coal reserves, the former USSR also accumulated the highest energy conservation potential in the world. The returns of cost-cutting investments were invisible in a situation of inefficient planning. Consequently, in spite of the potential to save much money, only small investments were made in energy efficiency measures. Studies performed by the Moscow Centre for Energy Efficiency have indicated that, if local energy prices were to approach world market prices, a vast number of energy efficiency measures could be implemented without any cost.

Economic and social gains would not be the only benefits of such measures. Energy efficiency improvement would also be the cheapest and most effective way of stopping any further environmental degradation. For instance, a reduction in the amount of pollution caused by oil and gas production and transportation could lead to a reduction in the number of oil spills, methane leakages, gas flaring and pipeline breaks that are currently typical of Russian petrochemical and gas industries (Bashmakov, 1992). Assuming that measures for emission reduction are not allowed to increase energy development investment costs by more than 15%, calculations based on models show that emission growth can be halted in the period between 1995 and 2000. Emission growth can be reduced by 14% by 2005, with a steady decline of 25% by 2020 and 35% by 2035 (Makarov and Bashmakov, 1990).

Apart from its large energy conservation potential, Russia is also important because of its current natural resources. The Siberian region, for instance, with its extensive forests, has a key role to play in the absorption and storage of CO_2. There is a serious threat that these forests will be cleared in order to bolster future economic growth. That would imply extensive releases of CO_2 in the atmosphere. Something similar might occur in the tundra in Northern Russia. Global warming could cause bacteria that inhabit the soil to speed up their metabolism and grow faster. In doing so large amounts of methane would be produced. Once in the atmosphere, methane gets oxidised resulting in CO_2 releases. Indeed, things may even get worse. The CO_2 that is released further contributes to global warming, which in turn affects the soil in Siberia, because of which methane releases increase, etc. So the initial change triggers further changes, ever more warming up the atmosphere. This is known as the *runaway effect*. It is not unique to the Russian tundra. Similar processes are expected to occur in the extensive permafrost areas in the far north of Russia.

The developing countries

Although greenhouse gas emissions from developing countries are low and their financial and technical ability to reduce these emissions limited, their position is nevertheless of crucial importance to the climate negotiations and to the implementation of subsequent treaties. First of all, the developing countries are faced with a considerable growth in their populations, which will exacerbate future greenhouse gas emissions. Developing countries currently generate roughly 25% of global anthropogenic CO_2 emissions and about half the world's methane and NO_2. Even with substantial improvements in energy efficiency, developing countries will still need to expand their energy production and CO_2 emissions in order to meet the demands emanating from population and economic growth.

Secondly, the greater part of the current global sink capacity for greenhouse gas is located in developing countries, primarily in tropical forests. At the current rates of deforestation, this important sink will soon vanish. Finally, developing countries are not only leading contributors to future climate change; they are also likely to be its chief victims. Many developing countries are extremely vulnerable to the impact of climate change. A relatively high proportion of their income is derived from climate-sensitive activities such as agriculture or fisheries. Furthermore, climate change is likely to hit poor countries the hardest because they cannot afford to pay for adaptation measures and do not possess the infrastructure and technology which are needed to implement them (see also Chapter 4).

The developing countries were also divided during the negotiations because of their widely diverging interests. Three main groups emerged:

1 the powerful and self-conscious semi-industrialised developing countries, such as India and China, which emphasised development, sovereignty and equity issues;
2 the oil-producing states, which forcefully questioned the need for strong commitments by either developing or developed countries and called for compensation;
3 the Alliance of Small Island States (AOSIS), representing the states most immediately at risk from climate change.

In addition to these three groups, several less distinct parties emerged, such as a number of African states which stressed the issue of desertification and drought, and Malaysia and Brazil which argued that forests should not be singled out from other greenhouse gas sinks. Only the three main groups will be discussed.

More than half the world's identified coal reserves are located in just four developing countries: South Africa, North Korea, China and India. China and India alone account for over 50% of global coal production. As an additional factor, almost 40% of the world's population lives in China and India. According to projections made by the World Bank, the size of their combined populations (i.e. 2 billion) is likely to increase by 50% by the year 2025 (Global Environmental Change Report, 1993). The current levels of strong economic growth will also lead to an increase in the level of prosperity, which will in turn inevitably have a considerable impact on the total demand for energy. The International Energy Agency (IEA) estimates that global consumption will jump to 45% over the 1990 level by 2010. Consequently, China is expected to become the number two CO_2 emitter within the next ten years. At present, its rate of growth of CO_2 emissions surpasses that of any other major country.

Present annual and per capita emissions, however, are relatively low. Annual CO_2 emissions in India and China are in the order of 1.5 tonnes per capita as compared with nine and 19 tonnes per capita in the EU and the US respectively. Nevertheless, improvements in energy efficiency could still help significantly to curb the release of greenhouse gases. Japanese researchers have estimated that, if all the world's existing coal-fired power plants were converted to efficient, clean coal technologies, CO_2 emissions from coal-fired electricity generation would drop by 30% (Global Environmental Change Report, 1993). For this reason, India, China and many other developing countries attach great importance to the issue of technology transfer. In their view, the developed countries should transfer advanced technologies to developing countries under the most favourable conditions and provide technologies to promote the renovation of energy industries as well as to achieve the effect of reducing CO_2 emissions as early as possible. Unfortunately, the negotiations did not result in distinct agreement on technology transfer. As has already been stressed, the convention does not define the terms on which such transfers will occur.

Apart from being potentially large emitters of greenhouse gases, India and China face a substantial threat from climate change. Their large populations are fed on the basis of domestic rather than foreign sources and their agricultural sectors are both largely dependent on the weather. Impact assessment indicates that China's agricultural production potential would be reduced by at least 5%. A rise in the sea level could also seriously jeopardise China's 18,400 km coastline, along which a number of its main economic activities are located (Guang and Zhihong, 1993).

However, the prospect that the developing countries would probably be the main victims was not a subject that was raised with any force by the major developing countries. Their position was dominated by the fear that the OECD countries would set a global regime for CO_2 control that would take away their opportunities for development. Because of this overriding concern, the major developing countries did not really press for action to reduce CO_2 emissions by OECD countries as they feared that OECD commitments would in due course start a process which would end with the developing countries also being asked to make commitments to curb the growth in greenhouse gases. This 'instinctive' behaviour meant that they sided mainly with the US when targets and timetables were discussed.

When it came to technological co-operation, though, they sided with the EU. The EU countries were a little more willing to give way on this issue than the US. Most of the developing countries took the view that climate change provided a new impetus for the transfer of money and technology from the 'selfish' OECD countries to the 'needy'

Plate 7.3 Coal-fired electricity plant in China. Energy policy in China will play a significant role in the debate on climate change. Photo: Alain le Garsmeur/Lineair

developing countries. The idea that the major developing countries could take action themselves to limit climate change was disregarded as an immoral proposal, under the argument that existing development problems far outweighed the long-term climate problems. If the developed countries did not take the lead by adopting domestic measures and changing the lifestyle of their populations, there could be no real argument for developing countries to take any action.

The group of small island states, which is represented in the AOSIS, is a transregional group of nations in the Caribbean, the Indian Ocean, the South China Sea, the Mediterranean Sea, the Atlantic Ocean and the Pacific Ocean. Their contribution to the increase in atmospheric CO_2 concentrations is almost nil yet the impact of climate change on the rise of the sea level is of major concern to them and other low-lying areas. Over 50% of the world's population live within 50 kilometres of the sea and 100-200 million people live in very low-lying areas that are potentially subject to annual flooding. If the sea level rises, many of these people will lose their homes, their means of livelihood and perhaps their lives.

The major dilemma regarding the vulnerability of the small island states and other low-lying areas is the fact that the adaptation of local conditions would be more effective in terms of damage limitation than would be the option of emission reduction. For this reason, several developing countries (particularly the AOSIS) proposed, during the climate convention negotiations, that adaptation should be included as a fundable activity under the Global Environmental Facility (see Box 3). The fund's guidelines, as currently interpreted, would not permit this and, although it takes a flexible attitude towards these conditions, many OECD countries have made clear that they do not want to be involved in funding adaptation costs (Heileman, 1993).

Although the AOSIS had an important position in the negotiations, the actual impact of the organisation, not being region bound, is considerably lessened by the UN-established geographically based regional representation system. Even though small island states make up close to one-sixth of the votes in the UN system, their population is much less than 1%. Traditionally, the economically more important countries have tended to be selected as locations for offices and decision-making units. Nevertheless, the AOSIS ensured in the G-77 meetings that some of its concerns were incorporated in the negotiating position of the G-77. This indirectly increased the influence of the small island states and other low-lying areas.

The Organisation of Petroleum Exporting Countries (OPEC) has an obvious difficulty in supporting any sort of CO_2 limitation. Its members are afraid that emission restrictions could reduce both the size of their market and the price of oil and coal and

---

3

The Global Environmental Facility

The Global Environmental Facility was established in November 1990 by the UN Development Programme, the UN Environmental Programme and the World Bank. It serves as an international facility that provides funding for schemes aimed at resolving global environmental problems.

that this would lower their national revenues. The oil-producing countries, led by Saudi Arabia, strongly opposed the incorporation of any substantive obligations in the convention and clearly would not have been unhappy to see the negotiations fail altogether. The OPEC countries were fairly successful in slowing down the process of reaching agreement on measures and policies to control CO_2 emissions. They were also very outspoken in their opposition to EU initiatives for introducing carbon and energy taxes.

7.5 Conclusion

Many governments and NGOs had set their sights too high at the early stages of the Climate Change Convention. Their expectation that it would go beyond existing international environmental agreements, for example by establishing a system of tradeable emission permits, and that it would create a basis for truly sustainable development proved unrealistic. 'Compared to these ambitious proposals, the FCCC is a modest achievement' (Bodansky, 1993). The Montreal Protocol, on emissions of substances that damage the ozone layer, for instance, is much more stringent, requiring the phasing out of most ozone-depleting substances within a decade. The FCCC does not even clearly require a stabilisation of greenhouse gas emissions in the industrialised world. However, the climate change problem is considerably more complex, both politically and from a scientific point of view. Thus, the current FCCC may be regarded as providing a good basis for further progress. It involves a variety of states, recognises the distinctive positions of the transitional economies and developing countries, strives for economic efficiency, preserves a certain degree of flexibility and lays a basis for future work such as national inventories and scientific research. The greatest disappointment, however, has been the absence of strict targets and timetables. The most important message of the convention is implicit, even in the absence of strict targets and timetables: business will not continue as usual.

The challenge of implementing the FCCC confronts society with much more than a climate problem. An effective climate policy requires changes in almost every sector of the economy: energy, transportation, industry, agriculture, etc. Increasingly, such remodelling will be conducted in an integrated manner, with trade-offs between the long-term benefits of environmental protection and the short-term concerns about international competitiveness (Reinstein, 1993a). The implementation of the FCCC will not be a sudden process, but is more likely to be incremental, as two contradictory tendencies can be observed in the international policy arena (Hisschemöller, 1993). On the one hand there is a tendency to wait for others to take an initiative. Disputed environmental problems such as climate change are particularly prone to such 'free-rider' behaviour. On the other hand there is a tendency towards the development of an environmental awareness that prompts people to act. Newly arising economic and technological opportunities serve to strengthen this tendency.

The product of these two tendencies is a fairly dynamic situation. As a result, there is likely to be an absence of clear leadership in the development of international climate policies. Until the Rio Conference, the EU had acted as a leading force, although this leadership was not irrefutable. The EU has never been completely united and most of all, the European Commission has neither the power nor the authority to implement a coherent programme. At present, the US and Japan are making better progress in designing and implementing their national climate action plans. Given the state of flux to which national politics are subject, the international policy debate on climate change will not be settled during the coming years.

Another reason for the implementation process to be incremental lies in the evolution of the scientific evidence on climate change. More signals will accumulate in the course of years. Uncertainties about the basic science will be removed only gradually and unexpected findings, which cannot always be explained conclusively, will frequently crop up. The key difference from other major environmental problems, such as acid rain and toxic pollution, is the absence of the fully visible signals of climate change that are capable of galvanising society into action. Although impacts are already occurring, these have not been fully associated with specific economic activities. Impacts such as extreme weather events have not yet been automatically related to anthropogenic climate change, though ever more proof is becoming available to corroborate this relation.

In other words, awareness of climate change and its impacts is a prerequisite for a climate policy to be successful. Efforts should be made to reduce scientific uncertainties and simultaneously to implement measures to reduce greenhouse gas emissions. At the same time, the dynamic international process of institutional structure building should continue in order to facilitate future developments. 'The UN Framework Convention on Climate Change makes a definite, albeit tentative, start along that road' (Bodansky, 1993).

In sum, the recent history of policy making attempting to deal with the problem of global climate change exhibits two fundamental features which are likely to impede progress. The first is the tentative state of scientific knowledge which presents ample opportunity for procrastination both over policy making and policy implementation on the part of those countries whose interests are threatened. The second is the inevitable clash between economic and environmental interests. Both the developed and developing countries are likely to give greater priority to the short-term demands for growth and development than to the longer-terms needs of the environment, no matter that these are, ultimately, interdependent. After all, governments must respond to economic interests if they are to survive. However, as awareness of the looming and inescapable problem of global warming deepens, governments will be able to act with assurance of support, even from hitherto opposed economic interests. When it is a question of survival, then erstwhile divergent interests will converge in the attempt to ward off the threat. The problem is that, by then, it may be too late.

Acknowledgements

The authors would like to express their appreciation to Joyeeta Gupta, Robert Reinstein, Roebijn Heintz and Joeri Bertels for their constructive criticism of the draft version of this chapter.

8

Conflicts over biodiversity

Nick Barnes

8.1 Introduction

There is one environmental issue that many environmentalists now believe surpasses all others in terms of long-term global impacts: the loss of our planet's biological diversity. Animal and plant species around the world are disappearing fast. Some scientists believe as many as 25% of the world's total complement of species could be lost over the next few decades (McNeely, 1992). Our planet is clearly facing a wide and disconcerting array of environmental problems and biodiversity loss is only one of them. Attempts to identify appropriate action present a daunting task. However, depletion of global biodiversity presents an urgent and unique set of concerns.

The key feature of this problem is the *irreversibility* of the damage (Cairncross, 1991). Whilst it might arguably be feasible to halt or even reverse other global problems by developing social and technological solutions, the loss of species cannot be mitigated by technological advances. According to some conservation biologists (e.g. Myers, 1993) we are witnessing horrifyingly rapid species extinctions, loss of habitats and even removal of complete ecosystems of an extent not seen since the disappearance of the dinosaurs some 65 million years ago. The irony of this tragedy is that it is occurring at a time when we are just starting fully to comprehend the diversity of living things and their immense potential uses.

This chapter explores the causes and consequences of and the possible solutions to the problem of world-wide biodiversity depletion. First it is necessary to establish what is meant by biodiversity, to understand the scale of the problem (section 8.2). When examining causes, we need to discuss the role of human activity in order to appreciate that biodiversity problems have both social and ecological dimensions (section 8.3). In the examination of the consequences of biodiversity depletion, the conflicts of interest which arise receive close attention (section 8.4). It will become apparent that the conflicts have both local and global implications that are relevant for biodiversity management. Management will be the subject of the final section (8.5), where I shall look at potential solutions by exploring important recent policy developments and their success. In the concluding section (8.6) I shall examine the future of global biodiversity.

However, as a preparation for these discussions we must first (briefly) establish an appreciation of what biodiversity is and how it has evolved.

8.2 Biodiversity: what is it?

Many nature lovers advocate biodiversity conservation on purely 'intrinsic' or aesthetic grounds, but it is also clear that biological resources can hold enormous immediate commercial value (Prescott-Allen and Prescott-Allen, 1982). Initial consideration quickly reveals a multitude of commodities of both direct functional value to human beings and wider indirect importance in the maintenance of the ecological processes on which human life ultimately depends. However, although less easily quantifiable, it would be prudent to avoid underestimating the recreational, aesthetic and spiritual value of biodiversity (Barkham, 1988). Before moving on to consider the major changes now facing global biological diversity and the causes of these problems, it is necessary briefly (but carefully) to consider how we should *define* the term biodiversity. Until recently, biodiversity was a word not widely heard outside circles of ecologists and conservationists but now it is almost a buzzword used by a wide spectrum of environmentalists and policy makers. Its wide use, however, does not detract from its essentially biological origins.

Defining biodiversity

The definition provided in Article 2 of the Earth Summit Biodiversity Convention (1992) provides a convenient starting point. According to it, biodiversity is:

> The variability among living organisms from all sources including, *inter alia*, terrestrial, marine and other aquatic ecosystems and the ecological complexes of which they are part; this includes diversity within species, between species and of ecosystems.

This is a complex definition that harbours quite a number of distinct elements.

Clearly, *variety* is an explicit component of biodiversity, but variety of what? Few would deny that the species notion is crucial to demarcating organisms and that it provides the very foundation for our appreciation of what is meant by biodiversity. However, as taxonomists and ecologists are well aware, organisms cannot always be neatly partitioned into groups of distinct species (see Box 1). Later in the chapter we will examine some more problems associated with attempts to measure (global) biodiversity and its rates of change. Here we need to recognise that species are not without variation themselves and that such variation may be hard to measure. For example, in botanical taxonomic classification a single species may be further categorised into subspecies or varieties. Variation is also not confined to the subspecific level. The familiar woodland bramble (*Rubus fruticosus*) belongs to an aggregate of species; in other words, it constitutes a group of species (or hybrids) which are morphologically (roughly: in their external appearance) similar and very difficult to distinguish from one another.

Attempts to impose structural order on the living world are also complicated by the existence of taxonomically problematic groups such as viruses, fungi and lichens. Lichens, for example, are composed of a fungus and an alga living in a symbiotic

What is a species?

Defining the concept of a species has turned out not to be an easy matter. The old concept was a typological one: a species was conceived of as collections of organisms that could unequivocally be distinguished from other such collections. All that taxonomists, i.e. biologists who classify organisms, had to do was stick names on those collections. Though there still is a need to give organisms collective names, the idea that all organisms could be named uniquely has turned out to be an illusion. The reason is evolution. As a result the boundaries between closely related species are often blurred. Biologists do have a criterion to distinguish species, even though it only works for sexually reproducing species: They call a group of sexually reproducing organisms a species when those organisms have acquired mechanisms for being reproductively isolated from other such groups. In other words, organisms that belong to the same species can have fertile offspring whereas organisms that belong to different species cannot. Of course, morphological criteria are used as a convenient proxy for this *reproductive isolation* criterion, as it is called.

relation (Galloway, 1992). However, there is no need to be scared off by such difficulties; rather, they serve to highlight the incredibly wide range of biological diversity we are attempting to understand, manage and safeguard. In simple terms, biodiversity is a measure that attempts to describe in a holistic way the total variety of life on the planet. Holistic or not, some broad classification is inevitably required and the following three components to biodiversity are frequently recognised.

Species richness and *species diversity* are used to describe the total complement of species present within a particular area or ecosystem. Species richness is the simpler one, as it only counts the number of species; species diversity is more complex in that it also takes the number of organisms for each species into account. Both measures of biodiversity have the advantage of being relatively straightforward. At the same time this is their weakness because attempts to describe biodiversity only in numerical terms almost certainly undervalue the variety concerned.

A more holistic approach recognises *ecosystem diversity*. An ecosystem may be defined as a community of organisms and their physico-chemical environment interacting as an ecological unit; in other words, an ecosystem represents the entire biological and physical content of a locality (see also Sloep and van Dam, 1995). This definition is useful because it highlights the critical importance of the interaction between species and their environment. Indeed, assessments of biodiversity in terms of its biological components only must be considered inadequate and hence any policies for biodiversity protection based on them as likely to be ineffectual. The ecosystem concept rightly emphasises the interaction of species within a biological community and with their wider physical environment. The complexity and interdependence of these interactions should be stressed in the recognition that ecosystems are continually developing and changing.

Genetic diversity represents the biological variation, or capacity for variation, within each species. It is critically important since it allows organisms to adapt to changing environmental conditions and, consequently, to evolve into new life forms. Genetic

Plate 8.1 Tropical rainforest in the south of Surinam, close to the Brazilian border. Photograph by Ron Gilling/Lineair

diversity is vital to the maintenance of ecological stability, enabling different species to respond to environmental change and to fulfil different functions within the biosphere.

Biodiversity is an abstract concept, yet it aptly encapsulates the immense variety of living things found on Earth. Indeed, it is important to extend our appreciation of life beyond the obvious, the appealing or (anthropocentrically) valuable. An endangered species of bacteria or slime mould is unlikely to have the same appeal to a concerned public as a panda, for example, yet their importance in ecosystem functioning may be more profound. Our appreciation of the diversity of micro-organisms may be far from complete, yet its inclusion in the biodiversity definition is no less critical (Hawksworth and Colwell, 1992).

The evolution of diverse biological systems

In all our attempts to preserve biodiversity, we should realise that it denotes an essentially dynamic concept. Even without human interference, biodiversity is bound to change, by natural causes only. Why this is so becomes clear when one understands how the present diversity of life has arisen. Central is the process of evolution,which may be defined as the accumulation of heritable changes in the characteristics of organisms or populations (see also Sloep and Van Dam, 1995). If large enough, such changes may result in speciation, that is, the creation of a new species (see Box 1). Such evolutionary processes are usually considered to operate over very long time spans and over wide geographical areas. However, environmental catastrophes and other forms of environmental 'harshness' (or stress) may also play a critical role in the evolution of new species.

The biodiversity in a given area is not determined by evolutionary processes only; ecological processes matter as well. These operate over short time periods (e.g. the lifetime of individual organisms) and on small spatial scales, influencing the extent to which species may coexist in the same area. Examples include the availability of resources such as food and space for territories. In situations where there is a high degree of environmental heterogeneity or where disturbance is a regular feature, it is likely that more species can coexist. The species diversity in a particular area or ecosystem is largely dependent on the range of different habitats available.

It is also important to recognise the role of human beings in creating new ecosystems and in modifying natural processes. Historically, this role has by no means been entirely negative for biodiversity. Many human activities were a critical component of the processes that gave rise to a diverse biota. However, recent trends in the ways in which human beings are choosing to manage biological resources are proving largely deleterious. Amongst the most important are the increasing emphasis placed on intensive forms of agriculture, wider use of special-ist methods of mass production, greater global movements of products and capital and less and less adequate methods of measuring the true value of biological resources or the impacts of their exploitation.

Of course, individual organisms have always had to adapt to changing environ-ments. Such adaptations drive evolution. Instability and environmental change are not new phenomena but rather continual processes, usually gradual in nature but some-times the consequence of catastrophic events (natural or of human origin). However, what is new is the rate and extent of environmental change that tax the ability of organisms to adapt to change beyond their capacities. We are consequently witnessing large-scale losses of species.

Recent trends of species and habitat loss

Whilst it is clear that large numbers of species are being lost every year, it is difficult to establish current *rates of extinction* with any certainty. This problem is compounded by our lack of knowledge of the present number of *described* species; recent estimates suggest it lies between 1.4 and 1.8 million species. About the total number of *living* species one is even less sure – estimates run from 5 to 15 million. The estimated total contemporary rate of extinction is placed between 10,000 and 20,000 species per annum (Stork, 1993).

Whatever the exact figures may be, conservationists believe that, unless current trends are reversed, anything up to 50% of the Earth's species will become extinct in the next 30–50 years. Alarming as this already is, a general estimate of this type inevitably masks the fact that species are being lost at much higher rates in some habitats than others. Particularly in the tropics, where terrestrial biodiversity is considered highest, in many places horrifying destruction of wildlife occurs daily.

As already discussed in the previous section, extinction also is a natural process. The vast majority of species that have ever lived on Earth are now extinct. However, it is not only the loss of species per se that is worrying, it is particularly the destruction and alteration of their habitats which is crucially important. Loss of habitat area and habitat diversity reduces the Earth's capacity to support viable populations. Indeed, the primary cause of biodiversity depletion in recent times has been the widespread destruction of habitats, as direct and indirect consequences of human activity. Although this destruction concerns an immense variety of habitat types we can single out a number of major habitat types and the principal threats that confront them.

Forests and *woodlands* are the first. They are cut for immediate exploitation of trees or cleared for conversion to agricultural systems, which are considered more productive. Clearance of rainforest for conversion to grazing has had devastating effects on biodiversity in developing countries. In the industrialised countries of Europe large-scale replacement of native woodlands has occurred as the consequence of the introduction of economically attractive monocultures. Remaining species-rich semi-natural woodlands are usually considered 'uneconomic' and left fragmented without further management, resulting in further depletion of variety in native woods. Semi-natural grasslands have similarly suffered from agricultural intensification. Application of fertiliser and other chemicals, reseeding, drainage and conversion to cultivation have all had major impacts on species-rich grasslands which are deleterious for wildlife.

Wetland areas come second. Belonging to the most diverse habitats, they nevertheless continue to be drained for conversion to agriculture, to be lost to development and to be disturbed by recreational and commercial activities. Many wetlands which have survived such impacts are undergoing ecological change from *eutrophication* (influx of nutrients) which often causes profound alteration of plant and animal communities.

Coastal zones, *coral reefs* and other diverse aquatic systems are also denuded as a consequence of increasing nutrient levels, pollution, 'reclamation' and other forms of degradation. Along the coasts of India, Pakistan, Sri Lanka and other countries, productive lagoons have become clogged with silt derived from the inland erosion of soil, mangroves have been stripped for firewood and estuaries affected by industrial and agricultural pollutants. In addition to the destruction of these habitats, wildlife faces further pressures from the over-exploitation of natural resources and a host of pervasive environmental influences such as acidification and climate change, which continue to pose questions about their long-term impact on global biodiversity.

Problems inherent in measuring biodiversity

For some, it might be surprising to learn that, in principle, it is not difficult to discover a new species of plant or animal (Attenborough, 1979). Biologists are certain that there are many new species yet to be discovered, mainly plants and invertebrates, but no doubt also higher organisms. However, without a reliable yardstick of current biodiversity, how can we be confident of estimates concerning rates of species extinctions or other rates of biodiversity loss? Yet, such estimates are the foundation upon which policy makers base their understanding of the global loss of biodiversity and their proposals for appropriate future environmental management.

Our brief examination of the factors which influence the evolution and coexistence of species should have made it clear that highly complex processes are involved, which are inherently difficult to measure. We find ourselves attempting to impose discrete structures (e.g. a classification system for species and habitats) on a continuous diversity of living organisms which by its very nature does not fit into sharply delimited categories. We must also avoid the trap of measuring only those things which are easily measured and valuing only those things which exhibit immediate or obvious merit. If we are not careful, it is only what is counted that counts.

A good example here is the comparison of micro-organisms with pandas or other large appealing animals. Soil-dwelling micro-organisms play a critical role in soil formation, nutrient cycling and other necessary processes in terrestrial (including agricultural) systems. Therefore, ultimately most other terrestrial organisms, plants and through them animals, rely upon them. The extent to which the diversity of these useful organisms is being depleted is, except in very small study areas, virtually impossible to gauge. The effects of their depletion, however, can result in clearly detectable environmental problems of immediate concern. Large-scale application of fertilisers and pesticides will, at least temporarily, increase crop yields but the effects of such chemicals on soil fauna are difficult to measure and impossible to predict precisely. In the medium or long term agricultural productivity may well decline irreversibly.

So, from a practical perspective, those concerned with measuring biodiversity have no choice but to adopt a broad brush approach. Resources, such as finance, time and expertise, are unlikely ever to be available in quantities adequate to provide detailed and accurate assessment of changes in biodiversity, even in the relatively prosperous countries of the North. Technological developments such as remote sensing techniques using satellites and geographical information systems (databases that portray their

Plate 8.2 The rhinoceros, an example of an endangered species, seen here at a water hole in Natal, South Africa. Photograph by Philip Schedler/Lineair

information on electronic maps) may help in assessing, for example, loss of broadleaved woodland in a given area. But loss of area is only part of the equation. A woodland may retain a given area but changes in the structure or composition of its floristic communities may only come to light after detailed ecological survey. Such changes may come about as a consequence of deliberate forms of management but may also arise in the wake of management neglect or, in other words, as a result of entirely natural ecological processes. Ecological processes which operate in the absence of human activity may have a large impact on biodiversity. Any gardener who has prepared an area of bare soil ready for planting and left it alone for a few weeks will be aware of the speed at which natural processes can bring about change in (local) biodiversity!

There is also a practical reason for seeking only broad measurements of change. Large-scale ecological surveys may be likened to painting a large metal bridge; once completed it is necessary to start from the beginning again. Consequently, any assessment of biodiversity is likely to become out of date very quickly, probably before it is even published (or rather, if it is published). Broad assessments are more likely to appear to retain their validity for longer periods, despite perhaps being inadequate reflections of the complex processes in operation.

Monitoring is therefore affected by constraints on the actions of policy makers. There are constraints on available resources and the constraints applied by the political necessity of achieving results and responding to further demands within a relatively short time span. But information provides power. What sections of society stand to lose or gain from adequate biodiversity monitoring? Who will see and use such information and to what ends? Potential conflicts arising from possession of information need to be examined critically during the policy-making process.

Regrettably, many countries, especially those in the South, face diverse and profound social and environmental problems and it is unsurprising therefore that politicians may see biodiversity monitoring as a low priority, even if resources are available to undertake the necessary work. Yet awareness and understanding of biodiversity is essential if biological resources are to be managed in the interests of long-term economic prosperity.

8.3 The causes of biodiversity depletion

Most, if not all, of the large-scale problems associated with losses of global biodiversity are linked to human activity of one form or another, in particular the endless consumption of natural resources of both physical and biological origin. Increasing demands placed on food production systems, spiralling consumption of energy, the inevitable requirement for clean water and ceaseless consumption of resources for the production of material items combine to pose huge threats to habitats and species. In this section, I shall investigate how human activities have influenced global diversity.

The role of human activity

Clearly, human activity has been causing immense negative impacts on biodiversity. However, the influence has not been all negative. Some of the most diverse selections of species can be found in habitats which have developed partly, but critically, in response to long-term management by humans. Examples include ancient broadleaved woodlands and species-rich semi-natural grasslands in temperate regions. The value of such habitats for diverse communities of plants and animals lies in the variety of ecological structures available. Importantly, human beings have been involved in maintaining a favourable environment for diversity whilst simultaneously exploiting resources.

Historically, human management of ecosystems has been sustainable in so far that impacts have been relatively local. Habitats were maintained to allow removal of natural products on a long-term basis. For example, exploitation of *coppice* products (woods of small trees, grown for periodic cutting) in long established woodlands was usually undertaken on a rotational basis, which only affected a small part of the wood at any given time. This resulted in a variety of coppice compartments at different stages of growth with consequent ecological opportunities for numerous plants and animals. Unfortunately, recent economic trends have now conspired to make low impact environmental management systems such as coppicing 'uneconomic'.

So, it is a mistake to believe that past human exploitation of ecosystems invariably had deleterious effects. Similarly, we should avoid the temptation of thinking that conflicts surrounding biodiversity are only new phenomena. Even during times of significantly lower population size, when lifestyles were less consumption orientated (for most people) than today, pressures to maximise resource exploitation were present. Historical records clearly show that many conflicts concerning ownership and common rights have surrounded the management of the countryside over the centuries (Rackham, 1986).

The consequences of human activity on biodiversity can be broadly divided as either *intentional* or *unintentional*, with positive and negative outcomes within each of these categories. Unintentional negative impacts on biodiversity frequently result from people's everyday activities. This problem has become more acute as people lose their direct contact with management of living resources, especially in the developed countries of the North. Most large-scale consumers of products no longer directly experience the consequences of their consumption habits. Consequently, biodiversity is often lost inadvertently, as the unintended side effect of the activities which provide benefits to people. Initially, we may be unaware of our impact on natural resources. It is only later that we will feel the effects and learn of the problems to which we have unintentionally contributed. The global applications of pesticides is a case in point (McNeely, 1992). Another example is the link between consumption of hamburgers (or other beef products) and the pressure to clear species-rich forests for conversion to cattle ranching in some areas of South America.

Intentional activities, such as direct exploitation of resources for obvious financial (or other) gain, may affect biodiversity negatively, as in the case of rainforest clearance for timber extraction. Effects may be positive too, however, as in the case of conservation management aimed at reinstating coppice management. Another example of the positive effects of intentional exploitation is the small-scale quarrying activities which were once commonplace across Britain and other European countries. Although initially there would have been some loss of existing crop or habitat, the longer term outcome frequently resulted in greater ecological opportunities for the development of

225

diverse plant and animal communities. Environmental harshness can contribute to wider coexistence of species and our example of a quarry offers numerous forms of environmental stress (e.g. proneness to desiccation, lack of soil, unstable substrate). Plant species and their attendant fauna which are capable of colonising such environments find that such quarries offer a sanctuary where they can avoid competition with the more vigorous species commonplace in less hostile environments. The longer term results may be demonstrably diverse communities of flora and fauna.

We also need to recognise the importance of *time* in these processes. The problems facing global biodiversity today are primarily attributable to the pace and extent of human-generated change. Relative to the total history of our planet, our own species *Homo sapiens* has been around for a very short period of time and our presence in large numbers covers an even smaller period of time. Whilst the impact of human activity on the biosphere, like the number of people itself, continues to grow exponentially, the capacity of species to adapt is limited. At present, the capacity proves largely insufficient to cope with the exponentially growing threats, resulting in the large number of extinctions now occurring.

The planet is now undergoing a human population explosion. However, growth is unevenly distributed between relatively stable populations in the developed North and rapidly increasing populations of the South. Population growth undoubtedly contributes to the pressure on natural resources everywhere but it makes life particularly difficult for the majority of people facing poverty in the South. Some indeed believe that the focus on population growth is misguided and that it has drawn attention away from the (environmental) issues which require most urgent attention (see also Chapter 4). These might include implementation of sustainable resource management, poverty alleviation measures, promotion of public health, social and economic development, land reform, reduction of resource consumption and minimisation of resulting waste.

Although population growth is greatest in the developing countries of the South, where the so-called *biodiversity 'hot spots'* are located (Mittermeier and Bowles, 1993), the populations of developed, affluent countries have the greatest impact on wildlife because of their rate and quantity of resource consumption. Waste, for instance, is a problem which is principally derived from the activities of people in developed countries. It has been estimated that the extra 57.5 million people in the North expected during the 1990s will pollute the globe more than the extra 911 million that are expected in the South (Farrow, 1994). As populations continue to rise in many areas of the South and the average environmental impact of inhabitants of the North also grows, biodiversity is under increasing pressure from both. This process of polarisation between numbers and consumption also seems set to continue, creating ever greater tensions between the North and South.

Increasing global trade

Trade is another cause of biodiversity depletion that gives rise to conflict between North and South. The international export value of particular components of a nation's biodiversity is relatively easy to quantify, at least temporarily. Many forms of biological resource have a readily attainable commercial value and for countries facing large debts and other economic, social and environmental problems, the export of such products is highly attractive. Increasing such exports may yield short-term financial benefit but it will ultimately generate its own problems (see Box 2).

Expanding global trade is bringing ever greater threats to biodiversity but this is not restricted to problems which arise from overexploitation of a particular species or product in particular nations. More insidiously, global trade brings devastating impacts to local, sustainable management systems of biodiversity which primarily supply local needs from local ecosystems. As international economic competition grows more intense, pressures for commercial interests to keep costs down also heighten. Furthermore, as international capital movements become more widespread, investors inevitably seek out opportunities to exploit cheap resources, notably labour. This results in a two-way pressure on biodiversity.

First, habitats are converted to more 'productive' systems of agriculture (at least initially) in an attempt to gain competitive advantage. Such systems invariably mean either complete conversion (as in deforestation for commercial ranching) or conversion via application of chemicals, input of energy, introduction of non-local species or a combination of these. Second, as goods become cheaper to obtain, local industries become uncompetitive relative to those in other nations and eventually have to cease operation. Experience and knowledge used in these local sustainable systems is then lost as local people move to other, usually urban, areas in search of alternative employment.

Both these pressures can bring devastation for existing native wildlife communities and usually a simultaneous increase in unemployment, with consequent increased social and economic problems. Many economists hold the belief that an efficient agriculture is one that produces the most food for the least cost, using the smallest possible number of people. Agricultural intensification is therefore favoured. The ensuing significant reduction in the number of people employed on the land results in the socially undesirable desertion of rural areas. If a forest ecosystem on which a given community depends is clear-cut for cattle pasture that community must either import foreign or regionally made products to replace those that were lost. Local independence is lost and sustainable management may be disrupted.

Goldsmith (1993) estimates that approximately 3.1 billion people make a living from the land. If intensive agriculture continues to grow as a result of free trade measures, he believes that anything up to 2 billion of these people will become redundant. Some will inevitably move to urban slums, but the capacity for such problem areas to accommodate yet more people is limited. The only available alternative is mass migration. Inevitably, such mass movements of people attempting to cross national borders in search of biological resources which can provide the basis of their livelihood increases the scope for conflict between nations. The problem is exacerbated by rapidly growing populations in many developing countries, resulting in severe unemployment and low labour costs. This leads to the ever increasing number of (economic) refugees, as we are already witnessing.

Goldsmith and others conclude that global free trade will simultaneously ravage developing nations and impoverish and destabilise developed countries (see also Faber, 1996). However, free trade between nations and regional groups of nations is widely regarded by policy makers and economists as an unquestionable objective. They argue that the total absence of *tariff barriers* provides the conditions for the

Export of frogs from Bangladesh

2

In the mid-1970s Bangladesh, along with India and Indonesia, was amongst the most important exporters of frogs' legs. The destination was primarily the US and other Western countries which were importing an incredible 6500 tonnes of frogs' legs a year. Estimates of frog numbers in Bangladesh were put at 1 billion, a massive biological resource which had successfully exploited the vast areas of paddy fields which were primarily farmed by smallholding peasants. For over ten years Bangladeshi farmers exploited these amphibians on a massive scale. By 1988 it was estimated that more than 50 million frogs a year were being exported from Bangladesh and only some 400 million frogs remained. Environmentalists recognised that the trade was not sustainable on this scale and the frog populations were facing imminent devastation.

The complexity of ecological interactions means that the consequences of wildlife exploitation are difficult to predict. Nonetheless, environmentalists pointed out that in Bangladesh's paddy fields the frogs played a key role in controlling insects, which included vectors of disease and many crop pests. Even so, the role of frogs in the nutrient cycles of these agricultural systems had not been adequately understood. Nobody, however, heeded their advice and, as frog numbers declined and pest-related problems increased, farmers looked to chemical forms of pest control to replace the biological control exerted by frogs. Between 1977 and 1989 imports of pesticides cost the country an equivalent of over 89 million US dollars. It became apparent that expenditure on chemicals was significantly outstripping the income derived from exporting frogs' legs. The government was spending some 30 million dollars a year to earn only 10 million dollars from the trade. Worse still, social problems associated with the poverty of peasants were exacerbated because traditional smallholders could no longer compete with large landholders, since the latter had access to cheaper chemicals by purchasing in bulk. The situation became so bad that smallholders were paying about 5 dollars on chemicals for every 2 dollars they made from catching 100 frogs. The wider environmental problems which this trade contributed to were incalculable, with no adequate way of estimating the impacts of pesticides on other biota, including humans.

Despite these ecological and social consequences the trade continued, driven by the Westerner's willingness to pay highly for these delicacies. Large profits were made by restaurateurs and traders but little of this found its way to the Bangladeshi smallholders. Who were the exporters of the frogs' legs who took the substantial part of the profits? According to Friends of the Earth (Vidal, 1994), they were none other than the companies which were profiting from importing chemicals. After finally realising the untenable nature of the situation and the environmental damage stemming from the actions of commercial vested interests, the Bangladeshi Government banned the export of frogs' legs. Within a short period imports of pesticide fell dramatically as frog populations started to increase. Unsurprisingly, the powerful pesticide companies soon lobbied hard for an end to the ban.

Frogs are just one illustration of the issues involved in world trade. Countless other biological 'commodities' are exploited with little appreciation of the wider environmental consequences. Production processes and transport also exert environmental pressures. These costs are 'externalised' and effectively passed on to the people as a whole, including future generations. Neither are the wider ecological consequences of biodiversity exploitation fully appreciated, predicted or accounted for, as aptly demonstrated in the smallholders' increased need for pesticides.

optimal, and therefore most efficient, allocation of resources enabling countries to specialise in the production of commodities in which they have a comparative advantage over other countries. Not only environmentalists, though, predict the increased environmental problems which such policies seem set to bring. In many developing countries large numbers of ordinary people are poised to lose both their livelihoods and the biological resources on which they are based if the effects of free trade policy continue to grow.

As this process continues, it is important to distinguish between populations on the one hand and ruling elites on the other. Free trade may bring benefits to a select few via the increased profits available from exploitation of lower labour costs, but the net effect will be a downward trend in wages (Daly and Goodland, 1992). The principal reason for this is the rapidly increasing populations of developing countries. The result will be that workers in Northern developed countries will simultaneously face greater job insecurity and lower wages, whilst labourers in developing Southern nations will stay largely impoverished. Clearly, pressures to exploit natural resources will grow in rich and poor countries alike. In Britain and other developed countries, where species-rich habitats are reduced to a tiny fragment of the land area, many of those remaining continue to be under threat of development from commercial interests. Powerful arguments about 'job creation' meet ever more passionate pleas to conserve threatened species and habitats.

In developing countries, areas rich in biodiversity may (presently at least) be relatively extensive but the pressure to address urgent social and economic problems means that development and trade which generate international currency are highly attractive options for policy makers. Short-term 'solutions' to these economic problems, which are frequently based on the exploitation of biological resources, become more feasible as international barriers to free trade are reduced.

Chief amongst the instruments which have sought to achieve global free trade is the General Agreement on Tariffs and Trade (GATT) now replaced by the World Trade Organisation (WTO). The aim of both is to lead to global economic integration, increasing the volume of world trade by freeing it of the barriers erected by countries or regions. Goldsmith and others criticise the WTO as an unelected, uncontrolled group of international bureaucrats, identifying their detachment from the people who are likely to suffer as a consequence of their policies. However, efforts have been made by the WTO to identify ways in which trade and environment policies can be effectively integrated. What hampers such efforts is the fact that biodiversity protection will only be possible if it can be financed from economic growth. Unfortunately, economic growth depends more and more on global trade which, as we saw, is such a potent threat to biodiversity.

As attempts to foster free trade and break down tariff barriers gather pace we may expect a continuation and intensification of the deleterious consequences for biodiversity we have already witnessed. Now that movement of goods and capital occur on a scale never witnessed before, the capacity of the global natural resource base to support such activity comes increasingly into question.

8.4 Consequences of biodiversity depletion

So far we have been looking at the processes that underlie biodiversity losses. Now we shall turn our attention to the consequences of biodiversity depletion, particularly to the conflicts of interest to which they give rise. First, we shall focus on impacts on the resources themselves, then on the impacts on society.

Impacts on resources

Even a cursory examination of the values that biodiversity has for human societies will reveal the impact of its depletion. Most immediate in this respect is biodiversity's function as *foodstuffs* of both plant and animal origin, including meat, fish, vegetables, nuts, fruits, flavours and spices. The recent depletion of rice and wheat varieties, for example, has caused many ecologists to raise questions about the capacity of crops to withstand new diseases and climate change. The potential *medicinal value* of plants, both as unprocessed herbal material and as complex biochemical extracts, remains unknown without proper evaluation. Many examples are available of 'new' medicines originating from plants which had previously been considered 'expendable'. Numerous *fuel sources*, *fibres* and other natural materials can be added to the list of commercially valuable natural products.

By focusing on such single products, however, we should not forget the critical importance of diversity in the ecological processes which underpin living systems (Box 3; see also Box 2). Amongst these 'indirect' functional values we can identify many locally and regionally important roles of biodiversity, including retention of groundwater in highly variable climates, the evolution of natural pest control mechanisms and protection of coastal areas from erosional processes. However, from a human perspective the most important ecological process is *soil production* which is reliant on a multitude of different micro-organisms. As discussed in the previous section, without the proper functioning of these microecosystems terrestrial-based life, including that of agricultural systems, would be threatened.

Nations and regions experience the results of biodiversity depletion in many ways. These experiences ultimately generate conflicts of interest, particularly between the North and South. In developed countries such as the UK the vast majority of species rich semi-natural habitats have already been lost and it is now expected that underdeveloped countries should simultaneously conserve and exploit such resources. For underdeveloped nations, their remaining natural areas may be the only immediately available resource and, faced with problems of debt and internal social tensions, the pressure to exploit them is intense. Affluent nations may have the luxury of being able to care about their remaining fragments of species-rich habitats, yet poor nations, understandably, aspire to similar affluence and the trend of biodiversity depletion continues. The consequences will be further disparity of wealth, more environmental degradation and increasing tensions between North and South. Arguments that technological development and increased scientific understanding will allow appropriate measures to be taken to 'offset' the environmental problems associated with biodiversity depletion should be questioned. Technological approaches ultimately depend on a biological basis and their application and benefits are invariably not shared equitably.

Declining amphibian populations – a global or local problem?

Alarming declines in natural populations of amphibians have been reported in many areas of the world in recent years (Blaustein and Wake, 1990; Phillips, 1990; Hedges, 1993). The decline in amphibian populations has also become evident in the United Kingdom where populations of two of the six indigenous amphibian species have declined dramatically over recent decades (Halliday, 1995). Numbers of the crested newt (*Triturus cristatus*) and the natterjack toad (*Bufo calamita*) are now sufficiently low to warrant protection under the United Kingdom Wildlife and Countryside Act 1981 but local declines have also become apparent in more widespread species such as the common frog (*Rana temporaria*) and common toad (*Bufo bufo*). Inevitably, declines have caused considerable concern amongst herpetologists, wildlife conservationists and researchers, which has generated considerable media attention (e.g. Barnes, 1993; Privor, 1993; Reed, 1993) reflecting a wider concern amongst people who value amphibians. The problem is now seen as sufficiently serious by the International Union for the Conservation of Nature to warrant the instigation of a worldwide Task Force on Declining Amphibian Populations (Vidal, 1991), with the aim of obtaining more information about the status of the global amphibian populations and the possible causes of their decline.

A number of explanations have been suggested as possible causes of decline. Habitat loss and modification are clearly partially responsible. However, these cannot offer a complete explanation since decline has also occurred in protected areas such as nature reserves. It is thought that amphibians may be particularly susceptible to environmental change for two reasons. Firstly, as a result of the nature of their lifecycles, amphibians are potentially exposed to environmental hazards in both terrestrial and aquatic habitats. Additionally, a soft permeable skin may make them particularly vulnerable to pollutants (Cooke, 1981). For these reasons some scientists believe amphibians may provide useful *bio-indicators* of environmental change, providing early evidence of global change. Other herpetologists believe that the scale of 'natural' fluctuations inherent in amphibian populations precludes their use as environmental indicators (Barnes and Halliday, 1993). One thing is certain: evidence (albeit often anecdotal in nature) continues to arise which confirms that many amphibian populations are in a long-term process of decline.

Part of the problem concerning the quantification of declining amphibian populations lies in the shortage of long-term monitoring studies in defined study areas. Long-term studies of field populations of amphibians are rare (Pechmann *et al.*, 1991), a situation which needs to be rectified if a proper assessment of the extent of amphibian decline is to be made and the causative factors understood. This paucity of long-term information about amphibians also highlights a more general problem for biodiversity managers attempting to evaluate population changes and their causes. Where information is available it can still be extremely difficult to establish cause and effect. A comparative survey of over 120 amphibian breeding habitats (ponds) in Milton Keynes showed that approximately one-third of these habitats had been lost over a ten-year period (1984–94) of development in the city (Barnes and Halliday, submitted). Despite this loss of habitat, one species of amphibian was found in a greater proportion of the remaining ponds, although populations of other species were apparently in severe decline presumably as a consequence (partially at least) of reduced habitat availability.

Impacts on society

Persistent and debilitating international debt, increasing global trade, rapidly growing populations in underdeveloped nations and intense patterns of consumption in developed countries continue to conspire to place ever greater pressures on global biodiversity. Such pressures may be expressed as social and political problems both within and between countries and the scope for local, regional and international conflicts consequently heightens. Against a background of these tensions, the role of biodiversity has become central, primarily because it provides the natural resource base of ecological support systems which underpin the coexistence of communities, nations and ultimately regions.

Some observers make the important point that biodiversity has a critical role to play in the maintenance of global political stability, a concept termed by some as *ecosecurity* (Mittermeier and Bowles, 1993). In developing countries, loss of biodiversity causes direct hardship to local people. Shortages of fuelwood, food or other biological products cause social and economic difficulties which may initially be localised but gradually spread and coalesce. As people move, searching to fulfil their basic needs, the political impact of biodiversity loss is felt across wider and wider areas. It is not difficult to see that such problems can soon spread across national barriers which in turn creates greater social tensions and scope for conflict. If not adequately addressed, relatively small-scale degradation can, through a feedback process, result in national and even regional conflicts.

In addition to the social and economic pressures already recognised, the scope for international conflict has been increased as a consequence of environmental trends which are physico-chemical in nature and global in scale. Acidification of surface waters, atmospheric pollution and widespread habitat loss add further unquantifiable environmental stresses on biodiversity in all parts of the world. The extent to which these phenomena are responsible for species extinction or the global decline of populations of plants and animals remains a central topic of much research and considerable speculation. If we are unsure of the scale of environmental problems and the loss of biodiversity associated with them, how can we be sure of the scale needed for the most appropriate policy response?

Attempting to separate the extent to which global phenomena (e.g. acidification) are responsible for population decline as opposed to local causative changes can be extremely problematic. However, without such an evaluation it is obviously difficult to establish international agreement about what (if any) concerted action is required. With this in mind, I will now turn to an investigation of possible solutions to the biodiversity loss problem.

8.5 Solutions to biodiversity depletion

Having recognised the central role that humanity plays in the development of biodiversity and its loss and having surveyed what the consequences of the losses are, it is appropriate to move on to consider *biodiversity management*. The question to be solved is, how can we reverse current trends of habitat loss and species extinction? In an attempt to answer this question, I shall first look at the possible role of the concept of sustainable management, before moving on to explore two important areas of international policy development which have evolved recently in an attempt to address the need for a collaborative approach to biodiversity management. At a global level the Earth Summit was an attempt to achieve a collaborative approach to the management of biodiversity. Similarly, the European Community has attempted such management at the regional level.

Sustainable management of ecosystems

The principal problem with the concept of *sustainable management* is the difficulty of defining it in practical and operational terms. The term 'sustainable' is likely to mean different things to different people but the idea of continuation over prolonged time periods is a central one, if insufficient on its own. We need, somehow, to include an element above and beyond purely existing (at least for human beings) and to accept that a definition for sustainability is probably only possible relative to each particular circumstance. The role of management, however, in sustainability is critically important. It is a common misconception that wildlife can be effectively conserved by merely leaving it alone and erecting barriers between habitats and external pressures. Unfortunately it is rarely that simple and in many situations diverse habitats can only be effectively conserved by active management, both within and across ecosystems. It is necessary to recognise that no ecosystem exists in complete isolation and, in some ways, the notion of an ecosystem is inadequate in that it implies separation and self-contained regenerative capacities which are not always inherent. It therefore becomes apparent that effective management of biodiversity frequently requires a transnational perspective, highlighting the need for international policy and co-operation (but see Box 4).

Central to the theme of sustainable management of biodiversity is the concept of *carrying capacity* or, to put it in a more familiar way, *living within our means*. Intuitively it is easy to see that the potential for exploitation within a given environment is limited by its capacity for ecological production. It is possible to extend this concept to a global dimension and estimate the scope for the Earth's capacity to support increased human numbers and economic activity (Daly, 1992). Such analyses are

---

4

Sustainable management by indigenous people

Interestingly, it is the indigenous peoples of developing countries in the South which offer the most convincing examples of low impact, long-term sustainable living and biodiversity management. It is informative to note that in some sectors indigenous peoples are often portrayed as 'primitive' with cultures in need of 'development'. How did such images arise and whose interests do they serve? Here we should briefly note that development may imply new markets (or consumers) and potentially cheap supplies of natural resources, including biodiversity in a variety of forms.

complex and necessarily based on many assumptions but they prove valuable in that they highlight the essentially limited nature of ecosystems on a global scale.

A practical demonstration of this can be observed when grasslands are overgrazed. A small paddock may provide adequate grazing for (say) three horses on a long-term basis. Addition of more animals will soon lead to overgrazing with consequent problems such as damage to flora due to the intensity of grazing or compaction of soil. Ultimately this might lead to severe deterioration of the grassland; possibly the grassland may lose its capacity to support any animals at all. In this example, the carrying capacity of the paddock would obviously depend on other factors beside density of grazing animals, such as composition of floristic communities, soil type, mineral status, size of grazing animals and external factors such as weather. The factors involved in this simple example demonstrate the potential for the complexity involved in sustainable biodiversity management. The implicit core idea, however, is that systems must be managed (or exploited) within, not beyond, their carrying capacity.

The quest for sustainability in the management of global biodiversity, like sustainable management of other planetary resources, is now confronting policy makers everywhere. Whilst it is clear that the practicalities of sustainable management are dependent upon the details of each particular situation it may be possible to recognise general approaches and characteristics which are widely applicable. What are the characteristics of such approaches?

Firstly and critically, there must be adequate natural resources available. This might be expressed in area, extent, size of population, diversity of species or a variety of other biological characteristics. Having recognised the resource at our 'disposal', there is a need to engage appropriate expertise in the management process. Recruitment should not only be directed to persons with skills and knowledge from formal qualification, but also (and critically) to those with expertise gained from long-term contact with, and use of, diverse ecosystems (e.g. the local indigenous peoples). Furthermore, the desire to maximise exploitation needs to be tempered with wisdom, realism and a longer term perspective of sustainability. Ideally we might hope that such guidance could come from policy makers who have based their decisions on adequate research and well-informed advice! Finally, the necessary social and political structures for resolving any conflicts, which would inevitably arise, need to be in place to ensure outcomes which are seen as fair and appropriate.

In conclusion, sustainability needs to be implemented rather than just seen as a convincing theoretical objective. The urgent problems facing biodiversity require solutions which are achievable by ordinary people in all nations. It is becoming clearer that biodiversity plays a critical role in global processes including climate regulation, watershed protection and sequestration of carbon. Policy makers confronted with the breakdown of these systems need to orientate policies so that practical actions for sustainable biodiversity management can become part of the daily experience of most, if not all, people.

Recent international policy developments

During the last ten years biodiversity has been the subject of increasing international attention and this expressed itself most notably through the gathering of representatives of over 160 nations at the Rio Earth Summit in 1992. After decades of relative

Plate 8.3 A scientist working in the growth room for mangrove clones at the M.S. Swaminathan Research Foundation in Madras, India. The foundation conducts research into methods for promoting sustainable agriculture and marine biology, including, for example, the restoration of coastal mangrove forests. Photo: Heldur Netocny/Lineair

obscurity, the biodiversity issue began to gain momentum. At first, it was confined mainly to biologists with a professional interest in conservation issues. Later it became the concern of increasingly large numbers of local people who are on the 'frontline' of habitat destruction and witness first hand the reality of biodiversity loss. As the biologists came to influence larger sectors of the scientific and professional community and the group of local people grew rapidly in size, policy makers became more aware of the problems facing biodiversity and of the need to address them. This process culminated in wide-scale support for the Convention on Biological Diversity at Rio. A number of signatory countries attempted to put policy into action quickly. Ironically, much of the international attention which focused on the convention during the Summit and immediately after arose as a result of the initial unwillingness of the United States to sign the convention.

The convention requires each contracting party to:

> … develop national strategies, plans or programmes for the conservation and sustainable use of biological diversity, or adapt for this purpose existing strategies, plans or programmes which shall reflect, *inter alia*, the measures set out in the Convention relevant to the Contracting Party concerned. (Article 6A)

This highlights the role of each individual signatory state, allowing each nation to decide how best to go about implementing the obligations of the convention, which is simultaneously likely to have positive and negative outcomes for biodiversity management (RSPB, 1994). Like all international initiatives, its success will fully depend on the commitment and expertise of the individual signatories. Although the new Global Convention on Biodiversity is an important international policy instrument, inevitably it does not contain everything that conservationists would like to see included (Holdgate, 1992).

Some consider that the financial resources available to implement these obligations will be inadequate with available finance being administered through the Global Environment Facility. This facility for administering resources originated when the World Commission on Environment and Development (better known as the Brundtland Commission) identified a serious lack of funding for projects that directly addressed biodiversity conservation or sought to improve the resource base for development. One of the recommendations of the Brundtland Commission was that consideration should be given to the development of a special banking programme or 'facility' to fund conservation projects. Following this recommendation, the United Nations Development Programme (UNDP) commissioned the World Resources Institute to undertake a study to evaluate the situation and propose new recommendations for the financing of international conservation (World Resources Institute, 1989).

The report suggested the creation of an international environmental facility. Its brief would be to identify conservation projects and provide assistance to their realisation. The facility would act as an intermediary between the numerous organisations and agencies involved in large-scale international projects. Chief amongst these agencies are the non-governmental organisations (NGOs) usually responsible for implementing the work, aid organisations, multilateral development banks which allocate finance, intergovernmental agencies and government representatives. There are inevitably complex and contentious issues associated with international conservation projects, which involve diverse political interests and aspirations. But it was hoped, at least, that such a facility would facilitate real progress. A year later, in 1987, following a proposal from the German and French governments, a Global Environmental Facility was created. Two principal agencies are responsible for its implementation: the World Bank and the United Nations Development Programme, with the United Nations Environment Programme serving as secretariat for an advisory panel to the Facility's Scientific and Technical Advisory Panel.

Conservation of biodiversity was one of the four main environmental issues which were the remit of the Global Environmental Facility (the others being reducing the quantity of ozone-depleting emissions, addressing global climate change and protecting international waterways; see also Chapter 7). The allocation for biodiversity conservation was approximately 40% of the total of 1.3 billion US dollars, which is significant when compared to previous allocations to international conservation projects. In fact, this is the largest commitment ever made to this issue. Of course, it remains to be seen how effectively it is used. The political complexity of the role of the facility was further compounded when it was designated the interim financial mechanism for the Biodiversity Convention. Nevertheless, considerable hope and expectation were generated in some quarters of the conservation community as a consequence of the scale of support now available for biodiversity protection. Others, with past experience of working with the agencies responsible for its implementation, may be less optimistic. Whatever the perspective, there are a number of important questions surrounding the Environmental Facility: who will decide policy, who will oversee its implementation, and for whose benefit will these projects be undertaken?

There is a clear challenge to all international and national institutions concerned with biodiversity protection and management to work together to make the objectives of the convention become reality. Given the disparity of political viewpoints and the inequalities in economic prosperity amongst signatory nations, the challenge is daunting. We can only hope that the immense problems facing biodiversity and the ultimate consequences for all nations will be a sufficiently powerful incentive for policy makers to overcome these differences.

If plans for a concerted and effective global response to the biodiversity issue are considered too problematic, can adequate policy measures be implemented on a regional basis? Over the last 20 years or so, a range of measures have been agreed by the member states of what initially was called the European Community and later became the European Union. In the main, these measures initially developed in response to the need to address pollution issues of air, water and land, which inevitably involved transnational boundary considerations. Whilst these measures indirectly have implications for EU biodiversity, there have also been a number of measures agreed to deal explicitly with the protection and management of European flora and fauna. The environmental policy of the EU has developed in response to several main objectives which centred on the protection of human health, maintenance of acceptable environmental quality, promotion of rational natural resource use and fostering international co-operation (Department of the Environment, 1992).

The original principal concern of the European Commission was the promotion of free trade in the region and there was initially no specific mention of environmental issues, including biodiversity. It was not until 1987 that the Single European Act gave the EU's environmental policy explicit legal backing for the first time. Measures to conserve wildlife and landscapes were, until recently, taken at the national level of each member state but EU policy concerning biodiversity is now increasing in importance. Policies originally orientated towards the protection of particular species have, through recent legislation, shifted in emphasis to address the conservation of important habitats and endangered species generally. There are a number of important measures which have been directly aimed at the protection and appropriate management of European biodiversity. The Birds Directive, implemented in 1979, was the first piece of major EU legislation dealing specifically with an aspect of biodiversity. It aimed to provide adequate protection for all birds and in particular to control the hunting and killing of wild birds, as well as outlawing the taking of eggs from nests. The directive recognised the critical importance of habitat availability and requires the provision of sufficient area and diversity of habitat to support bird populations.

The CITES Regulation aims to ensure that the Convention on International Trade in Endangered Species is uniformly applied across the Union. The convention utilises a licensing system to attempt to regulate or prohibit trade in species which have been identified as endangered. It extends its cover to products which are derived from listed species.

The Habitats Directive was published in 1992. It addresses the conservation of natural habitats and wild flora and fauna in EU countries (Faulks, 1994). Building on the measures taken in the Birds Directive, it outlines a new system for creating an ecological network of special areas of conservation in Europe ('Natura 2000'). The network comprises a range of important and threatened habitats including those already designated under the Birds Directive. In addition to habitat protection measures, a number of species of plant and animal are identified as being of Union-wide interest and are afforded explicit protection.

Finally, we can recognise a measure which, rather than implementing protection for a particular species or habitat, seeks to ensure that adequate appraisal of biodiversity is undertaken prior to development work, together with assessments of their potential impacts. The Environmental Impact Assessment Directive imposes a legal requirement for developers engaged in major projects to commission and publish statements concerning the environmental impacts of the proposed work. Examples of such projects include power stations, motorways and sites used for storage of toxic wastes. The statement must evaluate the potential effects on biodiversity directly, as well as wider impacts on landscapes, water quality and other physico-chemical components of the environment. The directive also explicitly recognises the critical importance of the relationship between living things and the habitat they need in order to survive.

We should also note that the EU played a key role during the negotiations at the Earth Summit for the development of the Convention on Biodiversity, highlighting the potential value of regional co-operation on the world stage. The role of EU measures continues to increase in scope and complexity in an attempt to implement appropriate regional responses to environmental management issues. Directives, regulations and other measures become increasingly potent forces for the protection and appropriate utilisation of biodiversity in member states. It is therefore important to question the extent to which these have (so far) been successful. We have already recognised that pollution and other environmental problems frequently fail to respect national boundaries and, consequently, an EU-wide approach should be considered an essential part of our attempts to provide solutions. Conversely, we must also recognise the validity of the argument that imposing large-scale regional solutions will always fail to be a completely adequate response. Such solutions can never be completely appropriate for all biodiversity which is inevitably placed in a context of different social and environmental pressures in each individual country.

Integrating conservation with economics

Many conservation biologists believe that most of the economic analyses of biodiversity which have been conducted so far focus too heavily on the foreign exchange value of biological resources (Mittermeier and Bowles, 1993). I will argue that the full potential of ecosystems and their uses to humanity have been inadequately explored. Indeed, a recognition of the wider values of natural resources would lift many of the threats currently facing biodiversity (see Boxes 5 and 6). I will also argue in favour of the widely held belief among environmentalists that the existing emphasis on the short-term *trade* value of biodiversity needs to change quickly and fundamentally if biological resources are to be protected adequately in the future.

The wider economic values of biodiversity **5**

Bennet and Reynolds (1993) examined the economic and employment value of selected tropical forest areas (mangroves) in Sarawak, Malaysia. In addition to the conservation arguments often advocated for rainforest protection, they identified strong economic incentives for conserving these areas, in particular exploitation of fisheries, timber production, tourism potential and employment relating to these forms of commercial activity. The important role of mangroves as coastal protection areas also needs to be taken into account since highly expensive civil engineering works would be necessary to avoid coastal erosion, flooding and other environmental problems.

Attempting to convert the mangrove areas to other economic uses such as aquaculture or oil palm plantations have been suggested, but the researchers predict that this would result in decreased revenues if all factors were taken into consideration. The area is recognised as an important refuge for flora and fauna in Sarawak but it is the economic, employment and coastal protection values which may offer the most compelling evidence to planners for its protection and appropriate management. Such factors, which are in addition to the species conservation arguments, are likely to be more effective agents for the protection of the mangroves.

One form of recognition of the wide value of ecosystems are the so-called *debt for Nature swaps*. These are agreements under which a developing country's debt is effectively written off in exchange for a commitment to protect some of its biodiversity assets. Such a transaction may have the dual benefits of reducing the debt burden of impoverished countries and simultaneously promoting wildlife conservation. It is clear that such deals offer considerable potential as the basis of international agreements for the preservation of global commons, including rainforests and other biodiversity 'hot spots'.

There have been a number of large-scale debt for Nature swaps involving developing countries such as Ecuador, the Philippines and Costa Rica. The first occurred in Bolivia in 1987 when Conservation International bought $650,000 worth of Bolivian debt from Citicorp Bank at a highly discounted price. The debt was then 'swapped' in exchange for promises from the Bolivian government to conserve an area of some 9 million hectares of rainforest. In addition, Bolivia agreed to set up a trust fund to provide local currency to finance the administration of the new reserve. Possession of the land is still retained by the Bolivian government, although where title deeds have been recognised, indigenous Chimane Indians have regained some ownership rights.

Critics of these deals argue that the swaps have the unwanted side effect of legitimising what was illegal or of doubtful legitimacy to begin with. First, debt for Nature swaps do not address underlying problems concerning current models of development in many poor countries of the South. Reducing some of the debt burden, so the argument goes, will only open the door for further loans to be taken on in the future. This may result in new development projects of the type which have already caused destruction of biodiversity. Another argument levelled at these deals concerns the 'legitimacy' of the original loans. Some environmental groups point out that these

> **6**
>
> # Example of biodiversity products proving economically viable
>
> Munthali and Mughogho (1992) explore the economic viability of two forms of wildlife-based enterprise in Malawi, namely beekeeping and caterpillar utilisation, and consider their value in relation to conventional forms of the country's agriculture (e.g. maize, beans and groundnuts). These latter forms of management have depleted biodiversity outside protected areas and have not, generally, been effective in raising the living standards of most rural people.
>
> Although a significant part of Malawi's biodiversity is protected in national parks and other designated reserves, local people have developed negative attitudes to wildlife as a consequence of their removal from these areas and denial of access to protected natural resources. Utilisation of honey and caterpillars by rural people in Kasungu National Park offers an example of how economically advantageous activity can be integrated with conservation management in protected areas, thus fostering more positive attitudes to biodiversity. The study suggests that there are strong economic incentives for rural people to engage in wildlife management to provide additional forms of income to those gained from subsistence agriculture alone. The researchers argue that this could be most effectively achieved if the Malawi Department of National Parks and Wildlife introduced economic incentives for the integration of biological conservation with economic development.

were often incurred by unelected regimes which resulted in financial benefits for ruling elites but left many poor people facing severe environmental degradation. As such, these original loans may be considered 'immoral' and therefore have no place in further transactions which may again bring benefits to large financial institutions.

If debt for Nature swaps involve land which has traditionally been used by indigenous tribal peoples there are likely to be serious problems if these people seek to re-establish their own rights to the land. As these areas become the focal points of intergovernmental dealings in the course of which commitments are made to future management strategies, ownership claims by local people may be highly jeopardised. Finally, there may be important internal economic consequences for poor countries which have committed themselves to paying significant funds in local currency for the management and administration of new reserves. This can cause additional inflationary pressure in economies which are often already suffering very high inflation and where currencies may be facing severe difficulties on international markets.

8.6 The future for biodiversity management

Some observers believe that the only appropriate way forward to safeguard adequate reserves of biodiversity is to set priorities which focus heavily on the protection of those areas which are considered richest in species and under greatest immediate threat. Methods for the setting of such priorities have already been developed and commonly quoted amongst these is the *threatened hot spots approach* (e.g. Myers, 1988). This approach focuses mainly on terrestrial habitats, in particular tropical rainforests, as these are considered the richest ecological systems. The logic of such an approach may seem convincing, although this is inevitably a reactionary rather than proactive course of action. Constant re-evaluating of which areas are richest or most threatened and targeting the modest resources available to address their problems may alleviate some of the worst symptoms of a problem in the short term. Essentially, however, it is a frustrating and never-ending process because it fails to address the fundamental reasons for biodiversity loss. There can be no argument that resources available for biodiversity conservation (whether modest or generous) should be targeted after a process of rational appraisal and priority setting. However, given the social and economic causes of the problem, should we not attempt to deal with these causes at the same time? Pessimists would argue that the ever more desperate attempts to safeguard priority areas of species-rich habitat, which are becoming ever more isolated and remain under continuous threat, may be likened to rearranging deck chairs on a sinking ship.

A set of more overarching approaches have been suggested by McNeely (1992) and others. They stress the need to integrate a number of lines of action which can be succinctly expressed as a *'Five-I' approach*: *Investigation, Information, Incentives, Integration* and *International support*. The first two of these go hand in hand with appropriate research and investigation, generating the information necessary for informed decision making. The use of economic incentives to provide support and pressure in favour of biodiversity conservation will help ensure that ordinary people can play a positive role.

The need for integration stresses the importance of cross-disciplinary expertise. In this chapter we have examined some of the social, economic and ecological elements involved in biodiversity depletion and if policy is to provide effective solutions, it must necessarily be based on an understanding of all such relevant factors. Finally, as we have also seen, the international dimension of environmental problems surrounding biodiversity will inevitably require international co-operation if they are to be adequately addressed. Again, the 'Five-I' approach offers appeal not least because it advocates a need for coherence and integration. In the end, however, whilst being of high theoretical value, it needs careful interpretation in different circumstances and conversion to appropriate action on the ground. A critical step is the development and introduction of new accounting systems which attempt to determine the full value of biodiversity and its environmental functions or the full costs incurred when habitats and species are lost (Aylward and Barbier, 1992). This will not be easy, not least because of the highly complex nature of biodiversity which makes evaluation difficult. But it will also be difficult because conflicts are bound to arise with the powerful vested interests whose continuing benefit and prosperity lie in the status quo.

References

AGRICULTURAL BOARD FOR LIVESTOCK AND MEAT, POULTRY AND EGGS (1993) *Livestock, Meat and Eggs in Focus*. Reist Produltschap voor Pluimuee en Eieken.

AGRICULTURAL ECONOMICS INSTITUTE (1994) *IKC Pig Farming*. Rosmalen Experimental Station.

ALCAMO, J. (1992) *Coping with Crisis in Eastern Europe's Environment*. Lancs, UK: The Parthenon Publishing Group Limited.

ALONSO, W. (ed.) (1987) *Population in an Interacting World*. London: Harvard University Press.

AMANN, M., HORDIJK, L., KLAASSEN, G., SCHIPP, W. and SORENSEN L. (1992) Economic restructuring in Eastern Europe and acid rain abatement strategies. *Energy Policy*, December, 1186–97.

ANNIS, S. (1992) Overview. In Annis, S. *et al.* (eds), *Poverty, Natural Resources and Public Policy in Central America*. Washington DC: Overseas Development Council.

ARIZPE, L., COSTANZA, R. and LUTZ, W. (1992) Population and Natural Resource Use. In Dooge, J.C.I. *et al.* (eds), *An Agenda of Science for Environment and Development into the 21st Century*. Cambridge: Cambridge University Press, pp.61–78.

ATTENBOROUGH, D. (1979) *Life on Earth*. London: BBC Books.

AYLWARD, B. and BARBIER, E.B. (1992) Valuing environmental functions in developing countries. *Biodiversity and Conservation*, **1**, 34–50.

BAKER, J.P.C. and MACFARLANE, W.A. (1961) Fuel Selection and Utilization. In K. Barker *et al.* (eds) *Air Pollution,* New York: Columbia University Press, pp.345–63.

BARKHAM, J. (1988) Developing the spiritual. *Ecos*, **9**(3), 13–20.

BARMENTLO, J. (1988) *Shell als Succesvol Lobbyist (Shell as a Successful Lobbyist)*. Undergraduate thesis, Department of Organisational Sociology, Leiden.

BARNES, N.J. (1993) Milton Keynes ponds back under the magnifying glass. *Urban Wildlife News*, **10**(2), 4.

BARNES, N.J. and HALLIDAY, T.R. (1993) *Declining Amphibian Populations*. Report of a Workshop held at the Department of Biology, The Open University. Milton Keynes, UK: Open University.

BARNES, N.J. and HALLIDAY, T.R. (submitted) Loss of amphibian breeding sites in Milton Keynes, central England 1984–94. Submitted to *Herpetological Journal*.

BARRACLOUGH, S. and GHIMIRE, K. (1990) *The Social Dynamics of Deforestation in Developing Countries: Principal Issues and Research Priorities*. Discussion Paper 16. Geneva: United Nations Research Institute for Social Development.

BASHMAKOV, I. (1992) *Cost and Benefits of CO_2 Reduction in Russia*. Paper prepared for IIASA Workshop, Luxembourg, September.

BENNET, E.L. and REYNOLDS, C.J. (1993) The value of a mangrove area in Sarawak. *Biodiversity and Conservation*, **2**, 359–75.

BENS, P.A.M., BECKUS, B.B.C. AND JEHAE, I.A.M.A. (1994) *Varkenssector op een kruispunt* [*Pig sector at a crossroads*]. Rosmalen: Proktijkonderzeek Varkenshouderij.

BERNSTORFF, A. and PUCKETT, J. (1992) *Poland: The Waste Invasion*. Amsterdam: Greenpeace.

BERNSTORFF, A. and TOTTEN, K. (1992) *Romania: The Toxic Assault. Waste Imports 1986–92*. Hamburg: Greenpeace Germany.

BESSELINK, C., VEERING, W., UHO, F. AND VAN BENNEKOM, S. (1994) *The Netherlands and the World Ecology*. Amsterdam: IUCN.

BILSBORROW, R.E. and DELARGY, P.F. (1991) Land use, migration, and natural resource deterioration: the experience of guatemala and Sudan. In Davis, K. and Bernstam, M.S. (eds), *Resources, Environment, and Population: Present Knowledge, Future Options*. Oxford: Oxford University Press.

BILSBORROW, R.E. and GEORES, M.E. (1990) *Population, Environment and Sustainable Agricultural Development*. Rome: FAO.

BIRNIE, P.W. and BOYLE, A.E. (1992) *International Law and the Environment*. Oxford: Clarendon Press.

BLACK, D. (1984) *Investigation of Possible Increased Incidence of Cancer in West Cumbria*. Report of Independent Advisory Group chaired by Sir Douglas Black. London: HMSO.

BLAIKIE, P. and BROOKFIELD, H. (1987) *Land Degradation and Society*. London: Methuen.

BLAUSTEIN, A.R. and WAKE, D.B. (1990) Declining amphibian populations: a global phenomenon? *Trends in Evolution and Ecology*, **5**(7), 203–4.

BLOWERS, A. (ed.) (1984) *Something in the Air: Corporate Power and the Environment*. London: Harper and Row.

BLOWERS A. (ed.) (1993) *Planning for a Sustainable Environment*. London: Earthscan.

BLOWERS, A. and GLASBERGEN, P. (1995) The search for sustainable development. In Glasbergen, P. and Blowers, A. (eds), *Environmental Policy in an International Context. Perspectives on Environmental Problems*. London: Edward Arnold.

BLOWERS, A. and GLASBERGEN, P. (eds) (1996) *Environmental Policy in an International Context: Prospects for Environmental Change*. London: Edward Arnold.

BLOWERS, A. and LEROY, P. (1994) Power, politics and environmental inequality: a theoretical and empirical analysis of the process of 'peripheralisation'. *Environmental Politics*, **3**(2), 197–228.

BLOWERS, A, LOWRY, D. and SOLOMON, B. (1991) *The International Politics of Nuclear Waste*. London: Macmillan.

BLUNDEN, J.R. (1987) Conflict management in rural resource planning. In *Problems of Constancy and Change – The Complementarity of Systems Approaches to Complexity*, volume 1, pp.76–84. 31st Annual Meeting of the International Society for General Systems Research, Budapest, Hungary.

BLUNDEN, J.R. and CURRY, N. (1989) *A People's Charter?* London: HMSO Books.

BMA (British Medical Association) (1991) *Hazardous Wastes and Human Health*. London: BMA.

BODANSKY, D. (1991) Scientific uncertainty and the precautionary principle. *Environment*, **33**(7), 4–5 & 43.

BODANSKY, D. (1993) The United Nations framework: a commentary. *The Yale Journal of International Law*, **18**(2), 451–558.

BOLSIUS, E.C.A. (1993) 'De hamvraag' [The key question]. *Ruimtelijke Verkenningen* [*Land-use Surveys*]. The Hague: RPD.

BONGAARTS, J., MAULDIN, W.P. and PHILLIPS, J.F. (1990) The demographic impact of family planning programs. *Population Council Research Division Working Papers*, No. 17. New York: Population Council.

BOSERUP, E. (1981) *Population and Technology*. Oxford: Basil Blackwell.

BRESSERS, J.T.A. (1992) Milieubeleid is het begeleiden van maatschappijverandering ('Environmental policy means assisting social change'). *Milieu: Tijdschrift voor milieukunde*, **5**,133–4.

BROADS AUTHORITY (1986) *Report of the Landscape Group*. Norwich: The Authority.

BROADS AUTHORITY (1993) *No Easy Answers. Draft Broads Plan 1993*. Norwich: The Authority.

CAIRNCROSS, F. (1991) *Costing the Earth*. London: Economist Books Ltd.

CALVERT, L.D.E. (1993) *Norfolk and Suffolk Recollections: Away the Lads*. Norwich: Stylus Press Publications.

CALVERT, D. and CALVERT, L.D.E. (1992) *Norfolk Memories: Fishing, Factories, Farming, Fillies and Fellows*. Norwich: Stylus Press Publications.

CHANDLER, W.U. (1985) Energy productivity: key to environmental protection and economic progress. *World Watch Paper 63*. Washington: World Resources Institute.

'CHERNOBYL CONFERENCE' AT THE HEBREW UNIVERSITY, 4 June 1992. *Environmental Policy Review*, **6**(2), 21-2.

CLARK, A. (1993) International cooperation for wetland management, in *Assessing and Monitoring Changes in Wetland Parks and Protected Areas*, p.109. Proceedings of Wetland Workshop held in the Broads, October 9–13. Norwich: Broads Authority.

CONWAY, G. and BARBIER, E. (1988) After the Green Revolution: Sustainable and equitable agricultural development. *Futures*, 20, 651–70.

COOKE, A.S. (1981) Tadpoles as indicators of harmful levels of pollution in the field. *Environmental Pollution*, **25**, 123–33.

CROSSON, P. (1986) Agricultural development – looking to the future. In Clark, W.C. and Munn, R.E. (eds), *Sustainable Development of the Biosphere*. Cambridge: Cambridge University Press.

CUTTER, S. (1993) *Living with Risk*. London: Edward Arnold.

DALY, H. (1992) Sustainable growth? No thank you. *Resurgence*, **153**, 8–10.

DALY, H. and GOODLAND, R. (1992) *An Ecological-Economic Assessment of Deregulation of International Commerce under GATT*. Washington: World Bank.

DE BRUIN, W. and VAN OOYEN, D. (1986) Esso Helpt Beter dan Shell (Esso Helps More than Shell). *Milieudefensie*, December, 8–9.

DE FREITAS, C.R. (1991) The greenhouse crisis: myths and misconceptions. *Area*, **23**, 11–18.

DEPARTMENT OF THE ENVIRONMENT (1990) *Waste Management: a Duty of Care*. Consultative paper and draft code of practice. London: Department of the Environment.

DEPARTMENT OF THE ENVIRONMENT (1992) *Protecting Europe's Environment: The Environmental Policy of the European Community*. London: Department of the Environment.

DEWALT, B., STONICH, S. and HAMILTON, S. (1993) Honduras: population, inequality, and resource destruction. In Jolly, C.L. and Boyle Torrey, B. (eds), *Population and Land Use in Developing Countries*. Washington DC: National Academy Press.

DIAZ, H.F. (1991) Some characteristics of wet and dry regions in the contiguous United States: implications for climate change detection efforts. In Schlesinger, M.E. (ed.), *Greenhouse Gas Induced Climatic Change: A Critical Appraisal of Simulations and Observations*. Amsterdam: Elsevier.

DIETZ, F.J., VAN DER STRAATEN, J. and VAN DER VELDE, M. (1991) The European Common Market and the environment: the case of the emission of NO$_x$ by motorcars. *Review of Political Economy,* **3**(1).

DORNER, P. and THIESENHUSEN, W. (1992) Land tenure and deforestation: interactions and environmental implications. *United Nations Research Institute for Social Development Discussion Paper No.34.* New York: United Nations.

DYMOND, P.P. (1990) *The Norfolk Landscape.* Norwich: Alastair Publishing.

EBERSTADT, N. (1991) Population change and national security. *Foreign Affairs,* **70**, 115–31.

ECONOMIST (1992) *The question Rio forgets.* 30 May.

EHRLICH, P. and EHRLICH, A. (1990) *The Population Explosion.* London: Hutchinson.

ENVIRONMENTAL ACTION PROGRAMME FOR CENTRAL AND EASTERN EUROPE (1993) Document submitted to the Lucerne Ministerial Conference, Switzerland.

EUROPEAN COMMUNITY (1991) Council Directive of 18 March amending Directive 75/442/ EEC on waste. Brussels: EC.

EUROPEAN PARLIAMENT (1990) *Opinions on the Communication from the Commission to the Council and to Parliament on a Community Strategy for Waste Management,* PE 140. Brussels: Committee on Legal Affairs and Citizens' Rights.

FABER, G. (1996) International trade and environmental policies. In Blowers, A. and Glasbergen, P. (eds), *Environmental Policy in an International context: Prospects for Environmental Change.* London: Edward Arnold, Chapter 4.

FARROW, C. (1994) The people problem. *WWF News,* Summer, 4–5.

FAULKS, J. (1994) The EU Habitats Directive, a policy profile. *European Environment,* **4**, 12–13.

FESBACH, M. and FRIENDLY Jr., A. (1992) *Ecocide in the USSR. Health and Nature under Siege.* New York: Basic Books.

FISCHER, G., FROHBERG, K., PARRY, M.L. and ROSENZWEIG, C. (1993) Climate Change and World Food Supply, Demand and Trade. In Kaya, Y., Nakicenovic, N., Nordhaus, W.D. and Toth, F.L. (eds) *Cost and Benefits of CO$_2$ Mitigation.* Laxenburg: International Institute for Applied Systems Analysis.

FRANSEN, J. (1985) Bezwaren tegen Vergunning voor Luchtvervuiling door Shell (Objections to air pollution permits for Shell). *Natuur en Milieu,* **7/8**, 25.

FRIENDS OF THE EARTH (1990) Britain's buried poison. *The Observer,* colour supplement, 4 February.

FROUWS, J. (1993) 'Mest en Macht' (Manure and power). A political and sociological study of representing interests and policy formulation in relation to the manure problem in the Netherlands from 1970. In *Studies on Agriculture and Rural Area,* 11. Wageningen: University of Agriculture.

GALLOWAY, D.J. (1992) Biodiversity: a lichenological perspective. *Biodiversity and Conservation,* **4**, 312–23.

GAVENTA, J. (1980) *Power and Powerlessness: Quiescence and Rebellion in an Appalachian Valley.* Urbana: University of Illinois Press.

GILBERT, J. and VELLINGA. P. (1990) Coastal zone management. In IPCC-RSWG, *Climate Change: The IPCC Response Strategies.* Cambridge: Cambridge University Press.

GLASBERGEN, P. (ed.) (1995) *Managing Environmental Disputes. Network Management as an Alternative.* Dordrecht: Kluwer Academic Publishers.

GLASBERGEN, P. and BLOWERS, A. (eds) (1995) *Environmental Policy in an International Context: Perspectives on Environmental Problems.* London: Edward Arnold.

GLASBERGEN, P. and KLIJN, F. (1991) Integrated water and wetland management: towards a project approach. *Landscape and Urban Planning*, **20**, 257–62.

GLOBAL ENVIRONMENTAL CHANGE REPORT (1993) Clean coal technology for developing countries: can the barriers be broken? *Global Environmental Change Report*, **5**(11), 1–3.

GOLDSMITH, J. (1993) *The Trap*. Basingstoke: Macmillan.

GOLITSYN, G.S. (1993) Ecological problems in the CIS during the transitional period. *RFL/RL Research Report*, **2**(2), p.8.

GOPAL, B. (ed.) (1990) *Ecology and Management of Aquatic Vegetation in the Indian Subcontinent*. Dordrecht: Kluwer Academic Publishers.

GOVERNMENT OF THE HUNGARIAN REPUBLIC (1991) *National Report to the United Nations Conference on Environment and Development*. Budapest.

GREEN, M. (ed.) (1992) *Memories of Norfolk*. Norwich: Stylus Press Publications.

GREENHALGH, S. (1990) Towards a political economy of fertility: anthropological contributions. *Population and Development Review*, **16**, 85–106.

GRIGG, D. (1980) *Population Growth and Agrarian Change: An Historical Perspective*. Cambridge: Cambridge University Press.

GUANG, Xia and ZHIHONG, Wei (1993) *Climate Change and Its Technical and Institutional Adaptations: China's Perspective*. Laxenburg, Austria. Prepared for the International Workshop on Mitigation, Impacts and Adaptation to Climate Change held by the Institute for Applied System Analysis, 13–15 October.

HALL, R. (1989) *Update: World Population Trends*. Cambridge: Cambridge University Press.

HALLIDAY, T.R. (in press) Declining amphibians in Europe with particular emphasis on the situation in Britain. *Environmental Reviews*.

HARRISON, P. (1990) Too much life on earth? *New Scientist*, 19 May .

HARRISON, P. (1992) *The Third Revolution: Environment, Population and a Sustainable World*. London: I.B.Tauris.

HAWKSWORTH, D.L. and COLWELL, R.R. (1992) Microbial diversity 21: biodiversity amongst micro-organisms and its relevance. *Biodiversity and Conservation*, **1**(4), 221–6.

HEDGES, S.B. (1993) Global amphibian declines: a perspective from the Caribbean. *Biodiversity and Conservation*, **2**, 290–303.

HEILEMAN, L.I. (1993) The alliance of Small Island States (AOSIS): a mechanism for coordinated representation of Small Island States on issues of common concern. *Ambio*, **22**(1), 55–6.

HELWEGE, A. (1990) Latin American agricultural performance in the debt crisis: salvation or stagnation? *Latin American Perspectives*, **67**, 57-75.

HETTELINGH, J.P., DOWNING, R.J. and DE SMET, P.A.M. (1991) Mapping critical loads for Europe. In *CCE Technical Report No. 1*. Bilthoven: RIVM.

HEWITT, T. and SMYTH, I. (1992) Is the world overpopulated? In Allen, T. and Thomas, A. (eds), *Poverty and Development in the 1990s*. Oxford: Oxford University Press, pp.78–96.

HILZ, C. (1992) *The International Toxic Waste Trade*. New York: Van Nostrand Reinhold.

HISSCHEMÖLLER, M. (1993) *International Positions Concerning the Greenhouse Effect*. The Hague, The Netherlands. Paper prepared for Workshop on Policy Options Addressing the Greenhouse Effect, 16–17 November.

HMSO (1986) *Radioactive Waste. First Report of the House of Commons Environment Committee, Session 1985–6*. London: HMSO.

HMSO (1992) *The UK Environment*. London: HMSO.

HOLDGATE, M.W. (1979) *A Perspective of Environmental Pollution*. Cambridge: Cambridge University Press.

HOLDGATE, M.W. (1992) Biodiversity conservation after Rio. *Biodiversity and Conservation*, **1**, 346–7.

HORDIJK, L. (1991) Use of the RAINS model in acid rain negotiations in Europe. Besselink, C., Veering, W., Udo, F., van Bennekom, S., *Environmental Science and Technology*, **25**(4), 596-602.

HORDIJK, L., SHAW, R. and ALCAMO, J. (1990) Background to acidification in Europe. In Hordÿk, L., Shaw, R. and Alcamo, J . (eds) *The RAINS Model of Acidification; Science and Strategies in Europe*. Dordrecht: Kluwer Academic Publishers, pp.31–60.

HOUGHTON, J.T., CALLANDER, B.A. and VARNEY, S.K. (eds.)(1992) *Climate Change 1992 — The Supplementary Report to the IPCC Scientific Assessment*. Cambridge: Cambridge University Press.

HOUGHTON, J.T., JENKINS, G.J. and EPHRAUMS, J.J. (eds.)(1990) *Climate Change — The IPCC Scientific Assessment*. Cambridge: Cambridge University Press.

HOUSE OF COMMONS ENVIRONMENT COMMITTEE (1989–90) *Contaminated Land. First Report, Session 1989–90, vol 1*. London: HMSO.

IAEA (1992) *Radioactive Waste Management*. Vienna: IAEA.

IPCC–RSWG (1990) *Climate Change: The IPCC Response Strategies*. Cambridge: Cambridge University Press.

IVENS, W. (1990) *Atmospheric deposition onto forests*. PhD thesis, University of Utrecht.

IVERSEN, T., SALTBONES, J., SANDES, H., ELIASSEN, A. and HOV, O. (1989) *Airborne Transboundary Transport of Sulphur and Nitrogen over Europe: Model Descriptions and Calculations*. Oslo, Norway: EMEP/MSC-W Report 2/89.

IZRAEL, Y. (1991) *Climate Change Impact Studies: The IPCC Working Group II Report*. In Jäger, J. and Ferguson, H.L. (eds), *Climate Change: Science, Impacts and Policy*. Proceedings of the Second World Climate Conference. Cambridge: Cambridge University Press.

JANICKE, M., MUNCH, H., BINDER, M. *et al.* (1992) *Umweltentlastung durch industriellen Strukturwandel? Eine explorative Studie der 32 Industrieländer (1970 bis 1990)*. Berlin: Edition Sigma.

JANSEN, H.M., KLEIN, R.J.T., TOL, R.S.J., VERBRUGGEN, H. (1993) *Some Considerations on the Economic Importance of Proactive Integrated Coastal Zone Management*. Noordwijk, The Netherlands. Paper prepared for the International Conference on Coastal Zone Management, 1–5 November.

JANSEN, H.M., VAN DER MEER, G.J., OPSCHOOR, J.B. and STAPEL, J.H.A. (1974) *Een Raming van de Schade door Luchtverontreiniging in Nederland in 1970* (An estimate of the damage caused by air pollution in the Netherlands in 1970). Amsterdam: Instituut voor Milieuvraagstukken (Institute for Environmental Issues), Free University.

JOHANNESSEN, M., SKARTVEIT, A. and WRIGHT, R.F. (1980) Streamwater chemistry before, during and after snowmelt. In Drablos, D. and Tollan, A. (eds), *Ecological Impact of Acid Precipitation*. Oslo: SNSF Project, pp.224–6.

JONES, R. (1985) *Birds of the Norfolk Broads*. Norwich: Jarrold.

JONES, T. (1993) *Operational criteria for joint implementation*. Paris: Paper prepared for the Conference on the Economics of Climate Change, OECD.

KABEER, N. (1992) From fertility reduction to reproductive choice: gender perspectives on family planning. In *Discussion Paper 299*, Institute of Development Studies, University of Sussex.

KAMMINGA, M.T. (1995) Principles of international environmental law. In Glasbergen, P. and Blowers, A. (eds), *Environmental Policy in an International Context: Perspectives on Environmental Problems*. London: Edward Arnold, pp.109-29.

248

KATES, R.W. and HAARMANN, V. (1992) Where the poor live. Are the assumptions correct? *Environment*, **34**, 4–11, 25–8.

KHAZANOV, A. (1990) The ecological situation and the national issue in Uzbekistan. *Environmental Policy Review*, **4**(1), 20-8.

KLAASSEN, G. and OPSCHOOR, J.B. (1991) Economics of sustainability or the sustainability of economics. *Ecological Economics,* **4**, 93–116.

KNOOK, H.D. (1991) Coordination of EC assistance to the Black Triangle. *International Spectator*, **45**(11), 709-17.

KORNAI, J. (1979) Resource-constrained versus demand-constrained systems. *Econometrica*, **47**(4), 801-19.

KOTLYAKOV, V.M. (1992) Concept for preserving and restoring the Aral Sea and normalizing the ecological, public health, and socioeconomic situation in the Aral region. *Post-Soviet Geography*, **33**(5), 283-95.

KRIVSKY, Z. (1991) *Air Pollution in Northern Bohemia*. Unpublished paper. Usti nad Labem: The North Bohemian Economic Association.

LARGE AND ASSOCIATES (1992) Comparison of the radioactive waste arisings generated by reprocessing, encapsulation and storage of LWR and AGR irradiated fuels. *Greenpeace*, 14 December.

LEONARD, H.J. (1989) Overview. In Leonard, H.J. *et al.* (eds), *Environment and the Poor: Development Strategies for a Common Agenda*. Washington DC: Overseas Development Council.

LESTHAEGHE, R. (1986) On the adaptation of sub-Saharan systems of reproduction. In Coleman, D. and Schofield, R. (eds), *The State of Population Theory*. Oxford: Basil Blackwell, pp.212–38.

LIBERATORE, A. (1995) The social construction of environmental problems. In Glasbergen, P. and Blowers, A. (eds), *Environmental Policy in an International Context: Perspectives on Environmental Problems*. London: Edward Arnold, pp.58–82.

LOCKWOOD, M. (1991) Food security and environmental degradation in Northern Nigeria: demographic perspectives. *IDS Bulletin*, **22**(3), 12–21.

LOHMANN, L. (1994) Freedom to plant. In *Southeast Asia and the Globalization of the Pulp and Paper Industry*. Unpublished paper.

LUKES, S. (1974) *Power: A Radical View*. London: Macmillan.

LUTZ, W. and HOLM, E. (1993) Mauritius: population and land use. In Jolly, C.L. and Boyle Torrey, B. (eds), *Population and Land Use in Developing Countries*. Washington DC: National Academy Press.

MACEWEN, M. and MACEWEN, A. (1987) *Greenprints for the Countryside: The Story of Britain's National Parks*. London: Allen and Unwin.

MACKENZIE, J.J. and EL-ASHRY, M.T. (eds) (1989) *Air Pollution's Toll on Forests and Crops*. New Haven: Yale University Press.

MAKAROV, A.A. and BASHMAKOV, I. (1990) The Soviet Union. In Chandler, W.U. (ed.), *Carbon Emissions Control Strategies: Case Studies in International Cooperation*. Baltimore: World Wildlife Fund & Conservation Foundation.

MALSTER, R. (1993) *The Broads*. Norwich: Philimore Publishing.

MANNE, A.S. and RICHELS, R.G. (1991) Buying greenhouse insurance. *Energy Policy*, **19**, 543–52.

MANNE, A.S. and RICHELS, R.G. (1993) CO_2 *Hedging Strategies: The Impact of Uncertainty upon Emissions*. Paris. Paper prepared for the Conference on Economics of Climate Change, June 14–16.

MARCHAND, M. and UDO DE HAES, H.A. (1991) Introduction, selection of papers from 'The People's Role in Wetland Management', Leiden, 1989. *Landscape and Urban Planning*, **20**, 1–8.

MARPLES, M. (1992) Post-Soviet Belarus and the impact of Chernobyl. *Post-Soviet Geography*, **33**(7), 419-31.

MATSUO, N. (1992) *Japan*. In Pachauri, R.K. and Bhandari, P. (eds), *Global Warming: Collaborative Study on Strategies to Limit CO_2 Emissions in Asia and Brazil*. New Delhi: Asian Energy Institute.

MCNEELY, J.A. (1992) The sinking ark: pollution and the world-wide loss of biodiversity. *Biodiversity and Conservation*, **1**, 2–18.

MEDVEDEV, Z.A. (1980) *Nuclear Disaster in the Urals*. New York: Vintage Books.

MEDVEDEV, Z.A. (1990) *The Legacy of Chernobyl*. Oxford: Basil Blackwell Ltd.

METZ, L., JANICKE, M. AND PSCHK, J. (1991) *Die Energiesituation in der vormaligen DDR. Darstellung, Kritik und Perspektiven der Elektrizitätsversorgung*. Berlin: Edition Sigma Bohn.

MICKLIN, P.P. (1992) The Aral crisis: introduction to the special issue. *Post-Soviet Geography*, **33**(5), 269-82.

MINISTER OF PUBLIC HOUSING, PHYSICAL PLANNING AND THE ENVIRONMENT (1983-1984) *De Problematiek van de Verzuring* (The problems of acidification), 18225, Nos. 1 and 2. Den Haag: VROM.

MINISTER OF PUBLIC HOUSING, PHYSICAL PLANNING AND THE ENVIRONMENT (1984-1985). *Indicatief Meerjarenprogramma Lucht 1985–1989* (Indicative long-term programme on air), 18605, Nos. 1–2, and 8. Den Haag: VROM.

MINISTRY OF AGRICULTURE, NATURE CONSERVATION AND FISHERIES (1982) *Memorandum on Manure and Ammonia Policy, Stage Three*. Lower House of Parliament, No. 34. London: HMSO.

MINISTRY OF ECOLOGY AND NATIONAL RESOURCES OF THE RUSSIAN FEDERATION (1992) *National Report*. Moscow: 1992 UN Conference on Environment and Development.

MINISTRY OF THE ENVIRONMENT OF THE CZECH REPUBLIC (1990) *Environment of the Czech Republic, Parts l, 2 and 3*. Prague: Brzda Publishing House.

MINISTRY OF ENVIRONMENTAL PROTECTION, NATURAL RESOURCES AND FORESTRY (1991) *The State of the Environment in Poland. Damage and Remedy*. Warsaw: Ministry of Environmental Protection, Natural Resources and Forestry.

MITCHELL, J.F.B., MANABE, S., TOKIOKA, T., and MELESHKO, V. (1990) *Equilibrium Climate Change*. In Houghton, J.T. *et al.* (eds), *Climate Change – The IPCC Scientific Assessment*. Cambridge: Cambridge University Press.

MITTERMEIER, R.A. and BOWLES, I.A. (1993) The Global Environment Facility and biodiversity conservation: lessons to date and suggestions for future action. *Biodiversity and Conservation*, **2**, 637–55.

MONROE, S.D. (1992) Chelyabinsk: the evolution of disaster. *Post-Soviet Geography*, **33**(8), 533-45.

MORTIMORE, M. (1993) Northern Nigeria: land transformation under agricultural intensification. In Jolly, C.L. and Boyle Torrey, B. (eds), *Population and Land Use in Developing Countries*. Washington DC: National Academy Press.

MUNTHALI, S.M. and MUGHOGHO, D.E.C. (1992) Economic incentives for conservation: beekeeping and Saturniidae caterpillar utilization by rural communities. *Biodiversity and Conservation*, **1**, 143–54.

MYERS, N. (1988) Threatened biotas: hot spots in tropical forests. *The Environmentalist,* **8,** 187–208.

MYERS, N. (1991) The world's forests and human populations: the environmental interconnections. In Davies, K. and Bernstam, M.S. (eds), *Resources, Environment, and Population: Present Knowledge, Future Options.* Oxford: Oxford University Press.

MYERS, N. (1993a) Tropical forests: the main deforestation fronts. *Environmental Conservation,* **20**(1), 9–16.

MYERS, N. (1993b) Questions of mass extinction. *Biodiversity and Conservation,* **2,** 2–17.

NATIONAL INSTITUTE OF PUBLIC HEALTH AND ENVIRONMENTAL PROTECTION (1991) *Nationale Milieuverkenning 1990–2010* (National Environmental Outlook, 1990–2010). Bilthoven: Rijksinstituut voor Volksgezondheid en Milieuhygiëne.

NATIONAL RIVERS AUTHORITY ANGLIAN REGION (1993) *Broadland, A Flood Alleviation Strategy: Options and Impacts.* London: NRA.

NOWICKI, M. (1992) *Environment in Poland. Issues and Solutions.* Warsaw: Ministry of Environmental Protection, Natural Resources and Forestry.

ODÉN, S. (1968) Nederbördens och Luftens Försurning dess Orsaker, Förlopp och Verkan i Olika Miljöer. Statens Naturvetenskopliga Forskningsråd. *Ekologikomitteën, Bulletin,* **1.**

OECD (1977) *The OECD Programme on Long-Range Transport of Air Pollutants – Measurements and Findings.* Paris: OECD.

OECD (1988) *Decision of the Council on Transfrontier Movements of Hazardous Wastes,* 685th Session, C(88)(Final). Paris: OECD.

OECD (1991) *The State of the Environment.* Paris: OECD.

OECD (1991) *Environmental Data Services,* June 1992. Paris: OECD.

OECD (1993) *Environmental Performance Reviews. Germany.* Paris: OECD.

OLTHOF, L. (1988) Milieu-organisaties in Beroep tegen Milieuvergunningen voor Nieuwe Kolencentrales (Environmental groups appeal against environmental permits for new power plants). *Natuur en Milieu,* September 22.

OPSCHOOR, J.B. (1974) *Economische Waardering van Milieuverontreiniging* (Economic valuation of environmental pollution). Assen: Van Gorcum.

OPSCHOOR, J.B. (1987) *Duurzaamheid en Verandering* (Sustainability and change). Amsterdam: Free University.

OPSCHOOR, J.B. and VAN DER PLOEG, S.W.F. (1990) Duurzaamheid en kwaliteit: hoofddoelstellingen van milieubeleid (Sustainability and quality: the chief aims of environmental policy). In: CLTM, *Het Milieu: denkbeelden voor de 21ste eeuw.* Zeist: kerckebosch.

OVERSEAS DEVELOPMENT ADMINISTRATION (ODA) (1991) *Population, Environment and Development.* An issues paper for the Third UNCED Preparatory Committee: ODA.

PEARCE, D. (1991) Population growth. In Pearce, D. (ed.), *Blueprint 2: Greening the World Economy.* London: Earthscan, pp.109–37.

PECHMANN, J.H.K., SCOTT, D.E., SEMLITSCH, R.D., CALDWELL, J.P., VITT, L.J. and GIBBONS, J.W. (1991) Declining amphibian populations: the problem of separating human impacts from natural fluctuations. *Science,* **253,** 892–5.

PETERSON, D.J.(1993) *Troubled Lands. The Legacy of Soviet Environmental Destruction.* Boulder: Westview Press.

PHILLIPS, K. (1990) Where have all the frogs and toads gone? *BioScience,* **40**(6), 422–4.

PIERCE, J.T. (1990) *The Food Resource.* Harlow, Essex: Longman.

POTTER, D. (1995) Environmental problems in their political context. In Glasbergen, P. and Blowers, A. (eds), *Environmental Policy in an International Context. Perspectives on Environmental Problems*. London: Edward Arnold.

PRECODA, N. (1991) Requiem for the Aral sea. *Ambio*, **20** (3–4).

PRESCOTT-ALLEN, R. and PRESCOTT-ALLEN, C. (1982) *What's Wildlife Worth?* London: Earthscan.

PRIVOR, (1993) The missing leap: frogs and toads are disappearing. *USA Today*, 4th January, p.10.

RACKHAM, O. (1986) *The History of the Countryside*. London: Dent.

REED, C. (1993) Farewell to the frog? *The Guardian*, 15th January, pp.16–17.

REINSTEIN, R.A. (1993) Climate negotiations. *Washington Quarterly*, Winter.

RIJNMOND REGION PUBLIC AUTHORITY (1983) SO_2 *nota* (SO_2 memorandum). Rotterdam: OLR

RIJSBERMAN, F.R., GUPTA, J., FARAG, T., SZERDAHELYI, G. and POOS, M. (1993) *Energy Use and Carbon-dioxide Emissions in Hungary and in the Netherlands: Estimates, Comparisons, Scenarios*. Budapest and The Hague: Dutch Ministry of Housing, Physical Planning and the Environment and Hungarian Ministry for Environmental and Regional Policy and Hungarian Ministry for Industry and Trade.

ROBERTS, S. (ed.) (1993) *Dangerous Liaisons. Western Involvements in the Nuclear Power Industry of Central and Eastern Europe*. Based on research for Friends of the Earth by Tim Jenkins. London: Friends of the Earth.

ROCHON, R., ATTARD. D., and BEETHAM, R. (1990) Legal and institutional mechanisms. In IPCC-RSWG,. *Climate Change: The IPCC Response Strategies*. Cambridge: Cambridge University Press.

ROYAL SOCIETY FOR THE PROTECTION OF BIRDS (1994) *Biodiversity Challenge: An Agenda for Conservation in the UK*. Sandy: RSPB.

ROUVIERE, C., WILLIAMS, T., BALL, R. *et al.* (1990) Human settlements; the energy, transport and industrial sectors; human health; air quality; and changes in ultraviolet-B radiation. In Tegart *et al.*.

SADIK, N. (1990) *The State of World Population 1990*. New York: United Nations Population Fund.

SANDS, P. (1992) The United Nations framework. *Reciel*, **1**(3), 270–7.

SCHEPERS, S. (1991) *Greenhouse Policies in the European Community and in the Member States the United Kingdom and the Netherlands*. Utrecht: University of Utrecht.

SCHIPPER, L. and MEYERS, S. (1992) *Energy Efficiency and Human Activity: Past Trends, Future Prospects*. Cambridge: Cambridge University Press.

SHAW, R.P. (1992) Population's success story, environment's nightmare. In Bergesen, H.O. *et al.* (eds), *Green Globe Yearbook 1992*. Oxford: Oxford University Press.

SIMMONS, I.G. (1989) *Changing the Face of the Earth*. Oxford: Basil Blackwell.

SLOEP, P.B. and VAN DAM, M.C.E. (1995) Science on environmental problems. In Glasbergen, P. and Blowers, A. (eds), *Environmental Policy in an International Context: Perspectives on Environmental Problems*. London: Edward Arnold, pp.30–57.

SMIL, V. (1993) *Global Ecology: Environmental Change and Social Flexibility*. London: Routledge.

SMITH, Robert Angus (1872) *Air and Rain: the Beginnings of a Chemical Climatology*.

SPRANG, U., DIJKSTERHUIS, H. and KLUGKIST, J. (1990) *Van Thaise cassava tot Europees veevoer; balans van een bedreigde handelsstroom [From Thai cassava to European animal feed; report on a threatened trade flow]*. Amsterdam: NIO Association.

STAIRS, K. and TAYLOR, P. (1992) Non-governmental organizations and the legal protection of the oceans: a case study. In Hurrell, A. and Kingsbury, B. (eds), *The International Politics of the Environment*. Oxford: Oxford University Press.

STOLWIJK, H.J.J., WIERENGA, K., WIJNANDS, J.H.M. *et al.* (1992) *Volumebeleid in de veehouderij; een verkenning van de economische en milieuhygiënische gevolgen (Volume policy in livestock farming; a survey of the economic and environmental effects)*. The Hague/Bilthoven: Central Planning Office/Agricultural Economics Institute/National Institute of Public Health and Environmental Protection.

STORK, N.E. (1993) How many species are there? *Biodiversity and Conservation*, **2**, 215–32.

TAMISIER, A. (1991) The Camargue: in search of a new equilibrium between man and nature. *Landscape and Urban Planning*, **20**, 263–7, .

TELLEGEN, E. (1986) The Soviet press on wastage, conservation and recycling. *Zeitschrift für Umweltpolitik und Umweltrecht*, **3**, 231-46.

TELLEGEN, E. (1989) Perestroika and the rational use of materials and energy. *The Environmental Professional*, **11**, 142-51.

TOL, R.S.J. and DE VOS, A.F. (1993) Greenhouse statistics – a different look at climate research. *Theoretical and Applied Climatology*, **48**.

TONNEIJCK, A.E.G. (1981) *Research on the Influence of Different Air Pollutants Separately and in Combination in Agriculture, Horticulture and Forestry Crops*. Wageningen: IRO Report R 262.

UI (1993) Briefing No. 93/2. London: The Uranium Institute.

UNITED NATIONS (1992) *Earth Summit, Agenda 21, The United Nations Programme of Action from Rio*, The final text of agreements negotiated by Governments at the United Nations Conference on Environment and Development (UNCED), 3–14 June 1992. Rio de Janeiro, Brazil: The Regency Press.

UNITED NATIONS GENERAL ASSEMBLY DOCUMENT (1991) Cross-sectoral issues. The relationship between demographic trends, economic growth, unsustainable consumption patterns and environmental degradation. In *A/CONF.*, 151/PC/46.

UNITED NATIONS POPULATION FUND (1991) *Population, Resources and the Environment: The Critical Challenges*. London: UNPF.

VALLETTE, J. and SPALDING, H. (eds) (1990) *The International Trade in Wastes*. Washington: Greenpeace USA.

VAN DER STRAATEN, J.(1990) *Zure Regen, Economische Theorie en het Nederlandse Beleid* (Acid rain, economic theories and Dutch policies). Utrecht: Jan van Arkel.

VAN DER EERDEN, L.J., TONNIEJCK, A.E.G. and WIJNANDS, J.H.M. (1986) *Economische Schade door Luchtverontreiniging aan de Gewasteelt in Nederland (Financial losses in agriculture due to air pollution)*. IPO Report R324. Wageningen: Instituut voor Plantenziektekundig Onderzoek (Institute for Research into Plant Diseases).

VAN DER STRAATEN, J.and GORDON, M. (1995) Environmental problems from an economic perspective. In Glasbergen, P. and Blowers, A. (eds), *Environmental Policy in an International Context: Perspectives on Environmental Problems* . London: Edward Arnold, pp.130–58.

VELLINGA, P. and GRUBB, T.M. (eds) (1993) *Climate Change Policy in the European Community*. Report on a Workshop held in October 1992. London: The Royal Institute of International Affairs. Energy and Environmental Programme.

VELLINGA, P. and SWART, R. (1991) The greenhouse marathon: proposal for a global strategy. In Jäger, J. and Ferguson.H.L. (eds), *Climate Change: Science, Impacts and Policy*. Proceedings of the Second World Climate Conference. Cambridge: Cambridge University Press.

VERBRUGGEN, H. (1995) *Mondiale duurzame ontwikkeling: efficiëntie en verdeling* (Global sustainable development: efficiency and distribution). Amsterdam: Inaugural lecture, Urÿe Universiteit Amsterdam.

VERMEULEN, A.J. (1977) Verzuring van de Neerslag: Oorzaken en Gevolgen (Acidification of precipitation: causes and effects). *Natuur en Milieu*, **6/7**, 12–21.

VERNON, R. (1993) Behind the scenes: how policy making in the European Community, Japan, and the United States affects global negotiations. *Environment*, **35**(5).

VIDAL, J.L. (1991) IUCN species survival commission establishes declining amphibian populations programme. *Herpetological Review*, **22**(3), 76.

VIDAL, J.L. (1994) Frogs, farmers and free trade. *Earth Matters*, **22**, 8–9.

WARRICK, R.A. and OERLEMANS H. (1990) Sea level rise. In Houghton, J.T. *et al.* (eds), *Climate Change – The IPCC Scientific Assessment.* Cambridge: Cambridge University Press.

WATSON, R.T., RODHE, H., OESCHGER, H. and SIEGENTHALER, U. (1990) Greenhouse gases and aerosols. In Houghton J.T. *et al.* (eds), *Climate Change – The IPCC Scientific Assessment.* Cambridge: Cambridge University Press.

WEALE, A. (1992) *The New Politics of Pollution.* Manchester: Manchester University Press.

WEINER, D.R. (1984) Community ecology in Stalin's Russia. 'Socialist' and 'bourgeois' science. *ISIS,* **75**, 84-96.

WOLFSON, Z. (1994) *The Geography of Survival. Ecology in the Post-Soviet Era.* New York: M.E. Sharpe.

WOLTERS, G., SWAGER, J. and GUPTA, J. (1991) *A Brief History Of Global, Regional and National Policy Measures.* The Hague: Ministry of Housing, Physical Planning and the Environment.

WORLD BANK (1990) *World Development Report 1990.* Washington DC: IBRD.

WORLD BANK (1992) *World Development Report 1992.* Washington DC: IBRD.

WORLD RESOURCES INSTITUTE (1989) *Natural Endowments: Financing Resource Conservation for Development.* Washington DC: WRI.

WORLD RESOURCES INSTITUTE (1990) *World Resources 1990–91.* Oxford: Oxford University Press.

WORLD RESOURCES INSTITUTE (1992) *World Resources 1992–93 – a Guide to the Global Environment. Toward Sustainable Development.* New York: Oxford University Press.

WYNNE, B. (1993) Implementation of greenhouse gas reductions in the European Community: institutional and cultural factors. In Rayner, S. (ed.), *Global Environmental Change: Human and Policy Dimensions,* **3**(1) .

WYNNE, B, WATERTON, C. and GROVE-WHITE, R. (1993) *Public Perceptions and the Nuclear Industry in West Cumbria.* Lancaster: Centre for Study of Environmental Change.

YABLOKOV, A. (1990) The current state of the Soviet environment. *Environmental Policy Review*, **4**, 1–4.

YANITSKY, O. (1993) *Russian Environmentalism: Leading Figures, Facts, Opinions.* Moscow, Mezhdunarodnyje Otnoshenija Publishing House.

YEARLEY, S. (1991) *The Green Case: A Sociology of Environmental Issues, Arguments and Politics.* London: Routledge.

ZWERVER, S., BOVENKERK, M. and MAK, P.J. (1984) ·Verzuring: Nationalen Internationale Ontwikkelingen (Acidification: national and international trends). In Adema, E.H. and van Ham, J. (eds), *Zure Regen, Oorzaken, Effecten en Beleid.* Wageningen: Pudoc.

Index